C0-AWF-455

Under the editorship of

DAYTON D. McKEAN

University of Colorado

OTHER TITLES IN THE SERIES

The Government of Republican Italy
JOHN CLARKE ADAMS and PAOLO BARILE

British Parliamentary Democracy
SYDNEY D. BAILEY

The Federal Government of Switzerland
GEORGE A. CODDING, JR.

Government and Politics in Israel
OSCAR KRAINES

Contemporary Government of Japan
THEODORE MCNELLY

Government and Politics in Malaysia
R. S. MILNE

The Mexican Political System
L. VINCENT PADGETT

The Indian Political System
NORMAN D. PALMER

Contemporary Government of Germany
ELMER PLISCHKE

South Vietnam: Nation Under Stress
ROBERT SCIGLIANO

Norwegian Democracy
JAMES A. STORING

The Political System of Chile

FEDERICO G. GIL
THE UNIVERSITY OF NORTH CAROLINA

HOUGHTON MIFFLIN COMPANY · BOSTON

PRINTED IN THE U.S.A.

CONTENTS

PREFACE

Politics in Latin America can no longer be adequately interpreted simply in terms of struggles for power, prestige, and plunder within the narrow circle of semifeudal landowners, the Church's hierarchy, army men, and parasitical politicians. A more adequate explanation may be that the patterns of political behavior now developing in Latin America are best regarded as class struggles, taking different forms in the several countries in consonance with their varying economic and social structures.

Evident similarities exist between these emergent patterns of political behavior and the metamorphoses through which many countries that have been more nearly in the main line of the economic, social, and political development in the Western world have passed. This suggests that the methods of comparative analysis may be fruitfully applied in the study of Latin American politics. In the present stage of development of the techniques of scientific investigation of political phenomena, Latin America may, indeed, occupy a unique and therefore peculiarly important position. Genuine advancement in the theoretical aspects of comparative politics has been made by the recognition of a relevant distinction between the politics of Western and non-Western countries. For better or for worse, however, Latin America does not fall neatly into either of these categories. Although in some countries the Indian and African heritages provide distinctly non-Western elements in the culture, Latin America can certainly not be appropriately classified as non-Western in cultural characteristics or background. Yet, perhaps because of a time lag, for geographical reasons, or other causes not easily discovered, the patterns of economic, social, and political institutions and behavior that have developed there can certainly not be called typically Western. For this reason, the countries of the area have in many ways been just as definitely influenced from the outside in the past century by the impact of Western culture of the late nineteenth and twentieth centuries as the countries of Asia, the Middle East, or Africa which were until that period distinctly non-Western in their culture.[1]

The study of Latin American political institutions has been dominated to this date by a legal, philosophical, and historical emphasis. As is the case in much of Europe's political literature, Latin American students of government, with all of their fine legal tradition, have

[1] Federico G. Gil, *Genesis and Modernization of Political Parties in Chile* (Gainesville: University of Florida Press, 1962), pp. 1–2.

tended to detach themselves from reality and to place too great an emphasis on the formal aspects of institutions and processes. Even surveys of the structure of government are lacking in some countries, to say nothing of realistic studies of the functioning of political institutions. Because most of the work done until now has been characterized by the historical and legal-analytical methods, it can be expected that the functional approach will yield new and rewarding insights into the general political system of Latin America.

The objectives of this book are modest. No attempt has been made to develop analytical concepts for systematic comparison. Instead the purpose has been to provide a comprehensive description and analysis of the operation of the Chilean political system while relating it at the same time, in a somewhat sophisticated fashion, to the physical, economic, cultural, and social contextual elements.

Chile is a country that has come to have a fairly mature political system with all its characteristics of respect for legality, free elections, high voter turnout, and parties that constitute an integral and effective wheel of the political machinery. It is also a country in which genuine issues, arising earlier than in other Latin American states, have produced authentic and significant socio-economic differences among political groups. Although not altogether absent, personalism has come to be overshadowed by ideology and discipline. Consequently, popular and democratic representation has become more nearly a reality and Chileans have made long strides toward perfecting systematic party organizations. In addition, the highly complex Chilean scene offers the best example of a multiparty system in Latin America. And yet, this country seemed, in the last few years, to be on the verge of a social earthquake which the traditional political structures did not appear able to prevent. An effort is made in this volume to trace the impact on the political system of these economic and social forces that have caused the upheaval, without, however, attempting to delve into the intricacies of all social change.

It is obvious that this book has emphasized comprehensiveness of coverage rather than depth of detail. In situations in which the researcher finds himself practically without predecessors whose work can provide him with the most basic data, there is always the temptation to turn every stone before beginning to excavate. There is some comfort in the assurance that colleagues working in non-Western areas are also finding it necessary to accumulate, in steps preliminary to intensive research, a great variety of data of a descriptive nature, which the workers in the more thoroughly cultivated vineyards of political research in Western Europe and the United States find already on hand in orderly and well-organized array. The conclusion is inevitable that the usefulness of any pioneering research enterprise is to be found precisely in the comprehensiveness of its exploration and its exposure of leads for future scholars to investigate in greater detail.

This volume could never have been completed without the assistance of a great many people. It is based on field research undertaken in the course of eight extended visits to Chile. A special grateful word is due to the author's many Chilean friends, and to the more than two hundred government officials, political leaders, and plain citizens whom he interviewed. Without their help this study could not have been written. It is impossible to thank each and every one by name. Of particular help were Professors Clodomiro Almeyda, Gustavo Lagos, and Ricardo Cruz-Coke. A very special debt of gratitude is owed to the late Professor Mario Bernaschina, good friend and scholar of excellence, who read many portions of the manuscript and spent innumerable hours of pleasant political discussion with the author. Of particular help also were Jorge Tapia Videla, Santiago Benadava, Luis Quirós Varela, and Ricardo Tichauer, who assisted in gathering research materials. The author wishes to acknowledge the encouragement and continuing support of his colleagues, Professors Frederic N. Cleaveland, Charles B. Robson, and Alexander Heard. A special word of thanks is extended to Howard Webber and Mrs. LeeAnn Matthews for their expert assistance in the final preparation of the manuscript. The Rockefeller Foundation, the Social Science Research Council, and the Research Council of the University of North Carolina at Chapel Hill provided financial support for which the author is deeply indebted. Finally, thanks are due to Professor Dayton D. McKean, editor of this series, and to the editorial staff of Houghton Mifflin Company. The inadequacies of this volume are, of course, the sole responsibility of the author.

FEDERICO G. GIL

Chapel Hill
April 10, 1965

Caracas
TRINIDAD (BR.)
Port-of-Spain
VENEZUELA
Orinoco River
Georgetown
Paramaribo
Cayenne
GUIANA
BR.
NETH.
FR.
Bogotá
COLOMBIA
Quito
ECUADOR
Manaos
Amazon River
Iquitos
BRAZIL
São Francisco River
PERU
Lima
Brasília
La Paz
BOLIVIA
Rio de Janeiro
PARAGUAY
São Paulo
Asunción
CHILE
Paraná River
Uruguay River
URUGUAY
Santiago
Buenos Aires
Montevideo
ARGENTINA
South America
FALKLAND ISLANDS
(BR.)
Strait of Magellan
SOUTH GEORGIA
(BR.)

1

Land, People, and Politics

It would be exceedingly difficult to give an accurate impression of the political system of Chile without first providing some understanding of its physical framework, for its highly differentiated geography and climate have strongly influenced its institutions and form of government.

Although the idea of geographical determinism may be debatable, the existence of an interrelationship between physical environment and economic, racial and political conditions is too obvious to be denied. In Chile, for instance, distinct major geographical zones or regions easy to identify correspond to administrative entities created by a long politico-economic process, and physical features have lent peculiar characteristics to the social development in each section. Its physical differences can be related to economic, social, and political distinctions.

Politics and the Geographical Setting

A country of extravagant shape, Chile is located at the southern end of the Andean range, second loftiest in the world and the dominant physical feature of the South American continent.[1] Its ribbon shape is the result of the physical framework of this part of the continent. Although it has been described as the Western or Pacific slope of this majestic mountain range extending from Cape Horn northward to Arica to latitude 17°5, the description is not accurate, for the Andes are seldom a single range but more often two or three parallel ridges. Chile's fantastic length (2,600 miles) extends through 38° degrees latitude to contrast with its narrow width (110 miles). While this width compares approximately to that of Italy, its length is four times that of France and is equivalent to the distance between Denmark and

[1] Benjamín Subercaseaux, *Chile o una loca geografía* (Santiago: Ediciones Ercilla, 1944), is a poetic but accurate geographical description of the country.

the Sahara Desert. This strip of land running between formidable mountain heights and abysmal ocean depths extends over 286,396 square miles, an area greater than that of any European country except Russia, and smaller only, in South America, are those of Uruguay, Paraguay and Ecuador.[2] Its population at mid-1963 was estimated at 8,290,000.[3] Chilean claims to the Antarctic territory between 53° W. and 90° W. would add 1,250,000 kms² and 202 persons.

With natural frontiers of desert, ocean, and a great cordillera, and being relatively far removed from the commercial centers of the world, Chile lived in near isolation for over three centuries. The Chilean people, it has been said, are in reality islanders. "The entire history of Chile unfolds like that of an archipelago," said one writer. And indeed, this land with its inhabitants "clinging to the mountains in order not to fall into the sea" is like an island, or a group of islands cut off from the world by the Pacific and the Andes.[4]

This republic, pressed between the ocean and the mountains, is a land of many physiographical and climatic contrasts. South from Arica a white desert, barer than the Sahara but with rich nitrate and other mineral deposits, is followed by a transitional zone of mining and agriculture, presenting an austere and sober landscape. Farther south there is the beautiful and fertile central valley with green vineyards and orchards and dry stimulating air. Next is a colder, rainy, heavily wooded area of varied topography followed by an almost uninhabited wilderness of islands, foggy channels, rocks, glaciers, and ice. At the southernmost point there prevails "an almost eternal succession of furious westerly gales, which appear to chase one another in an unending procession round and round the Southern Pole."[5]

From the sea, the long Chilean coast offers two highly differentiated sections: the northern and central, and the archipelagic southern third. The former, extending south to Chiloé, is fairly regular but only occasionally provides a good port, such as Corral, Talcahuano, Coquimbo, Caldera, and Mejillones. Most of its cities, such as Antofagasta and Valparaíso, are too open and exposed to strong northwest winds. Along this coastal section there are few islands, although westward in the Pacific there are the groups of Juan Fernández and the

[2] Elías Almeyda Arroyo, *Geografía de Chile* (Santiago, 1955), p. 10. Some older geographical treatises are Pedro Lucio Cuadra, *Geografía física y política de Chile* (Santiago, 1868); Enrique Espinosa, *Geografía de Chile* (Santiago, 1903); and, Luis Galdamés, *Geografía Económica de Chile* (Santiago, 1911).

[3] Estimated by the Inter-American Development Bank on the basis of preliminary returns from the 1960 census.

[4] Almeyda, *op. cit.*, p. 9.

[5] G. F. Scott Elliot, *Chile* (London: T. Fisher Unwin, 1911), p. 6.

Easter Islands. The greatest ocean depths of the eastern Pacific Ocean lie off the Chilean coast. A line running east-west just north of the port of Taltal in northern Chile has the greatest difference between height of land and depth of ocean in a short distance anywhere in the world. From the peak of Llullaillaco on the Chilean border to the Richards Deep the difference is just over 46,000 feet. Such critical differences in the land's surface make for great instability of the earth's crust. Chile has suffered some of the most tragic earthquakes for this reason.

In the southern third, where the sea has inundated the continent, leaving only mountain peaks unsubmerged, the coast line is the reverse of that of the northern and central sections. Its labyrinth of sounds, fjords, and landlocked harbors makes it one of the world's most jagged coasts. On its southward course it becomes more and more inhospitable and tempestuous until finally it reaches the Strait of Magellan and gives Chile an opening to the Atlantic Ocean.

Topographically the country is divided into three parallel sections: the Andean range on the east; the lower and more broken coastal range; and the great central depression, hardly defined in the north, perfectly developed as a longitudinal valley in the center, and invaded by the ocean in the south. The Andean cordillera, in the northern part of Chile, is a lofty plateau (Puna de Atacama), which gives way in the south to the parallel chains of very high peaks. These chains decrease farther south and are interrupted by numerous passes, lakes, and rivers. At its southern extreme the cordillera borders the sea and is fringed with glaciers which sometimes terminate in the water.

The lower coastal cordillera, which parallels the Andes and the sea, consists of a series of rounded hills and mountains close to the sea shore. They are the worn-down remnants of a great mountain range which existed before the great fold in the earth's crust, now the cordillera of the Andes, was forced upwards.

Between the cordillera of the coast and that of the Andes lies the central depression which, in the north, consists of a large plateau separated by deep ravines. South of this meseta there is a transverse valley crossed by mountain ranges which join the Andes to the coastal sierra. Farther south, at 33° S., the central depression assumes the form of a perfectly longitudinal valley, 600 miles long and 45 miles at its widest part. At its southern extreme the valley submerges into pronounced fjords. At this point, the Chiloé Islands and other islands along the seaboard continue the line of the coastal cordillera right down to Cape Horn.

The climate of Chile is very different at various latitudes and influences the whole economic life of the country. Physical structural units, already described, combine with the transversal climatic zones to form the nation's environmental patterns.[6]

Rainfall is the key to climatic division. Chilean rainfall depends almost entirely upon the Pacific and is brought by westward winds. The north is practically rainless; the center enjoys a Mediterranean climate, rainy in winter and dry in summer, and the south is drenched by heavy rains.[7] Accordingly, temperatures from north to south range from tropic heat to sub-Antarctic cold.

These three major climatic regions, known respectively as Desert Chile, Mediterranean Chile, and Forest Chile (a fourth one known as Atlantic Chile and consisting of the land on both sides of the Strait of Magellan, adjoining Argentina, is sometimes added), are the convenient bases of any geographical study of the country.[8] For analytical purposes, they can in turn be subdivided into smaller regions, each with its own characteristics. This is a particularly useful method for outlining the interrelationship of physical environment and sociopolitical problems.

Desert Chile

The first climatic region, Desert Chile, which stretches from the Peruvian frontier to Coquimbo, is one of the most unmitigated deserts of the world, in part of which no rain falls for years in succession. This great desert has provided a strong wall of defense, giving Chile a natural strategic advantage from the days of the Incas to those of the war with Peru.[9] Although temperatures are high throughout the year, variation exists between coastal locations with favorable maritime influences and the interior with extreme seasonal and diurnal changes of temperature. The coast rises in bare cliffs, 3,000 to 3,500 feet from the Pacific, like a straight pink-colored wall. Inland, there are the bolsones or enormous dry basins between the Andes and the coastal range. Here are the great nitrate deposits which are one of Chile's main sources of revenue.

Two distinct zones can be distinguished in this region: the *Norte Grande* (Big North) and the *Norte Chico* (Little North). The former

[6] See Benjamín Vicuña Mackenna, *Clima de Chile* (Valparaíso, 1877).

[7] See Mack Jefferson, *The Rainfall of Chile* (New York, 1921).

[8] Gilbert J. Butland, *Chile* (London: Royal Institute of International Affairs, 1951), p. 11.

[9] This region of Chile has always fascinated world travellers. Narrative accounts and physical descriptions concerning the desert are numerous. Examples are Hiram Billinghurst, *Geografía de Tarapacá* (Santiago, 1886); Francisco San Román, *Desierto y cordilleras de Atacama,* 2 vols. (Santiago, 1896); and Rodolfo Philippi, *Viaje al desierto de Atacama* (The Hague, 1860).

is composed of the provinces of Tarapacá and Antofagasta which were incorporated into Chile after its victory over Peru and Bolivia in the War of the Pacific. These two provinces occupy about 24 per cent of the national territory and have 5 per cent of the total population (336,755) of which 226,388[10] live in urban centers, seaports or mining towns. Urban concentration is particularly accentuated in the province of Antofagasta where 89 per cent of the people are city dwellers. (In Tarapacá province it is 60 per cent.) The largest cities are Antofagasta and Iquique. Mining is the chief economic activity. Agriculture has been reduced to the oasis type due to the arid character of the region, although there is some stock-raising of species typical of the Andean plateau. Energy resources are almost nonexistent so that this area depends almost entirely for foodstuffs on the provinces of the center zone. In turn, the *Norte Grande* is the chief producing center of natural sodium nitrate and one of the world's greatest sources of iodine. Nitrate production, at present, is centered at two or three important *salitreras,* near Tocopilla and Antofagasta, and at other small ones in Tarapacá province.

The inhospitable conditions of the desert combine with the characteristics of mining exploitation to determine hard living conditions which give a certain unstable air of camps to all settlements, large cities included. Also, the total dependence on foreign market fluctuations has led to a high degree of insecurity among the population. The typical *nortino* (northerner) is a rough, frugal, and courageous individual.[11] He forms the backbone of a strong, fighting, well-organized proletariat that developed in this area representing one of the principal nuclei of the early labor movement. The first unions, which provided recreational facilities in a hostile physical environment, did much to develop organizational identification. The two provinces, despite their small population, have about 16 per cent of Chile's unionized labor force.[12] It is also in this region that the Communist Party was first organized. The fact that these two provinces constitute the main sources of national revenue but receive little and disproportionate attention from the central government accounts for the development of strong regionalistic feelings.[13] Although yet unmeasurable and with-

[10] These and all other regional population figures are based on preliminary returns from the 1960 census. See Dirección de Estadística y Censos, *Algunos Resultados del XIII Censo de Población y II de Vivienda* (Santiago, April 1962).

[11] For an interesting essay on man and environment in Chile, see Mariano Latorre, *El paisaje y el hombre* (Buenos Aires, 1941).

[12] Ricardo Cruz-Coke, *Geografía electoral de Chile* (Santiago, 1952), p. 23.

[13] See "El Norte Grande pide la palabra," *Panorama económico,* XI, No. 175 (September 13, 1957), pp. 546–571.

out political manifestations, this regionalism may become a force of some significance. Continuous instability and dependence on foreign markets have resulted in a pronounced leftism in the politics of the *Norte Grande*.

The *Norte Chico* is the transitional zone between the desert and Mediterranean Chile, and extends to 30°5. It is here that the extensive high plateau of the North begins giving way to a series of transverse valleys watered by some small rivers. It has a steppe vegetation, and small wooded sections begin to appear. Comprised of the provinces of Atacama and Coquimbo, which represent 16 per cent of the national area, the *Norte Chico* has a small population: 420,661 (about 5.7 per cent of the total). In contrast to the *Norte Grande* there is a more even spread of population in urban and rural areas. In Atacama province the urban percentage is 52, while in Coquimbo it is only 39. The chief activities of this population are mining and agriculture, which lend greater economic stability to the area. However, the frequent droughts sometimes produce effects as disastrous as those caused by the sharp fluctuations of the nitrate and copper markets in the *Norte Grande*.

The average person — miner or small farmer — is by tradition and socio-economic circumstances, an individualist. There are no great labor organizations. Politically, the influence of a few powerful families with mining interests is a factor of significance. One of the strongest nuclei of the Radical Party developed among this group during the nineteenth century.

Mediterranean Chile

The territory stretching from Coquimbo (30°5) to the Bío-Bío River (37°5) constitutes the central part of the country or Mediterranean Chile. It includes ten provinces (Aconcagua, Valparaíso, Santiago, O'Higgins, Colchagua, Curicó, Talca, Maule, Linares and Ñuble) which form "the heart of the Chilean nation" and the home of 90 per cent of the population. This was the Chile of colonial and early republican days, enclosed by desert, ocean, mountains and forest, fertile and blessed with mild climate. This Chile grew northward and southward only in the second half of the nineteenth century, and only recently were the two extremes of the republic incorporated into the nation.

In this region there are the expected differences between the coastal areas, the central valley and the Andes. The coastal range is lower than in the north, but the seashore maintains its regular unbroken outline. Valparaíso and Talcahuano are the only ports of any importance. The central valley is formed by alluvial fans created by the

Andean rivers which, fed by snow, have cut into and worn away the hills. The soil is an incredibly rich blend of the infinitely varied rocks and deposits of the Andes. The climate, truly Mediterranean, is delightful. There are *fundos* (farm-estates) for wheat and other cereals, orchards, vineyards, and livestock enterprises.

These farms, for the most part, belong to large landed proprietors under a system of land tenure which developed in colonial days and has survived with minor alterations. The inherited land tenure system is oppressive in many ways, among them the failure of the landowners to use their property to the best productive advantage.[14]

Many of these properties, because of their large size, cannot be rationally utilized, a fact which contributes toward fixing a low level of productivity.[15] It is significant to note that in the "provinces of Santiago, Valparaíso, and Aconcagua, 7 per cent of the properties cover 92 per cent of the agricultural lands, while the smaller properties making up almost 85 per cent of the total number of farms occupy scarcely 3 per cent of the land area. For the country as a whole 9.7 per cent of the properties comprise 86 per cent of the agricultural lands."[16]

As a result of the Chilean *hacienda* system a strong paternalistic relationship between peasants and owners developed and is a major factor in the politics of the Chilean valley. The region is also the stage upon which the transition that Chile is presently undergoing stands out more vividly: the change from an agricultural, traditional society dominated by a land-owning oligarchy with a semi-servile class at its service, into an industrial, complex, modern society. The re-structuration of society seems more evident here as a result of the appearance of new groups which demand participation in the whole realm of public affairs.

This changing process can be better illustrated by describing the central region in terms of three clearly defined sections which can be identified within it: one in the north, a second, also in the north, and a third located in the south. The northern rural section includes the provinces of O'Higgins, Colchagua, Curicó, and Talca. This territory

[14] K. H. Silvert, "The State of Chilean Agriculture" (Santiago: American Universities Field Staff, July 1, 1957), p. 9. This series of AUFS letters, written in an excellent, light style, is a remarkable collection of social science essays. Professor Silvert's shrewd and perceptive observations, and his wide background of reference, make these newsletters one of the most interesting and valuable documents available on contemporary Chile. The author is much indebted to them for much data and many suggestive insights.

[15] Instituto de Economía de la Universidad de Chile, *Desarrollo económico de Chile* 1940–1956 (Santiago, 1956), p. 104.

[16] *Ibid.*, p. 104.

contains 4.2 per cent of the republic's area and 10 per cent of its population (729,767) (plus 25 per cent of its hydro-electric resources and a good share of its metal production). Except for Talca and Rancagua, there are no important urban centers, and the population is mainly rural (approximately 67 per cent). Industrial workers are relatively few; there is one large mining center (Sewell), and the rest of the population is engaged in agricultural pursuits. These agricultural workers have until now participated only slightly in the organized labor movement, and have received small benefits from the existing protective legislation.[17] The great political influence of the landlord class has excluded these workers from whatever protection and benefits are received by the industrial laborers. The *inquilinos* (tenant farmers) under the paternalistic rule of landowners still labor here under crude conditions.

The second section of the Central Region is formed by the province of Aconcagua and the great urban centers of the provinces of Santiago and Valparaíso, with populations of 2,427,539 and 613,405 respectively. The total population of this area is 3,182,822 — 43.4 per cent of the total Chilean population in 4.4 per cent of the national land area. Between the censuses of 1940 and 1952, the population of Santiago province increased 38.35 per cent and that of Valparaíso 17.22 per cent, while Chile's total population was augmented 18.10 per cent. The city of Santiago grew from 952,075 to 1,350,400 inhabitants during the same period. This is 42.40 per cent of the total Chilean urban population. Today Santiago has a population of 1,914,539 — more than seven times the population of the next largest city. If the capital city continues to grow at the present pace, it will have a population of 3 million by 1980.

The trend toward urbanization, which had made urban dwellers of 66.5 per cent of all Chileans in 1960, is accentuated in this region by a corresponding industrial concentration. This growth has caused forebodings which have led to studies of multiple and varied problems such as food supply, transportation, energy, and housing.

Under the auspices of the University of Chile, a "Seminar on Greater Santiago" with the participation of fifty private and government organizations was held in 1957. For the first time were gathered doctors, sociologists, economists, lawyers, engineers, architects, and others seeking answers to the complex and varied problems created by this phenomenal demographic, economic, cultural, and institutional concentration in the capital area and its surroundings. Some interesting facts came to light in the course of the discussions: forty people arrive in Santiago from the country every day, resulting in an average of

[17] See José Vera Lamperein, "Sindicalización campesina," *Panorama económico,* XI, No. 177 (October 11, 1957), pp. 651–654.

15,000 newcomers per year; 30 per cent of the city's population lives in unhealthy conditions because of lack of housing and sanitary facilities; 75,000 persons live in *poblaciones callampas* (literally, mushroom towns), the name given in Chile to shanty towns, while another 60,000 live in *conventillos* or tenement houses.[18]

Today, Santiago is chiefly an industrial center. Its share of the national production is 60 per cent, and one third of its inhabitants are engaged in industrial activities. According to statistics, about 48 per cent of all industrial workers are found in the provinces of Santiago and Valparaíso. However, the number of office workers is also high (53 per cent in the two provinces) and, given the political and administrative centralization, the proportion of government workers is even higher. These figures serve to remind us that Santiago and Valparaíso, despite the mass of workers that form part of their populations, are also strong middle-class centers. The great proletarian strongholds are to be found in the mining areas of the north and the coal zone of Concepción, not in Santiago, where the differentiation born of the variety of industrial enterprises has impaired to some extent the development of the labor movement.[19] The emphasis that we have placed upon industrialization should not mislead us into neglecting the importance of Santiago and Valparaíso as agricultural provinces, shown by the fact that Santiago's agricultural production is greater than that of any other province.

The third section within the Central Region is formed by the provinces of Maule, Linares and Ñuble. Conditions here are slightly less favorable than in the northern areas because of the great portions of poor eroded land, particularly near the coast. In this section, representing 3.9 per cent of the country's surface, lives 7.3 per cent (534,098) of the population. The region is chiefly agricultural with little or no industry and mining. Sixty-six per cent of its population lives in rural areas. Chillán, its biggest city, has only 82,947 inhabitants.

Forest Chile

The rainy southern region of forests and grazing lands, known as Forest Chile, is structurally a continuation, in its northern portion, of the physical framework of Mediterranean Chile, except that it features a number of beautiful volcanoes and lakes bordering the Andean foot-

[18] "El Gran Santiago: quebradero de cabeza nacional," *Ercilla,* May 8, 1957. See also the series of studies made by the Instituto de Economía of the University of Chile entitled *Ocupación y desocupación,* Publicaciones del I. de E., Nos. 16, 26, 28, 35, 37, 40, 41, 44, 45, 48, 53, 54, 57, 58, 61, and 63.

[19] Cruz-Coke, *op. cit.,* p. 26.

hills. The southern extreme consists of many islands, a narrow coastal strip, the Strait of Magellan, and the larger part of Tierra del Fuego. Forest Chile begins south of the Bío-Bío River, along the colonial frontier between Spaniard and Araucanian. This is essentially "backwoods" country of a temperate character. Dense woods cover the land, which is rich in alluvium.[20] Rainfall increases southward where a generally cooler temperature prevails down to the southern archipelagic zone. Rain falls there in enormous amounts.

This is a frontier region which reveals an economic and social pattern quite distinct from that of the rest of the country. This pattern can be better shown by considering separately three sections: Concepción and la Frontera, the Lake Region, and the Channel Region.

The Concepción section includes the provinces of Concepción, Arauco, Bío-Bío, Malleco, and Cautín, all of which have one of the greatest natural increases of population among the Chilean provinces. Concepción and Arauco are also, next to Santiago and Valparaíso, the largest industrial centers of the country. Manufacturing at Concepción is primarily textiles and some food and glass and accounts for 9 per cent of the national production. The area which produces practically all of Chile's coal is south of Concepción, a decided advantage for the development of heavy industry. With the completion of a steel plant and subsidiary industries, the importance of the region is rapidly increasing. There is no question that the new steel industry at Huachipato marks the most significant milestone in Chilean progress in industrialization.

The population of these five provinces is 1,361,434 — 18.6 per cent of the total population in 7.4 per cent of national land area. The rural population prevails with the exception of Concepción, where 76 per cent is urban. Since 1940 Concepción has increased its population 33.52 per cent, the second highest population increase, Santiago being first.

For three centuries this section was the stage for the war against the Araucanian Indians and marked the southern frontier of Chile. In colonial days it was also the only counterweight to Santiago's political and economic predominance, and a very important army center. Economic factors as well as historical considerations imply profound differences with the traditional Central Region. Concepción with 136 unions has 36,000 trade union members.[21] The coal miners and the nitrate miners in the north were among the pioneers of the Chilean labor movement.

[20] Scott Elliot, *op. cit.*, p. 12.
[21] Butland, *op. cit.*, p. 87.

Bío-Bío, Malleco, and Cautín are prosperous agricultural areas, 77 per cent of the land being suitable for pastoral or agricultural activities; cattle farming is well developed, accounting for about half of the nation's cattle production. A large area is devoted to cereals, especially wheat, the nine forest provinces growing two thirds of the Chilean crop. Oats, rye, maize, and peas are also important. The region is fortunate in having abundant energy-providing resources resulting from the heavy all-season rainfall from Concepción to Puerto Montt.

The Lake Region is composed of the provinces of Valdivia, Osorno and Llanquihue. With practically no dry season and a wooded landscape, it features numerous lakes connected by rivers. It contains 565,023 (7.7 per cent of the total) people in an area covering approximately 6.2 per cent of the national territory. Important population increases have taken place within the last twelve years (Valdivia 21 per cent; Osorno 14 per cent; Llanquihue 19 per cent) accompanied by the usual urbanization trend. However, the bulk of the population, about 65 per cent, remains in the rural areas. The region's farming economy is similar to that of the Frontera, although the rainier and cooler climate determines a less diversified agricultural output. Abundance of rich pastures has meant the development of cattle farming. Wheat production is about half of that of the Frontera section, climatic conditions are favorable to oat growing, and 30 per cent of Chilean timber originates here. Osorno and Llanquihue are famous for their potatoes which constitute 40 per cent of the country's crop. The city of Valdivia is the only industrial site of any importance.

This region had neither been colonized nor explored until the German colonists began to arrive about one hundred years ago. From 1846 to 1926 some ten thousand German immigrants, sent by colonizing agents or coming of their own will, settled in the territory situated between Valdivia and Puerto Montt. They received plots in the unsettled lands of the state, either directly from the state or through concessionaires who, under certain conditions, were in possession of portions of public land. This German colony not only survived times of trial and distress but left a very deep imprint on the total culture of the southern regions.

Partly because this colonization established the policy of smaller land holdings in consonance with the immigrants' European experience and with the type of crops they were accustomed to, and partly because of its late assimilation to the rest of the country, the land-tenure system in this area contrasts with the large holdings type which is typical of traditional, older Chile. There are some large properties, to be sure, but a much greater variety in the size of holdings exists, and small farms are the general rule. Thus, this region supports an agricultural economy unlike that of the central valley both in type of products and in land-tenure systems. The different socio-economic basis of Forest Chile has, in turn, supported political attitudes often in conflict with those of the established interests of central Chile.

The southward archipelagic extension known in Chile as the Channel Region lies between Chiloé and Cape Horn and is administratively divided into three provinces: Chiloé, Aysén, and Magallanes. It occupies one third of the national area and is inhabited by only 208,784 people, 2.8 per cent of the Chilean population. However, in the last twelve years the population of Aysén has increased 54 per cent. Chiloé and Aysén are predominantly rural (82 and 56 per cent, respectively) while the reverse is true in Magallanes province (81 per cent urban) which includes Punta Arenas, founded in 1843 and the only city of any size in the southernmost extreme of Chile (52,595 inhabitants). Most of this region is an almost uninhabited wilderness, the climatic characteristics of which have already been described. The territory on both shores of the Strait of Magellan, sometimes referred to as Atlantic Chile, is oriented in many aspects to the Atlantic. Although politically Chilean, it is strongly linked to the economic life of Argentina. In general, communications are frequently more expeditious with Argentina, and there is an appreciable migration of seasonal workers, and even Chilean colonists, to the *estancias* of Argentine Patagonia in search of well-paid jobs. Although less significant than in times past when nearly an entire region of Argentina, the territory of Neuquén, was populated by emigrants from Chile, this migration is a constant drain on the economic life of the region.

Agriculture and cattle raising are the chief activities. On Chiloé Island as well as in Aysén province, wheat, oats, and potatoes are grown, but the dense forests of the west coast of the island effectively bar agricultural exploitation. There are parts of the region, specifically northern Tierra del Fuego, the Magallanes pampa region, and some sections of Aysén province, which are of some pastoral value, but the land suitable for sheep and cattle is small in proportion to the total area. However, on some fifteen million acres of pasture land described by some as the finest natural sheep country in the world, are raised about three million sheep, representing 53 per cent of all the sheep in the country.[22] Frozen mutton, wool, skins, and tallow are exported or distributed in central Chile. There is some dairy farming and a fair production of vegetables.

Politically and socially, Chiloé differs from the rest of the region, for while Aysén and Magallanes are new, industrial and pioneering areas, the island has traditions of long-standing.[23] Its middle class

[22] *Ibid.*, p. 69.
[23] Alfredo Weber, *Chiloé* (Santiago, 1903).

(teachers, government officials, priests) is relatively numerous, and its politics have always been characterized by a certain belligerence and vigor. Indeed, it is notorious for bribery and political fraud and a general untrustworthiness in electoral matters. Given the strength of the Catholic Church in the region, religion provides a common ingredient in Chiloé's political battles.

Industrialization of sheep raising has given quite a different character to the population of Aysén and Magallanes. The latter is already exploring and exploiting coal and oil, and it is probable that oil production will expand with the discovery of new fields. In this region, contrary to Chiloé, large land-holdings are prevalent, so that a few individuals or companies control economic life without checks other than the ineffectual action of the far-removed central government, and the defense of its interests by labor organizations.[24]

Population

Regions as diversified and varied as those which have been described were occupied by various races and groups of natives long before the time of the Spanish conquest. Historians' estimates of the total Indian population upon the arrival of the conquistadores fluctuate between 400,000 and 1,500,000. This primitive population was, as is the case with the present inhabitants, mostly concentrated in the central valley, growing denser from north to south as vegetation increased. The far north was occupied by the Atacameño, Chango, and Diaguita tribes, which probably belonged to the aboriginal race of Bolivia and northwest Argentina, and have long been extinct. In the far south were the Chonos in the Archipelagic zone, the Patagonians in Patagonia, and the Fuegians in Tierra del Fuego (a group which has never mixed with the rest of the population and is now almost extinct). More important were the Huilliches from Valdivia to Reloncaví and the Pehuenches between the Bío-Bío and the Copiapó.

The central zone of Chile was occupied by the Araucanians, the most numerous and characteristic of Chile's native races. In the fifteenth century, conquered by the Incas from the Andean highlands, they were either subdued or pushed south into Forest Chile which in turn became the heartland of the Mapuche, the common name given today to all native groups. It was there that until 1887 they heroically and fiercely resisted the white man's penetration. This region contains the 130,547 pure-blood Indians who formed the Araucanian population in 1952 and constituted 26.2 per cent of the population of Cautín and 12.1 per cent of the population of Malleco.

The Araucanian type has been described as "of medium height, with well-proportioned limbs, large head, round face with narrow forehead,

[24] Cruz-Coke, *op. cit.*, pp. 33–34.

small eyes usually black, short and flat nose, large mouth with thick lips and white teeth, thin, short beard, pronounced cheek bones, medium-sized ears; and completing the whole, a grave, sober manner, at times mistrustful but showing resolution and commanding respect."[25]

Indeed, many of these characteristics can be recognized in the present native Chilean, for into this basic Araucanian population came the Basque and Andalusian adventurers and settlers who intermarried with the Indians. The process of racial intermixture known as *mestizaje* took place early and fairly completely, thus originating the nearly homogeneous Chilean racial type of our time. Cutting across social structure it is not difficult to recognize in the mass of the people of all social strata the typical *mestizo,* the true representative of this common Araucanian-Spanish racial heritage.

The European population received its greatest increase during the eighteenth century, when an abundant immigration from the Basque provinces of northern Spain joined the heretofore almost exclusively Castilian element, principally Andalusians, who had established themselves in Chile. The Basque immigrants were robust, vigorous, and industrious. Coming from a territory very similar to Chile in topography and climate, they made an extremely valuable contribution to the progress of the country. The families that they established came to acquire considerable influence because of their wealth and culture, as witnessed by the great number of Basque names to be found today among Chile's most prominent political and intellectual leaders.

Small numbers of other European immigrants, principally Swiss, German, Italian, French, British, and Yugoslav, who settled chiefly in the pioneer regions during the nineteenth and twentieth centuries, made additional contributions to Chile's racial make-up. This immigration, however, was never on a large scale, in contrast to the mass migrations which characterized the development of Argentina, Uruguay, and Brazil, and therefore anthropologically its impact has been inconsequential. Despite this fact, the influence these foreign groups have exerted in all facets of national life is worthy of consideration, especially in the southern regions where their influence is not at all proportionate to their actual size.

Today the number of foreigners is insignificant. According to the 1952 census, there are 7,936 nationalized Chileans and 96,511 resident aliens (1.5 per cent of the total population). Contrary to common belief, the majority lives in Santiago province (58.9 per cent), in Valparaíso (12.3 per cent) and in Antofagasta (5.1 per cent). The largest contingent of foreigners comes from Spain (22,366) followed

[25] Luis Galdames, *A History of Chile* (Chapel Hill: The University of North Carolina Press, 1941), p. 6.

by those from Germany (13,044), Italy (11,607), and Argentina (9,537).[26]

The census of 1952 (the most recent complete census available), remarkable for its detail and objective analysis, indicates some significant demographic trends. In the first place, the Chilean population has increased steadily, as shown by the censuses of 1920, 1930, 1940, 1952, and 1960, from a total of 3,714,887 in 1920 to 7,375,200 in 1960, which is more than double that of 1900. In 1963 the Chilean population was estimated at 8,290,000. The annual population increase is about 2.5 per cent — average for Latin America. Population will reach 9.7 million by 1970 if this annual growth rate is maintained. Second, despite the fact that agriculture remains the basic national activity, there has been a significant urbanization of the Chilean population which suggests that the country is emerging from its underdeveloped economic status.[27] From 1940 to 1952, the urban percentage increased from 52.5 to 60.2, so that during this period, of every thousand persons who lived in the rural areas, 77 passed over to the urban.[28] In 1960 the urban population constituted 66.5 per cent. (See Table 1.)

Composition by age groups reveals that for every thousand persons, 372 are less than 14 years of age, 584 are between 15 and 64, 40 are over 65, and 4 are unknown. These figures, compared with previous statistics, show a drop in the death rate which is certainly related to the urbanization growth. The average life expectancy is about 51

Table 1

Population, Rural and Urban

				In percentages		
	1940	*1952*	*1960*	*1940*	*1952*	*1960*
Total	5,023,500	5,933,000	7,375,200	100.0	100.0	100.0
Urban	2,637,300	3,573,100	4,902,500	52.5	60.2	66.5
Rural	2,386,200	2,359,900	2,472,700	47.5	39.8	33.5

Adapted from Instituto de Economía, Universidad de Chile, *La Economía de Chile en el período 1950–1963,* Vol. II (Santiago, 1963), p. 11.

[26] República de Chile, Servicio Nacional de Estadísticas y Censos, *XII Censo General de Población y I de Vivienda* (Santiago: Guttemberg Press, 1956), Vol. I, "Resumen nacional." Hereafter cited as *Census.*

[27] K. H. Silvert, "The Chilean Population and Housing Census" (Santiago: American Universities Field Staff Letter, October 20, 1956), p. 3.

[28] *Census,* p. 107. All figures are based on the 1952 census unless otherwise noted.

years, representing a notable improvement over 31, which it was thirty years ago. The infant death rate, however, is 119 per thousand live births, one of the highest in the world despite the drop from the 284 per thousand of 1919. As Chile makes progress in its campaign against infant mortality, the trend toward an older population may be expected to increase.

Sex ratio favors the female, with 964 men to every 1,000 women. Of every 1,000 inhabitants, the 602 who live in urban areas include 321 women and 281 men, and the 398 left in the rural sections are composed of 210 males and 188 females, the disproportion being explained by the large number of women in urban service industries and in household employment.[29]

Internal migration is fairly high: 1,461,407 persons live outside the provinces of their birth. Santiago imports and exports more than any other area, with a net gain of 450,001 persons. "The attraction exercised by the cities, owing in part to industrialization, in part to the areas of irradiation of mining operations, and the increase in services in the great urban concentrations, may be observed in notable proportions for Santiago, Valparaíso, Concepción, Antofagasta and Valdivia. In the south, the influence is exercised by the spontaneous, or directed colonization of Llanquihue, Aysén, and Magallanes because of agricultural expansion and oil exploitation."[30] The growth of Santiago since 1885 from a city of a little over 180,000 to one of 1,914,539 in 1963 is striking. Valparaíso and Viña del Mar have also grown rapidly, while in the Concepción-Talcahuano urban district there has been a spectacular rise from 29,210 to 174,881 in the period 1885–1952.

As seen before, the pattern of distribution of population is quite uneven and chiefly determined by the pattern of economic development. The national population density is 8 per square kilometer, the fourth highest in South America after Uruguay (14), Ecuador (13), and Colombia (11). However, the desert north contains a density of 1 person per square kilometer, the southern extreme has a density of 0.74, while Chile's center, the nineteen provinces from Coquimbo to Llanquihue including the central valley, has a density of 23 persons per square kilometer.

From the preceding discussion it becomes apparent that demographic trends have tended to magnify the dominance of the central region and its cities to the detriment of the rural areas. While the highly urban portions generally hold their own populations or increase them, there are some exceptions in the far north (Tarapacá, Antofagasta, and

[29] Silvert, "The Chilean Population," p. 4.
[30] *Census*, p. 121.

Atacama) and in the far south (Cautín, Valdivia, Osorno, Llanquihue, and Aysén). In the former cases, *nortinos* abandon their mining towns, pushed by cyclical economic factors as well as by conditions of the labor market in the nitrate industry, and move to the more attractive central valley. The southern agricultural areas with exceptionally stable populations are comparatively prosperous and are under a definite German influence. The major segment of the surviving unassimilated Indian groups lives here.[31]

The characteristic centralization of the unitary state results in an absolute dependence of the two geographical ends of the country on the middle zone. Chile's center views the development of the natural resources of northern and southern extremes with what may be termed a colonial mentality and approach. On the part of the national government, more efforts are needed in the direction of systematic and effective planning for the development of these zones, so rich in potential resources, for, in general, a great deal of indifference exists towards their problems and aspirations.

An interesting demographic feature is the large number of illegitimate births, which reached its highest index in 1917. Although since that time it has been reduced considerably, probably due to a wider spread of education, it was still 23.4 per cent in 1945.[32] Illegitimacy is, of course, related to income, which determines possibilities of family life. In Chile, almost 90 per cent of those persons receiving incomes cannot afford to maintain an average family at a minimum adequate standard of living. The situation at present may be even worse since Chile's per-capita real income since 1942 has gone down.[33] In spite of this, recent increases have been noted in the recorded marriage rate, probably due to more efficient systems of registrations, improved communications, and changes in the social structure. Of every thousand persons over 15 years of age, 399 were single in 1952; 476 were married; one had had a marriage annulled; 12 were either legally or informally separated; 34 were in extra-legal unions; 74 were widowed, and 4 were of unknown status.[34]

Figures on the religious affinities of the population are of some interest. The great majority is at least nominally Roman Catholic; the remainder is composed of some Indians, Protestant groups, and those of agnostic and atheistic tendencies. Of every one thousand persons, it was found in 1952 that 896 were Catholics, 41 Protestant, 2 Jewish or Greek Orthodox, 31 listed themselves as freethinkers, agnostic, or

[31] Silvert, "The Chilean Population," p. 6.

[32] Juan Crocco, F., *La población chilena* (Santiago: n.p., 1947), p. 278.

[33] Silvert, "The Chilean Population," p. 4.

[34] *Census*, p. 134.

atheists, while the faith of 29 remained unknown.[35] The central provinces appear to be the most loyal to the Catholic Church, and those from Ñuble province to Llanquihue showed the highest number of Protestants. The populations of the northern mineral provinces and of the southern extreme indicated the strongest inclination to no religious ties. Arauco province showed 8.8 per cent of its population to be atheists, the highest rate in the republic. These figures, however, are to be accepted with caution for several reasons. The Chilean Catholic Church, although legally disestablished since 1925 and with its influence waning long before that date, is still very strong. The number of people willing to declare themselves openly as not-religious is relatively large because of a strong anticlerical tradition, but this condition does not necessarily affect social status. Furthermore, Catholicism in a social sense has developed along peculiar lines. For instance, the number of professed Catholics who are, at the same time, Masons, is said to be significant.[36] Religious beliefs, however, do play a role in politics, as will be shown later, affecting not only party ideology but also social characteristics of party membership. It seems clear that political affiliation of Chilean voters, for instance, is not determined by national origin, but rather by religious beliefs. Thus, in southern Chile, Catholic Germans seemingly join the Conservative Party, while Protestant Germans are recruited by the traditionally anticlerical Radical Party.

Of Chile's total population in 1952, 2,155,293 persons or 36.3 per cent of the population over twelve years of age were considered economically active.[37] Three fourths of these were men. The occupational breakdown of the economically active population is shown in Table 2.[38]

Another useful classification of the population, shown by the 1952 census, on the basis of "habitual occupation," appears in Table 3.[39]

A summary of the figures below may provide a glimpse into social structure. Of the total active population, 10.7 per cent could be classified as directive personnel, 7.5 per cent as white-collar employees, 2.5 as salesmen and the like, and 79.3 per cent as the great mass of

[35] *Ibid.*, p. 199.

[36] Silvert, "The Chilean Population," p. 9. Professor Silvert poses the question of whether there is any truth in the statement commonly made by Chileans that a person must be a Mason in order to become President of the country.

[37] By "economically active" persons is meant those who, according to the *Census*, "exercise an economic activity, producing goods or services at the time of the census."

[38] *Census*, p. 230.

[39] *Ibid.*, p. 251.

Table 2

Type of activity	*Persons*	*Per cent*
Totals	2,155,293	100.0
Agriculture, hunting and fishing	648,054	30.1
Mining	101,368	4.7
Manufacturing industries	408,713	19.0
Construction industries	102,317	4.8
Public utilities	20,464	0.9
Commerce	222,880	10.3
Transportation, storage, communications	95,274	4.4
Services	478,913	22.2
Other not specified	77,310	3.6

Table 3

Occupation	*Total:* 2,155,293
Professionals, technicians, etc.	92,195
Managers, administrators, directive personnel	137,616
Office workers, and the like	160,621
Salesmen and the like	54,801
Farmers, fishermen, hunters, lumbermen, etc.	608,390
Miners, etc.	60,044
Transport workers	52,385
Manual laborers, day laborers and other similar	40,119
Service workers, etc.	300,068
Unspecified and miscellaneous	136,255

laborers.[40] As regards occupational position and ownership, salaried laborers form more than half of the total active population (53.1 per cent) and self-employed workers come next with 21.6 per cent. White-collar employees constitute 19.4 per cent, and employers are only 2.1 per cent of the total, the remainder being unknown.[41]

Education

Statistics concerning the economically active population and its occupational breakdown, of course, can be related to the type of educational training available. Analysis of the last census returns indicates very high literacy rate which contrasts with comparatively low secondary school and university populations. Nothing reveals more clearly Chile's intermediate stage of development than this very contrast.[42] Some 75 per cent of the Chilean population over six years of age are

[40] *Ibid.*, p. 253.

[41] *Ibid.*, p. 260.

[42] Silvert, "The Chilean Population," p. 10. See also Eduardo Hamuy, *Educación elemental, analfabetismo y desarrollo económico* (Santiago: Editorial Universitaria, 1960).

literate, and if illiterate children of school age (from six to fourteen years) are excluded, since they are about to enter school or are already enrolled in it, the rate goes up to 85.4 per cent. On a rural-urban basis, the expected differences appear with 86 per cent of urban persons over six years of age literate, and only 58 per cent of rural persons literate in the same ages.[43] The census also indicates that of every thousand persons attending school, 806 are in the primary level, 119 in secondary schools, 59 receive special vocational training, and 16 attend universities.

In 1920 primary education was made compulsory in Chile for those between the ages of seven and fifteen, but even now, about one fourth of all children from ten to fourteen years of age do not attend school, and of the seven-to-nine group approximately one third are also absent. Only about 30 per cent of the students who begin school complete this level. Nevertheless, Chile's educational progress has indeed been remarkable. In 1949 there were 5,200 primary schools, 96 colleges of secondary education, 185 *lycées,* 14 normal institutes, 19 industrial schools, 29 artisan schools, 24 commercial schools, and 14 technical schools for girls.[44]

The number of schools throughout the country, particularly in the rural areas, has increased at a remarkable annual rate in the last thirty years, but is still not sufficient. School construction has not yet caught up with the increase of the school-age population. In 1960 the school-age population was 1.42 million, but only 1.16 million were enrolled in elementary schools. Some 260,000 children were thus not being educated. Other economic factors, besides the lack of schools and teachers, help explain school absenteeism. The province of Magallanes records the highest percentage of literates, followed by those of Antofagasta and Santiago.[45] The farm provinces of Arauco, Colchagua, Malleco, Bío-Bío, and Cautín have the highest indices of illiteracy, indicating the pressures of the agricultural environment on children of school age.

The Chilean educational system features a very high degree of centralization, but government authorized private schools fill an important place in the national educational scheme. The fact that many of these private institutions are under the control of religious orders has caused issues and policy in the whole realm of education to become often critically involved in politics. The issue of free education versus the "teaching state" (*estado docente*), as Chileans prefer to call a state-

[43] *Census,* pp. 159–163.

[44] Julio Vega, "La clase media en Chile," in *Materiales para el estudio de la clase media,* Vol. 113 (Washington: Unión Panamericana, 1950), p. 79.

[45] *Ibid.,* p. 170.

controlled system, has been a real and touchy one in political battlegrounds for many years. It is an ideological as well as a practical question that has often embittered party rivalries, particularly between the Conservative and Radical parties. Furthermore, it is commonly conceded that the greatest sources of strength of the Radical Party have lain for many years in its control over the educational system and bureaucracy. This party, ideologically the product of nineteenth-century anti-clericalism, is, socially speaking, a provincial middle-class movement. Even more important is the fact that its leadership was formed in the government *lycées* (*liceos fiscales*) or secondary schools, the Pedagogic Institute (*Instituto Pedagógico*) for the training of personnel of secondary instruction, and the University of Chile under the influence of the great liberal patricians who were responsible for the secularization of Chilean education. To follow the trajectory of the Radical Party one must take into account the course of Chile's educational evolution since it was through the educational machine of the state that this party recruited substantial portions of its followers.

Chile has eight universities, including the University of the North which is under the Catholic University of Valparaíso. The state-supported University of Chile, generally recognized as one of the best institutions in Latin America, is the country's principal center of higher learning and awards more than 1,000 professional degrees each year. It is followed in importance by the Catholic University of Santiago, the University of Concepción, the Austral of Valdivia, and the two technical universities, the Santa María Technical University of Valparaíso, and the State Technical University. The enrollment of all university establishments totals 25,939 students, of whom 12,895 belong to the University of Chile. The Student Federation of Chile (FECH), the largest and most important student organization in the country, has been a part of the tradition of militant political activism among youth in Latin America, and has had a historically significant role in the political life of the nation. Politics within this organization often faithfully reflects politics on a national scale. As a sort of microcosmos of Chile's political system, the FECH is worthy of observation and analysis.[46]

There are many who maintain that Chilean education has failed to concern itself with the social and economic needs of the country and is still carried on within the aristocratic molds of nineteenth-century society. It is significant, for example, that "of every 100 students entering elementary school, 22 fail to enter second year, only 52 continue on for a total of four years, and only 33 finish the sixth year of

[46] Frank Bonilla, "The Student Federation of Chile: Fifty Years of Political Action," *Journal of Inter-American Studies,* II, No. 3 (July, 1960).

elementary school. The fact that only 1.6 per cent of the Chilean population have a university education and 2.4 per cent have some other type of specialized training, shows the error of having an elementary school dedicated to preparing the student for college and a college organized to prepare him for a university which he will never attend."[47]

Higher education and advanced training received considerable impetus during the three years from 1960 to 1963. In addition to the expansion of the country's eight universities, creation of a system of regional university colleges was initiated by the University of Chile and has made facilities available to high school graduates in the provinces. Such regional colleges were in existence in Temuco and La Serena by 1962. A new unit was later founded at Antofagasta and others are planned for Talca and Ossorno. Advanced technical training was intensified through the Technical Cooperation Service (a part of the Development Corporation), the State Technical University and the University of Chile's Institute for Business Organization and Administration.

Other long-range and short-range measures have been taken recently to adjust the educational system to the country's requirements. The Human Resources Committee, established jointly by the Development Corporation and the University of Chile, is studying reform measures directed toward that end. This research is to determine Chile's needs for trained manpower on the basis of the production goals set in the Ten-Year Plan for Development, and to compare those needs with the production of technicians which may be expected on the basis of past trends. A large part of the basic data needed for educational reform had been accumulated by 1964. Examples of short-range measures are creation of the Educational Planning Commission to study plans for a functional and administrative reorganization of the Ministry of Education, and establishment by the universities, the Development Corporation and other organizations of a series of special training programs in fields where needs are obvious and urgent.[48]

The Social Structure

Strong class divisions and feelings are basic to Chilean society, if for no other reason than that status, prestige, power, and economic differences are always given preferential attention by Chileans. This high sensitivity to class stratification is easily perceived by the most

[47] J. Ahumada, *En vez de la miseria* (Santiago: Editorial del Pacífico, 1958), pp. 27–28.

[48] Inter-American Development Bank, *Social Progress Trust Fund, Third Annual Report, 1963* (Washington: Inter-American Development Bank, 1964), p. 187.

casual observer of the social scene, for Chileans tend to discuss public affairs almost invariably in terms of occupation, income, and prestige.[49]

The reasons for this sharp class awareness are partly historical. During colonial times and long after independence, Chile was characterized by a fairly rigid two-class society — a land-owning aristocracy descended from the original Spanish settlers, and a lower class formed by the large mass of peasants and domestic servants. The Indians lived as a nation apart. As race mixture proceeded, large numbers of *mestizos* appeared, some of whom acquired education and rose to occupy a middle position.

In the latter part of the nineteenth century, this middle category gradually enlarged. Its ranks swelled from many sources, including the old upper class, some of whose members had lost their estates and were being forced to enter business or the liberal professions, and newly arrived foreign elements. Stimulated by the growth of the population, accompanied by the trend towards urbanization and by general economic and educational development, this emerging middle group became, in less than a century and a half, one of the largest segments of Chilean society, estimated in 1949 at 1,100,000 persons or roughly one fifth of the total population.[50] There exist in Chile, then, three universally recognized groups or categories: an upper class, a middle or "employee" class,[51] and a lower class. All three categories are difficult to define precisely and to break down accurately, for another characteristic of Chilean class divisions is the lack of clearly marked boundaries. One of the difficulties of dealing with class structure is that local ratings do not always correspond among themselves or with those of a regional or national basis. More knowledge is needed about what the members themselves think of these groupings and how they classify themselves and others.[52]

In the first place two upper classes are distinguishable. On the one

[49] K. H. Silvert, *The Conflict Society: Reaction and Revolution in Latin America* (New Orleans: The Hauser Press, 1961), pp. 230–241, contains a series of accurate generalizations concerning Chilean society and very interesting interview material on the matter.

[50] Vega, *op. cit.*, p. 79.

[51] It is of some importance to note that the term "employee class" is commonly used in Chile to designate the middle segment. The reason is to be found in labor legislation which involves clear distinction between the *empleado* and the *obrero,* with charges and benefits derived from it also being different. Unquestionably, this occupational stratification, created by the law itself, is partly responsible for Chilean class-consciousness.

[52] Silvert, *The Conflict Society,* p. 231. Professor Silvert conducted a preliminary survey on this matter, among the Santiago population. Although the experiment was very limited and modest in scope, it is of intrinsic value because of the reality of the opinions revealed.

hand are the members of the old aristocracy of the land or remnants thereof, who have preserved their fortunes. On the other hand is what may be called a new-rich upper class (although here the difficulties begin). The latter group is chiefly formed of industrialists, merchants, politicians, and military men who either through business or politics or both have made fortunes which permitted them to arrive at the upper level. These members who have recently obtained power and prestige became more numerous after the sweeping political and economic reforms, started in 1920, deprived the landed aristocracy of its power monopoly and inaugurated a new era of broader-based politics.

The economic base of the country shifted with the impact of industrialization and modern technology, and the nature of politics also experienced a metamorphosis. Both factors provided access to the upper level to a new segment of the population.[53] Although the old landed aristocracy and the new moneyed upper class have power and prestige in common, they are opposed to each other in many of their interests, resulting in further fragmentation of the élite. The older group which is inaccessible except by marriage is chiefly concerned with the preservation of the semifeudalistic *latifundio* system. The new upper class, not nearly so tightly closed as the landowners, is generally open to all who are its financial equals, with ethnic and religious prejudice playing only a small part. In contrast with the old, the moneyed upper class is influenced by a diversity of interests and is generally interested in higher living standards and the increase of the population's ability to consume. It has no close ties with the Church and exerts its power through flexible organizational structures rather than rigid traditional structures.[54] This lower group is much more receptive to innovations and appreciative of technology than the old aristocracy, especially as regards business methods, and is politically more sophisticated.

Since there is a certain degree of mobility in the Chilean class system, many of the members of this class have advanced from the middle group, but being insecure in their lack of knowledge and experience, they will share some of the value complexes of the middle

[53] Francisco Walker Linares, "Evolución Social," in *Desarrollo de Chile en la primera mitad del siglo XX* (Santiago: Editorial Universitaria, n.d.), pp. 35–49. See also Joseph H. Fichter, *Cambio social en Chile. Un estudio de actitudes* (Santiago: Editorial Universitaria Católica, 1962), pp. 171–192.

[54] John Gillin, "Some Signposts for Policy," in *Social Change in Latin America Today* (New York: Council on Foreign Relations, Harper & Brothers, 1960), pp. 21–58. This article gives a general but accurate description of Latin America's social structure. Many of its observations are particularly fitting in Chilean societal structure.

group. Some of these newly rising persons are *turcos* (Turks), a generic name given to any people from the Levant who have accumulated fortunes that enable them to claim upper-class status. Since these persons are considered ethnically inferior, they may encounter difficulties, but access to the upper group is not impossible. They are among the wealthiest and more industrially advanced groups in the country, and their political influence is growing, especially through campaign financing.

The lower class may be equally divided into two groups: the farm laborers, and the industrial proletariat including factory workers and those in the mineral extraction industry. In addition, a third category, that of the "aristocrats of labor," such as the steel workers, may be differentiated. There seems to be some tendency toward skin-darkening as one goes down the occupation-income scale. As Benjamín Subercaseaux has stated, the Chilean lower class is distinguished primarily by its color. This tendency is more pronounced in the rural areas where the great majority of the *inquilinos* or sharecroppers are obviously of mixed blood.[55] The artisan group which in colonial times was small and composed mainly of *mestizos* is still within the lower class. Despite their relatively high income the artisans who adopt a life style characteristic of the middle group are precious few. In general, the artisan maintains living conditions similar to those of the proletariat, although his children, taking advantage of the urban public school system, may often become primary school teachers, for example, and thus automatically move up the social scale. Both the artisan and the new labor aristocrats, with higher monetary income than other members of the lower class, may give their offspring better educational opportunities, thereby enabling them to climb to the middle level.

National origin may in itself be a class determinant. For example, artisans of European origin, especially Germans, are highly esteemed and have no difficulty in being accepted as members of the middle class. In general, the great majority of foreigners who have settled in Chile, with the exception of an insignificant number who almost immediately identified themselves with the upper group and an even smaller number who joined the lower class, have increased the ranks of the middle segments of society.

The large growing class between the two extremes of the social ladder is largely urban, although a nucleus of the rural population is also part of this group. That nucleus, composed of small landowners,

[55] An excellent description of social conditions in mid-twentieth-century Chile is found in Fredrick B. Pike, *Chile and the United States, 1880–1962* (Notre Dame: University of Notre Dame Press, 1963), pp. 271–93.

is insignificant in number since the greatest portion of small-holders must be included in the lower class because of their economic status, education, and living accommodations. There are probably not more than fifteen or twenty thousand small landowners who can be properly classified as members of the middle class. With their families they constitute around eighty thousand persons.[56]

The urban middle class is extremely varied in income, occupation, and foci of interest. It is composed of: more than 90 per cent of the professionals (physicians, lawyers, engineers, and the like), or about 15,000 persons; more than 90 per cent of the university faculties, and the entire body of teachers at the primary, secondary, and special levels, a total of 25,000 persons; the officers' corps of the armed forces and the police, about 8,000 persons; around two thirds of the civil service, about 20,000 persons (the rest belong to either the upper class or in the case of workers to the lower group); two thirds of the private employees, about 100,000 persons (the other third are not counted for the identical reasons stated above); and, finally, some small industrialists, merchants, and *rentiers,* or about 70,000 persons. The total, considering the families involved, is estimated at one million, which added to the 100,000 given for the rural middle class, makes a grand total of 1,100,000 members of the Chilean middle class.[57] The most typical of this class is probably the professional and civil service employee.

Persons at either end of this middle group are difficult to classify. For example, a certain group of aspirants to the upper rank may be hardly distinguishable from a group stabilized as upper middle class. Furthermore, there is a group of small merchants, peddlers, and the like, who wander in a no man's land between the lower and middle class. At any rate, less blurring seems to exist between middle and lower groups than between the middle and upper class, for although the class system has become more flexible in the last quarter of a century, it is generally accepted that social distance between the middle and lower classes has widened considerably in recent times. The standard of living of the middle segment has evidently gone up while the lower has been struggling to hold its own, and, in many cases, has gone sharply down. The country's efforts to industrialize and, at the same time, raise living standards, with consequent economic problems such as inflation, have caused serious dislocations. In comparative terms, of all social groups the heaviest loser seems to have been the worker's class.

56 Vega, *op. cit.,* p. 84.

57 Vega, *op. cit.,* p. 85. These figures are the latest available but probably need some revision in the light of the recent census.

As of now, however, this middle class lacks the characteristics usually ascribed to such groups in more developed countries. Although it holds some values in common, such as disdain of manual labor and a minimum definition of "decency" in living conditions, it has yet to develop a distinctive consciousness and ideology of its own. The urban middle sectors, in general, tend to assume upper-class attitudes and to defend the value judgments of the aristocracy. For this reason, the middle group has developed very little consciousness of itself as a distinct class. In Chile, says a Chilean sociologist, "formed of such heterogeneous professional and economic elements, the middle class has no ideological homogeneity. Although the majority has a center position, its members take part in all the political parties from the extreme Right where some of the most ardent defenders of the principles sustained by the upper class are individuals of the middle class, to the extreme Left where the Communist Party is directed, in large part, by elements of the middle class. . . . This extreme ideological diversity, as well as the economic differences, explain why there does not exist in this great social conglomerate a class consciousness."[58]

The preceding sketch of Chilean social structure accurately describes it as "a class system clearly based on occupational considerations for the lower and middle groups, and resting on occupation plus family and other prestige factors for the upper."[59] It is a highly mobile system, with upward mobility being perhaps more in evidence than downward-directed motion, an almost natural phenomenon given the expansive transitional nature of the economic structure.[60] Chileans are acutely aware of social distinctions, the reason, other than the historical one, being the impact of recent economic and political changes upon social structure.

From the political viewpoint this stratification is paramount for any analysis, but beyond certain class-oriented stereotypes, such as the representation of the Church and the landowners by the Conservatives, the big industrialists by the Liberals, the white-collar employee class by the Radicals, and the support of the parties of the Left by the labor unions, little is known about the interrelationship between social characteristics and political attitudes and behavior.[61] In subsequent

[58] Vega, *op. cit.*, pp. 90–91.

[59] Silvert, *The Conflict Society*, p. 236.

[60] There is, however, a certain measure of downward motion principally caused by urbanization, as in the case of the rural upper-class member who finds himself demoted when migrating to the great urban centers.

[61] A recent study is Guillermo Briones, "La estructura social y la participación política. Un estudio de sociología electoral en Santiago de Chile," *Revista interamericana de ciencias sociales*, II, No. 3 (1963), pp. 376–404.

chapters attempts are made to explore some phases of this interrelationship. However, a warning is in order. Due to the lack of social research and available data on the present shifting and restructuring of society, the student of Chilean politics is unable to delve into the intricacies of trends and predictions. Of necessity he must confine himself to studies which are mostly descriptive of the moment.

A final comment may be in order. The legalization of social stratification passed with the colonial era, although it continued in social customs for a long time after independence and some remnants may still persist. Chile's progress in the way of rendering "differences irrelevant to social status," has gained her an enviable reputation on the continent as an effective democracy. Equality before the law and before the ballot boxes regardless of social status is an important leveling measure which seems firmly entrenched in Chilean democracy. How far equality has progressed in other aspects is difficult to determine without more independent data. The country is still characterized by a close association between upper and middle classes which works to the detriment of the lower mass. There are many who feel that the gulf separating these two population elements is the chief cause of economic stagnation and that it carries with it the seed of violent social revolution.

In September, 1957, under the auspices of the University of Chile and, for the first time in the history of the country, a scientific survey was made among the Greater Santiago area population (almost one fourth of the national total) in an effort to learn something about their unstructured ideas on some fundamental questions. This survey was conducted by 99 students of the Pedagogical Institute, using a 44-point questionnaire.[62] Results are based on visits to 2,124 homes, which resulted in a net total of 1,640 interviews with persons over 18 years of age. Given the unavailability of a full-age historico-quantitative study of Chile, the results of this preliminary work in spite of its limitations are significant for social scientists in that they give some idea of attitudes, tendencies, and aspirations which until now could only be guessed.

A substantial part of the questionnaire was devoted to living conditions and identification of related problems. On this matter, 45 per cent of the *santiaguinos* listed the economic problem (*falta de plata,* lack of money) as their chief preoccupation. In decreasing order, others pointed to housing difficulties (22 per cent), unemployment (9 per cent), education of their children (7 per cent), and health (4 per cent) as their main worries. The majority felt their standard

[62] Alain Girard and Raúl Samuel, *Situación y perspectivas de Chile en Septiembre de 1957* (Santiago: Universidad de Chile, 1958).

of living had dropped, and 44 per cent stated that their economic status in 1957 was inferior to that of five years before. Only one fourth of the informants thought that their economic position had improved. It is interesting to note that the "economic problem" seemingly affects virtually all social categories.

On the subject of housing, the workers and *empleado* classes showed greater sensitiveness than the upper group. One half of the interviewees stated satisfaction with their housing accommodations. The other half considered them *regular*[63] (not so good) (36 per cent), bad (9 per cent), and very bad (4 per cent). In a city with as many old houses as Santiago, it seems improbable that such a small percentage would consider its housing inadequate. Only 35 per cent of the people own their own homes.

More than half of those interviewed used the urban transportation system regularly; only 8 per cent owned automobiles, and 1 per cent had motor scooters. Somewhat surprising are the facts that among the professional and employer classes, 45 per cent made use of public transportation facilities; that 2 per cent of the workers had automobiles; and that 5 per cent used scooters or bicycles. Nearly half of the respondents believed the public transportation to be deficient.

Also significant were the answers related to expectations, for they gave a clear image of the typical *santiaguino's* vision of the future. To begin with, nine out of ten respondents believed that economic issues were Chile's number one problem. Only 7 per cent thought that political problems represented the number one problem. In general, young interviewees, particularly those between the ages of eighteen and twenty-four, were keen and willing to give opinions on economic subjects. About 60 per cent of all persons interviewed considered present conditions "bad," 35 per cent thought them *regular*, and only 4 per cent termed them "good."

Asked how they thought the economic situation would change in the next few years, 32 per cent stated it would be worse, 25 per cent said it would remain unchanged, and 35 per cent declared there would be an improvement. The sum of the first two percentages reveals an inclination towards pessimism and was considered by many observers as symptomatic of the majority's lack of confidence in the country's

[63] A certain margin of error should be taken into account in connection with the use of this term. The survey's directors' opinion is that *regular* should be taken as synonymous with "correct, although without excellence." However, it can be argued that in Chilean colloquial speech *regular* implies a complete scale of shades that runs from "the worst" to "the satisfactory." Only persons of unusual frankness would use the term *pésimo* to denote dissatisfaction if given the opportunity of using *regular*.

future development.[64] This is important, since psychological factors do play a role in stimulating the inflationary spiral, and since dissatisfaction may eventually lead to desires for drastic political solutions. It should be observed that not long after the survey was completed, the disastrous drop of copper prices in early 1958 undoubtedly added to the plummet of despair, making it doubtful that those who were then optimistic are still maintaining the same views. The survey indicated that women were more severe and more pessimistic than men in their judgment of the situation. It also showed that pessimism was espoused in inverse proportion to the social scale, being strongest among the lower groups. Among all classes, manual workers had the gloomiest views concerning the future.

In other fields of questioning, results were equally revealing. For example, it was found that 66 out of 100 persons had not finished their formal education, 33 of that 66 having gone no further than the third grade at the secondary school level, and 4 out of 10 not having gone beyond the third year. However, these figures are to be taken with caution because of the peculiarities of the Santiago population, and are probably not applicable on the national scene. In general, Chileans appeared satisfied with their educational system. More than half of those interviewed considered it "good," and 15 per cent superlative. Another field was newspaper reading which varies according to instruction level and class position. Of those responding 48 per cent were found to read the press daily, 46 per cent were irregular readers, and 10 per cent were non-readers. The proportion of homes with radios was 87 per cent, although the figure was even higher (98 per cent) among families in the higher status groups. Among the workers, the percentage of those with radios was 77.

Reactions to other questions were interesting as they revealed Chilean attitudes toward other nations. Among the Latin American countries, Mexico was preferred by 23 per cent, and Brazil, second, by 21 per cent. With respect to Argentina, 30 per cent were sympathetic while 23 per cent expressed dislike, women outnumbering men in the former group. Inclination toward Argentina was stronger among the low-income groups. Only small percentages were inclined toward Perú and Bolivia. Young men and workers made up a majority of those who expressed preference for Mexico.

In international politics, Chile's adherence to the Western camp seems well defined, with 35 per cent favoring the United States and only 4 per cent inclining toward the Soviet Union. After the United

64 See, for example, "Situación y perspectivas de Chile," *El Mercurio*, February 2, 1958, and "Preocupaciones dominantes en Chile," *El Mercurio*, February 8, 1958.

States, the preferred country was Germany (20 per cent), especially by men. Women tended to prefer the United States. The younger generation favored in order the United States, Germany, Italy, and France. Upper-class members manifested less disposition than others towards the United States but had no enthusiasm for the Soviet Union either. This can be explained among other ways in terms of the Catholic-Protestant division which Chilean Conservatives see exemplified as an "Anglo-Saxon" culture versus a "Latin" or "roman" way of life.[65] The least hostility toward the Soviet Union was found among the workers.

On the basis of educational level the picture was different. The higher the cultural level of the informants, the greater the esteem for Great Britain, Germany and especially France, and the lower the esteem for the United States and Russia.[66]

Questions relative to national character revealed an interesting self-portrait: "we are affectionate, kind, industrious, humanitarian, obliging, happily disposed, hospitable." Some added "intelligent, resigned, and patient." However, the flattering adjectives used to describe national characteristics were counterbalanced by the terms denoting the gravest national defects. Drinking was on top of that list, followed by laziness. Upper-class members joined in the belief that the Chilean workers are *flojos* (indolent) while the latter insisted they are the only truly industrious group of society. Other deprecating terms used were: vice-addicted, irresponsible, negligent, undependable, wasteful (8 per cent), and apathetic (5 per cent).

Many of these virtues and faults have, in fact, been mentioned by commentators on Chile, both foreign and native, and, in general, if one discounts a certain amount of self-flattery dictated by national pride, the image that Chileans seem to have of themselves is not too distorted. Perhaps a fair composite picture is the one given by a writer who speaks of the people as "generally independent and temperate of character, prodigal, hospitable, cautious, naturally suspicious, irregularly industrious, difficult to develop enthusiasm, who have little sentimentality, and who are conservative in praise and rude in censure."[67] This image would justify the appellation "Englishmen of South America," often given to Chile by those who have wanted to

[65] For an interesting discussion of the anti-United States feelings of the Chilean upper classes see Pike, *op. cit.*, pp. 250–256.

[66] For an interesting account of Chilean opinions concerning the United States, see K. H. Silvert, "The Eagle Inside" (Santiago: American Universities Field Staff Letter, May 26, 1957).

[67] Alberto Cabero, *Chile y los chilenos* (Santiago: Editorial Lyceum, 1948), p. 155.

emphasize the less imaginative and passionate but more practical and active nature of Chileans as compared with that of tropical Latin Americans. Somewhat abhorrent of so-called "tropicalism," Chileans have always cultivated more successfully those literary genres in which reasoning is more important than imagination. Humor, although witty, is characteristically crude rather than elegantly salted. Their orators are scanty in expression and consciously avoid verbosity. Even political speechmaking is usually characterized by sobriety and simplicity, a striking contrast to the pyrotechnics of most Latin American campaign oratory. It is true that the Chilean ideal type of *homo politicus* of the nineteenth century, symbolized by austerity and represented by political figures such as Montt, Varas, or Matta, has given way in the present, because of the social and economic upheaval, to a more jovial and emotional specimen typified by Arturo Alessandri. But numerous signs of this tendency to severity in the Chilean character can be found in the country's history. Further evidence has appeared in recent years with the success of *políticos,* like Jorge Alessandri, who appealed to this innate Chilean ordered way of looking at life.

The portrait can be completed by mentioning some of the reigning myths illustrative of the Chileans' version of themselves. Like all national myths, these contain elements of fact and fiction and are sometimes contradictory. In general, they are accepted and recognized by all Chilean writers.[68] In the first place Chileans are proud of their intellectual achievements and consider themselves particularly apt for the arts in general.[69] This belief is substantiated by literary figures of international fame, and a Nobel-prize winner, the poetess Gabriela Mistral. Second is the conviction that education is the best means of remedying social ills, of overcoming and altering those conditions which militate against progress. Education will counteract the weighting-down effect on society of the poorly educated segments. Third, although not third in importance, is the persuasion that Chile is basically an effective institutional democracy. Every now and then, this idea is partially shattered by political actions which are technically legal but which need stretching to fit within democratic bounds. Nevertheless, this state of mind is firmly founded in reality, for Chile has developed a fairly mature system of politics, including respect for legality, free elections, high voter turnout, and effective parties which are an integral part of the system. Chileans are also proud of not

[68] K. H. Silvert, "Coda" (Buenos Aires: American Universities Field Staff Letter, September 21, 1957) gives an excellent analysis of Chilean national myths. Our listing is suggested by Professor Silvert.

[69] Cabero, *op. cit.,* pp. 137–138.

being subject to violence in politics and of having few revolutionary changes of government on their record. The myth of race homogeneity, not as well founded as other myths, is responsible for Chileans feeling more fortunate than other Latin Americans because they have no Indian problem and are not *mestizos* (actually, one third of them are).[70] They extoll the virtues of a "Chilean race," and point to the tough qualities of their Araucanian, Basque, and Catalan ancestors,[71] with almost as much pride as Miguel de Unamuno had when he gave his own people, the Basques, credit for two great creations: the Jesuit Order and the Republic of Chile.

Two other characteristics should be mentioned which relate to military affairs. In this area, the Chilean says of himself that his innate courage, disciplinary sense, patriotism, and endurance are all qualities of the good soldier. He believes in Chile's military invincibility, well based in view of the notable set of national heroes that Chile has acquired in the course of international wars.[72] Coupled with this is the opinion that these very military qualities have caused an antimilitarist feeling, a desire to restrict the military to its true function, keeping it from active participation in affairs other than its own. This opinion holds up well, as shown by the country's scarcity of military dictators.[73]

The overall picture denotes a fine set of attitudes and a serious, disciplined, and strong people — a character portrait more reminiscent of Sancho than of Don Quixote in Cervantes' immortal work, with the tone set by an admirable permeating, practical good sense. As one writer puts it: "When a national views itself as civilian-oriented, nonviolent, anxious to remain within institutional norms, cultured and possessed of a fine assortment of ethnic materials, it is reflecting, at least, partially mature, and soft self-appreciations and norms."[74]

Social and economic shifts and the pressure of inflation have brought other changes, which are difficult to define and measure.[75] The most obvious, perhaps, is a new bitterness and shortness of temper, regardless of class or fortune, which strikes the person revisiting Chile. It is a bitterness sometimes bordering on almost insane animosity against all things and all strangers (foreign or native), and is similar to the state of mind reportedly found by visitors to postwar France. It is, of course, a manifestation of profound discontent, "the blowing

[70] Silvert, "Coda," p. 8.
[71] See Cabero, *op. cit.*, pp. 45–112.
[72] Silvert, "Coda," pp. 8–9; Cabero, *op. cit.*, p. 144.
[73] Cabero, *op. cit.*, pp. 147–148.
[74] Silvert, "Coda," p. 11.
[75] See Alberto Baltra, "Los factores sociales y el desarrollo económico," *Panorama económico,* XI, No. 181, (December 6, 1957), pp. 785–790.

off of steam which threatens to explode the boiler"; and the "pressure is relieved by skinning the other fellow, lamenting bad fortune all the while."[76] Some claim that a major source of this bitterness is the inefficiency of the public administration system, but, for obvious reasons, it is unjust and inaccurate to blame the government for all the national troubles and seems more fruitful to seek explanations in the value system. Often it is said that the price for human progress is the disruption of old ways and the acceptance of new ones. Accordingly, a keen observer of Chilean society proposes the idea that Chileans live in a "wrenched, twisted society," because their "value system has not kept pace in its adjustment to the rapidly changing institutional structure," or, to put it differently, "the myths of the new society have not had time to form about the technical innovations of the twentieth century."[77] This theory does much more than explain the phenomenon of Chilean irritation, which after all, is not important, and has far-reaching implications. Since Chile, like all societies, cannot remain at a standstill with static contemporary conditions, the price for progress will have to be fully made and may mean, politically, a drastic social restructuring of Chile's power groups.

[76] Article by Alejandro Tinsly in *El Mercurio,* January 24, 1957. This article, by a Chilean humorist, deals in a light vein with this phenomenon. A more detailed and serious treatment is K. H. Silvert, "On Civil Discourtesy" (Santiago: American Universities Field Staff Letter, February 5, 1957).

[77] Silvert, "Coda," p. 11.

2

The Pattern of Political Development*

Many of the features of the system of Spanish colonial government, which remained in existence for over three centuries, endured to become conditioning elements in the social, economic, and political development of modern Chile. The *latifundio* system, the social structure, the all-pervading influence of the Church, the characteristics of the frontier, and many political institutions, survived separation from Spain and continued to influence government in the republican era. This chapter is devoted to a general description of the historical pattern of Chilean socio-political development since the colonial era and to an appraisal of substantial changes at particularly significant periods.

The Early Republican Era

The revolution for independence in Chile was almost accidental, in the sense that it was precipitated by the succession of events that occurred in Spain after 1808. There is no evidence that there existed in Chile before these occurrences any strong desire for political innovations. Among the Chilean Creoles there was no doctrinal or philosophical movement aimed at independence, and only a few of their revolutionary leaders were actually cognizant of the political meaning of the revolutionary era in the Old World. With the Creoles divided in allegiance, the winning of independence, as in most of Latin America, was marked by civil war. Spanish authorities mustered into service

* This chapter includes portions of a monograph by this author entitled "Genesis and Modernization of Political Parties in Chile" (Gainesville: University of Florida Press, 1962). Copyright 1962 by the Pan American Foundation, Inc. Used by permission.

Creole loyalists and enrolled recruits without regard to previous social status; and patriot leaders, in turn, enlisted soldiers from all social classes. In the war for independence there was no social upheaval involved, nor was there any basic change in institutions. When the struggle ended, Chile found itself free from all political ties to Spain, but its social structure emerged intact — at one end of the social scale, a respectable aristocracy united by blood ties and common interests, whose political experience was insignificant; at the other end, an ignorant and servile mass incapable of understanding or practicing the rights and duties of a free people.

It was only to be expected that at the outset, the military leaders of the successful revolution having won great prestige and the new army being the only organized force in the country, these elements would prevail over the rest of the colonial aristocracy, occupied as it was in recovering from the material losses it had suffered. Consequently, during the period from 1817 to 1823, Bernardo O'Higgins, the distinguished military hero, headed a government legally constituted under an autocratic institutional system. When, believing that in order to institute a real republic it was necessary first to modify society, O'Higgins attempted reforms, he was confronted with revolt in 1823. Rather than subject the country to civil strife, he resigned his authority.

O'Higgins' renunciation marked the appearance of two distinct political tendencies which were later to result in the creation of Chile's early parties. One favored a real republic, free and democratic, and the liberalization of social institutions accordingly, regardless of the lack of traditions in political habits; the other demanded a strong centralized government, as opposed to the federalization advocated by its opponents, and aspired, in general, to a system which would not break completely with colonial traditions, one which would not modify the existing structure of society, and which, in short, would not be different from the one maintained under Spanish control.

All of those who were supporters of the first tendency were known as the *liberales* or *pipiolos* (liberals or novices), while the group who subscribed to more conservative ideas became known as the *pelucones* (bigwigs). Except for a short period after the fall of O'Higgins, the *pipiolos* were in the ascendant until 1830. After a series of constitutional experiments, which included an attempt to establish a federal form of government, a liberal victory in an election of deputies to a new constituent assembly and consequent prospects of social reform were among the causes of the civil war of 1829. This war brought success to the conservatives and the inauguration of an "autocratic republic." At this time there were not yet in existence any well-defined political organizations, but only confused and vague aspirations for a constitutional system. These took only such forms as existed in the broad tendencies that have been mentioned.

The Autocratic Republic (1830–1871)

In the midst of the chaos a new group, the *estanqueros,* made its appearance under the leadership of a remarkable man, Diego Portales, who was to lead Chile out of anarchy and into strong, solid, and orderly government. A man of intuition, Portales understood the necessity of giving a social foundation to the political structure, of grouping all social forces in support of an impersonal regime of legitimate tradition which could offer legal regularity, decorum, and circumspection, a guarantee of order, and, finally, good government.[1] To Portales, constitutional techniques were only accessory; the essential issue was to set up what he called "the mainspring of the machinery" — traditional authority, a quiet and silent force, loyally obeyed and respected, eternal, above any *caudillos* and factions.

Portales' task of restoring peace and establishing a strong, stable government was facilitated by various factors. In the first place, Chile was, of all the former Spanish colonies, the one with the most compact social and geographical unity. Its territory, confined to what today is central Chile, was relatively small; most of its inhabitants lived in the area between La Serena and Bío-Bío. This population was racially homogeneous, most Indians having been pushed south of the Bío-Bío River and the remaining ones having mixed with whites. In addition, Chile already had a political and social head, the city of Santiago, which stood far above all other cities in influence and wealth.

Not only the geographical conditions of the country and the relative simplicity of its social structure were important in the consolidation of the state built by Portales, for no less significant were its isolation from the world and the relative backwardness of the Chile of 1830. These conditions account for the survival of the colonial spirit of passive obedience and respect for hierarchy which, in time, made possible the restoration by Portales of the monarchical and aristocratic traditions of colonial Chile under a new legal framework, outwardly republican. The old social order had been preserved by what Portales, using a picturesque expression, often called "the weight of the night," that is, Chile's traditional habits of obedience and respect for authority, ingrained by centuries of colonial domination.

The Chilean aristocracy provided the base for the authoritarian structure created by Portales. Just as geographical conditions tended

[1] Alberto Edwards, *La fronda aristocrática* (Santiago: Editorial del Pacífico, 1952), p. 51.

to encourage unity and stability, historical accident had also created a social encouragement. The Chilean aristocracy was significantly different from the aristocracies of other Latin American countries in that it was already a mixed aristocracy, at the same time bourgeois and feudal, in which at the advent of independence there were successfully intermingled the old families of *conquistadores* and landowners with new stocks of enterprising Basque immigrants who had become successful businessmen. There was not a bourgeois class in Chile because it had fused with the old nobility, forming only one group after 1750. The wealthy bourgeois and the aristocrat could not clash because they were one. From the combination of landowners and merchants, this mixed aristocracy derived its virtues as well as its defects. Industry and economy and a good practical sense, narrow-mindedness and lack of imagination, essentially bourgeois qualities, were mixed in the Chilean aristocrat with the ambitions for power, pride in independence, and rebellious spirit inherited from his feudal ancestors.[2] Portales was to be the providential leader of this aristocracy. The legal framework was provided by the constitution of 1833, which with some alterations was to remain in force for almost a century. During the ensuing forty years, the powers of the executive were without an effective counterweight. Under that instrument, Chile was to acquire a reputation for stability in striking contrast to the reputations of other Latin American republics which were periodically rent by revolutions and military dictatorships. For approximately twenty years the oligarchy made no attempt to oppose the presidential absolutism created by Portales. However, after 1849 and up to 1891, in the words of a Chilean political writer, "The politics of Chile [were] synthesized principally in the conflict between two organic spiritual elements, both of which belonged to the past: the aristocracy and the monarchy." Alberto Edwards has, in his admirable discussion of this struggle between the feudal-bourgeois oligarchy and executive absolutism, almost invariably peaceful in nature, used the term *fronda aristocrática*. He compares it with the phenomenon which in Europe, especially after 1848, transformed the traditional monarchies based on the divine right theory into parliamentary regimes dominated by the bourgeois plutocracy.[3]

According to Edwards, survival of the monarchical and aristocratic traditions of colonial Chile after its independence made it possible to organize the country under a political system which, after 1830, did not necessarily rest upon forcible seizure of power or upon arbitrariness and cruelty in the use and abuse of this power. Slowly this system was to develop into parliamentarism, at the same pace as the

[2] *Ibid.*, p. 17.
[3] *Ibid.*, p. 15.

aristocracy became stronger than the presidents, until finally the *fronda* defeated executive absolutism. Chile became an exception among the former Spanish colonies, enjoying political stability precisely because of having preserved intact its colonial past. It was, in this sense, socially the most backward of them all.

It is not possible to speak of well-defined political parties in reference to that period of Chilean history. Rather than real parties, there were alignments and groupings dictated by the common interests of the restricted circle which constituted the oligarchy and created as instruments to influence the government.[4] As a matter of convenience, the development of political parties in Chile can be divided into four periods. From 1830 to 1860, political organizations (not actually political parties in the true sense) participated very little, if at all, in a system in which presidential authority was all-pervasive.[5] From 1860 to 1890, the presidents governed with support of parties, and there existed a sort of unstable equilibrium between executives and the groups which supported them. During the third period, the period of the "parliamentary republic," from 1891 to 1920, presidential influence became almost extinct, and parties ruled at will. The fourth, beginning in 1920,

[4] They were "general staffs without soldiers" since the great mass of the people were not participants. The electoral system provided by the authoritarian scheme of the Constitution of 1833 placed an irresistible power in the hands of the chief executive who named all the election administrators, and who had unlimited means of action to dispose of political opponents. According to the law, individuals with the right to vote, who wished to make use of that right, had to register with their respective town councils (all composed of presidential appointees), from which they received a certificate or ticket called a "qualification." This qualification had to be presented by the citizen upon voting. Under such circumstances, no candidate could hope to win an election without the support of the government. For example, in the 1864 elections the total number of qualified voters was 22,261. Shortly before the elections took place, agents of the chief executive (intendants, governors, *subdelegados* and National Guard commanders) were holding 13,000 "qualification" certificates, a number more than sufficient to assure election of the government's list of candidates.

[5] The Conservative Party, born of the *pelucones* and of the organizational genius of Portales, was to govern the country after the revolution of 1829 almost without interruption for the next thirty years. The *pipiolos* or liberals as well as the followers of O'Higgins and the federalists were completely excluded from any influence in the government, and their leaders dismissed and intimidated by Portales' iron hand. "Twenty years of strife had not only conquered but crushed them as well, and under an authority which stifled by the aid of force the slightest manifestation of discontent, they no longer had hopes of renewing the struggle." Luis Galdames, *A History of Chile* (Chapel Hill: The University of North Carolina Press, 1941), p. 256. As the country recovered and prospered, it began to rejoice over the work of the revolution; the Conservatives won prestige, and their opponents gradually disappeared from the political scene.

has been marked by the rebellion of an electorate, until then submissive, and the appearance of new party types.

The thirty-year period beginning in 1830 witnessed the orderly ten-year "reigns" of three successive Presidents.[6] General Joaquín Prieto (1831–1841), elected under the auspices of Portales, who was to die at the hands of assassins in 1837; Manuel Bulnes (1841–1851); and Manuel Montt (1851–1861). Long before the end of this period, however, divisions began to arise in the conservative camp.[7]

The material progress of the country was a most powerful agent in an intellectual movement which began in 1842. This intellectual awakening of Chile was to have immediate consequences in its political life. The progress of education, especially after the founding of the University of Chile, in 1842, the influence of foreign exiles, particularly from Argentina, the appearance of several periodicals, and the emergence of national writers and poets were significant in awakening public interest in social and political reforms. A new liberal spirit, which had little in common with the approach of the early liberals, was growing in a new generation. This spirit was strongly apparent in the works of Francisco Bilbao and José Victorino Lastarria, whose criticisms of the past, including religion as well as politics, were quite severe. This liberal current was confined to academic circles and at first had little influence upon parties. However, in 1849, a new group, the Liberal party, growing out of the intellectual renaissance of 1842, arose under the guidance of José Victorino Lastarria.[8] Some of the old *pipiolos* were also incorporated into this group. By 1849 it was represented in the Congress by some brilliant men of liberal ideas who were, however, not party members. At the same time, a Reform Club aimed at bringing about some constitutional reforms had a brief existence. In 1850 a new political group, known as the *Sociedad de la Igualdad* (Society of Equality) was established by Francisco Bilbao. For seven months this Society, which attracted a large number of workers, carried out an intense campaign in favor of freedom of suffrage and civil liberties and against the governmental candidacy

[6] Since the constitution permitted re-election for a second period of five years, all presidents availed themselves of the opportunity. Re-election was always achieved without difficulty.

[7] The excessively restrictive policy in excluding their opponents who were, after all, members of their own class, was not unanimously approved by all members of the party. A moderate faction, representing a conciliatory tendency, appeared in 1835 on the occasion of the presidential election in which General Prieto was re-elected for a second term. This faction, known as the *filopolitas* (after the title of their newspaper), was short-lived and was soon brought into submission by Portales' strong will.

[8] Fernando Campos Harriet, *Historia constitucional de Chile* (Santiago: Editorial Jurídica de Chile, 1956), pp. 251–265.

of Manuel Montt, chosen by the Conservatives to succeed General Bulnes. Equalitarians and liberals joined forces to combat the government, and held public meetings until finally the government declared the Society of Equality dissolved and sent the leaders of the liberal movement into exile. During this period there also emerged the figure of an early champion of social reform, Santiago Arcos. A young disciple of French utopian socialism, Arcos was the first national writer to study Chilean society in a systematic manner. Anticipating the later labor movements, he believed that a proletarian party representing the interests of the working classes might be formed and proposed that drastic economic reforms, beginning with land distribution, would have to precede changes in the political system, if these were to be given solid foundation. Inspired by self-denying love for the poor, he vigorously defended their cause. "Everywhere in the world," he said, "there are the rich and the poor, but not everywhere are there poor like those of Chile. In the United States, England, and in Spain there are people who are poor, but in these places poverty is an accident, and not a normal state, while in Chile, poverty is a condition of life."[9]

The ten-year period of Montt witnessed remarkable economic progress and with it the development of a new and vigorous group of wealthy mining and merchant families who, rebelling against the existing semifeudal system, began to demand liberal reforms. Economic development had built up new wealth and created new power structures.[10] The clergy, a powerful group since colonial times, and the nobility were consequently weakened, and a new governmental ideal more in consonance with social development began to arise — the liberal-democratic program calling for respect of civil liberties, freedom of suffrage, secularization, and limitation of executive authority.[11]

The period is one of transition between two types of economy: the feudal and the capitalist. It is a critical period in that it is marked by changing ideas and by the development of a strong opposition to the heretofore unquestioned authority of those in power.[12]

At the end of the period of the "aristocratic republic" it was clear that questions of moral and constitutional import were determining

[9] Domingo Amunátegui, *El progreso intelectual y político de Chile* (Santiago: Editorial Nascimento, 1936), p. 84.

[10] See Alberto Edwards, *El gobierno de don Manuel Montt* (Santiago: Editorial Nascimento, 1932).

[11] Julio César Jobet, *Ensayo crítico del desarrollo económico-social de Chile* (Santiago: Editorial Universitaria, 1955), pp. 40–43.

[12] Galdames, *A History of Chile*, p. 256.

the delimitation of political camps. "While for the conservatives political authority and religious dogma were the two fundamentals of well-being and of collective progress, for their adversaries liberty in politics and liberty in belief and ideas were conditions indispensable for social development."[13] The social transformation which was needed to permit the passing from the "autocratic republic" to the "liberal republic" had occurred. The growth of the new mining and commercial bourgeoisie, and consciousness of strength newly acquired by this class, were determining factors in the ensuing era of moderation in which political parties began to take a more active role in the nation's life. Until this time, Presidents had been able to rule without the assistance of organized political forces. With the rise of liberalism, this was no longer the case; the presidential authoritarianism could not continue to function independently without this assistance. During the "liberal republic" the President felt impelled to seek the support of at least one of the existing political groups, although, thanks to his decisive influence in the electoral machinery, he was to remain undisputed master of his own political faction. Although still far from party government, the system required at least some participation of organized groups in national politics.[14]

In the elections of 1861, José Joaquín Pérez, National Party candidate, was favored for the presidency. A man of conciliatory inclinations, he first attempted to govern wtih a cabinet in which all political groups — liberals, conservatives, and nationals — had representation. Having failed in this attempt, Pérez finally dismissed the National Party and turned for support to Montt's former adversaries, the Liberal-Conservative fusion, and the clergy, driving into the opposition the party which had elected him.

A new political organization which has existed up to the present time was born in 1861 during Pérez's first year in office. This new political group, calling itself the Radical Party, was formed by the most advanced or orthodox liberals, who wanted political reforms at all costs and who were ready to launch a vigorous opposition campaign.[15] The foundations of the Radical Party, destined to play a great role in Chilean politics, had been laid by Pedro León Gallo, a rich miner of the north who led an unsuccessful revolt in 1859, and by the Matta brothers, Manuel Antonio and Guillermo. At first only

[13] *Ibid.*, p. 303.

[14] Julio Heise González, *Historia constitucional de Chile* (Santiago: Editorial Jurídica de Chile, 1954), p. 77.

[15] Edmundo Montecinos Rozas, *Apuntaciones para el estudio de la evolución de los partidos políticos chilenos y de su proyección jurídica* (Santiago: Imp. Dirección General de Prisiones, 1942), pp. 66–67. This work is a useful historical sketch of party development in Chile up to 1939.

a small group of dissident liberals, the party was soon to grow into a formidable force as lower-middle-class intellectuals, Masons, members of "reform clubs," and small merchants began to swell its ranks. In the beginning the Radical Party program included four essential points: constitutional reform, state supervision over education, administrative decentralization, and freedom of suffrage. Later the Radicals were to acquire the strong anticlerical taint which became a distinctive mark of this political group. Socially and economically, then, the Radical Party was at first the expression of the political demands of the new wealthy bourgeoisie produced by the development of mining in the north and subsequently became the focus of the resistance by the agricultural provinces of the south to the centralization of power in Santiago. Later it was reinforced by the other social groups which merged as a middle class began to develop in the cities.

The Liberal Republic (1871–1891)

After 1864 the so-called "theological questions" became the crucial issue in Chilean politics. By this time, conflict and upheaval were open and common, and the period was to witness a fierce political struggle which ended with victory for the liberal cause. The opposition's campaign in behalf of freedom of instruction, strongly resisted by the conservative elements which formed part of the administration of Federico Errázuriz Zañartu (1871–1875), precipitated the split of the government coalition.

Other religious questions contributed to this division. The reforms which were advanced by the liberal elements included suppression of the ecclesiastical *fuero,*[16] "secularization" of cemeteries, civil marriage, and separation of church and state.[17] "The political struggle degenerated, therefore, into a religious struggle, and the Conservative Party was transformed into a clerical or 'ultra-montane' group, as its adversaries branded it, opposed to the other extreme party, the radical or 'red,' as it was nicknamed."[18] Finally, in 1873, the Liberal Conservative coalition definitely broke up; Errázuriz dismissed the Conservative Party and formed a cabinet composed entirely of liberal parliamentarians.[19] The new coalition, composed of the Liberals, the Radicals, and the Nationals, called itself the Liberal Alliance and now sup-

[16] The right of the clergy to be judged by their own tribunals.

[17] See Ricardo Donoso, *Las ideas políticas en Chile* (Mexico: Fondo de Cultura Económica, 1946), pp. 174–326, for an excellent treatment of events concerning the religious issues.

[18] Galdames, *op. cit.,* p. 317.

[19] For constitutional reforms during this period see Alfredo Meynet González, *Estudio histórico de las reformas constitucionales de la administración Errázuriz Zañartu* (*1871–1876*) (Santiago, 1946).

ported the government. The new group, so heterogeneous in composition, was, nevertheless, bound together by a common demand for religious reforms, and "in more general terms, by their common belief in and devotion to the nineteenth-century ideal of progress."[20] With the exception of the religious question, it lacked a definite program and carried within itself the seeds of discord, represented by the various circles in which its members were divided.

The old conservatives, embittered by defeat, were to become more intransigent than ever, to the point of desiring, once displaced from power, even the destruction of the authoritarian structure created by Portales, which was now the stronghold of their enemy.[21] With the coming of elections in 1876 to choose Errázuriz's successor, a new party, the Liberal-Democratic, made its appearance. It was a small group, hastily organized to support the candidacy of the illustrious publicist Benjamín Vicuña Mackenna, but it almost wholly disappeared shortly after defeat at the polls.

When Aníbal Pinto, the new President elected by the Liberals in 1876, took office, the country was passing through a severe economic crisis. The seriousness of the situation forced what amounted to a temporary truce in political battles. These halted altogether when, in 1879, Chile entered upon the greatest of all the conflicts in its national existence, the War of the Pacific. Had this national crisis not occurred, it is possible that revolution would have ended Pinto's administration. As a consequence of its victory over Peru and Bolivia, Chile remained in possession of rich nitrate and copper territories, the development of which had been the cause of the conflict. The newly acquired wealth meant for the country the opening of an era of expansion and economic development which was to have repercussions in the structure of society as well as in politics. Chile had increased its territory by more than a third, and the revenues derived from nitrate began increasingly to augment private wealth and public revenue. With the end of the war came also the end of what has been called "The Golden Era of Liberalism," which had given a new veneer to the old authoritarian political system, making it acceptable for a few more years.[22]

The new President, Domingo Santa María, was a true exponent of political authoritarianism and religious liberalism, the essence of liberal

[20] John Reese Stevenson, *The Chilean Popular Front* (Philadelphia: University of Pennsylvania Press, 1942), p. 16.

[21] Alberto Edwards and Eduardo Frei, *Historia de los partidos políticos chilenos* (Santiago: Editorial del Pacífico, 1949), p. 78. This volume binds together Alberto Edwards, *Bosquejo histórico de los partidos políticos chilenos,* first published in 1936, and another study by Eduardo Frei, which covers the period 1891–1938.

[22] Edwards and Frei, *op. cit.,* pp. 80, 82.

thought of the time. Although the Santa María administration was far from being characterized by political liberty (it freely used executive control over elections), the reform spirit which animated the regime resulted in the enactment of anti-clerical laws and legislation extending suffrage to all Chilean males of twenty-five years of age and removing the income and property restrictions imposed by the Constitution of 1833.[23]

The War of the Pacific had opened an era of prosperity, evidenced by the fact that in ten years the income of the Chilean treasury was nearly quadrupled (from 15 to 60 million pesos).[24] This prosperity radiated to all the social classes, but it was in particular concentrated in the upper classes of society. With the riches of the public treasury at its disposal the government undertook public works programs, opened new roads, promoted immigration, established war pensions, and increased wages of public employees. Currency problems, however, were aggravated because of the government's failure to redeem paper money issued as an extraordinary measure during the economic crisis in the Pinto administration and later employed to finance the war. The peso dropped 50 per cent by the end of the war, compounding the existing currency weakness. The cost of living increased, and the mass of consumers became the victims of monetary depreciation. Such was the origin of the chronic inflation which has affected Chile to this day.

The nitrate revenues, however, were applied to everything but the redemption of paper money issues. This policy seemed clearly in the interests of the upper classes, since it saved them from the necessity of levying taxes on themselves. The systematic depreciation of the currency favored the interests of the great landowners and commercial magnates by permitting them to pay the salaried and laboring classes the same wages in depreciated money, while increasing the profits they themselves received for Chilean exports sold in the world market.[25] Thus currency manipulation became a habit and "probably the most subtle and at the same time the most effective of the various exploitive techniques of the oligarchs."[26] It led one deputy to make in Congress the following statement: "In Chile, there exist two indus-

[23] For a study of the Santa María administration see Humberto Alegría Reyes, *Orientación política de la administración Santa María* (Santiago, 1946).

[24] Galdames, *op. cit.*, p. 359.

[25] Jobet, *op. cit.*, pp. 60–63. See also Julio Valdés Cange (Alejandro Venegas), *Sinceridad: Chile íntimo en 1910* (Santiago: Imprenta Universitaria, 1910).

[26] Stevenson, *op. cit.*, p. 25.

tries. One is that of the *rotos* [poor], who saw-off guns to rob the rich, and another, that of the rich, who saw-off *pesos* to rob the *rotos*."[27]

If the mining wealth meant the salvation of the ruling class by assuring its political and economic dominance, it also brought a grave risk — an exaggerated dependence upon foreign markets which was in the future to unbalance Chile's internal economy. In addition, it marked the arrival of large foreign investments.

Another event of significance during the period was the complete pacification of the Araucanians which occurred with the opening of a large area of southern Chile. A significant number of nationals and immigrants from Europe began to flock to the new territories. A new human type developed in this region, the "frontier man," tough and courageous, but, in contrast to the conservative and patriarchal farmer of central Chile, receptive to new influences. The frontier was to become the main source of strength of the Radical Party. These new provinces found in this party the means of expressing their demands for greater autonomy against the centralization of Santiago. Ideologically, they were to find in the same way expression for their anticlerical ideas. The varied social-economic base of the newly opened Chile soon supported political attitudes in opposition to those of the traditional interests, resulting in further amplification of political activities confined almost exclusively, until then, to the great landowning and commercial class.

With most of the religious issues settled by the end of the Santa María administration, the liberal forces, left without the anticlerical banner, began to disintegrate. It was in 1891, during the administration of José Manuel Balmaceda, that a split in the Chilean aristocracy culminated in civil war. Now that the religious problems were definitely settled, the historical issue which divided the ruling élite was whether a strong executive was to control the power of the parliament representing this aristocracy, or whether the power of that parliament was to prevail over presidential power, establishing itself in undisputed predominance.

There was no great social reform involved in this conflict. Neither Congress, which was the focal point of the antipresidential movement, nor the President spoke for the lower classes. Both represented one single economic group which had monopolistic political control. The Civil War of 1891 marks the end of the conflict between the authoritarian monarchical tradition and the Chilean aristocracy which had begun in 1810. "When Balmaceda, in the anguish of the final battle with feudalism, wished, like the kings of old in Europe, to appeal to

[27] Deputy Francisco Palma Tupper. Quoted in Jobet, *op. cit.*, p. 226.

the people, to democratic sentiment, events proved that the ill-fated President had requested the protection of something which did not exist."[28]

Balmaceda took the lead in constitutional reforms which broadened the right of suffrage, but political disorganization prevailed, and the old parties, splitting more and more into splinter groups, refused to come to an understanding with the executive. All parties helped to bring down the political system created by the old *pelucones* and characterized by presidential omnipotence. It had already been weakened by the reforms of the liberal era, but despite modern innovations, the cornerstone of the system, i.e., presidential dictatorship, though no longer legal, nevertheless effectively subsisted in obsolescence.

Other considerations of an economic nature played a part in the complete annihilation of presidential omnipotence. Balmaceda's attempts to implement measures designed to put an end to currency depreciation, to parcel out land to small holders, and to curtail the growing influence of foreign investments encountered the violent opposition of the landowners and big exporters on one hand, and on the other, the hostility of the influential foreign nitrate interests.[29]

Balmaceda has been characterized by some as a champion of a new middle class in the effort to promote a peaceful bourgeois revolution on the European model. A more accurate portrait of the unfortunate President appears to be the one that depicts him neither as an enlightened reformer nor as an autocrat, but as a composite of both, a nationalist who was ideologically a little of everything, "an eclectic true to the patchwork nature of the Chilean economy," who was destined for failure as the representative of no one socially and politically potent segment of the population."[30]

The Parliamentary Republic (1891–1925)

The revolution of 1891, led by a rebellious Congress, and portrayed to the country at large as one to depose a tyrant who had placed himself above the Constitution, succeeded in gaining the support of the great majority of the population. The President responded by establishing a stern dictatorship, which after about eight months of long

[28] Edwards, *La fronda aristocrática,* p. 179.

[29] Jobet, *op. cit.,* pp. 80–94. See also Edwards and Frei, *op. cit.,* pp. 121–130; Frank W. Fetter, *La inflación monetaria en Chile* (Santiago, 1942). Hernán Ramírez Necochea, *La guerra civil de 1891: Antecedentes económicos* (Santiago: Editorial Nascimento, 1943), throws much light on the influence of economic interests in the civil conflict of 1891.

[30] K. H. Silvert, "A Political-Economic Sketch of Chilean History from 1879" (Santiago: American Universities Field Staff, January 27, 1947), p. 9.

and bloody military operations, finally collapsed and led to Balmaceda's suicide. His death marked the end of the old presidential regime and the beginning of another era, the era of the parliamentary republic. In place of the old omnipotence of the executive was substituted the supremacy of Congress. From then until 1920, presidential authority was to disappear almost entirely; political parties were to multiply rapidly, and the oligarchs in Congress were to wield unrestricted power.

With these events, the political party picture became more complex. Even before the conflict, the economic changes brought about by the new national resources caused a certain amount of political restructuring. With the opening of the northern mineral regions and the coal mines of the south, a populist trend appeared and with it a primitive pattern of political unionism developed. In the south, foreign immigration and colonization were fostering the development of a class of small farmers. A new political organization, the Democratic Party, was formed in 1887. Essentially protectionist and pro-industry, this party aimed at the political organization of the artisan class, a small nucleus of workers in the cities, and some segments of the middle class. At its first convention, held on the one-hundredth anniversary of the French Revolution, it adopted a Declaration of Principles which stated that "the Democratic Party has as its object the social, political, and economic emancipation of the people."[31] It elected its first deputy in 1894. Its membership was to grow appreciably, but either because the artisan class was small in size and socially insignificant or because of the moderate tone of its ideology, the Democratic Party was destined to play only a subordinate role in Chilean politics.

The relatively simple partisan divisions of the earlier periods with the establishment of the parliamentary republic gave way to a multitude of political organizations. During the period of Conservative domination, there existed two parties: the Conservative and the Liberal. During the Liberal period there had been four: Conservative, Liberal, National, and Radical, to which the Democratic was added in 1887. But after the victory of the congressionalist forces in the civil war, seven parties appeared.[32] Among the older parties, Conservatives and Radicals emerged substantially stronger after the revolution, while the Liberals almost disintegrated. The Conservatives were stronger because of the high degree of cohesion among their forces which recent political developments had changed but little. The Radicals had grown to represent a wide range of socio-economic interests. Their dissident

[31] Jobet, *op. cit.*, pp. 97–98.

[32] In addition to the five listed above: the Liberal-Democratic or Balmacedista formed by the followers of the late president, and the Liberal-Independent, a small personalist group with no electoral base.

Liberal and middle-class base had first been strengthened by the southern agricultural interests resentful of both the ruling élite's exclusive concern with its own interests in the central valley, and the absorbing centralization which was maintained from Santiago. Later, the Radical Party had been further envigorated by the appeal that it began to exert upon the newly developed proletariat.

The existence of multiple parties required the formation of blocs in order to secure parliamentary majorities. These coalitions were subject to such kaleidoscopic changes as to make lines of responsibility unclear if not nonexistent. Give the absence of a central issue around which factions could rally, politics became little more than struggles for personal advantage.[33] Only between Radicals and Conservatives did there seem to exist clear lines of demarcation, determined in this case by the different attitudes of these two groups toward education and religion. Public education, except at the primary level, had been directed since 1879 by a corporation, the University Council, which acted independently of the government and was composed of men from all parties and ideological tendencies. The Conservatives believed that the state should have as little to do with education as possible, and from the religious point of view, allow individuals complete freedom to teach. Carried away by their independent spirit and ultraradical and systematic opposition to the government, the Conservatives gradually withdrew from the University and eventually established their own institutions of learning. The Radical Party, on the other hand, advocated the so-called *estado docente* (teaching state), maintaining that the state should have exclusive trust of education, and that instruction at all levels should be obligatory, free and secular, but permit teaching by private individuals if subject to state supervision.[34]

The gradual withdrawal of Conservatives from state educational institutions meant the conversion of the University into a sort of "church of spiritual liberalism, independent, but supported by the public treasury," and made it possible for the University to become "the political citadel of the Radical Party."[35] As for religion, the Radicals supported the idea that the state should maintain full freedom, even to the point of separation of church and state.

Government in Chile reached its lowest ebb during the period of parliamentary rule. The degree of ministerial instability is shown by the fact that while from 1831 to 1886, a 55-year period, the Chilean

[33] René León Echaíz, *Evolución histórica de los partidos políticos chilenos* (Santiago: Editorial Ercilla, 1939), pp. 126–130.

[34] Galdames, *op. cit.*, p. 365.

[35] Edwards, *La fronda aristocrática*, p. 211.

government was headed by 31 Cabinets, in the 33-year period of the parliamentary republic there existed 121 different Cabinets with a total of 530 ministers.[36] Instability was accompanied by deplorable financial waste in administrative organization. Even worse than irresponsible government was the posthumous influence of the parliamentary system upon electoral habits. Immediately after their victory in 1891, the congressionalist forces enacted a new Law of Municipalities and another law, given the name of "parliamentary incompatibilities," designed to destroy presidential intervention in electoral affairs. The first ended control of elections by the executive; the second prevented office-holders appointed by the President from becoming candidates for seats in the Congress and thus removed a means of securing support of the administration in that body.[37] The principle of electoral freedom now formally established, bribery and fraud became substitutes for the earlier governmental intervention. Although punishable by law, vote-buying became a common practice, and people from all social classes came to accept it as natural. The custom of selling votes had some effect also upon the composition of the ruling élite, by accentuating its plutocratic tint. Until this time, it had been possible for men of intellect but modest means to have access to public life and to gain political and social recognition. The governments had availed themselves of such citizens and often elevated them to public office, thanks to presidental control of elections. After 1891, however, persons who were capable but not rich no longer had this opportunity, for great sums of money were indispensable in getting elected to office, the amount depending on circumstances. For the sake of prestige, seats in Congress were bought by wealthy aristocrats in the same way that their ancestors had purchased titles of nobility. Civic spirit and patriotism seemed to be lost, and the masses submitted to the congressional oligarchy with the same resignation with which they had accepted presidential absolutism after 1830, apparently indifferent to the neglect of the national interest and to administrative inefficiency and political corruption.

Six Presidents, mere shadows of their predecessors, presided over this sad state of affairs during the period from 1891 to 1920, each as politically inert as the oligarchy which wielded power.[38] By 1915, however, a harsh reaction in civic spirit became noticeable and the

[36] Heise González, *op. cit.*, p. 108.

[37] W. W. Pierson and F. G. Gil, *Governments of Latin America* (New York: McGraw-Hill Book Co., 1957), pp. 167–168.

[38] These were: Jorge Montt (1891–1896), Federico Errázuriz Echaurren (1896–1901), Germán Riesco (1901–1906), Pedro Montt (1906–1910), Ramón Barros Luco (1910–1915), and Juan Luis Sanfuentes (1915–1920).

presidential election of 1920 was transcendental. The campaign revolved around clearer issues and developed chiefly as a struggle between the partisans of stability in the prevailing order and those who favoured profound social and political changes — a "new system," as Arturo Alessandri, their candidate, called it.

The tendencies toward "democratization" and reform of Chilean national institutions that caused the destruction of oligarchical domination and the victory of Alessandri had a gradual development. Despite the many vices of congressional rule, the three preceding decades were a period of preparation for change rather than a complete social stagnation.[39] In the first place, it is interesting to note that there prevailed throughout the period a scrupulous respect for civil liberties, which made possible political debates and a public airing of new social doctrines[40] and, in general, of all political problems. In many ways the parliamentary era afforded an excellent opportunity for the civic schooling of the Chilean people. Its political peace and juridical normality contrasted with the unrest of other states of Latin America during the same period. It must also be noted that some of Balmaceda's reforms were retained, particularly those related to education and religion. Although redemption of paper money was rescinded and the country settled back into the course of continuing inflation, the development of urban industrial and commercial interests was renewed under the influence of uncontrolled expansion. A systematic protective policy succeeded in giving stability and energy to agriculture and national manufacturing. Except for a temporary setback during the crisis of 1907, Chile's economy continued to be characterized by constant growth. Prosperity, evident in the increase of fiscal receipts, was also evident in all phases of national activity, for it brought a certain measure of improvement in the well-being of the general population.

Paralleling these economic changes, profound alterations were also taking place in the social-political complex, leading to a great social and economic upheaval. The social restructuring affected all levels. The aristocratic oligarchy transformed itself gradually into a plutocracy, as the commercial and industrial bourgeoisie continued to swell its ranks. A new mentality, more enterprising but also more utilitarian than the old patriarchal one of the early nineteenth century, began to characterize the aristocracy, which developed a new set of values and a new attitude toward politics and life in general. The prosperity

[39] Silvert, *op. cit.*, p. 10.

[40] An example: the famous debates in 1915 between Luis E. Recabarren and Father Merino in a public square of Iquique.

brought by nitrate and copper replaced its frugal and orderly manner of living with habits of luxury and idleness, and moved by the desire for wealth, the aristocracy lost its patriotic sense of social and civic responsibility.

Economic developments gave rise, in turn, to the integration of new and significant groups into the middle class, groups which contributed substance and vigor to it. Industrial and commercial growth created a considerable force of middle-class private employees; the expansion of the administrative machine of the government added an important segment of bureaucrats; expansion to the south and subsequent immigration furnished a valuable contingent of independent farmers to the middle-income groups; and finally, a new and growing intellectual nucleus resulted from the more active development of public education.[41] Of course, the rapid growth of the Chilean urban population after 1890 was a wider factor in the reinforcement of this social group. Formed by such heterogeneous elements, the middle class still lacked any real class consciousness and common ideology. However, since none of these new elements was accustomed to the tradition of passive submission to oligarchical domination, they became the vanguard of the movement for socio-economic reform.

It is also important to note that the middle class which was growing so rapidly was in a sense a "proletarized" group quite distinct from the middle classes in Europe, since it lacked the economic and social consistency of its counterparts. This "proletarization" of the middle class was chiefly the result of the prevailing land tenure system and of the peculiar characteristics of the mineral regions which prevented the healthy growth of a numerous class of small holders (comparable to the French *rentier* class) and of small industrial entrepreneurs. The systematic depreciation of currency under the influence of the oligarchy prevented, in turn, the emphasis on savings so distinctive of other middle classes.[42] In addition, a large "intellectual proletariat," as one writer calls it, was formed by the enormous expansion of the state-controlled education system. These individuals, who could not claim the privileges of birth and wealth and were denied the opportunities which the aristocracy had formerly afforded them, became the leaders of the masses.[43] This process played a part in aggravating the so-called "social question."

As economic development and democratization made progress after the revolution of 1891, the middle class acquired some measure of consciousness of its condition and, abandoning its former timidity and

[41] Heise González, *op. cit.*, pp. 124–217.
[42] Jobet, *op. cit.*, pp. 147–148.
[43] Edwards, *op. cit.*, pp. 212–213.

inertia, became the center of political agitation. In 1920, it was the backbone of the "revolt of the electorate," which gave the masses their first electoral victory.

The lower class was not less affected than the others by the restructuring brought about by economic changes. The rich northern mineral regions and the coal mines of the south had given rise to an industrial proletariat. According to the 1907 census, the salaried class, or proletariat, constituted almost one million persons.[44] The living and working conditions of this large conglomerate were deplorable. Despite Chile's material progress, they had remained far below the standards of other civilized countries. Many writers, both foreign and Chilean, have left accounts of the incredible fate of the nitrate workers.[45] Although their wages were higher than those of other workers, lack of adequate housing and of safety measures added to the iniquitous exploitation to which they were subjected in the *pulperías* or company stores, made their conditions comparable to that of the Indian who worked the gold washings in the colonial era. The lot of the urban worker was no better. Wages were low, and he lived in slum tenements, damp, close, and unhealthy, where he was subjected to numerous endemic and epidemic diseases resulting from lack of sanitation.[46] As for the rural workers, the situation of the *inquilino* (tenant farmer) and the migrant worker had in many respects worsened rather than improved, for they remained in a semi-servile condition while the relationship between them and the landowners underwent a significant change. The softening influence of traditional paternalism gave way to much more formal relations between employer and worker, with some oppression. The Chilean workers finally awakened to their plight. Gradually, they learned to give the middle class electoral support and began to supply "the necessary violence and strong-arm methods which the order-loving middle class could not have been expected to provide."[47]

This proletariat, which had at first only a confused, almost unconscious aspiration, to better its material being, had its strongest center in Valparaíso, with other principal nuclei in the provinces of Santiago — Tarapacá, Concepción, and Antofagasta. These early manifestations of a social crisis in the making were ruthlessly repressed by the administration in power. There occurred in Iquique in

[44] Jobet, *op. cit.*, p. 133.

[45] For some descriptions see Domingo Amunátegui Solar, *El progreso intelectual y político de Chile* (Santiago: Editorial Nascimento, 1936), pp. 146–149; Jobet, *op. cit.*, pp. 131–140.

[46] Life in the Santiago slums is vividly depicted in Joaquín Edwards Bello, *El roto* (Santiago: Imprenta Universo, 1929).

[47] Stevenson, *op. cit.*, pp. 26–27.

1907 a senseless massacre of 2,000 nitrate workers. Equally tragic were the events that took place in Puerto Natales in 1919, and in Magallanes in 1920, which served as further examples of the determination of the ruling élite to crush social unrest at any cost. Repression, however, made the situation worse rather than better, for it served as an effective catalyst for the revolutionary movement, generating thereby a further consolidation of its power. As the labor movement began to feel its strength, animosities grew more acute, and strikes became more frequent. From 1911 to 1920, there occurred 293 strikes involving over 150,000 workers.[48]

The first groups which were strictly trade unions in a modern sense began to appear at the turn of the century in the nitrate and coal mine industry, but only with the accelerated expansion of industry in the interval between the two world wars was the Chilean labor movement converted into a popular mass organization with a strong voice in politics.[49] Organizations such as the Worker's Social Center (1896), the Socialist Union (1897), the Francisco Bilbao Workers' Party (1898), and the Socialist Party (1901), and newspapers such as *The Worker, The Proletarian, The People,* although ephemeral, were among the early interpreters of the Chilean populist movement. Labor organization in Chile developed along the lines which are common to most labor movements in Latin America. It began with the establishment of mutual benefit societies (*mutualidades* or *mancomunales*) to attend to the workers' immediate needs which arose in case of illness, and to serve as activity centers for their meetings, lectures, night schools, and libraries. The next phase of development was marked by the rise of "resistance groups" which struggled for the improvement of labor conditions and against the influence of employers. These pioneering organizations were controlled by anarcho-syndicalist groups which later lost influences to the new socialist and communist elements. The first groups which were strictly trade unions in the modern sense began to appear at the turn of the century in the nitrate and coal-mining industry. During the first decades of the twentieth century, the labor movement was led by a capable and dedicated leader, Luis Emilio Recabarren, who performed the miracle of being elected to the

[48] Alberto Cabero, *Chile y los chilenos* (Santiago: Editorial Lyceum, 1948), p. 339.

[49] For the history of the Chilean labor movement see, among others, Hernán Ramírez Necochea, *Historia del movimiento obrero en Chile — antecedentes — siglo XIX* (Santiago: Talleres Gráficos Lautaro, 1956); Tulio Lagos Valenzuela, *Bosquejo histórico del movimiento obrero en Chile* (Santiago: Imprenta El Esfuerzo, 1941); and Moisés Poblete Troncoso, *El movimiento de asociación profesional obrera en Chile* (Mexico: Fondo de Cultura Económica, 1945).

Congress in 1906, but he found himself excluded from this body by decision of the aristocratic majority. He inspired the founding of the Workers' Federation of Chile in 1909, and founded in 1912 the first labor party, the Workers' Socialist Party, which was affiliated with the Second International. In 1919, Recabarren led the Workers' Federation into the central union organization of Moscow, laying the basis for the inception of the Communist Party several years later.

The pattern of Chilean society was changing, and changing rapidly. It was no longer to be characterized by the existence of a small élite and an amorphous and submissive mass, without ideas and aspirations. Now public opinion had been aroused, and new segments of the population were voicing demands for a fundamental redistribution of power.

This process of change had more emphatic effects upon the political scene after 1920. The existing political parties represented long-established classes and interests, and except for the educational and religious issues, no vital question separated them. What may be called a "right bloc" was formed by the Conservative, National, Liberal, and Liberal-Democratic parties. The Conservatives were the defenders of the landowners and of the Church. Political control over the tenant farmers on the great estates and over an appreciable segment of the middle class through the religious institutions, particularly in central Chile, assured the party substantial electoral support. Since governmental measures of reform never touched the *hacienda* economy, the Conservative Party was the least affected by the chaotic situation brought about by the parliamentary regime. The Liberal Party, socially and economically, was now intimately connected with the Conservatives. Separated in the past by religious conflict, no real barriers existed between them after the fall of Balmaceda. The Liberal Party represented no particular ideological position, but in practical politics it was the protector of the great grape growers, the nitrate and industrial interests, and big business in general. Its weak defense of state control of education was the only difference between it and the Conservatives.

The National Party was the political agency of the high bureaucracy. Its members were closely connected with the large private banks and commercial interests. Although at its birth the National Party had championed the cause of state supremacy over the Church, during the parliamentary era it sought the further weakening of presidential authority and invariably placed itself in the ranks of the Conservative bloc.

The Liberal-Democratic Party, heir in 1893 to Balmaceda's ideas, had soon become a group devoid of ideologies and engaged only in an opportunistic struggle for privilege in high office. Socially, it was composed of an aristocratic group of well-to-do families plus some upper-middle-class groups in the provinces.

The Radical Party had a broader base than any other political organization. It represented the interests of the southern region, but it principally spoke for the dissident upper middle class and the middle groups which have been described above. After the "doctrinaire" struggles of the period 1864–1884 ended, the Radicals, forgetting all ideological differences, had joined the parliamentary oligarchy in order to bring down Balmaceda's regime. The Radical program adopted at the party convention held in 1888 said nothing about socio-economic problems, except for a vague statement favoring the "improvement of the conditions of proletarians and workers." The failure of the Radicals to give a more explicit expression to the new social demands can be explained by the existence within their ranks of an intellectual nucleus which held advanced ideas but which was closely linked to the aristocracy. It was only after 1906, when the "socialistic" tendency, led by Valentín Letelier, triumphed over the extreme individualism represented by Enrique MacIver, that the party's program began to reflect the growing demand for reform which animated its followers among the middle class.

The Democratic Party was distinctive in that it was the only organization during the period with a popular base, but its congressional representation did not have any influence until long after its founding in 1887. Its program clearly advocated some economic and social reform, but in spite of its reformist program, the Democratic Party played with enthusiasm the political game of alliances and party combinations. Its failure to identify itself with the labor movement had serious consequences, for the Chilean worker, searching for leadership in the early stages of the labor movement and not finding it among the established political groups, turned to the Marxists. This explains why in Chile the organized labor movement assumed a totally revolutionary position in which communism was to have a preponderant influence, as it still does today.[50]

The Revolt of the Electorate

Such were the conditions in Chile in 1920 when oligarchical domination collapsed. Change had come swiftly — an industrial revolution and social upheaval hand-in-hand — the machine, the proletariat, the metropolis, and the intellectual middle class appearing almost simultaneously on the scene. While these changes were in the making, par-

[50] Edwards and Frei, *op. cit.*, p. 162.

ties remained alien to the social revolution. They were imposing structures without substance, too absorbed in political machinations and petty rivalries to grasp the significance of the transformation. The downfall of the system was inevitable. Its demise can be chiefly attributed to the revolt of the middle class supported by the new proletariat, the loss of its political prestige by the traditional oligarchy, administrative chaos, a government on the brink of bankruptcy, and the scandal of parliamentary majorities created by bribery and fraud.[51] To these, the impact of an economic crisis was added when the nitrate boom collapsed after 1910 with the development of synthetic production elsewhere. The country could no longer depend on nitrate revenue to finance the government, and if new taxes were necessary, the landowning interests might be affected. The mining workers had been hit hard, and the ranks of the unemployed were swelling daily. Furthermore, the agricultural interests of the central valley and the southern areas, deprived of their northern market, were in difficulty. Lastly, the influence of recent and successful social revolutions in Mexico and Russia was not insignificant.

At this point a new leader emerged to express the general dissatisfaction with this state of affairs and to become the champion of the common man, Arturo Alessandri Palma. It was he who led a modified Liberal Alliance to victory in the presidential elections of 1920. The Radicals and Democrats provided the basis for this coalition, with additional support from the Liberal faction and a few other small groups. Opposing Alessandri was a new rightist coalition, the National Union, formed of the Conservatives, a majority of the Liberals, some *Balmacedistas,* and the Nationals.

The campaign was characterized by emotion and enthusiasm, aroused to a fevered pitch by the flowery oratory and charismatic appeal of Alessandri. Election returns favored him by a narrow margin, and a Tribunal of Honor established by agreement between the contenders later awarded him the presidency. The significance of his victory was that it demonstrated that the passive obedience of the masses of the people to the old oligarchy had ceased to exist.

Alessandri's first message to the Congress contained proposals for administrative decentralization, abolition of the parliamentary system, presidential election by direct vote, and separation of church and state. In economic and social matters he proposed state control of banks and insurance companies, monetary stability, and social security. Faced with strong opposition in the Senate, Alessandri could not go far along the road of reform. Other causes combined with congres-

[51] Ricardo Donoso, *Desarrollo político y social de Chile* (Santiago: Imprenta Universitaria, 1943), p. 181.

sional obstruction to prevent realization of his program. Among them were the postwar slump, lack of foreign markets for Chilean mineral production, unemployment, and the inefficiency of the inexperienced group surrounding the President.[52] "As a result of economic depression, Chile's social-economic liberalism of 1920, like the United States' New Deal of 1932, was handicapped by the necessity of recovering and reforming at the same time."[53] Although the congressional elections of 1924 gave Alessandri a majority in both houses, the new Congress failed to act upon the President's messages submitted for its consideration. The matter came to a head when this Congress, instead of approving some urgent projects, voted itself pay increases in violation of the Constitution.

This astonishing action, which startled the country, moved officers of the Chilean army to intervene openly in politics for the first time in almost a century. The cabinet fell. In an hour and without debate "the suggestive rattling of army sabres in the congressional galleries"[54] obtained approval of a complete program of social legislation which had been pending for years in the Congress.

On the same day, the President, aware that his authority was now subject to military force, left the country. A military junta was established, and Congress was dissolved. This junta lasted but five months, when another military clique, led by young and reformist officers who desired the implementation of the reform program and a return to constitutional forms, took control of the government.[55]

The majority of the Chilean armed forces, composed of middle-class members in the officer corps and of men of proletarian origin in the rank and file, were sympathetic to the national cry for reform. Suspicious of the original junta's subservience to the oligarchy, the young clique recalled Alessandri.[56] With army support and free from political obstructionism, Alessandri returned in 1925 and began to rule by decree. He set about introducing economic and social reforms designed to protect the laboring groups. A graduated income tax and a permanent electoral register were established. The President, with the assistance of advisers from each political party and each national interest group, promptly concentrated his efforts on the reform of the Constitution.

52 Siivert, *op. cit.*, p. 11.
53 Stevenson, *op. cit.*, p. 35.
54 *Ibid.*, p. 37.
55 An interesting account of this period can be found in Juan Bennett A., *La revolución del 5 de septiembre de 1924* (Santiago: Balcells y Cía, n.d.), written by a member of the military junta.
56 Emilio Bello Codesido, *Recuerdos políticos* (Santiago: Editorial Nascimento, 1954) gives useful details of the military coup of January 23, 1925, and the period immediately following.

The new Constitution provided for a strong executive and put an end to the parliamentary system. Above all, the new instrument was designed to prevent the restoration of the old system under which a small group of powerful landlords ruled the whole country as though it were but one great *hacienda*. The new basic law deprived the legislative body of the power to depose cabinets by means of censure, although it authorized the lower chamber to bring impeachment procedures against ministers and in some cases even against the chief executive. It increased the presidential term to six years and provided for election of the chief executive by direct vote. It also declared incompatible the holding of a congressional office and a Cabinet seat, and created a permanent "qualifying tribunal" entrusted with the impartial supervision of all electoral matters. Along with guarantees of civil liberties, the 1925 Constitution included a definition of property as a social function, and provisions which definitely established the separation of church and state and freedom of worship.[57] The power of the oligarchy was diminished by the provisions which established widespread suffrage and the direct election of the President, and by those which gave the chief executive effective authority and control of finances. It was no longer possible for the Congress to dominate the presidency by its control over the national treasury.

Three features of the constitutional regime established in 1925 were to have great influence upon Chile's prospects for stable government: a system of proportional representation, the selection of the President by the Congress if any candidate failed to receive a majority, and the separation of the dates of congressional and presidential elections. Proportional representation has in practice encouraged party fragmentation and unstable congressional coalitions. Throwing doubtful presidential contests into Congress has meant that, in a multiparty system, the President has often owed his election to a parliamentary coalition. Because he has had to reward the various factions with patronage, squabbles over the spoils have frequently broken out, and the coalition has disintegrated. As a result, ministerial instability has persisted, and interference by party leaders has taken the place of interference by parliamentary cliques. Separation in the dates of congressional and presidential elections has meant that variable public opinion has sometimes elected a President and a Congress hostile to one another.

[57] A fuller analysis of the Constitution of 1925 is given in Chapter 3. A fine commentary on this text is José Guillermo Guerra, *La constitución de 1925* (Santiago, 1929). The following works by Mario Bernaschina are important contributions: *La constitución chilena* (Santiago: Editorial Jurídica, 1940); *Los constituyentes de 1925* (Santiago: Editorial Universitaria, 1945); and *Manual de derecho constitucional,* 2 vols. (Santiago: Editorial Jurídica, 1955).

Adoption of the Constitution on September 18, 1925, marks the official end of the anarchical years of the parliamentary republic and the re-establishment of a presidential regime. This was, however, "purely a structural restoration; it did not carry with it the restoration of the dominance of a given socio-economic class."[58]

A new party, destined to enjoy widespread support among the Chilean working class, appeared during Alessandri's presidency. Its roots were in the Workers' Socialist Party founded in 1912 by Recabarren. In 1921 this party's convention decided to join the Third International, accepting the twenty-one conditions established by the Comintern for admission, and changed its name to the Communist Party.[59] At this time the party had two members in the Chamber of Deputies and virtually controlled the Chilean Workers' Federation, which claimed 200,000 members. Returning from a trip to the Soviet Union in 1924, Recabarren lectured extensively on Russia's advances. Sometime later he committed suicide. During the military regime the Communist Party continued to be active. After Recabarren's suicide, his successor, Manuel Hidalgo, headed a group of six members of the Communist Party who participated in the drafting of the Constitution of 1925. During this period, the party opposed some of the measures in Alessandri's program, particularly the legislation which established social security funds for manual and white-collar workers.[60]

Incidents during the electoral campaign of 1925 ended Alessandri's regime three months before completion of his term. The presidential ambitions of Colonel Carlos Ibáñez and Alessandri's refusal to support him led to the President's resignation. When elections were held, Emiliano Figueroa Larraín, supported by all political parties, was elected. The fact that another candidate, José Santos Salas, without any party support, made a surprisingly strong race is extremely significant. In a few days of compaigning without any organized assistance, except perhaps from the Communists, candidate Santos Salas attracted over 100,000 votes, an indication that the existing parties did not appeal to a large mass of voters, particularly among the workers.

Within a short period, Ibáñez forced Larraín out and in 1927 established a dictatorship which was to last for the next four years. His regime gave impetus to the reform of public administration; state interventions and activities began to acquire new dimensions, while a

[58] Stevenson, *op. cit.*, p. 40.

[59] Fernando Alegría, *Recabarren* (Santiago: Editorial Antares, 1938), p. 155.

[60] Robert J. Alexander, *Communism in Latin America* (New Brunswick: Rutgers University Press, 1957), pp. 177–180.

vast plan of public works was completed. Foreign capital poured into Chile, and the need to finance new services and to satisfy new luxury demands pushed foreign trade to unprecedented levels. A sense of prosperity pervaded the country. There existed, however, a reverse side to the picture, which was characterized by political repression and arbitrariness. Political parties practically ceased to exist, and their leaders were deported, banished, or jailed, in accordance with the regime's publicly expressed notion that parties were useless to the nation. To take their place Ibáñez sponsored a strange conglomeration of "nonpartisan" forces, "a civic movement" known as the Republican Confederation for Civic Action (CRAC).

By 1930 a sharp economic depression began to be felt.[61] Public agitation and civil disturbances finally brought the collapse of Ibáñez' dictatorship in July of 1931.[62] Naturally enough, the fall of Ibáñez was followed by a period of political agitation and social unrest which witnessed the failure of nine different governments, two general strikes, and even a naval revolt, in the short space of fifteen months.[63] Ibáñez' successor, Juan Esteban Montero, remained in office only five months. A coup d'état of military men and civilians led by Colonel Marmaduke Grove proclaimed a "socialist republic," dismissed Congress, and formed a governing junta. These revolutionaries were not able to accomplish much during the brief period of their rule (December, 1931, to September, 1932), but they did decree some important measures. They proposed to nationalize the coal, copper, and nitrate-mining industries, and they gave strong encouragement to the trade union movement. Some of this reform legislation long survived the government which enacted it.[64]

A new military coup put an end to the socialist republic in September, 1932, one hundred days after the accession of its President,

61 A League of Nations study of 39 countries representing 90 per cent of world trade showed that Chile, in all Latin America, was the most severely affected by the world depression.

62 For details of the overthrow of Ibáñez, with personal observations, see C. H. Haring, "The Chilean Revolution of 1931," *Hispanic American Historical Review* (May, 1933). See also Carlos Saez M., *Recuerdos de un soldado* 3 vols. (Santiago: Editorial Ercilla, 1934). An interesting personal account of the Ibáñez dictatorship is given in Vol. II. René Montero M., *La verdad sobre Ibáñez* (Buenos Aires: Editorial Freeland, 1953) is a biography of General Ibáñez written from a sympathetic point of view.

63 See Saez, *op. cit.*, Vol. III, for details covering this period.

64 For a scathing treatment of the revolutionary movement of June 4, 1931, see Alfredo Guillermo Bravo, *4 de Junio: El festín de los audaces* (Santiago: Empresa Letras, n.d.). Another critical account is Manuel Aránguiz Latorre, *El 4 de Junio* (Santiago: Zig-Zag, 1933).

Carlos Dávila, to power, and turned over the government to the Chief Justice of the Supreme Court. In the same month, new elections were called.

Forced out of the political arena by the repressive policies of Ibáñez, political parties had reached a maximum point of disorganization during the period of the socialist government. The "social question" had then completely displaced all other political issues, and parties, after a decade of disorder and experimentation, were confronted with the necessity of reorganizing themselves before taking their battle positions.

Among all parties, the Conservative Party came out of the turmoil better than any other organization, principally because of the high degree of cohesion among its members, but also because recent political developments had scarcely affected the interests that it represented. At no time, despite the revolutionary ferment, had the land system been in danger of dissolution, expropriation, or heavy taxation. The economic base of Conservative power had emerged intact from all the harrying confusion. In the 1932 convention, the Conservatives reaffirmed their traditional ideological position, opposed to liberalism, particularly of the socio-economic kind. In practical terms, the Conservatives unmistakably associated themselves with the extreme Right.[65]

Fragmentation within the Liberal Party was unprecedented. The several factions which existed before the dictatorship had now multiplied into new numbers. In reality, nothing differentiated the majority of the Liberals from the Conservatives, for beyond the façade of political factionalism there was the fundamental fact that both represented identical economic interests and the same social stratum. The membership of both parties had the same characteristics: their leaders belonged to the old Chilean aristocracy; they were the owners of the vast majority of the agricultural lands, a fact which was the base of their electoral power; and they had practical control of the large banking and industrial enterprises. Economically, they represented capital, and socially, the old power élite. Politically, they were dedicated to the defense of the liberal-capitalistic economic system. Previous areas of disagreement between the two essentially conservative parties involved only politico-religious questions and the degree to which commercial or agricultural activities were to be the prime focus of governmental protection and encouragement. Now that these issues

[65] Ignacio Arteaga Undurraga, *Partido Conservador — XIV Convención — 1947: Notas para la historia política del Partido Conservador* (Santiago: Imprenta Chile, 1947), pp. 272–273. See also Edwards and Frei, *op. cit.*, pp. 223–226.

had been removed, having no barriers to separate them, the two parties were destined to unite in a powerful bloc of the Right.[66]

The acuteness of the class struggles during the preceding decade had had great repercussions in the Radical Party. This group, essentially individualistically oriented in the beginning, had now turned away from this philosophy and was inclining more toward the primacy of collective rights. While the rest of the parties represented a relatively narrow segment of Chilean society, the Radicals included northern liberals from the mines and southern large and small landholders, and was, at the same time, the stronghold of the urban middle class. The leftist inclinations of this latter group, the *petite bourgeoisie* of professionals and bureaucrats, prevailed over other segments in 1931. After that date it became clear that the Radical Party had taken the side of the proletarian class and that it advocated a system in which individualism would be replaced by social solidarity.

The struggle between these two currents within the Radical Party had actually begun in 1906. Until 1920, as we have seen, political parties tended to align themselves into two camps: a conservative coalition and a liberal alliance of which the Radicals were the backbone. The Liberal Party had fluctuated between both, as a center force, key to all majorities. Now that a compromise between Liberals and Conservatives had brought them together, the Radical Party ceased being liberalism's extreme wing to become the stronghold of the middle masses and part of the proletariat, with ideological inspirations which ranged the spectrum from moderate state socialism to communism. Having once been the vanguard of the liberal movement, the Radicals were to play a new role, that of the moderating or center force within the ranks of the new social-economic leftism.[67]

The extremely varied composition of the Radical Party played a large role in the continuous indecision and vacillation that are so characteristic of this group. With its middle- and lower-class elements dominating party assemblies and conservative interests prevailing in everyday politics, the party's position must necessarily reflect an ambiguity which stems from the dual nature which so troubles it. Its support of Masonry and distaste for the Church make it a natural enemy of the Conservatives. It has little affinity with Liberals, who reject state interventionism, but, at the same time, it cannot unreservedly line up with the Socialists who seek full collectivism. As a result, the Radical Party lives a double life. In the electoral arena it is fond of slogans and frequently allies itself with the Socialists and Communists. When in control of the government it often has a

[66] Edwards and Frei, *op. cit.*, p. 222.

[67] Jobet, *op. cit.*, pp. 227–228.

rightist twist, allying itself with Conservatives and Liberals in defense of the vested interests. A graphic expression used by one writer to describe this peculiar role is that of "lightning rod for the proletarian storm."[68]

While the Radicals veered to the Left, the first of the Populist parties, the Democratic Party, was undergoing a transformation in the opposite direction, slowly moving away from its proletarian base and becoming more and more a lower-middle-class organization. After reaching its peak of popularity during the first term of Alessandri, its influence began to wane steadily, particularly after it lent its support to the dictatorial Ibáñez regime. Two other Populist parties, however, were giving forceful and dramatic presentation of national socio-economic problems. They constituted formidable new forces, and they carried the banners of the newly born Chilean Left. With the overthrow of Ibáñez in 1931, a split in the Communist Party had become public, the result of the Stalinist-Trotskyite feud in the Comintern. Two groups, headed by Elías Lafferte and Manuel Hidalgo respectively, were organized as separate parties. Although somewhat weakened by this internal division, the Communists continued to grow, devoting all of their energies to the labor movement. Some years thereafter, the Trotskyite group, who had been living a very precarious life, merged with the Socialists, abandoning the camp to the Stalinists. Significant during the early 1930's was the adherence of a group of intellectuals to the Communist cause, marked by the designation of Carlos Contreras Labarca, a former leader of the students' federation, as the party's Secretary General.

After the "socialist republic" fell, there occurred a merger of the small groups which had contributed to the triumph of the socialist coup but which had failed to lend the government the needed support of a disciplined, well-organized political organization.[69] These formed

[68] *Ibid.*, p. 183.

[69] Many of the men who soon after the fall of the "socialist republic" in 1933 founded the new Socialist Party had had their initiation in politics in 1927, when under the organization known as the USRACH (*Unión Social Republicana de Asalariados de Chile*) they had supported the labor candidate José Santos Salas. This organization was dissolved by Ibáñez soon after the 1927 election. After the fall of Ibáñez and during the Montero administration, there was a proliferation of reformist groups, inspired by socialist ideology. Small and weak groups such as "New Public Action" (NAP) founded by Eugenio Matte, "Socialist Revolutionary Action" (ARS), the Marxist Socialist Party, the Unified Socialist Party, and "Socialist Order," contributed to the triumph of Grove's coup and the installation of a socialist regime. They were not capable, however, of lending that government the needed support of a disciplined, well-organized political organization.

the second of the leftist groups, the Socialist Party of Chile, on April 19, 1933. The new party was destined to play a very significant part in Chile's political life. Its membership grew with remarkable rapidity and for a time it became the strongest of all the mass parties. In its first declaration of principles, the Socialist Party avowed its allegiance to Marxism and advocated the collectivization of private property, the temporary dictatorship of the proletariat, and the economic and political unity of all the Latin American countries.[70]

Three other parties of relative importance made their political debuts early in the turbulent 1930's. A group of Radicals, discontented when their party joined the Conservatives in support of Montero, organized a leftist Radical Socialist Party. Another group, representing southern agricultural interests and composed of former Radicals and Liberals, established, in the early years of Ibáñez' rule, a Center-Right Agrarian Party destined to gain some importance in a later period. A third group, the *Partido Democrático,* an offshoot of the Democratic Party (*Partido Demócrata*) was born of dissatisfaction with the leaders who controlled the latter organization.[71]

The multiplicity of party organizations which had gradually become characteristic of the Chilean political system was evident in the election of 1932. Five candidates entered the presidential race. Among these, two represented the rightist forces, two the Socialist and Communist Left, and the fifth, Arturo Alessandri, the winner, represented the middle class, and received the support of most Center groups.

Considering that leading the country to constitutional order was his most urgent task, Alessandri, the champion of the people, during his second administration (1932–1938) was to yield more and more to the claims of the rightist parties and to detach himself from leftist support. In doing so, he was faced with strong opposition, and since there were constant demands for social and economic reforms by the forces of the Left, these were the principal victims of a policy of repression. The Radicals and other "popular" parties began to move together into unified opposition when it became clear that the "Lion of Tarapacá," as Alesandri was called, had ceased to roar and was not going to inaugurate a progressive program. The Alessandri administration, however, had some praiseworthy aspects. National

[70] The literature of Chilean socialism is abundant. Some examples of this early period are Oscar Schnake, *Política socialista* (Santiago, 1937); Julio César Jobet, *Significado del Partido Socialista en la realidad nacional* (Santiago, 1940); Luis Zúñiga, *El Partido Socialista en la realidad nacional* (Santiago, 1938). Also useful are Oscar Waiss, *Presencia del socialismo en Chile* (Santiago: Ediciones Espartaco, 1952) and Julio César Jobet, *Socialismo y comunismo* (Santiago: Ediciones Espartaco, 1952).

[71] León Echaíz, *op. cit.,* pp. 176–177.

finances under the management of Gustavo Ross, reputedly a financial wizard, experienced remarkable recovery. Unemployment was practically erased, economic nationalism received new impetus, bankruptcies decreased, and the economic depression nearly vanished by 1934. Although Ross had done much to re-establish economic stability, he also became a disturbing element since his autocratic methods and forceful manners made him the object of intense dislike by the opposition and an ideal target for political attack.[72]

The political ferment had given rise in 1932 to a substantial contingent of Nazis, rooted in Chile's small but influential German population. Fears among the aristocratic élite after the events of 1932, and the growing strength of the working class contributed further to the spread of the Nazi philosophy. The National Socialist Movement of Chile, organized by Jorge González von Marées, by 1933 had become a militant organization. Its principles were strongly injected with Hitlerian ideas, and according to its leaders, it differed basically from Marxist socialism in that it was spiritual and materialistic, and intended to establish and preserve a rigid social stratification.[73] After electing two deputies in the 1937 elections, whatever strength Chilean Nazism may have had dissipated when on September 5, 1938, an uprising directed by young Nazis ended in a massacre of the group and the imprisonment of its leader.

Another new group was to build up, in a short time, a new party with a promising future. Since the encyclical *Rerum Novarum* of Leo XIII, there had existed a new current among Conservative forces. After 1927, New Catholic social ideas began to gain acceptance in university student circles. The activities of Catholic Action organizations and the appearance of the *Quadragesimo Anno* encyclical gave further impetus to Christian Socialism. The younger generation among the conservative class, detached from party influences during the Ibáñez dictatorship, was highly receptive to the theories and philosophy emanating from European Social Christian movements. When this Chilean youth, following tradition, joined the Conservative Party, it had already developed definite reformist tendencies. The result was that a conflict soon arose within Conservative ranks between the progressive attitudes and ideas of the "Conservative Youth," which after 1935 banded together to unify these elements, and the attitudes and ideas of the traditional Conservatives. This conflict eventually led to a break in 1938.

[72] Stevenson, *op. cit.*, pp. 59–60, 63.

[73] Jobet, *Ensayo,* p. 195. For details on the Chilean Nazi Movement, see *El movimiento nacionalista de Chile* (Santiago, 1933) and Jorge González von Marées, *El problema del hambre* (Santiago, 1937) and *El mal de Chile* (Santiago, 1940).

By then the Conservative Youth movement had in any case practically become a separate political entity. After the split, it adopted first the name *Falange Conservadora* and later it became the *Falange Nacional*.

The success of the Chilean Christian Socialists in building a small but disciplined and effective political organization was remarkable. In a relatively short time, they attracted many followers in intellectual circles, in the trade union movement, and in the new industrialist class. "With its democratic political ideals, its roots in a traditional religion made consistent with the modern atmosphere, and its neo-socialistic economic doctrine,"[74] their party, calling itself subsequently the Christian Democratic Party, became in later years a major competitor in Chilean politics.

The Popular Front (1938–1941)

In the wake of severe repressive measures and the dissolution of Congress by Alessandri, following a wave of strikes sparked by railroad workers the parties of the Center and Left rallied together in preparation for the presidential election of 1938. The example of several successful Popular Front coalitions in Europe at this time gave impetus to a similar development in Chile. Obviously, the Comintern's decision in its 1935 Congress to recommend alliances with democratic parties, soon crystallized by the emergence of leftist fronts in Spain and France, must have exerted influence upon the forming of the Chilean counterpart. It seems true, however, that local conditions were the chief inducement.[75] Resisted at first by the more conservative leadership of the Radical Party, a proposal of the Socialists to form a block of the Left was eventually accepted.[76] Representatives of the Radicals, Communists, Democrats, Socialists, Radical-Socialists, and

[74] Silvert, *op. cit.*, p. 4.

[75] Up to 1936 the only attempt to unite the forces of the Left had been a congressional bloc known as "Bloc of the Left," and formed of Socialists, Democrats, Radical Socialists, and Trotskyites, but excluding the Stalinist Communists. Although its strength was relative, in 1934–1935, this bloc conducted an active anti-government and anti-Nazi campaign. Jobet, *op. cit.*, p. 198. The Radical Party, because of the different views held by its heterogeneous components, followed a vacillating policy in this period and supported the Right on most issues.

[76] The initial move was taken when the Socialist Party Congress, early in 1936, appealed to the Radicals and the Communists to join the "Bloc of the Left." A few days later, a Radical Deputy, Justino Sotomayor, formally proposed a Chilean Popular Front, which was enthusiastically received by the rank and file of his party, as well as by the leaders of the "Bloc," the Communists and labor organizations. For the relationship between the Radicals and the Popular Front see Alfredo Guillermo Bravo, *El Partido Radical y el Frente Popular* (Santiago, 1938).

the Chilean Labor Federation organized a directorate for this political alliance.[77]

The Popular Front was first tested in the 1937 congressional elections, where it made a surprising show of strength.[78] The rightist parties managed to preserve their majority in Congress, but thanks only to systematic bribery and wholesale vote buying. It was after this election that Radical Party leaders realized the political wisdom of throwing in their lot with an alliance which was beginning to awaken a mystical devotion among the masses. Being the largest party in the Popular Front combination as well as the most experienced and best organized, no other could dispute its right to have the controlling voice and to lead the alliance on the road to power. The parties of the Front, realizing the importance of nominating a candidate who could appeal to a broad range of voters, both in the working and in the middle classes, chose Pedro Aguirre Cerda, a member of the moderate wing of the Radical Party, to represent the coalition.[79] The Conservatives and Liberals failed to follow a similar course of wisdom and nominated the widely despised extreme-rightist, Gustavo Ross. Another faction also took part in the bitter electoral campaign. General Ibáñez had been allowed to return to Chile in 1937, and his candidacy was proclaimed by the newly formed Union Socialist Party. Ibáñez' candidacy, based on a more or less liberal socio-economic reform program, received the support of the Chilean Nazi Party. All the various elements supporting the former dictator joined together under the "Popular Liberating Alliance" in an effort to enlist leftist support. Their campaign put emphasis on Ibáñez' achievements in public works and social services during his last administration. However, after the failure of the Nazi coup, its leader von Marées as well as Ibáñez, both under arrest, ordered their followers to vote for the Popular Front candidate.

In the 1938 election, for the first time in Chilean political history, middle-class and proletarian groups were challenging the traditional parties that had governed the country for more than a century. This was no desperate attempt of the undisciplined masses, but a well-concerted effort of mature, well-organized political forces pledged to

[77] The best treatment of the birth, development, and record of achievements of the Popular Front is John Reese Stevenson's *The Chilean Popular Front.*

[78] The coalition won ten out of the 25 Senate seats, and 66 out of 146 positions in the Chamber of Deputies. The Socialist Party elected three senators and 19 deputies, with 45,000 votes. The Communists elected their leader, Lafferte, to the Senate, and seven deputies.

[79] Stevenson, *op. cit.,* p. 76. Also see Juan Fernández, *Pedro Aguirre Cerda y el Frente Popular chileno* (Santiago, 1938).

basic ideological principles. It was a closely fought contest because it afforded the electorate the opportunity of choosing between two different conceptions of government, and was, to a large extent, a national trial of the existing political systems. "The horizontal divisions of [Chile's] social and political map were never more in evidence than on this occasion."[80]

The Front's victory in the presidential race was not clear-cut, for both houses of Congress were lost to the rightist bloc, and its presidential candidate was defeated by only a few thousand votes.[81] But the leftist presidential victory did mean that Chile was to have its first president elected predominantly by the middle and lower groups of society.[82]

Coalition Politics (1941–1958)

The withdrawal of the Socialists from the Popular Front in 1940 brought the formal dissolution of the alliance early in 1941. The Popular Front had been weakened by an effective campaign of legislative obstructionism conducted by the Right and by the intra-governmental rivalry brought about by the contest for control over patronage and policy between the Radicals and the Socialists. Harmony among the government parties was further threatened by the acrid controversy between Socialists and Communists arising from early events of the Second World War and from their natural competition for control of the labor movement. The Communists chose to remain outside the government, criticizing it when criticism seemed advantageous, but at the same time claiming credit for its accomplishments.

In the early days of Chilean socialism there were two principal figures: Marmaduke Grove and Eugenio Matte, both of whom had participated in the twelve-day government of the Socialist republic. After the death of Matte in 1935, Grove assumed undisputed leadership of the party after defeating César Godoy. It was not too long after the installation of the Popular Front government that a strong faction led by Godoy began to feel that the party was losing prestige through its participation in the government and should, therefore, abandon the Popular Front. Finally, early in 1940, this group led

[80] Edwards and Frei, *op. cit.*, p. 247.

[81] Aguirre Cerda was credited with 212,000 votes to 199,000 for Ross.

[82] Aguirre Cerda also received support from many moderate rightists and independent voters. A man of humble rural origin, he rose rapidly in the education and political worlds, and had also built up for himself a comfortable economic position. Thus, while he aroused the fierce devotion of the poor man who could identify himself with Aguirre, he also had a strong appeal for intellectuals. Being an essentially moderate Radical and a well-to-do man, he did not arouse violent dislike among Conservatives.

by Godoy withdrew to form a new party, the Socialist Workers Party (*Partido Socialista de Trabajadores*).[83] This split was to be followed later by other serious Socialist divisions.

In terms of party interests, the Popular Front benefited two parties in particular, the Radicals and the Communists. The first enjoyed control of the government with the consequent consolidation of its political strength. The second, given an unprecedented freedom of action, made greater gains in the struggle for control of the labor unions and the workers' vote and reaped substantial benefits from the weakening of their chief rivals, the Socialists.

Despite the dissolution of the Popular Front, one or another coalition of the Center and Left managed to hold power until the end of the decade. Immediately after the dissolution of the Front, a new tripartite alliance directed by the Radicals was formed with the Democrats and a Socialist faction, the Radical-Socialists, for action in the congressional elections of March, 1941. Later, the Communist joined this electoral coalition as did the new Socialist Workers Party led by Godoy. Having been recently outlawed, the Communist Party took part in the election under a new name, the Proletarian Party. The Liberal and Conservative rightist forces, having first announced their intention of boycotting the election, decided to participate after leftist divisions gave them hope that control of Congress would not pass entirely into the hands of their opponents. The orthodox Socialists, under Grove and Schnake, went it alone.

The election, one of the most orderly ever held in the country,[84] was won by the leftist coalition. The most impressive gains were made by the Radicals and the Communists. The election removed the danger of future rightist legislative obstructionism although it did not guarantee the government coalition against internal dissensions. The cause of leftist unity was now more hopeful because of the influence of international events. The Communists' change of international position after the Nazi invasion of the Soviet Union resulted in improvement of their relations with other parties of the Left, particularly the Socialists. Future evidence of this new harmony was to be the lack of conflict between Socialists and Communists for control of the labor confederation at the Third Congress of the C.T.CH., held in 1943, when a joint ticket was presented.[85]

President Aguirre's withdrawal from office on November 10, 1941, for reasons of health, and his subsequent death shortly after presented

[83] In 1944, Godoy and other leaders of the Socialist Workers Party joined the Communists.

[84] Stevenson, *op. cit.,* p. 114.

[85] Alexander, *op. cit.,* p. 196.

a serious problem to the various leftist parties. Former dictator Ibáñez was again making a strong bid for the presidency, this time supported by Conservative and Liberal parties, and with the pledged support of the Nazis, who under the Popular Front's scrupulous respect for civil liberties, had acquired renewed strength. Under Radical leadership, and after some hesitation, a new political coalition was formed — the Democratic Alliance. It included not only the Radical and Leftist parties, but also Center elements such as the Falange, the Agrarians, the Democrats, and the Doctrinary Liberals. After a heated campaign in which international issues were given much emphasis, the Democratic Alliance's candidate, Juan Antonio Ríos, a moderate Radical, was elected President in 1942, by 260,034 votes against Ibáñez' 204,635. Ríos' triumph, however, did not mean a resurrection of the Popular Front. His candidacy had not come out of any convention of formally united parties, but was rather a result of a primary election held by the Radicals, by that time the nation's largest party, and later endorsed by action taken separately by all other parties except the rightist. The extreme Left, represented by the Communists and Godoy's Socialists, had joined at the last minute. It was only a week before the election that Ríos had been proclaimed the standard-bearer of this loose alliance of the united Left, the Falange, the Agrarians, and the Doctrinary Liberals. Furthermore, Ríos himself, a violent anti-Communist and a centrist Radical, was to push forward the trend towards moderation which had already been set in motion by the end of Aguirre's regime.[86]

Conditions of World War II, and the continuation of party feuds which often forced Ríos to govern with nonpartisan ministers, caused difficult problems during his administration (1942–1946). Some changes of importance took place during the remainder of the war. The Communist Party continued to gain in strength, chiefly as a result of further Socialist splits. In 1943 a serious schism among the ranks of the Socialists was brought on by differences of opinion concerning participation of the party in the Ríos administration and was aggravated by personality clashes between the party's sage Grove and other leaders. A final split took place in the middle of 1944. Grove's followers abandoned the party and organized a new force, the Authentic Socialist Party (*Partido Socialista Auténtico*), while his critics, led by Salvador Allende, remained in control of the majority of the organization. Since the anti-Grove faction kept control of the Socialist trade-unionists, rivalry between Socialists and Communists in the labor movement continued to increase.[87]

[86] Stevenson, *op. cit.*, p. 120.
[87] Alexander, *op. cit.*, pp. 196–197.

The battle for control of the organized labor movement was bitterly fought by these two factions. The majority of unions sided with the Communist-controlled C.T.CH., after a split which caused the Socialists to organize their own Confederation. Unions controlled by Radicals and the *Falange Nacional* also went with the Communists. Some unions split, with separate groups being established in both labor Confederations, and others dropping out of the labor movement entirely.[88]

The untimely death of President Ríos in 1946 resulted in the holding of new elections that year. With the unity of the populist parties a thing of the past, four candidates campaigned for the presidency. The Radicals again leading a coalition of the Center and Left, formed with the Communists, and several small factions, nominated Gabriel González Videla. A popular leader of the Social Christian wing of the Conservative Party, Eduardo Cruz Coke, was supported by that group, by the *Falange,* and by Grove's Authentic Socialists. The rightist parties, the Conservative and the Liberal, supported Fernando Alessandri, son of former President Alessandri. The Socialist Party went it alone, and nominated their leader Bernardo Ibáñez.[89]

González Videla, acknowledged political heir of Aguirre Cerda, received the largest number of votes, but failed to obtain the necessary 51 per cent majority,[90] and the election was thrown into Congress. Under these conditions, with congressional support almost evenly divided between González Videla holding the Radical and Communist votes, and the Conservative and Falangista parties pledged to Cruz Coke, the Liberal Party, which had supported Fernando Alessandri in the popular election became the key to the presidential succession. An accord between Radicals and Liberals finally assured González Videla's election by Congress. His cabinet contained three Liberal ministers, three Radicals, and three Communists — strange bedfellows, indeed. For five months Communist ministers had the rare distinction of participating in the government for the first time in Chile's history. That period marks the peak of Communist influence, and also the outbreak of violent clashes between Communists, Socialists, and Anarchists.[91]

The Radical-Communist-Liberal coalition had serious repercussions. The municipal elections of 1947 showed considerable gains by Com-

[88] *Ibid.,* p. 199.

[89] No kin to former President Carlos Ibáñez.

[90] The votes received by each candidate were as follows: González Videla, 192,207; Eduardo Cruz Coke, 142,441; Fernando Alessandri, 131,023; and Bernardo Ibáñez, 12,114.

[91] Alexander, *op. cit.,* pp. 200–202.

munists, Socialists, and Conservatives. It was clear that in the government coalition the only winners were the Communists. It also seemed clear that many who formerly had voted Radical were now becoming supporters of the Communists, while at the same time, because of the latter's high-handed tactics, many workers were returning to the Socialist fold. Furthermore, rightist voters who normally were adherents of the Liberal Party were strongly reacting against the alliance of this party with the Communists and, in disgust, had now turned toward the Conservatives. Soon after the elections, the Liberals abandoned the government. President González Videla dismissed the Communist ministers and organized an all-Radical cabinet. Definitely breaking with the Communist Party, the President obtained from Congress in 1948 the so-called "Law for the Permanent Defense of Democracy," which made illegal the Communist Party, ordered the removal of all Communist voters from the electoral registry,[92] and gave the government power to confine Communist leaders to remote areas of the country.[93] The Communists experienced serious setbacks in the labor movement, since the Law prescribed that those persons excluded from the electoral register could not belong to any union, but their party was not destroyed, and it even retained its congressional seats.

However, this Law for the Defense of Democracy was indirectly responsible for new divisions among the Socialists, just when they appeared to be moving toward unity, after the dissolution of the Authentic Socialist Party. Difference of opinion concerning this legislation and the question of whether or not they should participate in the González Videla government eventually resulted in the new Socialist offspring, the Popular Socialist Party (*Partido Socialista Popular*) formed by the anti-González Videla group led by Raúl Ampuero and Salvador Allende.[94]

By 1949, the Chilean political scene was characterized by an extraordinary multiplicity of parties. The political nomenclature was bewildering. Ten parties were represented in Congress. Another ten new parties had been duly registered for the congressional elections of that year. Final results of the 1949 elections, shown in Table 4, indicated the relative strength of those which secured congressional representation.

Of the new political forces, the most significant was the Agrarian Labor Party, which had apparently subsumed all the pro-Ibáñez votes and those of the defunct Nazi Party as well. As the 1952 presidential election approached and the political picture became more confused, ex-dictator Carlos Ibáñez, who was conducting a virulent campaign

[92] Accordingly, 26,384 Communist voters were eliminated.
[93] Alexander, *op. cit.*, pp. 202–204.
[94] *Ibid.*, pp. 204–205.

Table 4

1949 Congressional Elections

Political Party	*Deputies Elected*	*Votes Cast*	*Senators Elected*
Radical	34	100,869	5
Conservative	31	98,118	3
Liberal	33	83,582	6
Agrarian Labor	14	38,742	3
Radical Democratic	8	23,248	1
Popular Socialist	6	22,631	1
Democratic	6	20,682	—
Falange Nacional	3	18,221	1
Socialist of Chile	5	15,676	—
Peoples' Democratic	1	8,536	—
Traditional Conservative	2	7,485	—
Progressive Liberals	2	6,431	—
Authentic Socialist	1	5,125	—
Renovating Action	1	1,985	—

Source: Dirección del Registro Electoral, *Elección ordinaria de Congreso Nacional en 6 de Marzo de 1929* (Santiago: Imprenta Universo, 1949).

against the political organizations responsible for governing, began to acquire great popularity. The forces of *ibañismo,* as it was called, were heterogeneous and included splinters of varied political coloration. The Popular Socialist Party threw its support to Ibáñez, an action which in turn led to a new Socialist split early in 1952. Allende quit the party and returned to the other Socialist faction, the Socialist Party of Chile. In one of those bewildering shifts which are not too rare in Chilean politics, Allende, who had broken from the anti-González Videla faction, returned with his followers to his former party. He convinced the Socialist Party of Chile to back his candidacy for President and to accept the support of the Communists as well. "As a result, the *Partido Socialista de Chile,* which until then had been the most violently anti-Communist group in the Chilean political spectrum, joined with the Communists and small dissident factions of the Radical and Democratic parties to form the so-called People's Front (*Frente de Pueblo*), backing Salvador Allende for President."[95] Two other candidates joined Ibáñez and Allende in the presidential race. The nominee of the Liberal Party, Arturo Matte Larraín, was supported by the rightist forces. The Radical candidate, Pedro Enrique Alfonso, was backed by splinter groups of the traditionally leftist parties. Besides the majority of the Radicals, Alfonso was supported by a Socialist faction which had refused the alliance with the Com-

[95] Alexander, *op. cit.*, p. 205.

munists, the Democratic Party, and the Christian Socialist Falange Nacional. During the campaign, Ibáñez promised to repeal the legislation enacted by González Videla outlawing the Communist Party, and this pledge gained for him considerable Communist support. Ibáñez' major strength, however, came from the electorate's strong feeling of disillusionment with the existing parties and from the frustrations and hardships arising from the ever-increasing inflation.[96]

It had been in the presidential campaign of 1938 that a trend having its beginning in 1920 had finally crystallized into a definite alignment of Chile's political forces into three great blocs: the Right, the Center, and the Left. The Radical Party, numerically the largest political organization in the country and also the only one representing a wide range of social and economic interests, necessarily became the center of gravity of Chilean politics. The factors responsible for the central role of the Radicals were at the same time to make it exceedingly difficult for them to perform that role. There exist in the Radical Party, as we have seen, two divergent and even antagonistic currents. The numerical equilibrium of the two groups into which these currents divided the party permitted them alternatively to select leaders, to make policy, and even to modify ideological principles. One of these currents is definitely Marxist in orientation, and logically it seeks to place the party politically with the Left, even in alliance with the Communist Party. The other responds to traditional liberalism and rejects any contact with the extreme-leftist parties. According to this latter wing, the logical location for the Radical Party is precisely the center of the political spectrum, removed from extremism, and its logical role is to act as the nucleus of a moderate bloc capable of supporting a truly national government representing all Chileans. After the coalition of left-wing forces in 1938 grabbed political power from the aristocratic élite, the Radical Party dominated this coalition for fourteen years, while within the ranks of the party these two wings wrestled for supremacy.

The split personality of the Radicals served well to prevent dangerous extremisms. In affiliation with the leftist parties, it prevented a drift too far from center from approximately 1936 to 1950. When it linked itself to the rightist forces during the last two years of its administration, that split personality exerted the same restraining influence. However, Radical dependence on other political groups seriously jeopardized the party's future, for the cost of dependence on Right or Left for support in order to govern was hollow programs, full of generalities

[96] For an interesting psychological analysis of the "nonpartisan" public reaction which swept Ibáñez into power, see Alfonso Stephens Freire, *El irracionalismo político en Chile* (Santiago, 1957).

and born out of the "necessity to take color from coalition rather than from inner conviction directed outward in convincingly proposed policy."[97] The administrations of Radical Presidents, Aguirre Cerda, Ríos, and González Videla, were often pushed to the left by their contact with Socialists and Communists only to veer later toward the Right when confronted with the danger of the social upsets encouraged by the extremists. The effectiveness of government was bound to suffer.

Also significant in the years preceding 1952 was the disintegration of the once-great Chilean Socialist Party. In many ways this was inevitable, for the Socialist Party carried within itself the seeds of disintegration. There were in the Socialist Party pure Marxists, some of whom were Leninists and others Stalinists; there were anarcho-syndicalists, arch-enemies of Marxism; and there existed also a major group composed of those who could be called social-democrats, whose position corresponded to what is now sometimes referred to as "humanistic socialism," as typified by certain currents of French socialism and particularly by Léon Blum. Once victorious, the prerogatives of power, petty jealousies, and personal ambition prevailed over party interest and ideology, corrupting Socialist ranks. But also important in causing the Socialist decline was the tenacious and effective competition of the chief rivals of the Left, the homogeneous and highly disciplined Communist Party. With the splitting of the Socialist Party, the Communists became during this period the principal political force among Chile's workers. Even after enactment of the anti-Communist law by González Videla, the party managed to preserve its position, and when it gained relative freedom to operate after 1952, it continued to work for control of the labor movement. As regards its political role, it should be noted that throughout this period, the Communists, because of their efficient organization and agile and effective campaign techniques, were always eagerly sought out at election time by other political groups, especially the Radicals.

As regards the forces of the Right, both the Conservative and the Liberal parties remained very strong. Their control of Congress throughout much of this period, as well as their domination of the nation's economic system, successfully prevented socio-economic reforms from being carried beyond a certain point. Periodic Radical dependence on rightist support permitted the Chilean plutocracy to recover at least part of the political power that it had lost in 1938. A key to the power of the rightist parties was the fact that their hold on the rural parts of Chile remained practically untouched. At no time

[97] Silvert, *op. cit.*, p. 16.

during the years of leftist predominance did the leadership of the temporarily allied government parties attempt any program involving the partition, the expropriation, or even the increased taxation of the landed estates. Preservation of the *latifundio* system assured the rightist parties of a sizable representation in Congress, since the great *fundo* owners were skilled in using their influence in the rural districts to secure the election of the local Liberal or Conservative nominees.[98]

Of some significance was the change of mentality of the traditionally malleable Chilean Right, for although the Popular Front victories drove many of its members to an ultraconservative and reactionary position, it is also true that those victories made the majority of the rightists start thinking in national terms, instead of exclusively in terms of class interest. Actually the term "oligarchy" could no longer be applied indiscriminately to the Right, and particularly to the landowning class, for the latter had lost their monopoly of political power in 1925 "and increasingly since then had been taking their place as one of several economic groups, along side the industrialists, mining and metal interests, commercial associations, and the representatives of the labor unions, among others."[99]

The presidential election of 1952 resulted in a remarkable victory for Ibáñez, the candidate who counted himself above politics. Election returns showed that he had received 446,439 votes, while the rightist candidate, Matte Larraín, who came in second, received 265,357.[100] Since no candidate obtained a majority, however, the election was thrown into Congress. As it had done in 1946, this body followed the established tradition of electing the candidate with the highest number of votes, and chose Ibáñez. The most significant thing about his victory is that for the first time the majority of the rural workers and tenant farmers defied the rightist landowners in order to vote for Ibáñez. This overwhelming support, across regular party lines, of a man who later came to represent property, uprightness, and strength but who waged a demagogic campaign can be explained only as an expression of the national demand for what political parties had been unable to do, namely, put an end to an ever-mounting inflation.[101]

By this time, leftist coalition politics had little to offer. "The economic development program was rolling along under its own power, and few new big and far-reaching ideas were being contributed. Population was going up at an increasing pace, urbanization was snow-

[98] Alexander, *op. cit.,* pp. 177–180.

[99] Silvert, *op. cit.,* p. 13.

[100] The Radical candidate, Pedro Enrique Alfonso, received 190,360 votes. Salvador Allende came in last with 51,975 votes.

[101] See Stephens Freire, *op. cit.,* pp. 27–33.

balling, agriculture was stagnant, prices were climbing inexorably, and economic desires far outstripped economic ability. The ultimate failure of the Left was that it did not know what to do with what it had helped build: its success, of course, is that it left Chile with much more economic power than it had before, contained within well-maintained democratic forms."[102]

Leftist coalition governments, however, failed to bring immediate and basic social changes and always fell short of their campaign pledges. No basic restructuring of society was ever attempted. However, if it is true that the social advances that the Left had been predicting failed to materialize, it is equally true that the Right's dark prophesies of chaos were just as wrong. The old keystone of the economic system, the *latifundio,* remained intact and unchallenged, and it is interesting to note that, under the Popular Front regime, an order was issued in 1939 that forbade the organization of rural workers into labor unions. This is more understandable when one considers the composition of the Radical Party and the fact that its leaders were, according to their socio-economic status, political anomalies, for most of them were men of considerable means. Leadership of the Left by this type of man served to keep socio-economic demands within certain bounds, with the result that the Conservative opposition never felt compelled to resort to revolution in order to defend its interests. The Radical Presidents, all wealthy men, could sympathize well enough with the rightist leadership, and they were able to shape their policies so as not to drive the opposition to extremes.

It was in its efforts toward economic development and industrialization that the Center-Left coalition achieved its greatest success. The crowning achievement was the creation of CORFO (Chilean Development Corporation), which marked the beginning of a state-directed program for economic development. In other fields of governmental authority, the period of leftist coalition politics witnessed the entrenchment and extension of the social welfare structure founded in the early regimes of Alessandri and Ibáñez, a considerable increase in trade union organization, a notable acceleration of educational programs, and tenacious adherence to constitutional procedure.[103]

[102] Silvert, *op. cit.*, p. 19.

[103] It should be noted, however, that legal exiling for political reasons was frequent as were declarations of emergency and consequent censorship. Radical Presidents frequently used, at first, the Law of Internal Security, passed over leftist opposition in Alessandri's second administration, and later, the Law for the Permanent Defense of Democracy, not only to control Communists, but also to silence or constrain other political critics of the regime. Nevertheless, these acts, if not in spirit in the letter, were taken strictly within the framework of the Constitution.

But whatever hopes the Chilean voters may have had, when, on the verge of desperation and doubting the efficacy of party government, they elected Ibáñez, they were not fulfilled. If in 1952 these voters tried to escape their responsibilities by electing a father-figure who would take upon himself all their worries, they were soon disappointed, for his administration turned out to be weak and ineffectual. The President was faced with the necessity of making frequent Cabinet changes; in fact, he made forty-one such changes in the first thirty-three months of his term. Eventually, he discarded the normal procedure of choosing ministers from the parties and formed cabinets of "nonpartisan extras." Like his Radical predecessors, he began his administration with the support of left-wing parties but ended it with the support of the rightist parties. Toward the end of his term his popularity dwindled, and, deserted by all the political groups that had been carried along with him to victory in 1952, he was a lonely figure. Strangely enough, the man who ruled as Chile's strong man from 1927 to 1931 and who had attempted to bring off a Fascist coup d'état in 1938, this time, contrary to all expectations, made no effort to establish a dictatorship and presided over two exemplary elections.[104]

Returns of the congressional elections of 1953, which occurred when the Chilean electorate's feelings against the traditional major parties were at their peak, reflected a high degree of political dispersion. All twelve political organizations represented in the Congress at the time of the election managed to survive the test,[105] although some saw their representation drastically reduced. Of the twenty-four newly registered parties, eight elected members to the Congress and the remainder, having failed to do so, were automatically removed from the official registry.[106]

[104] A good study of the second Ibáñez administration is Donald W. Bray, "Chilean Politics during the Second Ibáñez Government, 1952–58" (doctoral dissertation, Stanford University, 1961).

[105] These were: Agrarian Labor, Conservative, Traditional Conservative, Democratic of Chile, Democratic of the People, Falange Nacional, Liberal, Progressive Liberal, Radical, Socialist of Chile, Popular Socialist, and Renovating Action of Chile.

[106] The nomenclature of these new parties did not carry much meaning: Agrarian, Doctrinary Democratic, Feminine Progressive, National Christian, Labor, Feminine Chilean, Doctrinary Radical, Popular Unity, National Ibáñista Movement, Social Christian Movement of Chile, Popular National Movement, National Union of Retired Employees Movement, National Renovating Movement, National Movement of the People, National Independent Alliance, Reformist, National Democratic, Peasant Organization, National Union of Independents, National Araucanian, Liberal Reform, National Unity, New Public Action, and Association of Fruit Merchants (as a social entity).

Election returns in 1957 were in striking contrast to those in 1953. Eighteen political organizations participated in the contest. The losers of 1953 were this time the winners. It was obvious that another one of those great shifts in Chilean politics had taken place and that, after the *ibañista* fiasco, the voters were willing to put their faith again in the long-established political organizations.

The Radical Party recovered its position as Chile's major party. The Christian Democrats (*Falange*) made impressive gains. Among the rightist parties, the Liberal resurgence was indeed remarkable. The surprising vote rolled up by its candidates was evidence of some success in its bid for the labor vote. The Liberal Party, more flexible than its traditional Conservative ally, had for some time been trying to adjust its thinking to fit the interests of broader segments of the population. The Liberal efforts apparently were being rewarded with support from sources other than the interests that had traditionally supported it.

During the Ibáñez administration, there were some important party developments. Prior to the 1957 elections, the parties of the Left entered into an alliance and called themselves the Popular Action Front (*Frente de Acción Popular,* or FRAP). Included in this group were the two major factions of the Socialists,[107] and the Labor Party (*Partido del Trabajo*) and the Democrats of the People (a splinter of the Democratic Party). Also included in the Front were the Communists, prevented as they were then from operating under their own banner. Before long the Socialists were able to bury their differences and to unify their forces into a single well-organized party, which soon emerged as a powerful political force. On July 28, 1957, a new party, the Christian Democratic Party, was officially constituted. This organization was the result of the fusion of *Falange Nacional,* the energetic Left-Center party which under the leadership of Eduardo Frei had made such impressive show of strength in the 1953 elections, and the Conservative Party (Christian Socialist wing of the traditional Conservatives; the traditional Conservatives now called themselves United Conservatives).

As the presidential election of 1958 approached, four major groupings became the contenders. The Conservatives and Liberals, having found a strong champion in Jorge Alessandri, another member of the famous family, made what was clearly their strongest bid for the presidency since their defeat in 1938. The Christian Democrats, having in Eduardo Frei a figure of great appeal among intellectuals, technicians, and non-Marxist leftists, as well as Catholics, waged an active

[107] The Popular Socialist Party and the Socialist Party of Chile.

campaign after having attracted several of the small Center parties. The Left, fortified by the unification of the Socialists, assumed an independent position, and, rejecting the possibilities of a new Radical-Left coalition, placed its hopes in its leader-candidate, Salvador Allende. As matters turned out, the unified Left came close to winning the presidency. The Radicals made some attempts to accommodate themselves once again to their leftist partners as in so many past electoral battles. No longer able to make a strong appeal to independent elements of the Left and unwilling to make the necessary concessions to permit this *rapprochement,* they found themselves isolated for the first time, and fought a hopeless battle for their candidate, Luis Bossay. When the returns were counted, Alessandri had won.

Revolution by Ballots (1958–1964)

Alessandri's victory was a narrow one, for he edged out Salvador Allende by only 33,500 votes. If an independent candidate, Antonio Zamorano, a defrocked priest known as the "priest from Catapilco" (*el cura de Catapilco*), a little village not too far from Santiago, had not entered the contest, Allende would have won. Had all the votes for Zamorano gone to Allende, which would have been logical to expect, he would have led Alessandri by 8,000 votes. Zamorano got 41,304 votes from the poor farmers and slum dwellers[108] who in 1957 had elected him to the Chamber under the FRAP banner.

During the Alessandri administration, Chile's economy showed little improvement, while popular demands became more pressing. The administration relied on import restrictions, wage ceilings and currency controls, all unpopular measures which were only partially successful. In spite of Alessandri's great personal popularity the period was characterized by governmental irresolution. The rightist forces in control of the administration, even if they conceded the need for social reform, remained generally committed to the past and proved unable to carry out the radical alterations demanded by Chilean society. Reform measures, passed by the Congress, were generally denounced in all circles as too mild and inadequate and did little to ameliorate the lot of the lower groups. In August, 1961, the Radical Party joined the Conservative-Liberal alliance and in October, 1962, the three parties formally constituted the Democratic Front (*Frente Democrático*).

As the presidential elections of 1964 approached, discontent was general and pressures grew stronger for adjustments in a political sys-

[108] The vote was distributed as follows: Jorge Alessandri, 389,909 (31.6 per cent); Salvador Allende, 356,493 (28.9 per cent); Eduardo Frei, 255,769 (20.7 per cent); Luis Bossay, 192,077 (15.6 per cent); and Antonio Zamorano, 41,304 (3.3 per cent).

tem which many had come to consider defective and ineffectual. The electoral campaign began early. Salvador Allende again became the standard-bearer of the leftist FRAP coalition. Eduardo Frei was the Christian Democratic nominee, and Julio Durán, a member of the Radical Party, was the candidate of the Center-Right (Radical, Liberal, Conservative) administration coalition. A polarization of the electorate soon developed as a result of a congressional by-election in agricultural Curicó Province. The candidate of the FRAP garnered a surprise victory. The upset victory in normally conservative Curicó reflected the growing disenchantment with the government and in the opinion of many observers portended a strong shift to the Left in national politics.[109] The *Frente Democrático,* expecting a victory for its candidate, had publicly staked its prestige on the outcome of this election calling it "a national plebiscite." As a result of this stunning defeat, the government coalition disintegrated. The Radical Party announced severance of ties with the Alessandri government and Julio Durán withdrew from the race as a candidate of the *Frente Democrático.* Although the Radicals later decided to maintain Durán's candidacy in hopes of wielding decisive power if the election were thrown into the Congress, Allende and Frei were left as the only serious presidential contenders. Concerned with the possibility of a leftist victory, Liberals and Conservatives threw their unconditional support to Frei. Until the eve of the election the outcome of the close race between Allende and Frei still appeared uncertain. When the ballots were counted on September 4, victory had finally gone this time to Eduardo Frei.

The most significant developments of the early 1960's were the impressive gains made by the left FRAP coalition and by the Christian Democrats. A strong shift of the electorate toward the moderate and extreme left became clearly detectable in the congressional and municipal elections of 1961 and 1963, respectively. The leftist coalition continued to make inroads among the agricultural workers of central Chile. In 1961, the FRAP obtained 31 per cent of the total vote and received 27.5 per cent of the seats in the Chamber of Deputies.[110] With nearly 11.3 per cent of the vote in the 1961 elections, the Communist Party more than doubled its parliamentary strength. In the 1963 elections, rightist strength heavily declined. The Conservative Party

[109] Oscar Naranjo Arias, the FRAP candidate received 9,578 votes, while Rodolfo Ramírez, the government coalition representative, received 7,955. The Christian Democratic candidate, Mario Fuenzalida got 6,619 votes. The votes of the opposition candidates combined was almost 70 per cent of the total vote.

[110] *Statistical Abstract of Latin America, 1963* (Los Angeles: Center of Latin American Studies, University of California, 1963), p. 36.

received only 11 per cent of the vote (compared with 25.8 per cent in 1950) and the Liberals' percentage dropped to 12.7 from a high of 18 in 1949. The Radicals, after their reversal at the height of Ibáñez' popularity, when they polled only 13.3 per cent, have maintained just slightly more than 20 per cent (21.6 per cent in 1963). The Socialist Party polled 11.5 per cent of the 1963 vote. The Communist Party's percentage increased to 12.7 in the 1963 elections. The Christian Democrats, by reason of their success in attracting new voters (particularly women) and thereby developing mass support, became in 1963 the country's largest major party. While in 1950 it had received only 4.7 per cent of the vote, in the 1963 municipal elections it led all other parties for the first time, receiving 23 per cent of the vote. An avowedly reformist party, it had created a "development mystique" of strong appeal as an alternative to the revolutionary program of the Marxist Left.

The 1964 election was a "revolution by ballots." By casting their votes for the revolutionary program of the Christian Democrats, the Chilean masses expressed their choice for a new socio-economic order to be created within the principles of Western democracy.

3

Governmental Institutions and Political Processes

The Early Constitutions

The adoption of a formal Constitution in Chile was delayed by war and dissension. In 1812, a provisional constitutional ordinance, generally known as the Constitution of 1812, was proclaimed. So the country organized under a republican form of government. Executive powers were vested in the junta of three members, and legislative powers were given to a senate of seven. José Miguel Carrera, although officially only a member of the three-man junta, continued in power virtually as a military dictator.[1]

After a brief period during which the country fell under control of Spanish arms (1814–1817), liberation was finally assured at the battles of Chacabuco and Maipú, and demands for a constituent assembly became widespread. They were met by a decree appointing a commission to prepare a provisional Constitution, and the provisional instrument was promulgated by O'Higgins on October 23, 1818. Although the provisional Constitution created a senate of five members which was granted legislative powers and charged with the responsibility of safeguarding the Constitution, it also legalized the dictatorship of O'Higgins. To him as *Director Supremo* was entrusted military control, the collection and expenditure of public funds, and the direction of foreign affairs. He personally named members of the Senate and of a supreme judicial body, and there was no formal limit to his authority. The colonial system of administration, courts, and municipal government was preserved.[2] Shortly after the promulgation

[1] Fernando Campos Harriet, *Historia constitucional de Chile* (Santiago: Editorial Jurídica de Chile, 1956), pp. 109–137.

[2] Ricardo Donoso, *Las ideas políticas en Chile* (Mexico: Fondo de Cultura Económica, 1946), pp. 51–52.

of this Constitution public unrest forced O'Higgins to convene a constitutional assembly, which drafted a new document, the Constitution of 1822. Opposition to this Constitution, which was never put into actual force, resulted in revolution.

The government of General Freyre replaced that of O'Higgins after the latter's resignation. The Freyre government brought forth the Constitution of 1823, a curious document, chiefly the work of Juan Egaña. It provided for three branches of government. A supreme director exercised executive powers in close association with a legislature composed of two houses — a senate of aristocratic composition and functioning permanently and a chamber of deputies functioning only by special summons. A distinguishing feature of this Constitution was the authority it gave the government to protect customs and morals. This charter lasted only half a year. Clashes between the director and the legislative body, the precarious state of public finances, and issue of the relation between church and state, as well as the questions of liberalism and federalism, brought about the fall of Freyre's regime in 1826.

A new Congress established a federal system that year. A new Constitution was drafted under the guidance of the apostle of Chilean federalism, José Miguel Infante. The establishment of the federal system, despite the fervor of its adherents, threw the country into anarchy, although the federal Constitution was never formally adopted or applied to the country at large.[3] Federalism continued for some time to be urged by liberals as a way of progress, but the misfortunes of the experiment turned public opinion against it.

A new constituent assembly adopted the Constitution of 1828, for which the Spaniard José Joaquín de Mora was chiefly responsible. For its representation of the consensus, its symmetry, and its logical arrangement, this Constitution is an admirable document. It permitted Catholicism to enjoy a privileged status as the state religion but provided that no one would be molested because of his private religious opinions. In an obvious effort to compromise with federalism, it established autonomous provincial assemblies, but the provincial administration was to be in the hands of officials named by the President from nominees presented by the assemblies. The chief executive, who was elected indirectly, would serve five years and be ineligible for immediate re-election. Final judicial power was vested in a Supreme Court. Legislative power was vested in two houses, which were intended as representatives of the people. The legislature was amply endowed with authority, including the right to censure the executive, but the

[3] Luis Galdames, *La evolución constitucional de Chile, 1810–1925* (Santiago: Imprenta Balcells y Cía, 1925), p. 732.

executive branch was given sufficient powers for the effective administration of public affairs.[4] This Constitution also established an electoral system much broader than those provided by previous charters. In practice, the number of qualified voters was doubled, since registration in the militia was made sufficient grounds for acquiring the right to vote. One unforeseen result was that militia chiefs obtained control of a vast number of votes. This Constitution, then, as a consequence of the electoral practices it established, ultimately benefited the aristocratic cliques in control of the government during the nineteenth century.[5]

Like all those that preceded it, the charter of 1828 had a basic fault, namely, that it was too far ahead of the society of its time.[6] It attempted to mold people to the Constitution, rather than to adapt the Constitution to the possibilities of the existing society.[7]

Meanwhile, growing dissatisfaction with political disorders, the ascendancy of the planter and mercantile interests, and the rise to leadership of Diego Portales finally carried the conservative group into power. As a consequence of the conservative success in the revolution of 1829, the country after much discussion and deliberation adopted the Constitution of 1833, which, with modifications, was destined to remain in force until 1925. A committee chosen to draft the Constitution was occupied with this task for a year. Two texts were chiefly considered, one attributed to Manuel José Gandarillas and the other to Mariano Egaña. The final text was influenced by both of these drafts.

The charter of 1833 provided for a unitary form of government. It laid down the principle that sovereignty resides in the people and that the powers of the government are limited to those delegated to it by the people. It established Roman Catholicism as the state faith. Concerning suffrage, it ruled that voters must be twenty-five years of age, must be able to read and write, and must enjoy an income determined by a separate law or must possess property. A Congress of two

[4] Jaime Eyzaguirre, *Historia constitucional de Chile* (Santiago: Editorial Universitaria, S.A., n.d.), pp. 95–98.

[5] Julio Heise González, *Historia constitucional de Chile* (Santiago: Editorial Jurídica de Chile, 1954), pp. 50–51.

[6] For a description of this constitution, see Ramón Briseño, *Memoria histórico-crítica del derecho público chileno desde 1810 hasta nuestros días* (Santiago, 1849), pp. 204–224.

[7] For some opinions, see F. Erráguriz, *Chile bajo el imperio de la constitución de 1828* (Santiago, 1861); J. V. Lastarria, *Obras completas* (Santiago, 1906–1909), Vol. I, p. 202; and C. Gay, *Historia de Chile* (Paris, 1854), Vol. VIII, p. 116. Also P. V. Shaw, *The Early Constitutions of Chile, 1810–1833* (New York: Chile Publishing Company, 1931).

chambers, with the deputies chosen directly and the senators indirectly, was provided.

Since the chief goal of the makers of this Constitution was the preservation of internal order, they sought to create a powerful executive. The President was chosen by special electors for a term of five years and could immediately be re-elected for an additional, consecutive term. As "supreme chief of the nation" he was charged with maintaining public order in the interior, guarding the constitution and the laws, and protecting the country against foreign attack. He could appoint and remove at will ministers, counselors of state, diplomats, intendants, and governors. Among the powers of the President, one was particularly significant: in the event of domestic upheaval, upon authorization of the Congress, or, when it was not in session, of the council of state, he could declare a state of siege in the areas affected. This declaration automatically suspended some specific constitutional guarantees. Also, the Congress might grant the President extraordinary powers for a specified time and with certain limitations. During the ensuing forty years, after the promulgation of the Constitution of 1833, the powers of the President were without an effective counterweight.

The judicial power was vested in a supreme tribunal of justice, with the guarantee of permanent tenure and responsibility for its judges. Members of the courts were named by the President from lists proposed by the council of state. Spanish private law and both the military and ecclesiastical *fueros* were left unchanged.

Provincial assemblies were suppressed, and provincial and local administration was entrusted to presidential appointees who were agents and direct representatives of the executive. The system was therefore a highly centralized one. The administrative subdivisions were the province, headed by an intendant; the department, by a governor; the subdelegation, by a *subdelegado;* and the district, by an inspector. These officials formed a sort of political hierarchy, each being responsible to and removable by the next highest in the scale. As for the municipalities, their elective councils had a strictly limited set of powers, and any action by them found to be contrary to the public interest could be invalidated by the central authorities.

Other provisions described individual rights and re-established the the system of primogeniture. They created a *Comisión Conservadora* (standing committee) — composed in the beginning of seven members of the Senate and later of representatives of both houses, to be in session during the recess of the Congress — and a Council of State. The former was to oversee the observance of the Constitution and the laws, to report to the executive concerning these matters, to approve or disapprove certain presidential appointments, and, by subsequent amendment, to report to the Congress at its next session. The Council of State, composed of the ministers, two members of the judiciary, one member of the clergy, a general of the army, an officer of the treasury, two former ministers or diplomats, and two former local government officials, was charged with making nominations for appointments to judicial and ecclesiastical positions, among its other duties. Rather than as a check on the executive, this body was designed as a support for the President. Lastly, the power to interpret and construe the Constitution was vested solely in the Congress.

Such, in the aggregate, was the Constitution of 1833, under which Chile was to acquire a reputation for stability. Notwithstanding the criticisms which can be made of it, the fact is that it was highly successful in bringing about the permanent organization of the republic. That was the case because the constitutional scheme was well suited to the social conditions of its time. If it established an oligarchic republic based on the colonial tradition of authoritarianism, it did not do more than recognize the social reality. Although as an operative instrument of government, this constitution evoked contradictory appraisals, present judgment has come to be favorable to it, precisely because, far from being an idealistic and impractical document, it faithfully reflected prevailing social conditions. So well did it fit historical reality that thirty-eight years were to pass before an amendment to it was adopted, and although it was modified on many later occasions, it remained in force for a total of ninety-two years.[8]

The Constitution of 1925

The manifesto of January 23, 1925, issued by the military junta stated the objectives and program of the revolutionary movement. Included among these was a proposal for a complete change in national institutions, based upon an entirely new constitution. In the famous "telegram from Rome" by which President Alessandri agreed to return to the country, he also stated his intention to secure the reform of the Constitution. After his arrival, an assembly of 108 persons representative of all political groups and national activities gathered to discuss the subject. In the absence of electoral registries, the holding of immediate elections for delegates to a constituent assembly was considered impractical. Consequently, President Alessandri appointed a "Consultative Commission" (finally composed of 122 persons) and entrusted to this body the discussion of constitutional reform. The Consultative Commission held only three plenary sessions. At the first

8 The text of this constitution is given in Briseño, *op. cit.*, pp. 489–510, and is discussed in the same work, pp. 230–265. See also Galdames, *op. cit.*, I, pp. 863–970.

session it appointed a subcommittee of about fifteen persons which, together with Alessandri and two of his ministers, prepared the draft of the new constitution.[9] This draft, together with another plan sponsored by the Radical and Conservative parties and featuring a restricted parliamentary system, was submitted to a plebiscite on September 12, 1925. A curious system of voting was used on this occasion: voters in favor of the "constitutional reforms advocated by the President" were to use red ballots; citizens desiring the maintenance of the parliamentary regime were to us blue ballots; and those opposing all reforms were to employ white ballots. The Conservative and United Liberal parties decided to abstain from all participation in the plebiscite. The Liberal, Liberal-Democratic, and Democratic parties agreed to support the subcommittee's proposal, while the Communist Party was the only organization which endorsed the reform plan that included a parliamentary system. With fewer than one half of all qualified voters participating in the balloting the results were: 127,483 for Alessandri's project (red ballots); 5,448 for the parliamentary regime (blue ballots); and 1,490 against reforms (white ballots), making a total of 132,421.[10]

Approval by the voters of what was virtually a new Constitution marked the end of the parliamentary system which had prevailed for thirty-three years. The new law instituted a presidential regime, although not in pure form. It created a very strong executive, and it deprived the Congress of the power to depose ministries by means of censure. It suppressed the so-called "periodical laws" which had formerly to be approved every year and which had therefore served very well to assure congressional predominance. Only the budget law was now discussed yearly, but Congress could not delay its passage since it was automatically approved under certain circumstances. The revision proscribed dual office-holding as both congressman and minister. It also authorized the Chamber of Deputies to bring before the Senate accusations against the President and his ministers for abuses of power, and the upper house was empowered to take action against them if the charges were upheld.

Other changes introduced by the new Constitution were the suppression of the Council of State and the *Comisión Conservadora,* the creation of an electoral court (*Tribunal Calificador de Elecciones*) and a system of administrative tribunals, and the re-introduction of provincial assemblies. These provisions have not all been implemented, the electoral court being the only one of the new institutions which has

[9] This subcommittee began working April 18, 1925, and held 33 sessions.
[10] Mario Bernaschina González, *Manual de derecho constitucional* (Santiago: Editorial Jurídica de Chile, 1955), pp. 17–29.

actually functioned. Of special interest is the provision permitting full religious freedom and separating church and state. The Church was to maintain all legal rights over property acquired prior to the adoption of the Constitution; and, as compensation for the loss of its privileges, it was granted an annual subsidy for a five-year period.[11]

Along with the traditional constitutional guarantees of public freedom and individual rights, the new Constitution, although timidly, embodied some new social concepts already accepted in other countries. It recognized the inviolability of property, but its provisions implied that individual rights related to private property could be limited when social need demanded. It also assured protection to labor and industry and stressed the duties of the state in matters of health and education, declaring that "each inhabitant shall enjoy a minimum standard of living, adequate to the satisfaction of his personal needs and those of his family." It also declared that the state would take measures to achieve the subdivision of land and expressed the concept of the homestead or place of family abode.

The Constitution of 1925 introduced other important changes. Terms of deputies and senators were extended to four and eight years respectively (they had formerly been three and six). A system of proportional representation was established in place of the cumulative vote system. Instead of leaving to the Congress the power to judge the validity of the elections of its own members and of the chief executive, it created for this purpose a permanent "qualifying tribunal" composed of five members whose terms were renewable every four years. As to the Senate, after much debate by the subcommittee which drafted the project, Alessandri's idea of converting this house into a merely consultative body composed of technicians was abandoned, and the powers of the senators were left intact. However, the number of senators was fixed at forty-five.

The lawmaking process was also modified, and a special mechanism for consideration of urgent legislative measures was introduced. Another provision made possible the use of mixed committees (like the so-called "Conference Committee" of the United States Congress) of deputies and senators to harmonize divergent views of the two houses on legislative matters.

The new Constitution established direct election of the President and extended his term to six years. Judicial branch reforms included a new system for the election of judges that provided for nominations by the judiciary as a way of protecting the independence of the courts.

[11] According to Bernaschina, *op. cit.*, p. 33, this formula was worked out by Alessandri in direct negotiations with Cardinal Gasparri, the Vatican's Secretary of State.

These elections had under the 1833 Constitution been a function of the now-extinct Council of State. Other significant provisions simplified procedure for constitutional reform. Two chapters of the new Constitution dealt with two distinct administrative subdivisions: one with regional government (provinces, departments, subdelegations, and districts) and the other with local administration (provinces and *comunas*). Although provision was made for a gradual decentralization of government, the power of the central government permeates all local administration in Chile to this day, and the provision for provincial assemblies remains to be put into effect.

The process of amending the Constitution is simple. Each legislative chamber must approve a proposed amendment by an absolute majority. Sixty days later the amendment is voted on in a joint legislative session without debate. If a majority of the legislators are not present on the first day set for this joint session, a vote is taken on the following day, regardless of the number of legislators then present. A simple majority vote is required for approval in either case. The approved amendment is then forwarded to the President, who may suggest changes. If these changes are rejected by a two-thirds vote of each house, the President must either promulgate the amendment as it stands or submit the points of disagreement to a plebiscite for a final decision.

The new Constitution went into force on October 18, 1925, and has remained as Chile's fundamental law to this day. Since its promulgation, only once has it undergone a substantial alteration. In 1943 an amendment was passed giving the President exclusive authority to initiate legislation concerning changes in the political and administrative divisions of the country, the creation of new public services and remunerative offices, and salary increases for government employees. This amendment drastically curtailed congressional initiative in matters of public expenditures, although it also established certain restrictions as well upon the President's powers to make appropriations by decree.[12]

Although it is far from a perfect document and has been severely criticized from time to time, the Constitution of 1925 has permitted Chile to carry out, within legal bounds, many of the necessary economic and political readjustments demanded by conditions in the twentieth century. By providing for electoral practices that were more just and extending the right to vote to all literate males over twenty-one, among other methods, the 1925 law has opened a new era in which government has become more nearly representative of public

[12] A 1959 amendment increased the term of office for municipal councilmen to four years (it was formerly three) and specified that municipal elections be held two years after congressional elections.

opinion. It has also paved the way for important socio-economic achievements.[13]

The Executive Branch

As in all the Latin American countries, the Chilean governmental system is based in principle on the classical concept of separation of powers.[14] In practice, however, separation of political powers is not rigidly observed. This practical departure from the principle combines with the ample constitutional authority granted to the President to produce a system chiefly characterized by the dominant role played by the executive branch in all governmental processes. A Chilean President exercises such wide political, administrative, legislative, and, on occasion, even judicial power that, in fact, the system might be designated as a "legal autocracy."[15] Although part of the supremacy of the executive is extra-legal, by far a larger part is prescribed by the Constitution itself, as cursory examination of the constitutional authority of the President will suffice to demonstrate.

Qualifications

To begin with, the Constitution specifies that a presidential candidate must be a native born Chilean citizen and over thirty years of age. He is elected by direct vote for a six-year term and cannot succeed himself for the following term. In case no candidate obtains a majority of the popular vote, the Congress in joint session will make its choice between the two candidates obtaining the largest number of votes. Elections are by secret ballot. The President nominates a Vice-President from among the members of the Cabinet when ill, absent from the country, or personally in command of the armed forces; but if the President dies in office new elections are to be called in sixty days. Order of preference of the members of the Cabinet for nomination as Vice-President is specified by statute, and in the absence of all

[13] For detailed commentary on this constitution, see Guillermo Guerra, *La Constitución de 1925* (Santiago: Balcells y Cía, 1929). An interesting study of the constituents of 1925 is given in Mario Bernaschina G., and Fernando Pinto L., *Los constituyentes de 1925* (Santiago: Universidad de Chile, 1945). Also useful is Mario Bernaschina G., "Génesis de la constitución de 1925," *Anales de la Facultad de Ciencias Jurídicas y Sociales,* III, No. 5 (1957). For the debates of the Consultative Commission, see Ministerio del Interior, *Actas oficiales de las sesiones celebradas por la comisión y sub-comisiones encargadas del estudio del proyecto de nueva constitución política de la República* (Santiago: Imprenta Universitaria, 1925).

[14] Jorge Guzmán Dinator, *Derecho constitucional* (Santiago: Editorial Universitaria, S. A., 1950), pp. 66–70.

[15] Bernaschina, *op. cit.*, p. 62.

these officials the president of the Senate, the president of the Chamber of Deputies, and the Chief Justice are nominated in that order. In practice, the Minister of the Interior is usually the one to assume the office of Vice-President. Often the incumbent minister resigns and another person is named minister expressly so that he can pass on to occupy the presidential office. In recent decades, persons other than members of the Cabinet have twice assumed the office. In 1931, at a time of upheaval, the president of the Senate, Pedro Opazo Letelier, became acting President, and in 1932, again in a period of anarchy, the president of the Supreme Court, Abraham Oyanedel, served as chief executive until the second inauguration of Alessandri.[16]

Powers

The constitutional powers and responsibilities of the President can best be described according to whether they are administrative, legislative, or judicial in nature. The ordinance power (*potestad reglamentaria*) is the essence of the broad administrative authority of the executive. By it, the President frames regulations to supplement the laws enacted in general terms by the Congress. The various types of executive orders used for this purpose are theoretically limited to implementing and applying existing laws. In practice, however, the Chilean President frequently uses his ordinance powers in such a fashion as to make changes which affect not only the form but the spirit of the laws as well.

There are basic differences among the three types of executive orders used. The general species is the *decreto* (decree), which is a written order of the President issued to implement a specific law, countersigned by the appropriate minister, and concerning matters within the President's authority. The *reglamento* is a variety of decree. It is a body of overall rules and regulations created to implement a law or part of it. The *decreto* deals with the particular, as for example the appointment of an official or his removal. The *reglamento,* on the other hand, consists of administrative norms for the application of the law and can only be modified by another *reglamento* and not by a simple decree. The third type of executive order, the *instrucción,* is lowest in hierarchical order and can be issued by Cabinet members as well as by the President. The *instrucciones* are simple directives to administrative officials concerning the application of the law by government agencies.[17]

[16] Bernaschina, *op. cit.,* pp. 337–338.

[17] Bernaschina, *op. cit.,* pp. 343–348. Also Rafael Raveau, *Tratado elemental de derecho constitucional chileno y comparado* (Santiago: Editorial Nascimento, 1939), pp. 290–292.

The President is the administrative chief of the government in law and in fact. In a scheme of administration which is highly centralized, he usually has, as would be expected, ample powers of appointment. He is, of course, authorized to appoint ministers and other public officials. He can also remove appointive officials at his discretion, with the exception of those that are removable by impeachment only. In addition, the President is the commander-in-chief of the armed forces. His military powers, however, are somewhat restricted. He cannot personally command the armed forces without consent of the Senate. He can only "dispose, organize, and distribute" these forces, and their number is fixed by the Congress. Similarly, troops cannot be sent out of the country except by a congressional act which must stipulate a time for their return. As to military appointments, the President must have the approval of the Senate for those above a certain rank. In addition, his authority is limited by a law of 1953 which regulates in detail recruitment, appointment, and promotion of military personnel. This legislation reduces to a minimum the practical role of the President in military affairs.

The Role of the Army

Unlike other Latin American countries, soldier-presidents have not been common in Chile. The fact that President Ibáñez (1952–1958) was a general was only incidental to his political career; of the last seven chief executives, he is the only one who was a military man. Participation of the armed forces in politics from 1924 to the fall of the Ibáñez dictatorship was a rare occurrence. In fact, the involvement of the military forces in the civil sphere had not taken place for a century. It did not even occur for a short period after the collapse of the Ibáñez regime. To be sure, the Chilean army performed an active political role in the early and difficult period of republican organization. After the dictatorships of O'Higgins and Freyre, it continued to play an important part in the period of anarchy between 1826 and 1830. However, after that date, only in the civil conflicts of 1851 and 1891 did the armed forces undertake any active participation in public affairs. In both of these conflicts, once the conflict was over, the army returned to its barracks without attempting to retain control of the government. During the period from 1924 to 1932, the military forces returned to the political arena, and, sometimes with the support of civilian groups and of public opinion, exercised power, making and unmaking governments.

If we seek an explanation of the general political abstention of the Chilean military, we find it above all in the lack of interrelationship between the aristocratic oligarchy and the leaders of the armed forces, a phenomenon which was already distinguishable in early republican days. The political power of Concepción, at that time, was chiefly owing to the fact that in that region this was not the case, and the old Concepción aristocracy was intimately connected with the military class. There is further historical evidence that the Chilean aristocracy was never able to count on the support of the army when the interests of the élite were endangered. Neither in 1859 nor in 1891 and 1920 did the military side with the aristocracy; always it maintained a loyalty of traditional and monarchical sorts. If in 1920, for instance, the Right was forced to accept electoral defeat when a few measured actions by those in authority could have tipped the balance to its candidate, it did so because it was not certain that the troops could be depended upon in the face of public unrest.[18] The military vocation, in general, is not identified with upper social groups. Although high military rank is the object of considerable prestige and is sometimes an avenue of admittance into the élite groups, the vast majority of the military men come out of the middle or lower classes. It was they who in 1924, seeing their economic condition impaired by the currency depreciation and the rise of the cost of living, became the interpreters of the discontent of those classes and thus initiated the military movement of September 5, 1924. Although it is true that there were attempts on the part of the aristocracy to use the movement in order to regain control, it is equally true that action by the military set in motion the economic and social reforms called for by the needs of the country. That helps to explain the at least passive and, sometimes, even active support which public opinion lent to the various de facto governments dependent on the support of the armed forces from 1924 to 1931. With the restoration of constitutional government, the military withdrew as active participants in politics in support of any other than their own specialized demands, becoming what may be best described as an important veto group in the Chilean political system. In spite of the development at one time of small Nazi-oriented groups within the army and the appearance of what has been called a "coup mentality" (*mentalidad golpista*) among some political organizations, the possibility of a coup d'état carried out by units of the military in conjunction with some political parties seems today — barring an economic debacle — only remotely possible.[19]

The fine organization and discipline of Chile's 45,000 man military force may also explain in part the country's tradition of military

[18] Alberto Edwards, *La fronda aristocrática* (Santiago: Editorial del Pacífico, 1952), p. 309.

[19] A group of this type, known as the *Línea Recta,* has occasionally been active in recent years.

nonintervention.[20] Frequent threats of war at the end of the nineteenth century and at the beginning of the present one led to reorganization of the military establishment. German officers introduced the Prussian regime and the most modern armament into the army. Similar reforms were made in the navy under the presidency of Jorge Montt after the revolution of 1891. Compulsory military service was first established in 1900. Splendid administration of the Chilean armed forces, plus the glorious traditions handed down by a group of national heroes, have undoubtedly contributed to the esteem of the military and, peculiarly, to the preservation of their nonpolitical role in society.

The Civil Service

We have already noted that only by virtue of a law of Congress can new public services be created, but this legislation must be initiated by the President, and executive initiative is also required to raise the salaries of public servants. As for removal from office, the President can only remove presidential appointees and needs the consent of the Senate to do so in the case of high officials. A civil service and merit system of sorts exists under a so-called *Estatuto Administrativo* (Administrative Statute) that is provided for by the Constitution. The *Estatuto* is in reality a whole body of laws composed of various decrees and statutes applicable to public servants. A decree promulgated in 1953 applies to civilian government officials and to University of Chile and school faculties; some of its provisions apply also to personnel of the judiciary and to military officials. Practically every branch of administration has its own *Estatuto,* covering its own personnel.

The President and Public Finance

The President's power to spend money augments his authority in other areas. The process of preparing and adopting the budget is standard. An objective of the revolutionary movement of 1924 was to put an end to the budgetary anarchy created by the frequent congressional delay in approving the budget, a tactic employed by parliamentary cliques against the executive. At present, if the budget is not approved by the Congress, the bill presented by the President becomes effective at the end of a four-month period. Shifts in funds and extensive use of supplementary appropriation laws have always been characteristic of the Chilean budgetary system. These practices have contributed more than any others to diminishing the effectiveness

[20] According to *Statistical Abstract of Latin America, 1963* (Los Angeles: Center of Latin American Studies, University of California, 1963), p. 41, Chile's armed forces in 1960 were: Army, 21,500 men; Navy, 17,000; Air Force, 6,100. The *carabineros* (police force) contained some 10,000 men.

and utility of the national budget. Although justified in cases of emergency, the enactment by Congress of increases in appropriations already voted and of additional appropriations (*fondos extraordinarios*) for services not provided for in the general budget and the executive practices of authorizing expenditures by decree and of shifting funds have always created serious fiscal problems. The President under certain circumstances may, with the approval of his Cabinet, make payments not authorized by law. The constitutional amendment of 1943 specified the emergency cases in which the President can exercise this power as: (1) public calamities; (2) foreign aggression; (3) internal disorder; and (4) exhaustion of funds necessary to maintain services which if suspended would seriously harm the country. The amendment also provided that the total of expenditures that can be authorized by decree cannot exceed two per cent of the amount of the expenditures authorized by the general budget law. Before the constitutional reform of 1943, the President frequently ordered payments from the treasury for a wide variety of purposes by simply meeting the formal requirement of having the fiscal decree countersigned by all members of his Cabinet. The freedom with which Chilean executives formerly exceeded budget authorization through the use of their emergency powers led to abuses and uncontrolled public expenditures, to say nothing of the effects of the significant reduction in congressional authority concerning fiscal policies that this situation produced.[21]

The Contraloría General

In the field of public finance, a very important agency in the Chilean government, and one with unique powers on the American continents, is the office of comptroller general (*Contraloría General de la República*). As a result of a recommendation of the Kemmerer Mission, an American advisory group engaged by the Chilean government in 1925, the *Contraloría* was created. It was first established in 1927 and was given constitutional recognition in a 1943 amendment. This autonomous agency is entrusted with the supervision of the fiscal management of the government and is headed by a comptroller appointed by the President with the consent of the Senate. The comptroller enjoys the same guarantees of tenure as members of the Supreme Court. He appoints a subcomptroller and all personnel of the *Contraloría.*

This agency, at once an administrative and judicial body, not only has custody of all national property and exercises supervision over the

[21] Carlos Estévez Gazmuri, *Elementos de derecho constitucional* (Santiago: Editorial Jurídica de Chile, 1949), pp. 264–299.

budget but it also has jurisdiction over financial legislation. Among its functions are: the conduct of the general accounts of the nation, the examination and closure of accounts of those responsible to the treasury, the denunciation before the proper authorities of any irregularity which may be observed in the management of public funds, and the countersigning of orders for payment. Most important, the Chilean *Contraloría* is vested with a significant power that permits it to exert effective control over the executive. It takes cognizance of executive decrees and pronounces upon their constitutionality and legality, if necessary returning them for reconsideration by the executive within twenty days from the time they are received. However, when decrees are rejected by the *Contraloría* the executive may in turn issue a "decree of insistence" bearing the signatures of all members of the Cabinet, and the *Contraloría* must accept the reaffirmed decree. In this case, it transmits all the pertinent information to the Chamber of Deputies so that this body can initiate proceedings against the executive if it so wishes. Flagrant abuse of the "decree of insistence" by chief executives resulted in the constitutional reform of 1943, which abolished all such decrees that involved expenditures other than those expressly permitted by the Constitution in cases of foreign attack, internal disturbance, public calamities, and so forth. The decrees were always to be, in addition, within the so-called "constitutional two per cent." The presidential power of "insistence," therefore, is now limited to those decrees which deal with expenditures authorized by law, and then only if there is no usurpation of powers belonging to the other branches of government.

The Chilean comptroller general is in fact the ultimate guardian of financial legality, and it is his duty to see that the Constitution is respected, the laws interpreted as they should be, and the *Estatuto Administrativo* observed. The management of public funds is entirely his responsibility, as well as the keeping of the general accounts of the country. To him falls the task of investigating charges brought against all fiscal institutions. All supreme decrees (*decretos supremos*) concerning the placement of public personnel, the execution of laws, and the collection and disbursement of public funds pass through his hands. It is he, in the final analysis, who decides if the foregoing operations are within the law. Although the acts of Congress itself are outside the scope of the comptroller general, he does pass judgment upon the executive decrees implementing legislation enacted by that body. In all matters involving management of funds his word is decisive.

The mere fact that such an institution exists in the first place speaks highly for the country's traditional respect for legality. What is more, the *Contraloría* has not encountered any serious interference with its work from the chief executive in its thirty years of existence, evidence of the high regard of the executive branch for the spirit and letter of the law. The *Contraloría General* has met with this success on a continent often torn by revolutionary upheavals. Far from resisting its authority, chief executives have augmented it, with the assent of Congress. An institution that simply began by supervising public accounts now plays a significant and even crucial role in all aspects of Chilean public administration. Although frequently Presidents and ministers have disagreed with the *Contraloría* and have criticized it publicly, they have ultimately submitted to its judgment, and its authority remains intact to the present day.[22]

The *Contraloría* has always been jealous of its prerogatives, and it has often found itself in conflict with the executive authorities. In 1956, for example, employing special powers delegated to the executive,[23] President Ibáñez announced a series of decrees the purpose of which was the reorganization and merging of several governmental agencies that performed similar functions. The *Contraloría,* maintaining that sixteen of these decrees exceeded the authority of the President, returned them. Although the executive could in turn have rejected the *Contraloría's* decision by issuing a so-called "decree of insistence," it chose instead to engage in a juridical-administrative argument with the comptroller general. In the course of the controversy, the Cabinet charged that the *Contraloría* by an exaggerated conception of its importance and role was attempting to make of the President "a prisoner of the laws."[24] Although the case in question, besides the problem of "insistence," involved some fine distinctions between two types of presidential decrees — simple decrees and decrees having the force of law (*decretos con fuerza de ley*) — the episode is cited here to emphasize the fact that, far from being merely an auditing agency, the *Contraloría* is an alert custodian of legality and a vigorous and efficient instrument capable of curbing, if necessary, the excesses of a President constitutionally endowed with a great deal of power.

Legislative Powers

About the legislative functions of the President, it should first be noted that some legislation that is large in importance is proclaimed

[22] An interesting account of the men who have occupied this important office is given in "La Contraloría General de la República," *El Mercurio,* March 9, 1958.

[23] Law 12,084 of August 18, 1956.

[24] For the text of the Cabinet's communication to the comptroller general, see "Insistencia del Ejecutivo para el trámite de decretos en Contraloría," *El Mercurio,* February 19, 1957. For a discussion, see "El fondo de una divergencia," *El Mercurio,* February 20, 1957.

by presidential decree rather than enacted by Congress. The use of legislative power by the President is associated in Chile with the issuance of two types of decrees: the *decretos-leyes* (decree laws) and the *decretos con fuerza de ley* (decrees having the force of law).[25] The first type is defined as an act of the executive by which legislation is enacted without authorization by delegation and in clear usurpation of the powers of the Congress. In Chile, numerous *decretos-leyes* have been issued by the various de facto governments since the adoption of the Constitution of 1925, giving rise to difficult juridical questions. For example, is such exercise of power by the executive to be justified by the argument of necessity in meeting an emergency? May the Congress invest the executive with powers to legislate by delegation previous to the issuance of decree-laws or by validation of them subsequently? A special committee of jurists declared on one occasion that a series of decree-laws issued in 1932 which were not validated by subsequent congressional acts were null and void. However, the Supreme Court has ruled that "during the period of the military movements of 1924 and 1925, in which no legislative organ existed, the courts applied decree-laws and accepted them without restrictions as obligatory and efficacious norms, emanating from the only authority in effective control of the government." Since 1932 the Supreme Court has maintained this view in numerous decisions, recognizing that presidential orders in times of constitutional abnormality were as valid as any other laws and accepting executive legislation by decree as a *fait accompli*.[26]

The *decretos con fuerza de ley,* on the other hand, are presidential decrees issued by virtue of a delegation of powers by the Congress. The constitutionality of such legislation has been the subject of controversy. From a strictly legal viewpoint, there is little doubt that the Constitution forbids the Congress to delegate its powers.[27] In practice, however, the cases of delegation of special or comprehensive powers have been numerous since 1925. In 1927, 1930, and 1931 the Congress often offered a broad delegation of its powers to the President. In 1942, the chief executive requested a general authorization to legislate, a privilege that, in view of strong parliamentary opposition, was given only after the Congress had set specific limitations upon it. Again in 1943, and more recently in 1953, the Congress

[25] Enrique Silva Cimma, *Derecho administrativo chileno y comparado* (Santiago: Editorial Jurídica de Chile, 1954), pp. 94–125, has a good treatment of executive decrees.

[26] José Domingo Amunátegui, *Tratado general de derecho administrativo* (Santiago, 1935), p. 98. Bernaschina, *op. cit.*, pp. 64–66.

[27] Article 4 of the Constitution of 1925.

authorized the President to issue *decretos con fuerza de ley* in this restricted way.[28] In practice, then, the executive is recognized as having delegated powers to issue decrees having the force of law. The Chilean courts do not distinguish as to source between laws passed by Congress and those proclaimed by the executive. The Congress is then, in practice at least, at liberty to delegate its powers. If delegation is made, it is a political decision. The political justification for such delegation has always been the necessity of meeting some kind of emergency. The courts decide cases involving the constitutionality of either class of legislation without regard to source. They declare their interest to be the substance. Thus, although the fundamental law of the country gives no formal recognition to these decrees, practice and custom have given sanction to them, and the courts by upholding or by refusing to decide on their unconstitutionality have definitely recognized them as sources of law.

The emergency powers authorized in the three special situations described in the Constitution are, of course, of great importance among the constitutional powers of the President. The exercise of these powers greatly enhances the effectiveness of the position of the executive in national life. The three kinds of formal responses to emergency situations are: the grant of extraordinary powers, the declaration of a state of siege, and the declaration of a state of assembly.[29] In addition, a law of 1942 deals with the establishment of "emergency zones," but the zones do not actually constitute an additional response since they are an instrument for the application of the grant of emergency powers. The law authorizes the President in cases of foreign attack, invasion, or sabotage to define an emergency zone and to place it under military control.

The Congress has the exclusive authority to grant extraordinary powers for six months in order to meet dangers arising from internal disturbances. The powers may be extended for a longer period if necessary. The constitutional guarantees that may be restricted under these powers are expressly specified: those affecting personal freedom, freedom of the press, and freedom of assembly.

A declaration of a state of siege differs from the grant of emergency powers in that the former may only affect the freedom of individuals and also in that the state of siege may be declared for a fixed time by the executive alone if the Congress is not in session. The circumstances which justify the use of this measure — foreign attack and

[28] See Laws 4,113 (January 25, 1927); 4,156 (August 5, 1927); 4,795 (January 24, 1930); 4,945 (February 6, 1931); 7,200 (July 18, 1942); 7,747 (December 24, 1943); and 11,151 (February 5, 1953).

[29] Constitution, Art. 44, No. 13; 72, No. 17.

domestic disturbance — determine also some further differences. Only the President can declare a state of siege in case of foreign attack.[30]

The authority to declare a state of assembly belongs exclusively to the President. It can only be declared in "case of war and when there is an invasion or threat of invasion of one or more provinces." The legal effect of a state of assembly is to put the government of the region affected under control of military authorities.

Extraordinary powers have been used frequently in Chile to meet grave dangers caused by domestic unrest. Although public opinion has favored restrictions in the use of these powers, some chief executives have employed their special powers in a repressive way. In practice, the country has lived for long periods under emergency powers. In the face of some domestic disturbance of little importance, the Congress has often acted hurriedly, and it has generally been too willing to grant these powers to the President. It is difficult to justify all these repressive actions on the noble grounds that they have been necessary to preserve constitutional government, for undoubtedly Chilean Presidents have not always been innocent of acting to increase their own personal power or on behalf of their own political interests. Emergency powers were last granted in 1957 on the occasion of the grave riots in Santiago and other cities. However, a few days later, order having been re-established, President Ibáñez reported to the Congress that emergency powers were no longer needed.

With reference to other legislative functions of the President, it may be added that he has the power to extend the ordinary sessions of the Congress as well as to issue calls for extraordinary sessions. The role played by the President in the ordinary lawmaking process is also important, since he is authorized to initiate legislation in the form of messages to the Congress. This power to initiate legislation is freely used by Chilean Presidents. As we have seen, it is in fact the exclusive prerogative of the executive to propose legislation dealing with the budget, to create new administrative positions, and to increase government salaries. Furthermore, the President can designate any bill he proposes as "urgent," in which case the house receiving it must take action on it in a period of thirty days. This expediting identification of "urgency" can be continued throughout the entire process of lawmaking. Each house, upon receipt of a presidential request for urgent consideration of a given bill, will determine if it is to be labeled *simple urgencia* (urgent), *suma urgencia* (very urgent), or *extrema*

[30] The state of siege does not automatically end with the meeting of Congress. It is necessary for this body to reject specifically the President's declaration. See Facultad de Ciencias Jurídicas y Sociales, *Constitución y leyes políticas* (Santiago: Editorial Jurídica de Chile, n.d.), p. 107.

urgencia (extremely urgent). The *extrema urgencia* designation obligates the respective houses to discuss and dispatch the bill in a very brief period of time. The periods allowed for the three categories are twenty, ten, and three days, respectively, in the Senate; and fifteen, five, and three in the Chamber of Deputies.[31] However, failure to act within the specified times does not mean that the bill is automatically approved.

The designation of urgency can be an effective weapon in the hands of the President. In April, 1958, for example, the Center and Left parties, alarmed by the unexpected strength shown by the forces of the Right in a by-election, organized a parliamentary block to sponsor certain electoral reforms and other legislative measures designed to improve their chances in the coming presidential elections. The time that would be consumed by all steps in the ordinary lawmaking process made it certain that the desired changes could not be achieved before the September 4, 1958, elections. On this occasion, the chief executive came to the rescue by referring the project to the Congress as an "urgent" one, which made possible discussion and approval of legislation which allegedly was damaging to the electoral interest of the Right while it favored those of all other political groups.[32]

The President may, of course, veto the laws that Congress submits for his signature. The Constitution provides specifically for the item veto for all legislation. The President may veto a bill within thirty days after its passage. If Congress recesses within less than thirty days following the receipt of the bill by the President, a new veto period of only ten days is counted from the date of the opening of the following session. The presidential veto is only suspensive, and the Congress may enact legislation rejected by the President if it then is approved by a two-thirds majority of the members present.

The President and the Courts

Among the judicial functions of the President are the duty of watching over the conduct of judges and other members of the judiciary and of requesting the Supreme Court to initiate proceedings against them in case of misbehavior. However, it should be said that neither in law nor in practice is there any presidential interference in matters which are exclusively judicial, and that this presidential super-

[31] Bernaschina, *op. cit.*, pp. 298–299; Estévez, *op. cit.*, p. 246.

[32] "Proyecto que reforma la ley sobre inscripción electoral envió Ejecutivo al Congreso," *El Mercurio,* April 26, 1958; "Avanza la reforma de la ley de elecciones," *Política y Espíritu,* Año XIII, No. 199 (May 1, 1958), pp. 3–6.

vision applies exclusively to the administrative functions of the judicial officials. The President has also the power to appoint judges of the courts of appeal from panels prepared by the Supreme Court. He can also grant pensions, in accordance with the laws, and he has the power to grant juridical personality to private corporations. Lastly, he exercises the power of pardon.

The chief executive is responsible to the Congress for acts or omissions that violate the Constitution and the laws or for "seriously endangering the honor or security of the state." He may be accused only during his term of office or within the six months ensuing. During this latter period, he is required to remain in the country.[33] The procedure for impeachment is for the lower house, upon charges being preferred against the President, to appoint a committee of investigation. The committee reports to the house, and upon a majority vote of its members the case is presented to the Senate for trial. The Senate converts itself into a jury, a two-thirds vote being required for conviction of the President.

The Cabinet

As we have already seen, the President has the power to appoint his ministers and to remove them freely. No legislative confirmation of their appointment is required. Members of the Cabinet have the title of "ministers of state," and their total number is, at present, eleven. The departments making up the executive branch are: interior; foreign relations; development, economy, and reconstruction; public education; justice; national defense; public works; agriculture; lands and colonization; labor and social welfare; public health; and mining. Each one of these ministers has a "subsecretary," except that the Department of National Defense has three (war, navy, and aviation) and the Department of Development, Economy, and Reconstruction has two (economy and development, and transportation). Although the ministers forming the Cabinet are responsible to the President and cannot be members of Congress, they are authorized to participate in its sessions and secure precedence in debate, though they have no voting rights.[34]

Although after 1925 the Chamber of Deputies and the Senate were deprived of the power to depose ministers by means of votes of censure and ministers were made directly responsible only to the President, Congress is still able to force the resignation of a minister in an indirect

[33] Constitution, Art. 39, Cl. 1.

[34] Rafael Raveau, *Tratado elemental de derecho constitucional chileno y comparado* (Santiago: Editorial Nascimento, 1939), pp. 318–340.

way. The constitutional authorization given to the Chamber of Deputies to bring before the Senate accusations against ministers is frequently used for this purpose in Chile by a legislature long accustomed to having an influential voice and always eager to find ways of compensating for the lack of parliamentary responsibility of Cabinet members. Accusations against ministers, followed by separation from the Cabinet, are fairly common occurrences. During the Alessandri administration, Minister Salas Romo was twice charged, but the accusations against him were not successful. During the Aguirre Cerda administration, the rightist congressional forces, since they could no longer depose a cabinet by a vote of censure, proceeded to do the next best thing — to impeach individual ministers. Scarcely six months after Aguirre's inauguration, his Minister of the Interior was impeached by the Chamber in a 68 to 59 vote, but he missed being convicted in the Senate by a narrow margin.[35] In 1940 the Minister of the Interior, accused of intervening in a by-election in Valparaíso, was forced to resign. In 1945, the Congress obtained the removal of the comptroller general on grounds of neglect. Also in 1940, the Nazi sympathizer von Marées led a congressional move charging the Minister of Foreign Affairs with irregularities in the admission of Jewish refugees from Hitler's Germany. On that occasion, the charges were rejected by the Senate. As a result of the rightist offensive, four other Radical ministers resigned their posts even before impeachment proceedings were actually initiated.

The second Ibáñez administration (1952–1958) was often the target of congressional accusations. One of his ministers escaped charges in the chamber by a narrow margin (three votes). Two other ministers, who held the portfolios of the Interior and Lands, were charged but ultimately exonerated by the Senate. Charges against President Ibáñez himself were preferred in December of 1956 for alleged violations of the Constitution. The accusation, supported by the Radical Party, failed to find support among other parliamentary groups and was rejected by a vote of 48 to 30, with thirty-seven members abstaining.[36] The spectacular flight of a group of Peronist leaders, under custody while extradition proceedings requested by the Argentine government were being considered by the Chilean Supreme Court, gave rise in 1957 to accusations against two other members of Ibáñez' Cabinet, the ministers of Foreign Relations and Justice. The Chamber of Deputies favored the accusation by a vote of 100 to 8,

[35] John Reese Stevenson, *The Chilean Popular Front* (Philadelphia: University of Pennsylvania Press, 1942), pp. 97–98.

[36] "La semana política," *El Mercurio,* December 9, 1956.

and subsequently the Senate, although it cleared the ministers of the charges of compromising the national honor, convicted them for failure to comply with and enforce the laws, which resulted automatically in their separation from the Cabinet.[37]

Powers and duties of Cabinet members are both political and administrative. They include the following: to prepare bills, regulations, and decrees and to propose them; to countersign laws and other official papers authorized by the President, except those appointing or removing ministers; to attend sessions of Congress, to report to that body, and to answer questions from it; and to serve, in general, as agents of communication between the administration and the Congress. The latter function is, in general, actively performed, for in contrast with many other Latin American countries, Chilean ministers have made a frequent practice of attending sessions of the Congress. The legislature, in turn, is always most eager to subject Cabinet members to long interrogations which, in spite of the heat of partisan controversy that is often created, are sometimes fruitful in terms of policy.

The Congress

The legislative branch is composed of a Senate and Chamber of Deputies. The Senate is made up of forty-five members, elected for eight-year terms, and the chamber of 147 deputies, elected for four years. Members of both houses are chosen by direct, secret, popular vote. Senators are elected from districts, consisting of natural constituencies or groups of provinces so arranged as to give representation to all the national interests. Five senators are elected for each of nine regional groupings — (1) Tarapacá and Antofagasta, (2) Atacama and Coquimbo, (3) Aconcagua and Valparaíso, (4) Santiago, (5) O'Higgins and Colchagua, (6) Curicó, Talca, Linares, and Maule, (7) Ñuble, Concepción, and Arauco, (8) Bío-Bío, Malleco, and Cautín, and (9) Valdivia, Osorno, Llanquihue, Chiloé, Aysén, and Magallanes. The terms of half of the Senate members expire every four years, the senators from the odd-numbered areas in the list of nine regional groupings completing their service alternately with the senators from the even-numbered areas.[38]

The 147 deputies are elected by departments or groupings of departments; one deputy is allowed for each 30,000 inhabitants or additional fraction of 15,000 or more. Citizenship and the full enjoyment of civil and political rights are qualifications necessary for election to either house. In addition, the candidate may not have been convicted

[37] "Senado declaró culpables a los Ministros de Relaciones Exteriores y de Justicia," *El Mercurio,* October 27, 1957.

[38] Estévez Gazmuri, *op. cit.*, pp. 207–210.

of punishable crimes (*delito que merezca pena aflictiva*).[39] Membership in the Senate is restricted to citizens over thirty-five years of age. Naturalized citizens can be elected as deputies or senators provided five years have elapsed since the date of their naturalization. Certain persons are ineligible to serve in either branch of the legislature. Cabinet ministers, intendants and governors, members of the judiciary, and citizens who hold contracts with the government are so excluded. Each house has the exclusive power to decide whatever questions involving its own members arise out of these exclusions known as "inabilities" (*inhabilidades*), by a two-thirds vote of the members present. The office of congressman is incompatible with any other office remunerated by the state, province, or municipality, as it is likewise with formal association with any agency supported wholly or partially by public funds. However, this provision does not apply to staff members of educational institutions at the secondary and higher levels if they are located at the site of Congress (Santiago). In cases of incompatibility, the person elected to Congress has a fifteen-day period of grace, counting from the day of his election, in which he may rid himself of the conflicting office.[40] Also no member of the Congress, from the time of his election and for six months after the expiration of his term, can be appointed to any other office remunerated by public funds.[41]

Two issues of qualification and conflict of interest involving members of the Congress assumed a national importance in the recent past. One difficult legal question was created by the Law for the Permanent Defense of Democracy, which banned the Communist Party in 1948. Full application of the law voided the election of any one who may be considered a Communist. In the elections of 1957, the director of the electoral registry maintained that the law required the annulment of the election of practically anyone elected by the coalition of leftist parties known as the FRAP. Others contested the election only of the four or five candidates who were avowed Communists. Under the law, any citizen could denounce a candidate as a Communist within a given period of time (before June 1 in election years). Given the

[39] Interpreted as meaning conviction for crimes imposing a sentence of not less than three years and one day of confinement. See Art. 37 of the Penal Code. Also Irma Naranjo Quaglia, *El poder legislativo y ejecutivo* (Valparaíso, 1951), p. 14.

[40] Mario Bernaschina G., *Síntesis del derecho constitucional chileno* (Santiago: Talleres Gráficos, 1944), p. 64.

[41] Intendants and other local officials who run for congressional offices must resign their positions twelve months before the date of the congressional election. If they fail to do so, they are automatically removed but may continue as candidates.

complexities and peculiarities of the electoral system in force at that time, the possible advantages of voiding elections were significant, for, since votes were thrown out, the electoral quotient was changed and new opportunities were created for candidates whose position was otherwise hopeless. Since its promulgation the anti-Communist law was circumvented by the formation of loose alliances in which it was difficult to define who was and who was not a Communist or a neo-Communist.

In accordance with the Law for the Permanent Defense of the Democracy, electoral registrations of all members of the Communist and the National Progressive parties were cancelled. The law was invoked to declare null the election in 1948 of a deputy from Valparaíso, as well as to void the election of numerous councilmen in the municipal elections of 1953. In 1957, the polls had hardly been closed when the electoral authorities were flooded with petitions to declare void votes received by various candidates supposedly barred from participating in the contest by the provisions of the LPDD law. Even before the elections, the parties of the Right had been issuing warnings concerning their determination to contest the validity of the votes cast for certain leftist candidates.[42] The first legal question was one of jurisdiction, since some claimed that the Qualifying Tribunal of Elections lacked competence and only Congress itself was empowered to decide cases arising out of the LPDD law. By a vote of four to one the Tribunal decided it did have jurisdiction over such cases. In a series of further LPDD decisions, the Tribunal rejected petitions for the disqualification of five candidates for lack of proof and declared void the votes received by another four as Communists. A move to strike a Peronist from the list of victors was turned down for lack of evidence. In total, three deputies elected with considerable numbers of votes, all belonging to the FRAP, saw their votes invalidated and their victories declared void. After these and other electoral cases were disposed of and the reshuffling of votes required by these decisions was made, the party line-up in Congress had been significantly altered. The parties of the FRAP had their representation reduced from 25 elected members to 21; that of the Radical Party increased from 34 to 36; the Agrarian-Labor Party, the Liberal Party, and the United Conservative Party each gained one deputy.

In 1958, shortly before the presidential elections, with the support of the Center-Left parties and of President Ibáñez, the Congress repealed the Law for the Permanent Defense of Democracy. Commu-

[42] Both the Minister of the Interior and the Director General of the Electoral Registry had issued similar warnings indicating the government's intention to apply the law strictly.

nists were reinstated as voters and their party was restored legal status.

Another interesting issue related to the incompatibility of congressional offices originated with a law of 1946, no longer in effect, which provided that the Senate and the Chamber of Deputies each were to have two representatives on certain boards or commissions which administer all autonomous or semiautonomous state agencies.[43] This law, based in turn on another which established excepted commissions designated by the Congress from the constitutional principle of incompatibility,[44] was under attack for some time. Although the intent of the law was to facilitate fulfillment of the congressional duty to supervise the fiscal administration by giving Congress direct participation in the management and administration of autonomous or semiautonomous agencies, in practice, provided a rich source of political power for congressmen and their parties.[45] The so-called "invisible

[43] Law 8,707, December 19, 1946. There were 22 such institutions, each with 4 parliamentary *consejeros,* making a total of 88 such offices. These agencies were: Banco del Estado, Banco Central de Chile, Caja de Accidentes del Trabajo, Caja de Colonización Agrícola, Caja de Crédito Minero, Caja de Previsión de Empleados Particulares, Caja de Previsión de los Carabineros, Caja de la Marina Mercante, Caja de Previsión de la Defensa Nacional, Caja de Previsión de los Ferrocarriles del Estado, Caja de Previsión de los Empleados Municipales, Caja Nacional de Empleados Públicos y Periodistas, Consejo de Fomento e Investigaciones Agrícolas (CONFIN), Corporación de Fomento a la Producción, Corporación de Inversiones, Corporación de la Vivienda, Empresa de Transportes Colectivos del Estado (ETCE), Instituto Nacional de Comercio (INACO), Línea Aérea Nacional, Servicio de Seguro Social, Servicio Médico Nacional de Empleados, and Servicio Nacional de Salud.

[44] Law 6,922, May 19, 1941, extended the conflict-of-interest prohibition to offices remunerated by semipublic funds and to positions in autonomous agencies supported partially by public funds, but at the same time it established this exception.

[45] Having a seat, for example, on the board of one of the *cajas* meant considerable influence in personnel appointments and other favors. The congressman who was a *consejero* on the CORFO board received an insignificant monthly salary of 6,000 pesos, but he wielded vast influence as a dispenser of public favors. The CORFO had many affiliates, and some, like the CAP or ENDESA, were vast economic enterprises. Nothing prevented him from serving also on the boards of these concerns. A senator or deputy who sat as a *consejero* for the National Air Lines (LAN) could allocate speedy transportation for the particular needs of his constituency. Or, if he served in the Investment Corporation, he was able to influence financial policy in favor of projects in a given city. The congressman who was a *consejero* in the *Caja de Crédito Minero* had his re-election assured in the mining regions, and the one who served with the Merchant Marine *caja* could count on the gratitude of the voters of Valparaíso. A congressman in the National Defense *caja* or the *caja* of the *Carabineros* had as much influence among the military as a general.

power" derived from the *consejerías parlamentarias* meant that, at the opening of each Congress, a political battle royal was conducted among political parties for control of these positions.[46]

Opposition to the present system grew steadily, and demands were widespread for a restriction of the powers of congressmen as bestowers of favors, without any sacrifice of parliamentary supervisory authority. The Christian Democratic Party was long the chief advocate of reform. Finally a bill suppressing the *consejerías* but increasing the authority and functions of investigating congressional committees was approved by the Congress.

Organization

Officers of the lower chamber include a president and two vice-presidents, who compose the steering committee known as the *mesa directiva.* These officers are chosen in the house by an absolute majority for a term of four years, and they may be re-elected. This committee is important because it directs the debates and exercises general supervision over the activities of the house. The presiding officer serves as liaison between the chamber and other organs of government, and he also may succeed the chief executive under the established system of presidential succession. Former presidents and vice-presidents of the lower house may become members of the Qualifying Tribunal of Elections. The organization of the Senate is very similar to that of the Chamber of Deputies. Every four years, at the beginning of each legislative period, a president and a vice-president are elected. The presiding officer may exercise a great deal of control over the legislature by making use of such discretionary powers as those of regulat-

[46] The law provided that these representatives of Congress should be the two members who obtained the highest number of votes in a single ballot in each chamber. Given a clear-cut division among two great political blocs in Congress, this provision was supposed to assure the election of a *consejero* for the minority. In practice, however, this was not the case, and a powerful occasional majority, formed by temporary coalitions, always managed to devise its own minority in order to sweep up most of the *consejerías.* Thus, for instance, in 1953 the Agrarian-Labor Party, although it had 4 senators and 29 deputies, obtained only 11 *consejerías.* In 1957 the Radical Party became likewise a victim of these improvised blocs. The Agrarian-Labor group (PAL), allied to the rightists, the Left coalition of the FRAP, and the National Party (PN) — aided by the neutral position taken by the Falange — left the Radicals isolated between two formidable groups. On one side were Liberals and Conservatives (with 15 senators and 55 deputies), who became the first majority. On the other, the coalition of the FRAP, the PAL, and the Nationals (with a total of 16 senators and 40 deputies) secured the minority's *consejerías.* The Radicals, despite their 9 senators and 36 deputies, were left with no seats at all.

ing the duration of the sessions, recognizing speakers, and nominating members of the standing committees for approval of the total membership.

As in every legislature, there exist in the Chilean Congress a number of regular or standing committees created by the rules of the house and the Senate. The role played by these committees in the legislative process is of significance, since as a rule the bulk of legislation originates in them. Only occasionally are major changes made before enactment of important bills as reported by these committees. There are thirteen in the Chamber of Deputies, with thirteen members each, and fourteen in the Senate, each composed of five senators.[47] Although committee members are nominated by the presiding officer in each house, the real appointive body is in practice the party caucus.[48]

Besides investigating, mixed, and some special committees, there exist also the so-called parliamentary committees or party committees. According to the rules of the Chamber of Deputies, each political party must form a committee composed of one member for each twelve deputies of the party. Every deputy is obligated to belong to a "parliamentary committee," and those who are independent or who are members of parties with fewer than the number of representatives required to form a committee must join together in order to organize one, unless they prefer to attach themselves to one of the regular party committees.[49]

Sessions

In Chile each meeting of the Congress is known as a session; a series of sessions (ordinary or extraordinary, as the case may be) is called a *legislatura* (legislature); and the four-year period for which deputies are elected is designated as a "legislative period." The annual legislative session (*legislatura ordinaria*) lasts from May 21 to September 18. It can be extended by the chief executive, although this is a rare occurrence. In recent times only twice, in 1928 and 1952, has the President made use of this prerogative. In addition, the Constitution pro-

[47] The committees of the Chamber of Deputies are those for: Local Government; Foreign Relations; Constitution, Legislation and Justice; Public Education; Treasury; National Defense; Roads and Public Works; Agriculture and Colonization; Medical and Social Assistance and Hygiene; Labor and Social Legislation; Industry; Economy and Commerce; and Internal Government and Rules. The committees of the Senate are similar in title.

[48] Carlos Andrade Geywitz, *Las comisiones parlamentarias en la Cámara de Diputados* (Santiago: Imprenta Cultura, 1945), p. 41.

[49] For the rules of both branches of the Congress, see Facultad de Ciencias Jurídicas y Sociales, *op. cit.*, pp. 137–213.

vides for the call of extraordinary or special sessions (*legislatura extraordinaria*), a privilege which may be exercised either by the executive alone or by the president of the senate upon request of a majority of the members of either legislative house. The Congress, whenever assembled in extraordinary session, is limited to dealing exclusively with those matters that have been the subject of the convocation, unless the special session was called at the initiative of the Congress itself, in which case it is free to deal with all "pending business."[50]

Congressional meetings, according to the Senate rules, are divided into two parts, known as the first and second hours. The first part is devoted to legislative matters proper, while the second, also known as the *hora de incidentes* (incident hour), is concerned with any matters that senators may desire to take up. In the Chamber of Deputies the second portion is devoted especially to the administration and to debate on any other matters of public interest. In fact, this period is often used by party leaders to engage in political polemics.[51]

Meetings in which both houses of Congress sit together are held on specific dates for purposes determined by the Constitution. Joint sessions (*Congreso Pleno*) are required: (1) to inaugurate the legislative session on May 21 of each year; (2) to proclaim the President-elect, and to proceed to elect one, fifty days after the presidential election, in case no candidate has obtained a majority of votes; (3) to witness the presidential oath of office (sixty days after the election); and (4) to vote on constitutional amendments sixty days after the draft has been approved separately by each chamber.[52]

Foreign precedents and customs, especially those of France, have exerted some influence on the development of Chilean parliamentary practices. Often the writings of well-known French or other foreign authors are cited in support of parliamentary points. The quorum required in the Chamber of Deputies is one fifth of its membership, and in the Senate attendance of one fourth (eleven senators) is required. Penalties are imposed on absent members in case a session cannot be held for lack of quorum.[53]

[50] Constitution, Art. 57, Cl. 2, 3.

[51] This author found the examination of the records of *incidentes* one of the most revealing and useful methods for the investigation of party ideology.

[52] Constitution, Arts. 56, 64, 65, 70, 108.

[53] Law 6,922, Art. 2, and Law 10,343, Art. 22, prescribe a fine of 500 pesos for house or senate sessions and 200 pesos for absences in committee session, respectively. Fines imposed during the extraordinary session of Congress in 1957–1958 totalled approximately half a million pesos. These are fines automatically deducted from the congressman's monthly pay.

Congressional Immunities

The Chilean system recognizes a general legislative immunity from prosecution as the result of debates or votes. However, congressional rules place certain limitations upon language used in debate, and members may be reprimanded if they violate such regulations. As in most of the rest of Latin America, in Chile the scope of parliamentary immunity from arrest is very broad. Legislators are immune from arrest from the day of their election until the expiration of their terms, without authorization of the Court of Appeals (*Corte de Apelaciones*) with jurisdiction over the case, unless surprised *flagrante delicto.* The Constitution of 1925, to prevent the abuses of congressional immunities that are frequent under the system found in other Latin American countries, provides that such authorization, or *desafuero,* be given by the courts instead of the body to which the legislator belongs. In case of *flagrante delicto,* though congressmen may be arrested, they must immediately be placed at the disposal of the appropriate Court of Appeals. Decisions of this court can be appealed to the Supreme Court.[54]

It must be said that, in general, considering the remarkably broad basis of parliamentary immunity, there have been few abuses of these privileges by legislators. The courts, with few exceptions, have been as jealous in safeguarding members of the legislature as the Congress itself might have been had it been charged with the custody of the parliamentary *fuero.* It should be noted, however, that the courts have tended to interpret the immunity of legislators as applying only to opinions and votes expressed on the floor of Congress and have on some recent occasions condemned members of the legislature for publishing in newspapers views that were considered disrespectful of the chief executive. Also, in recent times a question of parliamentary immunity and freedom of the press arose simultaneously when two newspapermen were jailed for having published the unexpurgated text of a speech in the Chamber of Deputies containing statements of a nature insulting to the President. The offensive portions of the speech had previously been erased from the congressional record by decision of the chamber. Such incidents, having become more frequent during the period of tension between the legislature and the executive which characterized the last years of the second Ibáñez regime, gave rise to a movement in favor of constitutional reforms to

[54] For details, see Mario Bernaschina G., "La extensión del fuero parlamentario," *Boletín del seminario de derecho público,* No. 15 (First Semester, 1941), pp. 82–84.

extend congressional privileges outside parliamentary floors, but these have not yet materialized.[55]

Powers of the Congress

The disciplinary powers of both houses include measures ranging from reprimanding a member, calling him to order, or censuring him, to depriving him of the right to participate in debates for three consecutive sessions. Legislators, if incapacitated physically or mentally, can resign with permission of the respective house. A two-thirds vote is required for the acceptance of resignations. Congressional permission is also required if any member is absent from the country for more than thirty days. Only by special legislation can absences for more than a year be authorized.

To carry out its functions the Congress is endowed with a variety of specific powers. The Chamber of Deputies is charged exclusively with two principal functions: that of preferring charges in what in Chile is called the *juicio político* (political trial or impeachment) of government officials, of presenting, in other words, the case to the Senate for trial; and that of scrutinizing all acts of the government. In execution of the latter function, the chamber may by a majority vote express its will in the form of resolutions that are transmitted to the chief executive in written form but that do not affect the political responsibility of Cabinet ministers to the President. It has earlier been shown how the Chamber has utilized the first of these exclusive attributes in order to circumvent the lack of parliamentary responsibility of ministers. As regards the second power, it should be said that its exercise has not been significant, and that Chamber resolutions do not have much practical value.[56]

Among the powers that pertain exclusively to the Senate is that of hearing and deciding all impeachment cases. A two-thirds majority is necessary to convict the President. In all other impeachment cases, a simple majority vote is sufficient.[57] Other exclusive privileges of the Senate are to authorize the filing of civil suits by private persons against cabinet members and the institution of criminal proceedings against intendants and governors. In addition, the Senate must give its approval to certain presidential appointments and decide on jurisdictional conflicts between the administrative and political authorities and the highest courts.

[55] See "La semana política," *El Mercurio,* August 11, 1957.

[56] Bernaschina, *Manual de derecho constitucional,* p. 270.

[57] Guerra, *op. cit.,* p. 249. For details on the impeachment procedure, see Leonidas Vial Palma, *El juicio político* (Santiago: Talleres Gráficos San Vicente, 1934).

The general power of the Congress to legislate includes the authority to approve accounts of public expenditures presented by the executive; to discuss and approve the national budget; to authorize the President to be absent from the country; to accept the resignation of the chief executive and to declare him incapacitated; to levy and collect taxes, duties, imposts, and excises that may be necessary; to approve treaties; to authorize loans; to authorize the sale of public property or the renting or concession of this property for periods of more than twenty years; to create and abolish public offices, to determine their functions and fix their remuneration, to grant pensions, and to decree public honors; to fix the salaries of the members of Congress; to establish the number of armed forces and to permit the sending of troops outside the country, fixing a time for their return; to permit the entry of foreign troops into the national territory; to declare war at the request of the President; to restrict personal liberty and freedom of the press or to suspend or restrict the right of assembly whenever necessary for the defense of the state, the preservation of constitutional order and internal peace, for periods not exceeding six months; to grant general pardons and amnesties; and to determine the city in which the President must reside, the Congress hold its sessions, and the Supreme Court meet.[58]

The Legislative Process

Under the Chilean system laws may be introduced by any member of the legislative chamber or by the executive. Bills must be introduced by motions signed by not more than ten deputies or five senators, but in practice the majority of bills presented are signed by more than the prescribed limit of sponsors. As we have seen, the President has the exclusive right to initiate certain specific laws. The lower house has exclusive power to initiative legislation raising revenue or affecting military service, as well as the budget law.[59] Amnesty laws and general pardons can only be initiated in the senate. In contrast with other Latin American countries, the judiciary has no authority in Chile to propose measures dealing with justice and judicial procedure.

The procedure governing the passage of a bill is not complicated. Bills are presented in writing to the secretary, and the presiding officer then proceeds to assign them to the proper committee. Party leaders usually decide in informal conferences questions of procedure and in-

[58] Constitution, Arts. 43, 44. See also Jorge Hunneus, *La Constitución ante el Congreso,* 3 vols. (Santiago: Imprenta Los Tiempos, 1879–1880), Vol. I, pp. 186–189.

[59] Actually the budget bill is in practice first submitted to a mixed committee of deputies and senators.

dicate the preference to be given to proposals. There are several types of discussion that a bill may receive, the most common being "general," and "specific discussions." A "general discussion" takes place only once, and in the course of it, the project is accepted or rejected *in toto,* that is to say, the respective chamber approves or disapproves the idea of legislating on the matter in question. The bill then must be returned to the appropriate committee for re-examination and for study of proposed amendments and other suggestions.[60]

On presentation of the committee's second report, the bill undergoes a "specific" discussion by items and articles. During all types of debate, cabinet members and the committee member reporting on the bill are given unlimited opportunities to present their views. Other deputies can speak no more than two times about the same bill. In the general discussion, each two individual speeches is limited to thirty and ten minutes, respectively. During the specific discussion deputies can speak only for ten minutes each time. The discussion ends when the presiding officer declares the debate closed, if nobody asks for the floor; or when the time fixed for debate has expired; or when the respective chamber so decides. In the Senate, cloture may be moved only by members of that body in written form. On the other hand, in the lower house, Cabinet ministers and committees, as well as members, may at any stage of the discussion move orally or in written form that the debate be closed.

Voting may be public or secret; it is public when members signify their vote by standing or a show of hands (in which case it is called "economic voting," *votación económica*) or by roll call. Secret voting is effected by written ballot and by the use of white and black balls (*balotas*).

Approval of bills is by an absolute majority, except when specified otherwise by law. After a bill has been approved by one chamber, it passes to the other, which may return it with additions or amendments. If the chamber in which the bill originated rejects the amendment proposed by the revising chamber, this body may insist on modification by a special vote of two-thirds, in which case the other chamber may in turn reject the amendments only with a two-thirds majority. A mixed committee composed of an equal number of members of each house is appointed to work out compromises.

Proposals, after having been approved in the form described above, are transmitted to the President. Two more steps are necessary before a bill becomes law: its promulgation or sanction by the chief executive and its publication. The President may, of course, reject

[60] By a two-thirds vote, the legislative body may omit this requirement, in which case the bill is immediately submitted to the "specific discussion."

the bill by using his veto power. If he approves it, he signs it and orders it to be published. The act passed by the Congress and approved by the executive is then printed in the government publication known as the *Diario Oficial*. It is only after the bill has appeared in this official periodical that it becomes law.[61]

Although the constitutional system has entrusted the legislature with the power to enact laws and to determine public policy, the Congress, in reality, is not the center of political life in Chile. The executive, rather than the legislative branch, holds a position of preeminence in the present system. Logically this is so because of the almost omnipotent role that the legal system and political customs have deliberately assigned to the executive branch, but it is also the result of other factors, such as the nature of the class system, defective electoral processes, and the fragmentation and fluidity of organized political groups. In some periods of Chilean history, the Congress, by its factional quibbling and occasional lack of responsibility, incurred an unfortunate stigma and was regarded with contempt by the people who looked to the chief executive for order and leadership and condoned a presidential usurpation of authority. In this way the President sometimes assumed a major role in the determination of legislative policy with the tacit consent of the people and of the members of the congress.

The effectiveness of the Chilean legislature is impaired in several specific ways. The legislative powers of the President being so ample, the scope of congressional authority is necessarily restricted to a corresponding degree. The relative brevity of the congressional sessions tends to lessen the efficacy of the Congress as a check upon the other two branches of government. Party fragmentation frequently prevents the attainment of compromises and the ironing out of differences which are so necessary in all legislative chambers. In addition, there is always a strong tendency to depend upon direction from the executive in the enactment of legislation.

Despite the validity of these observations, it would be unjust to conclude that the Chilean legislature has always failed to fulfill its constitutional mandate. Unlike many Latin American legislatures, the Chilean Congress is not a rubber-stamp body. It is an independent,

[61] The terms "promulgation" and "publication" were until recently indiscriminately used, causing some confusion. Law 9,400 of October 6, 1946, settled the matter by declaring that they were two different things. Promulgation is by presidential decree, countersigned by the respective minister. After such a decree is approved by the *Contraloría General,* the law is published in the *Diario Oficial,* and it becomes effective on that day.

properly elected, deliberative assembly which often challenges the authority of the executive and participates actively in the determination of national policies. The pre-eminence acquired by the Congress during the period of the so-called "parliamentary republic," 1891–1925, was conducive to the establishment of a tradition of independence, and this may well account for the difference between Chilean and other Latin American legislatures. Although the parliamentary system disappeared after 1925 and was succeeded in form by a *sui generis* presidential scheme, executive omnipotence has never been a pure, unrelieved fact, except in times of constitutional subversion, and Presidents have had to count on the support of political parties as much as they needed congressional support in the past. Ministries were overthrown by the machinations of parliamentary cliques before 1925; they are now removed by decisions of party leaders, who may force the withdrawal of party members from the Cabinet. It can even be argued that in a way this new situation is a less desirable one, for at least the members of the old parliamentary cliques were the elected representatives of the people, while the party leaders who today make these decisions are not necessarily in the same category. However, the important thing is that the establishment of a parliamentary form of government, lacking only the disciplined relationship between executive and legislature in order to become effective, was fertile ground for the rooting of a congressional tradition of independence. The floors of the Congress are the best forum for political debate and the logical platform for party government, and the Chilean legislature has therefore managed to preserve at least a part of that tradition in contemporary times.

It would be extremely difficult even for the most casual observer not to be impressed by the austerity and sobriety characteristic of the daily routines of Chilean congressmen. Their debates are generally conducted, in spite of the bitter ideological differences sometimes involved, on the highest of planes, pervaded by an air of dedicated sincerity which is striking to one accustomed to the more pompous and ostentatious manner in which many of the congresses of Latin America deliberate. It is not at all uncommon for Chilean legislators, even though their financial status may permit them much greater luxury, to use public conveyances instead of private automobiles. It is interesting to note the air of cordiality and mutual respect which stand out even in the most informal gatherings of the members of Congress, such as the traditional *once* (tea time), at which it is common for political differences to be forgotten for the moment, amidst genuinely spontaneous and friendly conversation. There is no such thing as ostracism owing to opposing political affiliations. That this spirit of confraternity holds true among men at opposite political poles is exemplified by Eduardo Frei and Salvador Allende, leaders and presidential candidates of the Christian Democratic Party and the FRAP coalition, respectively. In 1957, Frei referred to Allende in private as "my aide-de-camp," and the latter referred jovially to Frei as "my minister." To further illustrate the point, one might mention the fact that Mrs. Gumucio, wife of the president of the Christian Democrats, stayed for a time in the home of the "Red" Allende.[62]

Scandal in the Chilean legislature very rarely reaches the levels unfortunately not uncommon in many of the Latin American countries. The all-too-familiar occurrence of senators and deputies becoming wealthy men during their terms of office is not a commonplace in the Chilean lawmaking body, or indeed in any other area of Chilean political life. The Latin American disposition to look after oneself while in political office — so formidable an obstacle to honest and efficient government — is not usual in Chile. Although peculations exist, to be sure, their frequency and extent never reaches the heights which characterize other governments.

The history of the Chilean Congress may be divided into three distinct periods: the first phase extends from the independence to the revolution of 1891, the second period from this date to 1920, and the third from 1920 to the present time. During the first period the Chilean legislature was nearly always a subservient instrument of the executive. The victory of the "congressionalist" forces in the Civil War of 1891 resulted in the "subjugation," in turn, of the executive branch to the legislative. The third period of development was significant by reason of the participation of the masses in the electoral process and the formation of new political parties which soon gained representation in the Congress as a result of electoral reforms. The tone of the legislature was then set by the activity of parties with a broad popular base, previously excluded as a result of corrupt electoral practices, and also by the appearance of new movements towards social justice and the rights of labor. On appraising the historical role of the legislative body, it may be observed that the Congress of the last period was a much less educated body but more representative of all elements of society than its predecessors.

As is the case in most Latin American countries, lawyers have traditionally been predominant in the Chilean Congress, but there are also other professionals among its members — physicians, engineers, journalists, and university professors. In fact it is not difficult to discern several categories among legislators. There are, in the first place,

[62] "La semana política," *Ercilla,* September 25, 1957.

the professional politicians, the political bosses, who, usually on a small scale, operate their own machines and who change party affiliation with great ease when expedient. There are also the wealthy landowners, the major industrialists, and the entrepreneurs who seek a place in Congress as a matter of business convenience. Then there are those legislators who represent economic groups which only recently have become influential, such as the labor unions.

The Chilean Congress, although not occupying the position assigned to the legislature in an ideal system of separation and balance of powers, is nevertheless an active body which plays a major role in the political system. The record of achievements of the Congress elected in 1953, which functioned from May 21 of that year to September 18, 1956, serves as a good illustration, since these dates include two periods characterized by sharply different political conditions: The first is marked by a vigorous conflict between the legislature and President Ibáñez and the second period by a coming to terms by the chief executive and a working parliamentary majority formed by the rightist parties and Agrarian-Laborites. Logically, the second phase was more fruitful in terms of legislative achievements. During the period which we are examining, the Congress enacted a total of 580 laws. Some of these were of utmost importance, such as the law freezing prices and wages; the so-called Copper New Deal law; the "nitrate referendum" law; and some tax reform acts.[63] Among other important pieces of legislation approved by this Congress were: an extraordinary appropriation of one billion pesos for activities of the Development Corporation; a bill increasing social security pensions; an appropriation of funds for the construction of airports, bases, and military buildings; a bill concerning the retirement of municipal workers; some housing bills; a law providing funds for school construction; additional appropriations for the universities of Santiago, Concepción, and Valparaíso; and a new law regulating coastal shipping. Many of these acts were the result of executive initiative, but there were some important bills presented by members of the Congress. Seven important treaties or international agreements were approved during this period. Among them were an economic treaty with Bolivia, an agreement with the United States concerning the purchase of American agricultural surpluses, and a treaty chiefly concerned with fishing with Ecuador and Peru. Aside from the budget laws, other important fiscal legislation was enacted resulting in a total increase of public expenditures of almost sixty-four billion pesos.

The Senate, exercising its privilege of confirming diplomatic appointments made by the President, rejected ten of these, while two

[63] Law 12,006 (January, 1956); Law 11,828 (May, 1955); Law 12,018 March, 1956); and Laws 11,575 and 12,084 (August, 1956).

others were withdrawn by the executive before Senate examination. Investigating committees were also active during the period. A committee appointed to investigate Peronist activities held fifty-seven meetings and heard a total of fifty-eight witnesses, bringing to light the extent of Peronist infiltration in Chile. A bicameral committee entrusted with investigating the conduct of the Chilean commission appointed to work on the Palena border conflict filed charges against the president of this commission — a general. Other investigating committees dealt with the rising food prices, tax evasion by industry, the administration's economic policy, butter imports from Argentina, a government purchase of buses, and the urban transportation system of Santiago.

The record also indicates that the legislature's powers of scrutiny were freely exercised, especially during the first years of the Ibáñez administration, when the President showed greater hostility toward the Congress. Two ministers and four former ministers of Ibáñez were formally charged by the Chamber of Deputies on constitutional grounds.

The same Congress the record of which we have been examining was called by the executive into an extraordinary session which lasted from October 9, 1956, to January 27, 1957. During this period the lower chamber held fifty-four meetings. Before the chief executive called this special session, the Chamber of Deputies had held a brief extraordinary session at the summons of its presiding officer upon request of twenty-nine deputies in order to discuss some incidents which occurred between nitrate workers and police at Pedro de Valdivia. Two hundred and sixty-two bills were enacted during the special session convened by the President. Of these, ninety were pensions granted to persons who had rendered special services to the country. Among the remaining 168 acts were those providing salary increases for government workers, funds to finish construction of a new school of medicine, and a plan for construction of new post office buildings. These records obviously indicate that the Congress in question was a hard-working body, much concerned with the vital issues of the period (something particularly shown by the predominance of legislation on economic affairs). They also show the presence of a certain measure of legislative vigor and independence capable of influencing the formation of public policy.

A final comment about the legislature and political parties should be made. Close examination of the record for the period under discussion reveals the frequency of changes in party affiliation. For example, in the Chamber of Deputies, the Agrarian Labor Party lost three delegates in this way; the Liberals increased their representation by two members; the Radical Party gained one; the Conservative Party lost two members who joined the United Conservatives; Falange Nacional gained one more deputy; the Christian Nationalists lost two; the Democratic Party increased its representation from five to eight. A new group, the National Party, was born in this period, represented by four senators and ten deputies. The National Independence Movement was left without congressional representation when its five deputies changed affiliation.

The Administration of Justice

The provisions of the Constitution respecting the judicial branch are supplemented by a judiciary act known as the *Código Orgánico de Tribunales*.[64]

The Court System

The highest court is the Supreme Court (*Corte Suprema*), composed of thirteen judges (*ministros*) and presided over by one of them as president. He is elected by his brother judges for a three-year term. The staff of the Supreme Court includes, in addition, a *fiscal,* a secretary, and three *relatores.* Judges have tenure for life on good behavior and are appointed by the chief executive from a list of five individuals nominated by the Supreme Court itself, provided that the two eldest members of the *Corte de Apelaciones* figure on the list.

The lower courts vary in number, designation, and structure. They are organized on the basis of the political divisions of the country in a pattern corresponding to the districts, subdelegations, departments, and provinces of the nation. The local courts, known as *jueces de letras* or *jueces letrados* (with one judge for each court), function in each department seat and have both civil and criminal jurisdiction. Important departments may have different sets of *jueces de letras,* one or more for civil cases and one or more for criminal cases. There are three categories of these courts, according to whether they function in departments, provincial capitals, or *asientos de corte* (localities in which there exists a court of appeal). In the rural districts and subdelegations there exist judges, called "inferior judges," who have no legal training and receive no compensation. They have jurisdiction over minor cases. Next to the *jueces de letras* in sequence are the *Cortes de Apelaciones* (courts of appeal), consisting of several *ministros* (judges). These are appellate courts but have original jurisdiction in certain cases. There are nine of these courts in Chile, each having jurisdiction over two or more provinces. From north to south, they are

64 The original judiciary act was the one of 1875. It was frequently modified by other laws until 1942, when the executive was authorized to compile all legislation dealing with the judiciary into a single code (Law 7,421).

located in Iquique, La Serena, Valparaíso, Santiago, Talca, Chillán, Concepción, Temuco, and Valdivia. The *Cortes de Apelaciones* are generally composed of four judges, each of whom serves as the presiding officer in his turn, the rotation occurring on the basis of seniority. Notable exceptions to the general rule of four-judge composition are the courts of Santiago, Valparaíso, and Concepción. In the case of the former, the court is made up of twenty-one judges who may sit as one body or as six separate divisions called *salas*. The Valparaíso and Concepción bodies consist of seven judges each and may also convene as single bodies or as two *salas* each.

The *jueces letrados* are appointed by the chief executive from a list of three names presented to him by the *Corte de Apelaciones* of the district concerned. This list is made up by the court after competitive sifting of candidates — the only requirement being that the name of the judge with seniority at the level immediately inferior to the vacancy to be filled must be included. The naming of judges of the *Cortes de Apelaciones* follows a like procedure — they are appointed by the President from a list of three names submitted to him by the Supreme Court. As in the former case, this list must contain the name of the ranking *juez letrado* immediately inferior to the vacant seat (in this case the *juez letrado de asiento de corte*). The functionaries in the court system — secretaries, *relatores,* and other auxiliary personnel — are appointed according to provisions of the judiciary act.

Formerly, under the Constitution of 1833, the appointment of judges was somewhat different. The system then in use exposed the judiciary to excessive political influence, since it entrusted the authority to make judicial nominations to the Council of State, a partisan political body. The Constitution of 1925 was a strong reaction against this method, which had brought the Chilean court system to a disreputable, chaotic state. In the way described above it gave the judiciary a decisive voice in the selection of its own personnel.[65]

In general, judges of the courts must be lawyers who are Chilean citizens and at least twenty-five years old. The judicial code specifies how long they must have practiced their profession, thus giving formal assurance of technical competence. Departmental judges must have been lawyers for two years. For members of the Supreme Court, the practice of law for fifteen years is required. Certain persons are ineligible to serve on the bench, such as the blind, deaf, or demented, and convicts. Judicial functions are incompatible with any other remunerated by public funds, except the teaching of law in the university and secondary schools.

[65] G. Troncoso Rojas, *Organización de los tribunales chilenos* (Concepción, 1949), pp. 12–21.

Judicial Independence

The independence of the courts is formally recognized in the Constitution and by the laws. This independence in a practical sense is safeguarded by tenure. A second protection of the courts is the removal — partially at least — of the selection of judicial personnel from the power of the executive and the establishment of a career judicial system, the so-called *escalafón judicial.* This merit system is divided into two branches: the *escalafón primario* includes all judges from those of the lowest rank to the justices of the *Supreme Court,* plus the *fiscales, relatores,* secretaries, and public defenders; the *escalafón secundario* is composed of notaries, *conservadores* or registrars, archivists, *procuradores,* and *receptores.* This *escalafón* is the basis for lists of nominations to fill vacancies in the general judicial system.

Judicial independence has a definite relationship to the power of appointment and the power of removal. Irremovability, except for a demonstrated cause to be established by formal process, is a further guarantee of judicial independence. In Chile, only the Supreme Court may declare the malfeasance of judges and, after hearing the accused and the respective court of appeals, may remove them by a two-thirds vote. The Constitution forbids the President to remove judges without the previous declaration of malfeasance by the Supreme Court. This tribunal must meet every three years for the purpose of "qualifying" all judges and deciding whether any must be removed for malfeasance or for lacking the efficiency, zeal, or ethical standards required for members of the judicial service. Those failing to qualify are required to resign their positions within sixty days. Judges can also be removed by a special procedure, called *juicio de amovilidad,* which is an exclusive power of the higher courts. In no case whatsoever can any other branch of the government but the judiciary initiate disqualification proceedings.

A corollary of the principle of independence is the principle of abstention from involvement in partisan political matters. That objectivity results from respect by the judiciary for the principle of the separation of powers. The idea that magistrates of courts of justice should not meddle in the affairs of partisan politics has long been accepted in Chile. A less formal safeguard of the independence of the courts has been, in fact, the respect of public opinion for the integrity and the tradition of the independence of the judicial power. The legal guarantees of independence and the constitutional and statutory tenure are always scrupulously respected. At the same time, Chilean courts have consistently been reluctant to intervene in matters exclusively political, and judges, in general, are careful to abstain from party politics.

Functions

The Supreme Court has some special budgetary responsibilities. In addition, it exercises certain kinds of supervision over the lower courts. Explicit budgetary authority is granted to the highest court over its own expenses and over those of other courts. Its powers of supervision and discipline are elaborately set forth in the *Código Orgánico de Tribunales*. The highest tribunal also decides conflicts of jurisdiction which arise between the political or administrative authorities and the inferior courts. (Jurisdictional conflicts between such authorities and the highest courts, courts of appeals, and the Supreme Court, are decided by the Senate.) The Supreme Court is also charged with the duty of arbitrating jurisdictional disputes between special courts or between these and the ordinary courts.

The most important function of the Chilean Supreme Court is that of judging the constitutionality of legislative acts. This right of interpreting the constitution, however, has limited practical effects, since the decision that a statute or executive act is unconstitutional as applied in a specific case does not constitute its total nullification. It is merely a declaration that the act is inapplicable to the case in question, so that only this particular case is affected. Vesting in the Supreme Court the important power of judicial review was one of the significant innovations of the Constitution of 1925. Earlier, the constitutional system afforded no way of reviewing legislation and executive acts that were contrary to the fundamental law. In consequence, some statutes which were obviously unconstitutional nevertheless went into effect, without any possibility of contesting them.[66]

The highest court can declare a law inapplicable on its own initiative in cases in which it has exclusive jurisdiction and also on appeal from the lower courts. In this way the declaration of unconstitutionality may occur in some cases without previous request from an afflicted party by the usual *recurso* or appeal. The majority of constitutional decisions, however, occur as the result of appeals. The prerequisites for the *recurso* are the existence of a case pending before a court and the attempt to apply in that case a legal provision contrary to the constitution. A *recurso* is not permitted if the case in question has been concluded by definitive sentence. Furthermore, only "legal precepts" — statutes, decree-laws, and decrees having the force of law — may be declared inapplicable. A *recurso* cannot be directed against regula-

[66] Guerra, *op. cit.*, pp. 455–462.

tions, decrees, or ordinances because there are other means of obtaining their invalidation.

Except where the Supreme Court has original jurisdiction, the issue of constitutionality can only be raised by the parties to the case, and the petition must specify the precept which is considered unconstitutional as well as the concrete case to which the decision must be directed. The restriction of the legal effect of any decision of unconstitutionality to a specific case has caused the Supreme Court frequently to declare that it does not have the power to decide whether the legislative branch can delegate its functions. As we have seen, the Court does not distinguish between laws enacted by the Congress and those proclaimed by the executive. Whether the Congress can delegate its powers or not is considered to be a political decision and therefore one not within the competence of the Court.[67]

Special Courts

There also exist in Chile some functional courts having special jurisdiction; their number has tended to increase over the years. Special jurisdiction usually exists in lower courts or those given original access to the cases in question, with appeals going to ordinary tribunals of a higher rank. The proliferation of these special courts might suggest that Chile, with all other Latin American countries, is returning to a modified version of the old *fuero* system. That however, is not the case, since the present aim is not to establish privileges for certain persons or groups but to supply a functional service through tribunals composed of experts in a field of law.[68] Some of the special courts deal with the military, lands and waters, food supplies (*abastos*), customs, and Indian problems. Examples of more modern special courts are those in electoral, juvenile, aeronautical, labor, and social law. It should be noted that some of the special fields of law have their own codes, as for example, the Labor Code. All of these courts are under the superintendence of the Supreme Court.

The Constitution of 1925 (Article 87) provides for the creation of a separate set of administrative courts to decide cases involving acts or decisions of administrative and political authorities not falling under the jurisdiction of other courts. However, the legislation needed to

[67] For details, see Marcos Silva Bascuñán, *La Constitución ante los tribunales* (Santiago: Dirección General de Prisiones, 1939); Horacio Carvajal Ravest, *La Corte Suprema* (Santiago: Imprenta El Esfuerzo, 1940), and Gustavo de la Cerda Plaza, *Recurso de inconstitucionalidad* (Santiago: T. Conelli y Cía, 1928).

[68] Bernaschina, *op. cit.*, p. 447. See also W. W. Pierson and F. G. Gil, *Governments of Latin America* (New York: McGraw-Hill Book Co., 1957), pp. 274–275.

implement this provision has not yet been enacted, and administrative courts have no officially recognized existence, although there exist several bodies endowed with judicial functions that in reality permit them to be considered as true tribunals of this kind.[69] Pending implementation of the constitutional mandate to establish these courts, the method of adjudicating controversies involving administrative issues is to use the ordinary tribunals, which have a separate docket for this purpose known as *contencioso-administrativo*.[70]

The Chilean court system may be the object of the criticisms that, in general, are also applicable to all Latin American judiciaries. In the main, these criticisms focus on delays in the administration of justice, the prevalence of written as against oral procedure, and the expense of the process of administration. The judgment that the Chilean courts are impotent is not justified. Those who would have the judicial branch act as a curb on the executive branch seek in effect to give the courts political obligations without giving them political power — which means, in the final analysis, control of political patronage, command of the army, and leadership in the dominant political group. The actual investment of courts with political power would obviously be dangerous. If the courts are to be truly independent, if they are not to meddle in partisan politics, and if they are to judge policy and not to create it, they cannot be constituted as political authorities and must not be expected to act as a political curb on the executive. The only appropriate question is whether the courts, as tribunals of law, judge cases independently and according to law.[71] In this respect, the consensus regarding the Chilean courts is unquestionably favorable.

The history of the Chilean judicial system after 1833 has three distinct periods. From 1833 to 1891 the courts, in general, adhered to standards which were fairly reflective of national ethics at that time. Unquestionably, many judges were inclined to be lenient towards members of the upper classes involved in criminal proceedings; they were often biased in favor of the government when the state was a party in litigation; and, above all they were consistent in showing partiality in electoral affairs. But, nevertheless, as a group these judges must not be condemned too severely. As private individuals, they led

[69] For example, the Customs Tribunals. The Directors-General of Internal Revenue and Public Health also operate in practice as administrative law judges.

[70] See Eduardo Alcayaga S., *De lo contencioso-administrativo* (Santiago: Imprenta El Esfuerzo, 1930), and Carlos Mondaca Kirkman, *Un proyecto de ley sobre tribunales administrativos* (Santiago: Imprenta Santa Laura, 1934).

[71] Pierson and Gil, *op. cit.*, p. 292.

impeccable lives, and their behavior on the bench was not necessarily incongruent to the moral tone that prevailed in the society of the time. In addition, their judgment of civil cases was without taint. Some of the judges of the period are recalled as ranking among the most distinguished jurists in the history of the nation.

After 1891 the picture changed completely: a shameful legal laxity and dishonesty came into being. Its causes are manifold. It was the natural result of the civil war and the inevitable weakening of the national moral fiber that accompanied it. Moreover, since the Congress had won its battle with the executive, it now assumed the leading role in the appointment of judges through its control of the Council of State. Inevitably, these nominations became political. The allegiance of judges was given to the political parties to which they owed their appointments, just as it had formerly been given to the chief executive in the preceding period. In many instances, the judges became political bosses in their respective districts. Finding political control in their localities too tempting an opportunity for financial gain, they became involved in financial manipulation, particularly in nitrate and stock speculations. There ensued of course a general demoralization, and the public lost its faith in and respect for the administration of justice. From a position among the most highly considered courts of Latin America, Chilean tribunals rapidly dropped to being the least respected.[72]

A reaction to this shameful state of affairs was inevitable. The main obstacle in the path of the much needed reforms was the difficulty in removing judges from their positions owing to the tenure granted them by the Constitution. The final solution was not forthcoming until the Constitution of 1925 was written. It set up the system of appointment and removal which is now in effect. Thanks to a firm public will and the installation of the new co-optative system, the Chilean courts underwent a process of regeneration that ultimately enabled them to regain their position in the forefront of the Latin American judiciary. In spite of the turmoil caused by revolutions and the establishment of various de facto governments during the initial years of operation of the Constitution, the courts preserved their integrity. They were the only enduring institutions untouched by those extraordinary and extralegal developments, and they have remained outside factional contests to this day.

Local Government

Territorial distribution of power in Chile, both political and administrative, follows lines laid down in the Constitution and in legis-

[72] Guerra, *op. cit.*, pp. 452–454.

lative acts.[73] The political units of local government are provinces, departments, subdelegations (*subdelegaciones*), and districts. The nation is divided into twenty-five provinces, which in turn contain eighty-seven departments. Departments are separated into subdelegations and these into districts. Each province is under the authority of an intendant (*intendente*), who is appointed by the President for a three-year term. As the President's "natural and immediate agent," he is entrusted with supervision and direction of all provincial administration.[74] Each department has as administrative head a governor, again nominated by the President for three years. However, the intendant of the department containing the provincial capital is also its governor. The *subdelegaciones* are under the authority of "subdelegates" subordinate to the governor of the respective department and appointed by him for terms of one year. These officials can also be removed by the governors. The smaller political units, known as districts, are each headed by an "inspector" appointed by the respective subdelegate and responsible to and removable by him.

For administrative, as distinct from political, purposes the country is divided into provinces, and these are further subdivided into communes (*comunas*). The number of communes may be determined by law, provided there is at least one for each subdelegation. Thus, the administrative unit known as the province corresponds to the political unit of the same name, while the *comuna* is also equivalent to the political subdelegation. The intendant directs provincial administration, supposedly with the assistance of a provincial assembly (*asamblea provincial*) composed of representatives from the municipalities within the province. The Constitution charged the provincial assemblies with ascertaining and presenting the needs of their respective regions to the President of the republic. They were also authorized to write ordinances and even to impose local taxes in order to satisfy those same needs. To the present time, however, these bodies have not come into existence because the legislation necessary to implement these constitutional provisions has not been enacted. All indications are that it will not be enacted in the future, since there is a strong sentiment favoring constitutional changes on the subject. Meanwhile, the provincial assemblies remain an unfulfilled constitutional mandate.

The administration of each commune or group of communes established by law is the function of a municipality, or municipal council (*municipalidad*), presided over by an *alcalde* (mayor) who in those

[73] Constitution, Arts. 88–107. There is among legislative acts one known as the *Ley de Organización de las Municipalidades* for the administration of cities.

[74] Raveau, *op. cit.*, pp. 345–350.

cities with a population of over 10,000 is a salaried official appointed by the President.[75] The total number of communes electing *municipalidades* is 263. The municipalities have from five to fifteen councilmen (*regidores*) elected by direct vote for a three-year period. Municipal councilmen must serve if elected and receive no remuneration. There were approximately 1,600 *regidores* in all the Chilean municipalities in 1963. Voters in municipal elections are all persons over twenty-one years of age, including aliens who have resided at least five years in the country. These municipal bodies have authority to legislate, within certain limits, over local matters, including health, educational, and recreational facilities, agricultural, industrial, and commercial development, and roads and public works (for which they may impose certain local taxes).[76]

The Law of Municipalities provides that certain actions taken by the municipal councils must be approved by the respective provincial assembly. Since this last institution has never come into being for lack of implementation, a law of 1942 ordered that until the provincial assemblies are constituted the intendants have the power to authorize, to approve, and to regulate actions and decisions of the municipal bodies. The constitutionality of this so-called "law of subrogation of the provincial assemblies" is very doubtful, but in practice it is applied every day. Besides its questionable constitutional validity, this law places intendants in a dual legal situation which is absurd: as substitutes for the provincial assemblies they may veto municipal acts, and as intendants they may equally veto decisions they themselves may make when acting in place of the provincial bodies.

The municipal council may be dissolved by the respective provincial assembly for causes specified by law. In case of dissolution, new elections are called by the President, who may also appoint a provisional "citizens' committee" (*junta de vecinos*). However, under no circumstances are intendants authorized to dissolve *municipalidades,* despite the fact that they are provisionally invested with powers which of right belong to the provincial assemblies.[77]

In spite of constitutional principles and theoretical implications, decentralization in Chile has never been a fact. Although many proposals have been made both by individuals and by political parties in favor of local self-government and although attempts have been made

[75] Bernaschina, *Síntesis del derecho constitucional chileno,* p. 94. Also Gustavo Lorca Rojas, *La administración comunal* (Valparaíso: Escuela Tipográfica Salesiana, 1934), p. 59.

[76] The best treatment of Chilean municipal government is Mario Bernaschina G., *Derecho municipal chileno,* 3 vols. (Santiago: Editorial Jurídica de Chile, 1952).

[77] Bernaschina, *Manual de derecho constitucional,* pp. 455–457, 460–461.

to place some of them in operation, in the main there has been a steady trend toward centralization — in spite of the existence of a real geographical and political sectionalism. The question is whether such a trend may result in a political system that is top-heavy or indifferent to the interests of the locality. The answer in Chile is definitely affirmative. Though constitutional statements of principle in favor of provincial and municipal home rule do exist, the fact remains that the promise for a greater degree of governmental autonomy for provinces and cities has not been redeemed.

Regarding the provinces, it has often been held that they are artificial institutions of little utilitarian value as political and administrative agencies representing local interests. Questions about the usefulness of provinces were raised in the committee which drafted the Constitution of 1925, and there was even some discussion about the possibility of abolishing them, dividing the country simply into departments, as in France. Beyond the extraneous justification that they provided offices for politicians and staff positions in the civil service not easily disposed of, the provincial organization was continued on weighty considerations of tradition and also because its abolition would have required drastic changes in the electoral system.[78] Changes in the administrative divisions of the country have often been made to gratify local sentiment or to further the schemes of politicians. It is generally agreed that probably the most satisfactory division with the greatest geographical advantage was the one introduced by Ibáñez in 1928. This division simplified considerably the existing pattern, providing for sixteen provinces and two territories, on the basis of communities with similar aims and interests and taking account of the development of communications. In the central region, for examples, provinces were based on river basins separated by thinly populated watersheds, rather than on river-divided entities. This system, however, did not last long. The historical ties of a system which had been in operation for so many years proved stronger, and a new division, carried out in 1936, restored in large measure the system in existence prior to 1928 and re-established the twenty-five provincial units.

It should be recalled that with the end of the Civil War of 1891 a new law of municipalities practically did away with the authority of the President's "agents" in the provinces. The "autonomous commune" law, besides putting an end to the central government's intervention in elections, granted municipal bodies very broad powers, more ample even than those that formerly belonged to the governors in their departments. As the municipalities were administered in absolute inde-

[78] Guerra, *op. cit.*, p. 468.

pendence of the executive power, the latter, which had previously controlled elections by means of intendants, governors, and *alcaldes* selected for its convenience, from that moment lost all influence. This reaction against official intervention in elections went so far to the extreme as to convert local executives into little more than simple figureheads without substantial authority. After 1925 there was a reaction, in turn, against this state of affairs. Although the Constitution of 1925 sought administrative decentralization and municipal autonomy, these principles are now present in the letter rather than the spirit of the Chilean polity. Legislation and political practice have more and more been buttressing the powers of the officials of the central government and restricting the activities and jurisdiction of municipalities to administrative matters of relatively minor importance. Centralization today has advanced to the point that self-government in municipalities has little or no reality. This trend toward centralization accounts in fact for the failure to implement the Constitution by providing legislation necessary for the establishment of the provincial assemblies. In consequence, provincial intendants, as direct agents of the executive, have become again "little presidents," in the manner that the Constitution of 1833 intended them to be. Their power, vanishing with the municipality law of 1891, was resurrected with the Constitution of 1925.[79]

In recent years strong regionalist feelings have developed anew. What may be called a sectionalist *fronde* is gradually extending from one end of the country to the other, giving rise in some quarters to fears that Chile is on the brink of disintegration. Recalling Ortega y Gasset's analysis of an invertebrate Spain torn by internecine struggles, there are Chileans who are alarmed by the constant growth of regional feelings and animosities, which in their extreme form may become a "war against the national entity."[80] These are invariably directed against centralization and the authority of the national government. Provinces are protesting angrily against the long neglect of their problems by the government in Santiago. Even natural disasters may be blamed on the disregard and negligence of the national authorities. Elsewhere in this work we have mentioned that, although yet unmeasurable and without political manifestations, this regionalism is a dormant force of some significance. What seems fairly certain is that regional divisions are likely to be exploited in politics by ambitious local demagogues who, unable to exert influence through national political groups, may choose instead to exacerbate local feelings. One encounters a tendency among some Chileans to exalt the virtues of a

[79] Guerra, *op. cit.*, p. 511.

[80] See for example "La semana política," *El Mercurio,* December 22, 1957.

federal system with a brashness that is excusable in the constitution-makers of 1828 but that at the present time is indefensible.

There are in reality some grounds for the belief that there is real danger of the weakening of national unity. It is likely, however, that such fears are exaggerated. After years of centralization, many outlying regions had lapsed into economic stagnation, and to combat it the government has resorted to stop-gap measures that in reality have not solved the problem but only alleviated it temporarily. In the north as well as in the south, regional tax exemptions were instituted in order to attract productive enterprises and an increased population to the affected areas. Arica, for instance, was declared a free port of entry. The results have undoubtedly been of some benefit to Arica, but at the same time grave problems for the national economy have been created. In the south, Magallanes was also declared a free zone, and the ultimate benefits of such action are similarly questionable. The two greatest problems brought about by these measures have been an increase in contraband trade (which has injured commercial interests in central Chile) and a dissipation of foreign currency reserves. Perhaps some of these consequences could have been avoided had the government embarked upon a systematic development program rather than introducing haphazard incentives. The establishment of free ports and duty-free frontiers has, in effect, contributed in some extent to the weakening of national unity. These measures have not actually solved regional problems, nor have they increased the national wealth, but in the main they have benefited only groups of middlemen and speculators, in the majority foreign.

In considering the dangers of exaggerated regional tendencies, it should be noted that, for historical reasons (the provinces of the north and south having only recently been incorporated), the feeling of nationality has not yet been sufficiently developed. The northern provinces of Tarapacá, Antofagasta, and Atacama have made a practice in recent years of negotiating agreements with neighboring areas across the Argentine border. In spite of the fact that an accredited diplomatic mission officially represented the government of Chile at the inauguration of President Arturo Frondizi of Argentina in 1958, these three provinces were also represented by delegations of mayors and presidents of civic and commercial organizations. The attempts by these provinces to come to direct understandings with adjacent countries in order to supply vital needs and the concern of these provinces for their own welfare regardless of the national interest are symptoms of an unhealthy tendency. Desires for a form of economic integration with Argentina that now are often expressed by residents of the region could some day become demands for political integration as well.

Autonomous and Semifiscal Agencies

The Chilean governmental system includes numbers of autonomous and semi-independent institutions carrying out a variety of activities. As noted elsewhere in this book, the government is very much involved in Chile's efforts for industrialization. It has supplied the necessary stimulus to industrialization, and credit and development agencies created by the government have participated in the planning, establishment, and operation of new industries. A very important part has been played in the economic expansion of the country by these state-controlled industrial and commercial corporations. A series of developmental and financing establishments have been set up as an answer to the problems of certain types of industry.

The increasingly larger share of participation in this area by the government and its assumption of more economic responsibilities are not solely a Chilean phenomenon, but their recent and rapid development in Chile are striking. The government is today responsible for a very considerable part of all Chilean economic endeavors, and governmental expenditures for this reason show a tendency to increase at a faster pace than the national income. Such a remarkable expansion of governmental activity into traditionally nongovernmental areas may be explained in terms of the need of government intervention to supply services, the reluctance of private capital to invest in certain industries, the elimination of foreign enterprise as an aim of nationalistic policy, or the mere and frequent fact that only the government is financially able to undertake certain enterprises. Government participation, however, is not limited to industry. It is extending more and more into finance, foreign trade, formal planning, the creation of a growing system of credit and banking institutions, trade control devices, and ambitious "plans" of assorted kinds.[81]

Significant among the recent trends in modern Latin American constitutionalism is the formulation of specific principles regulating the establishment and operation of agencies of this kind. Special chapters are devoted in some recent constitutions to autonomous entities and decentralized services.[82] This is not, however, the case in the Chilean Constitution — it contains no provisions of this type. Such agencies as we are concerned with here have been created by legislative action, and in each case the law regulates their respective organization and administration and, when necessary, determines the way by which

[81] The expansion of government activity in Latin America in general is discussed in Simon G. Hanson, *Economic Development in Latin America* (Washington, D.C.: Inter-American Affairs Press, 1951), pp. 456–458.

[82] Pierson and Gil, *op. cit.*, p. 403.

private capital may be invested in such enterprises and establishes the manner of participation by shareholders in their administration and management. In general, however, the so-called "organic laws" provide for the administration of these various services by autonomous councils or boards of directors.

The oldest and most influential of the development agencies, not only in Chile but in Latin America, is the famous Chilean Development Corporation (*Corporación de Fomento de la Producción* or CORFO), established in 1939. Numerous references to the activities of the CORFO are made in Chapter 4, and it will suffice here to comment only upon its organization and administration. The corporation is managed by a board of twenty-one members, which includes representatives of the government, business, and labor. The chairman is the Minister of Economy, Development, and Reconstruction. It is divided into five departments: agriculture, industries, mining, planning and studies, and finance. The corporation operates with great flexibility, since it is authorized either to do its work directly or to invite participation of private enterprise. It is able to finance existing or proposed industries by a variety of methods. It may acquire part of the stock of a private industry and participate in its management. It exercises practical supervision over all industry, since no new industrial operation or plant expansion is permitted if not authorized by the corporation. A basic policy principle is for the Development Corporation to discontinue its support and management voice as soon as new industries can dispense with its aid. The CORFO has been instrumental in the establishment of enterprises enjoying a high degree of autonomy in the execution of development plans. These industrial and commercial concerns have been established as mixed corporations. Among the principal affiliated organizations at present are the National Electricity Enterprise (*Empresa Nacional de Electricidad, S.A.*, or ENDESA) in hydro-electric power development; the National Petroleum Enterprise (*Empresa Nacional de Petróleo*) in petroleum exploration and exploitation; the Pacific Steel Company (*Compañía de Acero del Pacífico*, or CAP) in steel production; the National Sugar Industry (*Industria Azucarera Nacional, S.A.*, or IANSA); and the Service for Mechanized Agricultural Equipment (*Servicio de Equipos Agrícolas Mecanizados*). In close connection with some of these ventures a series of other entities has sprung up. For example, around the Pacific Steel Company there have emerged in Huachipato a number of enterprises like the *Fábrica de Carburo y Metalúrgica, S.A.*, the *Metalúrgica del Sur, and the Sociedad de Industrias Chilenas de Alambre.*

Besides the CORFO, other autonomous and semifiscal agencies related to the government through the Ministry of Economy are the

National Council of Foreign Trade (*Consejo Nacional de Comercio Exterior*), which authorizes and controls exports, imports, and international exchange; the National Institute of Commerce (*Instituto Nacional de Comercio,* or INACO), with ample powers in trade development and price controls; the Authority for Supplies and Prices (*Superintendencia de Abastecimientos y Precios*), which administers price legislation and combats speculation; the National Statistical and Census Service (*Servicio Nacional de Estadística y Censos*); the National Air Line (*Línea Aérea Nacional,* or LAN); the State Maritime Line (*Empresa Marítima del Estado*); and the State Urban Transportation Enterprise (*Empresa de Transportes Colectivos del Estado*).

Other agencies similarly related to the government but through the Ministry of the Treasury are the Central Bank of Chile (*Banco Central de Chile*), founded in 1953, as well as the Autonomous Fund for the Amortization of the Public Debt (*Caja Autónoma de Amortización de la Deuda Pública*).

Connected with the Ministry of Public Education are the University of Chile, the Technical State University (*Universidad Técnica del Estado*), the *Junta Nacional de Auxilio Escolar,* administering social services in public schools (meals, clothing, medical and dental assistance, etc.), and the *Sociedad Constructora de Establecimientos Educacionales,* an agency in charge of school construction. Under the Ministry of National Defense there are three important autonomous institutions: the *Fábricas y Maestranzas del Ejército* (Army Manufactures and Quartermaster Supply), which makes and distributes materials needed by the armed forces; the National Aircraft Factory (*Fábrica Nacional de Aeronaves,* FANAERO); and the Department of Security for National Defense (*Caja de Previsión de la Defensa Nacional*), the social service organization covering military personnel.

A very important independent agency related to the Ministry of Public Works is the Housing Corporation (*Corporación de la Vivienda,* or CORVI), which administers government housing schemes. Connected with the Ministry of Agriculture are the Council for Agricultural Research and Development (*Consejo de Fomento e Investigaciones Agrícolas*) and the Agricultural Cooperation Board (*Junta de Cooperación Agrícola*), devoted to the administration of the Agrarian Plan and the development of agricultural cooperatives, respectively. Related to the Ministry of Lands and Colonization is a colonizing and development agency known as the Fund for Agricultural Colonization (*Caja de Colonización Agrícola*). Those agencies having ties with the Ministry of Mining are the Mining Credit and Development Fund (*Caja de Crédito y Fomento Minero*); the Nitrate and Iodine Corporation (*Corporación de Ventas de Salitre y Yodo*); and the National Petroleum Enterprise (*Empresa Nacional de Petróleo*).

Lastly, the independent agencies related to the government through the Ministry of Public Health and Social Security are the National Health Service (*Servicio Nacional de Salud*); the Social Insurance Service (*Servicio de Seguro Social*); the National Corporation for Social Security Investments (*Corporación Nacional de Inversiones de Previsión*); the National Medical Service for Employees (*Servicio Médico Nacional de Empleados*); the State Insurance Institute (*Instituto de Seguros del Estado*); and the Society for Hospital Plant Construction (*Sociedad Constructora de Establecimientos Hospitalarios*). Also included in this group are the various *cajas* of public employees and journalists, *carabineros* or policemen, municipal employees, state railroad workers, and members of the merchant marine.[83]

The structure and operation of these institutions are as varied as their large number would lead us to suspect. They all, however, have certain features in common. In general, these organizations are administered by autonomous councils or boards of directors; some have a chief executive official, a director general. The composition of these councils varies a great deal, of course. Their membership generally includes a number of presidential appointees and representatives of the organizations and segments of the population interested in and affected by the particular type of activity. Very often such membership includes representatives of the workers. The *directorio,* or board of directors of the State Bank of Chile, for example, is composed of seven persons appointed freely by the President, two of whom are designated by him as chairman and vice-chairman of the Bank and of the board; the Vice-president of the Chilean Development Corporation; the president and vice-president of the Central Bank; five members representing agriculture, industry, commerce, and mining appointed by the chief executive from lists submitted by the organizations representing those fields; and two other members chosen by the Chilean president from nominating lists submitted by white-collar workers (*empleados*) and manual workers, respectively. Another general feature of these agencies, is that none of them may conduct any business foreign to that specifically assigned to it by law, nor may it devote any of its resources to purpose other than its normal activities. They are required in all cases to publish periodic statements which clearly indicate their financial condition.

Although it is not within the scope of this book to make any appraisal of the success or failure of government ventures for economic development or of the virtues or faults of the independent agencies as

[83] Details and useful organizational charts concerning these autonomous agencies are found in Ministerio de Hacienda, Departamento de Estudios Financieros, *Organización institucional de Chile, 1955,* 2 vols. (Santiago, 1955), Vol. II.

chosen instruments of policy, it must be noted that some serious obstacles have impaired, and probably will continue to impair for a long time to come, the effective attainment of the objectives pursued by such government enterprises. The lack of a well-trained staff of experts with high professional standards and a thorough technical knowledge of the subjects involved is an important factor. It must be said in this connection that Chile has produced in recent years a remarkable crop of fine economists and that the creation in the University of Chile of the School of Administrative and Political Sciences is an important step toward the creation of a capable body of public servants. A certain amount of corruption and mismanagement, though it is small, is a barrier to the effectiveness of government activities in economic fields, since it undermines the positive efforts made by the various economic agencies. It also causes a public skepticism about the agencies that reduces the popular support that is indispensable if development activities are to succeed. The spirit of expediency is also an important factor in explaining the difficulties encountered by the Chilean government when it undertakes any detailed economic planning.

A final comment concerning the increase in the range of governmental responsibilities as a consequence of significant developments in the economic field may be in order. This increase in the functions of government has given new impetus to the power of the presidency by investing this office with the authority to manage a great part of the economic affairs of the country. As we have seen, plans for economic development have resulted in the establishment of important government agencies which exercise general supervision over the economy. Although the Congress has played a significant role in the creation of administrative agencies and in the general expansion of government services, it has been often the responsibility almost entirely of the chief executive to initiate and undertake reforms in the administrative system whenever they became necessary. Some important phases of the program for industrialization have been placed under control of the executive branch. Administrative agencies, government-owned corporations, and mixed corporations entrusted with the control and direction of government investments, in spite of their autonomy, are inevitably in close contact with the executive branch. The growth and ramifications of governmental operations have therefore contributed to some degree to the aggrandizement of the powers of the chief executive, giving him a strong voice in the economic life of the country.

Of Chile's governmental structure, it may be said in general that there are no basic, irremediable faults in the political system that might impede the forward movement of the nation. When a country has come to have a system in which there is respect for legality, genuine popular and democratic representation, a President whose powers are legally limited, a judiciary not subject to undue pressure, and a Congress that goes about its business normally without restraints, a high degree of national maturity is evident.

It is, then, more the social system than the constitutional system that requires basic alterations if the gulf between the two distinct and coexisting modes of existence in Chile, semifeudalism and semi-industrialism, is to be narrowed. To be sure, modifications in the structure of government may be required in the near future in order to achieve a just social order, but the point is that Chile has at least already enlightened legal and political institutions which put this country well ahead of many of the Latin American nations on the path of political development. These institutions should, without basic changes, prove to be susceptible to sufficient adjustments to meet the requirements, within democratic channels, of a social revolution aimed at curing Chile's economic and social ills. What emerges most clearly from the preceding analysis of the forms of organization, the functions, and the operation of the government of Chile is the general impression of a fine assortment of materials constituting a moderately well integrated and effective political instrument for a democratic nation.

4

The Socio-Economic Setting

Resources

The land of Chile is generously endowed with natural resources. Among these, the most important have been minerals, to the extent that for most of its modern history the nation's economic existence has depended principally on their exploitation. Indeed, the mining extractive industry is so essential to Chile's economy that by furnishing close to 80 per cent of her exports, it is the principal source of the country's capacity to import what it needs. The national economy is very sensitive to changes in the world market conditions for minerals, since approximately one fourth of the fiscal revenues derive from mining. Nitrate and copper top the list of Chile's minerals, but there are others which also are important, such as iron and manganese. Most of these minerals have been found in North and Central Chile, but the possibility that vast mineral reserves may be found in the southern third of the country, particularly in the archipelagic section, is indeed very promising.

As has already been indicated, the resources of nitrate lie in the zone between Arica and Copiapó, and although production is at present centered at only a few *salitreras,* there is a vast area which could be profitably exploited. Iodine, sodium, and sulphate are also found in large amounts, and there are deposits of common salt and calcium borate. Nitrate deposits, however, account for 74 per cent of the value of the nonmetallic minerals; limestone represents half the remaining 26 per cent, while sulphur is third in value.[1]

Copper reserves are enormous; some 30 per cent of the world's copper reserves are located there, and the Chilean output contributes

[1] Gilbert J. Butland, *Chile: An Outline of Its Geography, Economics, and Politics* (London: Royal Institute of International Affairs, 1951), p. 48.

nearly one fourth of the world production. Three great mines located at Chuquicamata, El Salvador, and El Teniente supply the largest percentages of the country's production. Two United States companies own and operate these mines. Anaconda Copper Company operates those at Chuquicamata and El Salvador, and derives roughly two thirds of its world copper production from these Chilean operations. Braden, a subsidiary of Kennecott Copper, operates El Teniente, and its production is roughly 25 per cent of Kennecott's overall world total. Together these three big United States-owned mines turn out 85 per cent of Chile's copper. By 1964, nationalization of the copper companies had become a major political issue, with both major presidential candidates, Allende of the FRAP coalition and Frei of the Christian Democrats, favoring different approaches. While Allende advocated immediate nationalization through legislative procedures, Frei opposes nationalization at this time. His program includes doubling of production in the next six years through new investments, a requirement that the companies refine all Chilean copper in Chile, and control over sales of the copper abroad. After his election Frei successfully undertook negotiations for the acquisition of up to 51 per cent or a controlling interest in the Braden Copper Company, the subsidiary of Kennecott Copper Corporation, for a price of $80 million payable in twenty years, this amount to be totally reinvested in the industry. According to Frei's "policy of association," the Chilean government was also to acquire 25 per cent interests in two new United States mining ventures. Frei's copper policy contemplates some large investments in the future: $135 million in the mines of Chuquicamata and El Salvador of the Anaconda group; $81 million in the new *Compañía Minera Andina;* and, $200 million in El Teniente mine.[2]

Large deposits of iron are located at El Tofo, El Romeral, and Algarrobo. Production of iron, normally above one million tons annually, tumbled during World War II but later trebled 1940 figures as a result of internal demand created by the Huachipato steel plant. Gold has been part of the mining economy for almost a century, and is mined from many small scattered supplies, chiefly in the provinces of Santiago, Atacama, and Coquimbo. Huge resources of manganese exist in Coquimbo province, and silver mining, is concentrated in the province of Antofagasta; production of both minerals has shown a steady increase for the last fifteen years. In general, mining production has continued to increase in recent years. In 1961, mining output was 5.4 per cent above 1960. A recent world-wide overproduction of

[2] For details on Frei's plan for the copper industry, see "Proyecto sobre la Ley del Cobre," *Política y Espíritu,* Año XVIII, (November-December 1964), No. 287, pp. 45–52.

copper, however, contributed to a rapid decline in prices from the high 1954–1956 levels. Various measures were adopted by the large companies to stimulate investment and production.

The abundant distribution of energy-providing power resources with which Chile has been blessed is, in view of the present industrialization of the country, a matter of vital significance. The amount of hydro-electric power potentially available is said to exceed five times that of the United States. A greater proportion of water-power resources than that of any other country in South America has been developed, and yet it represents only 6 per cent of available reserves. Geographically, water resources are scarce in the desert region, but in more heavily populated central Chile there is fortunately a tremendous wealth of available water power. From La Serena to Puerto Montt there is a vast reservoir of potential power in the numerous Andean rivers and lakes. The narrowness of the country is an additional asset in that it makes possible an inexpensive distribution of the power produced.

Electrification has been a feature of economic development. The supply of electric power has doubled since 1940. In 1954 and 1955 forty-nine new electric plants were installed and account for more than two thirds of the power available at this time. A vast electrification plan was drafted by the Chilean Development Corporation (CORFO) and is being carried out by its subsidiary, the *Empresa Nacional de Electricidad, S.A.* (ENDESA). In the period 1940–1952, ENDESA built four large hydro-electric plants: Pilmaiquén, Sauzal, El Abanico, and Los Molles, representing a supply of 203,040 kw. Another plant with 101,400 kw has been completed at Los Cipreses, and four diesel-electric plants have been built at Copiapó, Vallenar, Ovalle, and Guayacán. Five other plants under construction in 1963 will provide an additional 716,600 kw.

Oil exploration in Chile, begun systematically in 1942, resulted in the discovery of fields in northern Tierra del Fuego. For a few years the CORFO, concerned with the need to reduce dependence on imported petroleum, continued exploration. Once there existed some assurance of the commercial possibilities of Chilean oil, the government created as a CORFO subsidiary, the *Empresa Nacional de Petróleos, S.A.* (ENAP), to take charge of exploration, extraction, refining, and marketing of oil. A refinery built at Concón has a capacity of one million cubic meters of crude petroleum per year. Half of this amount originates with Chilean reserves, and the other half is imported from Venezuela. The opening of this refinery in 1955 has meant savings in the amount of 4 million dollars, or one fourth of the total oil import value.[3] It is hoped that the Magallanes oil fields will soon supply nearly 50 per cent of all domestic fuel consumption.[4]

In contrast with its vast hydro-electric resources, Chile is comparatively poor in coal. As has been mentioned, the coal-producing area is located on the seaboard, south of Concepción, in the northern extreme of Forest Chile. Since the first half of the nineteenth century it has been exploited, and small reserves are expected to be exhausted in another fifty years. The industry is presently in decline due mainly to the lignitic quality of its coal, which restricts its use, to the lack of an adequate policy in developing the internal market, and to insufficient capital investment. The first of these handicaps is illustrated by the fact that the Huachipato steel plant must import part of its coal for lack of adequate Chilean resources. Furthermore, the coal industry, owned by domestic private capital, has no share of the substantial governmental assistance through CORFO to oil and hydro-electric enterprises.[5] There are, however, extensive coal reserves in Magallanes. The Chilean Development Corporation is planning construction of an experimental coal purifying plant at Valdivia to serve as a pilot plant in the exploitation of the Magallanes reserves.

Forests occupy about 22 per cent of Chile's total area, an estimated forty million acres, but very little has been done so far to exploit scientifically these valuable timber resources. Practically all forestry production comes from the provinces of Cautín and Valdivia, where forests are more accessible. The untrodden southern archipelagic and coastal forests have scarcely been scratched. Nevertheless, some hardwoods are exported to neighboring countries and to England, and wood imports have declined noticeably.

The long Chilean coast offers an abundant and varied maritime fauna which can be utilized for valuable protein foods and for opening new industries. Valparaíso, San Antonio, and Talcahuano are the most important bases of the fishing industry. Coquimbo, Valdivia, and Puerto Montt are next. Sardines, anchovies, and tuna are plentiful

[3] Instituto de Economía, Universidad de Chile, *Desarrollo económico de Chile 1940–1956* (Santiago, 1956), pp. 167–168. This study, prepared by the Instituto staff under the direction of Joseph Grunwald, is an excellent economic survey of the country.

[4] The role that foreign capital should play in the development of the oil industry is a controversial issue. For opinions see "Pro y contra en el proyecto sobre el petróleo," *Panorama económico* (July 19, 1957), pp. 406–412. See also Aníbal Pinto, "El petróleo: El problema de hoy y la experiencia del pasado," *Panorama económico* (August 2, 1957), pp. 439–441.

[5] Instituto de Economía, *op. cit.*, p. 168.

in the northern provinces. The annual catch increased more than five times from 1945 to 1955 and keeps increasing at nearly 60 per cent annually. Shellfish production has tripled during the same period. A government policy designed to stimulate the industry by means of favorable tax and currency exchange regulations is responsible, in large measure, for the industry's remarkable development. Canned products have practically eliminated fish imports. In 1955 there were seventy-seven manufacturing plants along the seaboard, the chief industrial centers being those at Puerto Montt and Talcahuano. The rapid increase of fish-meal exports in 1961 and 1962, coupled with a promotional program and a favorable world market outlook portends further expansion.

Lastly, two other natural resources of some importance should be mentioned: water resources and scenery. The former, represented by rivers fed by melting snows, which descend from the Andes into the central valley, is very valuable to Chilean agriculture and enables farmers to irrigate in the summer over two million acres of land by means of a complex system of canals. The spectacular scenery and the wonderful climate of Chile can, in turn, be the basis for the development of an international tourist industry which even at its present incipient state has already redounded in some economic advantage to the country.

Communications

The diversity of geographical and economic regions, the anomalous shape of the country, the concentration of population in a fairly compact area, and the volume of foreign trade are all factors which lend essential significance to the problem of communications. The utilization of fertile land not yet available to agriculture, as well as the development of remote areas, depends chiefly on the establishment of a net of efficient communications between the various regions of the republic.

Shortage of petroleum has somewhat restricted development of road transport services, and relatively little freight and few passengers move by road. Of a total of 51,456 kilometers, 63 per cent are of an unimproved earth type. It has been estimated that a "satisfactory" road system could be completed with the paving of an additional 7,000 kilometers and with the improvement of 18,500 kilometers of other roads. The government has coordinated all efforts to secure this "satisfactory" road system. In 1955 more than 100 road projects were underway amounting to a total of 1,700 kilometers.[6] The regions best

[6] *Ibid.*, p. 170.

served are, of course, the Santiago region and the Mediterranean Central Valley, but the mineral zones of the north now have fairly adequate roads. The provinces of Chiloé and Aysén need much road construction if they are to have larger settlement, while the situation in Magallanes is slightly better. There are two trans-andine roads to Argentina, one through the Uspallata Pass, and another from Peulla in the south; there are also roads linking Magallanes and Argentina. The Pan American Highway in Chile consists of 1,500 miles of road from the Peruvian frontier to the city of Los Andes, and on to the trans-andine Pass of Uspallata. In 1963 this highway was near completion except for the section running through Atacama province. Road connections between Santiago and Valparaíso have been greatly improved with construction of the Zapata Tunnel.

Since the middle of the nineteenth century Chile has developed an internal railway system which resembles a great spinal column. This system is indeed one of the three principal networks of South America. The two northern provinces are united to the rest of the country by railroads built and operated by private companies, while, with few exceptions, all other Chilean railways center on a main trunk line running south to the end of the central valley at Puerto Montt and are under a state system. There are offshoots from this main line to important towns and tourist resorts of the Lake region. There are also a private railroad serving the coal and industrial district of Concepción and some short lines on Chiloé island. The main problem confronted by the State Railways system is that of antiquated equipment. It was estimated in 1952 that a minimum of approximately $130 million was required if normal and efficient service was to be established. Although the average passenger-kilometers and ton-kilometers of freight totals have increased appreciably in recent years, they are still far behind the growth rates of the population and national production.[7]

There are also five international railway lines which link Chile with Argentina, Peru, and Bolivia. These unite Arica and Tacná, Arica and La Paz, Antofagasta and La Paz, Antofagasta and the Argentine city of Salta, and Los Andes and Mendoza. The latter, the famous Trans-Andean railway, is the most important international rail link. The Antofagasta-Salta railway has special significance since it should permit the desert provinces to import quantities of much-needed foodstuffs in exchange for copper and nitrate. A plan to modernize the railway system, prepared by CORFO, is now being implemented. Cost of this program during the period 1961–1970 is estimated at $114 million

[7] For proposals to modernize transportation see Robert T. Brown and Carlos Hurtado, *Una política de transportes para Chile* (Santiago: Instituto de Economía, Universidad de Chile, 1963).

and 208 million escudos. It includes electrification of the railroad between Santiago and Chillán. purchases of diesel equipment, construction of buildings and development of a modern communications system.[8]

Despite its elongated coast and the fact that 99 per cent of foreign trade is routed by sea, Chile has only a small merchant marine, with 102 ships and a little over 300,000 tons.[9] By law, coastal trade between Chilean ports is the almost exclusive privilege of Chilean vessels. However, Chile's share in international shipping is only 10 per cent of its own exports and imports. Despite governmental efforts to reserve for Chilean steamships 50 per cent of all international shipping, this objective is far from being achieved. Chilean merchant vessels are too old (34 per cent are thirty years old); adequate maritime legislation is needed; there is a lack of incentives, such as credit facilities and remunerative tariffs; trained personnel is not available in numbers, and most ports are poorly conditioned.[10] However, in 1961 new port facilities were planned by CORFO in Arica, Puerto Montt, Valdivia, and San Vicente.[11]

The coming of the air age has been of outstanding importance to Chile as to all Latin American republics; air traffic has risen spectacularly in the last fifteen years. Domestic air travel is practically monopolized by *Línea Aérea Nacional* (LAN), an autonomous governmental entity established in the late 1930's which has also started some international routes in recent years. The popularization of air travel within the country is shown by the increase in the number of passengers carried by this line from less than 10,000 in 1940 to over 180,000 in 1954. In 1960 this number had increased to 302,117. Passenger-kilometers soared from 3.5 million in 1940 to 254.2 million in 1960, and ton-kilometers increased from 15,900 to 2,061,906 in the same period.[12] In 1940, LAN had only six small aircraft, while by 1957 it had twenty-seven larger ships including six DC-6B's, each with a sixty-two seat capacity. Jet aircraft were put into service in LAN international flights in 1964.

[8] CORFO, Programa de Transportes, 1961–1970 (mimeographed, 1961).

[9] Claudio Véliz, *Historia de la marina mercante en Chile* (Santiago: Editorial de la Universidad de Chile, 1961) is an exhaustively documented analysis of Chile's failure from 1810 to 1921 to develop an important merchant marine and shipbuilding industry despite favorable conditions.

[10] Instituto de Economía, *op. cit.*, pp. 171–172.

[11] See Instituto de Economía, Universidad de Chile, *Eficiencia portuaria en Chile* (Santiago, 1960) for an interesting study of the efficiency of five main Chilean ports: Antofagasta, Coquimbo, Valparaíso, San Antonio, and Puerto Montt.

[12] Source: Departamento de Estadística de la Línea Aérea Nacional, *Movimiento de la Línea Aérea Nacional* (Santiago, 1962).

A chief problem in air communications is the need for more large landing fields which in turn require large capital investments. Present conditions are inadequate, with only two landing strips available to large airships, Santiago and Antofagasta, and in emergency cases La Serena's field. New airports have been completed in Punta Arenas, Puerto Montt, Arica, Valdivia, and Copiapó.[13] Traffic on international routes is mostly carried by foreign lines, especially American, British, German, and Swedish, although LAN carried 21,149 passengers in 1960.

The Agrarian Question

There can be little doubt that Chile, with the optimum climatic conditions and the highest amount of arable land per inhabitant in the hemisphere, should be capable of adequately sustaining its 8.7 million population. However, this is not the case, for among the economic maladjustments that beset Chile and retard its progress, the one which stands out is the system of land ownership.[14] Like many other Latin American countries, ownership of land in Chile has been the major economic basis for the exercise of power and one of the basic conditioning factors of government, because 30 per cent of the total active population depends directly for its living on agricultural and pastoral pursuits. Despite this fact, the agrarian system is characterized by a high degree of inequality in land ownership. In addition, agriculture has failed to fulfill its role in the economy in recent years. It contributes only about 12 per cent of the gross national product. The stagnation of agricultural and livestock production during the last few years has created pressure on the balance of payments by increased imports of food, agricultural raw materials, and livestock.

The Chilean agrarian structure retains economic and social traditions from the colonial period. Productivity per worker is lower in agriculture than in other sectors of the economy; moreover, it declined by 20 per cent between 1952 and 1962. The lack of incentives for the average worker to increase production, low technological levels, and the under-utilization of labor in some large holdings all contribute to low output in terms of both land and labor yields.[15]

[13] Instituto de Economía, *Desarrollo económico,* p. 173.

[14] G. M. McBride, *Chile: Land and Society* (New York: American Geographical Society, 1936) is an excellent study of Chile's agrarian problem. See also, Hugo Trivelli F., *Expansión y estructura agraria de Chile* (Santiago, 1941).

[15] Inter-American Development Bank, *Social Progress Trust Fund, Third Annual Report, 1963* (Washington, D.C.: Inter-American Development Bank, 1964), p. 179. See also David Félix, *Desequilibrios estructurales y crecimiento industrial: El caso chileno* (Santiago: Instituto de Economía, Universidad de Chile, 1958), pp. 9–25.

The large estate or *fundo* is the prevailing form of land ownership in Chile. Cultural factors have also influenced the land tenure system. An example is the concentration of large properties, contrary to expectations based on the physical and economic conditions, in the most highly populated area of the Santiago-Valparaíso region, and of smaller properties to the south. As can be expected, this abnormal distribution of land has had a profound effect upon methods of production. Strikingly enough, the major money crops in the former region are fruits, wine, and truck garden products, which permit intense cultivation with high productivity per land unit, while farther south wheat, rye, and other cereals are grown which require extensive acreage for greater productivity.[16] One simple explanation is, of course, the fact that early colonists settled around the capital and established the Spanish land use system, while the south was colonized much later and partly by other Europeans with their own ideas and experiences.

Monopolization of land, core of the plantation system, is still an important source of political power; the system, based on semifeudal social relationships, has been aggravated at times by religious conflict. The colonial land system has survived with all its antiquated agricultural practices and its many vices, i.e., absenteeism. Large holdings make up 62.8 per cent of all farm land, but only 1.4 per cent of all holdings. Thirty-seven per cent of the farm units, containing less than five hectares each, occupy only 0.3 per cent of the agricultural area.[17] The situation in the central region was described in the preceding chapter.[18] Some of the properties in that region are so extensive that the individual owner has little interest in the maximum exploitation possible by means of modern methods, or in the full education, training, and employment of the laborers.[19]

Chile has tried to broaden the basis of land ownership, but its efforts, as those of most Latin American countries, have been unsuccessful. There are formidable obstacles. Any attempt to alter the status quo is met with the determined and well organized power of the entire oligarchical landed group, which is highly skilled in political action. Any program of land reform inevitably arouses the hostility of this group, generally in alliance with other large vested interests. Their influence permeates all major political blocs. Even after the electoral defeat of the Conservatives in 1938 supposedly broke the power of the Right, the Popular Front and other leftist administrations which

16 Instituto de Economía, *Desarrollo económico,* p. 104.

17 United Nations, Department of Economic Affairs, *Progress in Land Reform* (New York, 1954), p. 43.

18 See p. 7.

19 Herman Finer, *The Chilean Development Corporation* (Montreal: International Labor Office, 1947), pp. 42–43.

followed it made no determined effort in the matter of agrarian reform. Plans for the colonization of new territories in the south have been only half-heartedly pursued since the last century. Only two major political groups on the Chilean political scene have conscientiously maintained the issue of land reform before the public eye: the Christian-Democrats, and the leftist agglomeration of parties known as the Popular Action Front (FRAP). But from a realistic viewpoint, even these two groups cannot do more than perhaps force landowners to assume a fairer share of the national taxation burden, put their lands to a more rational use, and accord their workers full benefits of social security legislation.[20] It is true that the Christian-Democrats advocate implementation of a thoroughgoing agrarian reform, giving it high priority in their platform, but it is doubtful that once in power they would be capable of implementing such a reform against the opposition of the farm interests. As for the FRAP, it is equally doubtful that it can achieve drastic reform without unleashing social and political upheaval. Therefore, the opinion is well founded that there cannot occur in Chile an agrarian reform such as that of the Mexican Revolution or even of the corporative type of the Guatemalan under the Arbenz regime. The problem in Chile requires a huge supply of resources, financial and otherwise, plus consummate political skill. One must agree that "it is only within the present tenure system as a 'given' that an overall improvement in productivity can be worked for without the payment of a very high price in political instability."[21]

Prior to 1962 efforts of the government to modify the agrarian structure had been largely directed toward settlement. The Colonization Office (*Caja de Colonización*), a semi-independent agency set up in 1928, was the principal agency for land redistribution. Its chief functions were to redistribute government lands, to encourage establishment of farm centers, and to furnish credit and other assistance to settlers and cooperatives. By the end of 1959 it had created some 3,600 new agricultural units involving a little over 400,000 hectares of land. The work of the *Caja* was restricted by lack of capital and by the serious inflation of recent decades. Reorganized in 1960, the *Caja* later subdivided and distributed about 550,000 hectares in the southern provinces.

Mostly as a consequence of the profound impact on the continent of the Cuban Revolution with its emphasis upon agrarian reform and the fears of social upheaval that it aroused, the Chilean government

[20] For an interesting study of land taxes see Instituto de Economía, Universidad de Chile, *La tributación agrícola en Chile, 1940–1958* (Santiago, 1960).

[21] K. H. Silvert, "The State of Chilean Agriculture" (Santiago: American Universities Field Staff Letter, July 1, 1957).

late in 1961 began to take steps directed toward formulating an agrarian reform program. A committee consisting of members of the Congress from the three political parties participating in the Alessandri administration (Radical, Liberal, and Conservative) was organized to study modification and supplementation of existing legislation. The process was slow and difficult. Early in 1962 studies were completed, and a series of bills was drafted. The program which emerged basically does not contemplate expropriating or breaking up the large private estates; it is based on redistribution of land already in control of the government. President Alessandri submitted to the Congress a *Normative Law* which would invest the executive with extraordinary powers to legislate on agrarian reform and to organize related agencies. Many modifications were made to this bill, and finally the Congress approved the Agrarian Reform Law in November, 1962.[22] Under the law the Colonization Office was converted into the Agrarian Reform Corporation (*Corporación de la Reforma Agraria,* CORA). The new law centralized all governmental activities in agriculture and the livestock industry in the Ministry of Agriculture. Under it, CORA is in charge of all matters related to land division and of the provision of credit and technical assistance to the "economic units" to be established.[23] The Agrarian Reform Law states that the following properties may be expropriated for agrarian reform purposes: (1) idle lands, as well as those which are poorly utilized and produced inadequate yields; (2) up to half of the lands irrigated by government facilities, provided the property is larger than one "economic unit" and is not impaired by expropriation; (3) those which have been publicly auctioned to credit institutions in payment of debts; (4) holdings belonging to public or private juridical entities and being worked in an indirect manner; (5) leased holdings where the lessor has not spent the legally prescribed percentage of income on soil improvement, irrigation, and fencing, or if some other provision of the Agrarian Reform Law has not been complied with; (6) flooded or saline lands conducive to drying and improvement and lands damaged by erosion or by dune formation; and (7) holdings designated by the Ministry of Agriculture as *minifundios* (uneconomically small holdings) for the purpose of regrouping and restributing them, preferably among former owners who wish to receive new land units. Other cases in which expropriation may be authorized include certain lands in the southern part of the

[22] Law 15,020, November 15, 1962.

[23] An "economic unit" is defined by the law as the idle portion of land which, when worked by the owner and his family, is enough to provide a living to such family if rationally exploited, with occasional employment of outside help.

country, lands on which certain desirable species of trees are growing, holdings which have defective titles, and those needed to complete a specific program of the CORA. Rural holdings not included in this list may also be expropriated if the expropriation is part of a "Regional Agricultural Development Plan" and the holdings are either divisible or are needed to supplement the subdivision of another tract. However, such expropriation can only take place within one year after the decree approving the respective Regional Development Plan is issued, and only if that year's budget includes allocations for that plan.

Every expropriation decree must state the amount of indemnity payable to the owner and to any third party. At the time of the adoption of the Agrarian Reform Law, the Constitution required that expropriated land be paid for in full at the time of expropriation. A constitutional amendment adopted in 1963 changed this provision to permit payment of 10 per cent at the time of expropriation, with the balance payable in equal annual installments over no more than fifteen years. This provision, however, is applicable only to land holdings which have been abandoned or are being poorly utilized. In all other cases the government will have to make prior cash payments.

Court procedures for expropriation are to be conducted before Special Tribunals for Agrarian Expropriation in each city where there is a Court of Appeals. Appeals are to be made to the respective Court of Appeals. The law also established a special agency, the Aysén Land Corporation, with jurisdiction over Aysén Province and over the Department of Palena in Chiloé Province. Its chief function is to advise the chief executive on granting titles to government lands in that region.

In 1963 as a result of the issuance of several decrees complementing the Agrarian Reform Law, two other new agencies were established. These are the Supreme Council for Agricultural Development (*Consejo Superior de Fomento Agropecuario*), and the Institute for Agricultural Development (*Instituto de Desarrollo Agropecuario*). The Council, composed of the ministers of Agriculture, Economic Affairs, and Land and Colonization among others, is to prepare national and regional plans for agrarian reform and rural development and to oversee the implementation of those plans. The Council is charged with conducting research on agrarian policy to insure achievement of the objectives of the Ten-Year Development Plan. Universities and research institutes are collaborating with the Council in the drafting of regional plans within the scope of the Ten-Year Plan. The Institute for Agricultural Development has been given the responsibility of providing technical supervision to small farmers, and of raising the living standards and production levels in areas of uneconomical small holdings.

Implementation of the Agrarian Reform Law is proceeding at a slow pace, and criticisms of its provisions, as well as dissatisfaction with what critics consider a too cautious approach to land reform have been mounting. The administrative machinery is moving sluggishly. From November, 1962, when the Law was enacted to the end of August, 1963, the Agrarian Reform Corporation had subdivided throughout the country 11 holdings with a total of 61,620 hectares to form 792 parcels classified as "economic units," 472 family garden plots, and 44 tracts for cooperatives. It was hoped that during the second year of operations an additional 4,208 parcels and 921 family gardens would be carved by CORA out of some 469,000 hectares of land.

A very significant phenomenon is the active role being played in agrarian reform by the Chilean Catholic Church. Concrete evidence of this institution's new concern with the need for social change is an agrarian reform initiated by the Chilean Church on its own properties in 1963. This program, although limited in scope, is being carried out dynamically by the Institute for Agrarian Development (*Instituto de Promoción Agraria,* INPROA) a private nonprofit foundation established in 1962 to contribute to the economic and social development of Chile.

It is maintained by some that the tremendous urge for industrialization which is so obviously an element of Latin American nationalist movements may be partially explained by the serious difficulties of solving the agrarian question. To a technician, it may be evident that opening new lands, improving agricultural techniques, and increasing capitalization are all steps which should precede industrialization if an orderly economic development is to take place. But most Latin Americans belong to two other schools of thought: one, the extreme nationalist that wants industries per se, as a panacea to all ills, and the other which rationalizes, with logic, that the landed groups loom so powerful politically and prestigiously that it is impossible to introduce drastic changes in the land tenure system without resorting to such violent political methods as would damage the measure of individual liberties which may have been obtained in any given situation. This being the case, they conclude, the only possible way out is to concentrate on building urban and industrial strength, and then to direct it back to the soil, using the tax revenues and coercive power derived from this strength to force payment for expropriated lands, purchase of modern equipment, credits, and public works programs.[24]

[24] Silvert, *op. cit.,* pp. 1–2.

In general, Chile's choice has been industrialization first and then modernization of agriculture, but the alternative is not that simple or exclusive, and the country has to be concerned with the many varied matters which interrelate industrial and agricultural activities. It is also attempting, in spite of financial limitations, to introduce modern agricultural techniques.

In recent years, while the population has been increasing by 1.8 per cent annually, agricultural production has risen only 1.6 per cent. The fact that agriculture employs more than 27 per cent of the labor force but contributes only about 12 per cent (1960) of the gross national product poses obvious difficulties for the international balance of payments. The failure of agricultural production to keep pace with increasing demands has been an important contributing factor to inflation and has forced Chile to import substantial amounts of foodstuffs. As food imports increase, the development of industry is retarded by the limited internal market, and migration to the urban areas is increased. The income per person active in agriculture is estimated at a little more than half of that found in industry and around a third of that shown in mining.[25]

Elements that characterize agricultural production are then distinct from those which are observed in industry. The number of persons in agricultural activities has diminished in relation to other sectors, while production has been practically stagnant and the total population has increased by nearly one million and a half. In addition, per capita income grew in 1961 and 1962 by about 3.3 per cent per year,[26] causing a greater demand for food than normal to meet the population growth. Furthermore, although the absolute number of agricultural workers has not diminished since 1940, its vegetative increase has been drained off mostly by the urban centers.[27]

It is a fact that for the last twenty-five years there has been a significant demand for food that warranted improvements in the level of agricultural productivity. Instead of meeting this challenge, the country, especially after 1947, turned abroad for food. From an exporter of food Chile turned into an importer. Exports of wheat virtually ceased after 1941, and a considerable amount is now annually imported from Argentina; more than 200,000 cattle and 200,000 sheep are also imported from Argentina to help feed the population of the central region. Other imports included those necessities which Chile cannot produce, such as sugar cane, bananas, coffee, and cotton. In 1954, for

[25] Instituto de Economía, *Desarrollo económico,* p. 103.

[26] CORFO, *Cuentas nacionales de Chile, 1950–1962* (Santiago: CORFO, 1963), p. 43.

[27] Instituto de Economía, *Desarrollo económico,* p. 103.

example, the imports of farm products for which there is also some national production were equivalent to one sixth of Chile's total imports.[28]

The stagnation of agriculture, assuming the country maintains its present dietary level, means that inevitably the deficit in the balance of payments will continue to increase. Since 1957 the unfavorable trend of the balance of payments has been worsened by a rapid rise of imports in the face of the relatively slow growth of exports. To be sure, this situation is not due exclusively to agricultural stagnation but is complicated by other adverse factors. The fact is, however, that by the end of 1963 the net international reserves of the banking system and of the official entities showed a negative amount of approximately U.S. $220 million.[29] Remedial action may involve in the future reduction of the diet per capita and a drastic limitation of imports such as machinery, raw materials and other essentials to normal economic life. The social and political repercussions of such drastic measures can be easily imagined.[30] Such gloomy prospects clearly call for a governmental policy of rectification as well as for an adjustment on the part of the predominant types of agricultural interests, whether they desire it or not, to conditions and needs of contemporary Chile.

Meantime, Chile has been receiving some foreign assistance, from intergovernmental and international agencies and from the United States, to alleviate the most urgent pressures and to carry out portions of its agrarian program. Through special agreements with the United States, large quantities of wheat, oil, cotton, and other items were received from surplus American farm production and payments were lent to the Chilean government for use in agricultural development.

Two thirds of Chile's total area, 74.1 million hectares, is wasteland. This large proportion of barren territory includes the extensive desert zones in the north and the Andean mountain lands. The usable[31] area is more than 56 per cent forest lands; 20 per cent is actually cultivated and the rest is left to natural pastures. The cultivated area, although a small percentage of the total, is one of the world's vastest in relation

[28] A good article on the failure of agricultural production is Ernest Feder, "Feudalism and Agricultural Development: The Role of Controlled Credit in Chile's Agriculture," *Land Economics,* XXXVI, No. 1 (February, 1960), pp. 92–130.

[29] Inter-American Development Bank, p. 177.

[30] Ministerio de Agricultura and Corporación de Fomento, *Plan de Desarrollo Agrícola y de Transportes* (mimeographed, 1954), p. 11, as quoted in Silvert, *op. cit.,* p. 5.

[31] The term "usable" is not employed in the sense of land that is "apt to be utilized" but rather it means "lands which have been utilized during a period of 10 years preceding the estimate."

to the total population and active farm population. In Chile, there is almost one hectare to each inhabitant, while in Europe the average is half a hectare or less per person.

However, since this apparent advantage cannot be translated into greater productivity, as we have shown, it becomes clear that the present underproduction is not the result of a per capita shortage of farm lands as such. The chief factor which prevents a better use of the cultivatable lands is, according to a report of the United Nations Economic Commission for Latin America, owner's lack of interest, followed in decreasing order by lack of water for irrigation, lack of working capital, ignorance of techniques, poor soils, and others.[32] Also significant is the fact that of the almost 6 million hectares of cultivatable land more than 46 per cent is in pasture, while the rest, approximately 3 million hectares, is used mostly for cereal crops and artificial pastures. Even with this excessive farming, imports of cereals and meat have increased more rapidly than any others, clearly indicating low productivity in the case of the former and specialization in dairy rather than meat products in the case of the latter.

Labor shortage is not usually considered a factor in the agricultural situation; farm workers are normally classified into the following: permanent workers which include the *inquilinos* (tenants), *medieros* (sharecroppers) and *afuerinos* or *voluntarios* (migrant workers); workers such as warehouse keepers, maintenance men, and the like, who are commonly called employees, whereas the law considers them workers; temporary workers who work part of the year on the farm and the remainder elsewhere; and, the small land holders who are unable to make a living out of their properties and therefore work as laborers part of the time.[33] There are about half a million rural families, 300,000 of which are landless and live a precarious existence, scarcely above subsistence level.

Of all farm labor the *afuerinos* receive the lowest pay in the country, U.S. 30–40 cents daily in cash and benefits. *Inquilinos* earn about U.S. 60 cents daily. Bearing in mind that international comparisons can be misleading, it should be mentioned that the per capita income in Chile for 1954 was a little less than U.S. $150, while in the United States it was $1,845. Since Chilean farm labor represents a third of the active population but receives only 11 per cent of the total wages paid, its per family share of the national income is quite small.[34] Ob-

[32] Instituto de Economía, *Desarrollo económico*, p. 107.

[33] Corporación de Fomento de la Producción, Departamento de Planificación y Estudios, *Cuentas nacionales de Chile 1940–1954*, (Santiago, 1957), p. 71.

[34] Silvert, *op. cit.*, p. 11.

viously any increase in the standard of living and purchasing power of this agricultural population would bring about a rapid significant demand for manufacturing production and be a powerful incentive for greater economic development.

The conditions which characterize at present the complex agricultural problem of Chile may be summarized as follows: agricultural production, while still absorbing the largest percentage of the total active population, is experiencing great difficulty in keeping pace with population growth. The basic feature of Chilean agriculture is its low productivity by comparison with other economic activities. This difference becomes more and more outstanding as the rhythm of industrialization accelerates in the present intermediate stage of the country's economy. Although there are still substantial possibilities of opening new lands for agriculture, the greatest increase in production could be attained through better utilization of the existing wide margin to improve productivity, and through the infiltration of modern techniques into the Chilean scene. It is also evident that Chilean agriculture is exceptionally sensitive to fluctuation in production and marketing of a few products because of the predominance of cereal crops, particularly wheat. The retarded growth of agriculture has caused serious repercussions on Chile's balance of payments. The effect is a two-sided one: imports have diminished and exports have gone up. Lastly, no substantial alterations can be expected within the traditional land tenure system without a drastic re-structuring of the political system. For the first time in Chilean history such institutional changes appear to be close to realization as Chile begins to move toward sweeping social revolution in the mid-1960's.

The Mining Problem

The importance of mining activities in Chilean economic development is evident from their role in the balance of payments, to which they contribute close to 80 per cent of the total exports, thereby providing the basis for the country's capacity to import. In addition, the mining industry is an important source of employment (about 100,000 workers and employees), and contributes approximately one fourth of the fiscal revenues. The factors which determine the export advantages of the mining industry are also responsible for serious ills in the Chilean economy, making it largely dependent on foreign markets, and therefore highly sensitive to cyclic fluctuations and to international events over which the country has no control.

Dependence on mineral activities still largely controls Chile's financial and economic policy, in spite of the fact that their contribution to the national income has been steadily declining for the last twenty years. Although the industry dates back to early colonial days, its greatest development occurred in the nineteenth century. This was especially true with regard to nitrate, which was paramount in the national economy for a couple of generations. After synthetic nitrate was produced in other countries and the world depression brought economic ruin to the nitrate industry, copper assumed the primary role in Chile's mining production.

Chilean law distinguishes between "large," "medium," and "small" mining concerns on the basis of size, nationality, and volume of capital.[35] The so-called "large" mining consists of a few enormous industrial enterprises dedicated to copper, nitrate, and iron, and characterized by a high degree of mechanization; they refine their own products, support a heavy taxation burden, and have a high productivity. The "medium" and "small" mining is formed by many small concerns of limited physical size, capital, and machinery. They usually have their products refined abroad and depend for survival upon preferential tax treatment. Production value of "large" mining is more than four times that of the other two combined.

Mining production has shown a constant decrease since the end of World War II when it reached its peak. In 1947, 1948, 1949, and during the Korean War, mining production rose significantly. Only in 1959 did it reach levels comparable to those of the World War II period. The number of persons, among the active population, occupied in mining activities has also diminished, this decline being sharpest in "large" mining, especially the copper industry. In 1940 mining laborers represented 6.6 per cent of the total labor force of the country, while in 1953 they accounted for only 4.6 per cent.[36]

Productivity in mining is considerably higher than in any other activity. It is twice that of industry and three times that of agriculture. It must be observed in this respect that annual output is much greater (five times) among "large" miners than in the "medium" and "small" categories.[37]

Copper production has been especially reflective of world conditions. It was estimated in 1958 that every one cent drop in the price of copper cost Chile $7 million in foreign exchange and a proportionate amount in taxes. After a peak output during World War II, copper production fell during the first ten postwar years. During that world conflict the industry had been encouraged by the United States de-

[35] Law 11,828 defines the term "gran minería del cobre"; Law 10,270 contains a definition of "pequeña minería" not restricted to a particular mineral.

[36] Instituto de Economía, *Desarrollo económico,* p. 154.

[37] *Ibid.,* pp. 154–155.

cision to fix the price of copper at $234 per ton, but this policy was cancelled in 1946 as demand diminished. Lifting of the United States import tax on copper in 1947 strengthened the industry, and Korean War demands later brought on a slight recovery. More recently, weak market demands have caused new setbacks, including a serious crisis in 1957 when President Ibáñez cancelled a state visit to Washington after the United States Secretary of the Interior proposed to restore the long-suspended copper tariff. These severe fluctuations clearly influenced the economic life of the country.[38]

Legislation enacted in 1955 and known as the "New Deal for the Copper Producing Companies" (*Nuevo Trato a las empresas productoras de cobre de la gran minería*), was intended to stimulate production and attract more capital.[39] It must be remembered that at this time over 90 per cent of the total copper production was owned by foreign enterprises. The mines at Chuquicamata, El Salvador, and El Teniente are owned respectively by the Chile Exploration Company, Andes Copper Mining Company, and Braden Copper Company. All of these are American concerns, the first two being subsidiaries of Anaconda Mining Company, and the second of Kennecott Corporation. The *Nuevo Trato* did away with all previous taxes on production and imposed instead only one direct profit tax which grows smaller as output increases. Modifications in matters of foreign exchange favorable to the copper company were also introduced by this law. As a result, the copper companies are engaged in ambitious plans which contemplate large investments. In 1956, new investments amounted to approximately $92 million. It was hoped that these investments would result in an annual output of 550,000 metric tons, as against 391,000 in 1955.

[38] An exhaustive analysis of the copper industry is contained in a series of articles by Carlos Arangua R., under the general title "Situación y perspectivas del cobre," published in *Panorama económico,* X, Nos. 163, 164, 165, 166, and 168 (March-June, 1957), and XI, Nos. 170, 171, 173, 175, 179, and 181 (July-December, 1957). More recent are: *Libro del cobre* (Santiago: Braden Copper Company, 1960), which contains facts and figures, descriptions of the mining process, and the complete texts of pertinent Chilean laws; and Mario Vera Valenzuela, *La política económica del cobre en Chile* (Santiago: Ediciones de la Universidad de Chile, 1961), in which the author urges forcing the companies to increase output and to refine the copper in Chile.

[39] Two new amendments to the New Deal Copper Law of 1955 went into effect in January, 1965. These amendments were proposed to finance costs of a bill increasing salaries of civil servants. One amendment no longer allowed U.S. import duties paid by American companies to be regarded as deductible expense for the purpose of estimating Chilean income tax liability. The other provided for a tax of 2 cents a pound on exports of all copper except electrolytically refined and fully processed copper.

Iron-ore production has also reflected world conditions. Because of shipping difficulties during World War II it fell from its normal output (approximately one million tons) to an insignificant amount. In the postwar years the industry experienced a remarkable expansion furthered by the internal demand created by the Huachipato steel plant. Annual iron production for the period 1950–1954 was almost twice the average for 1940–1941. In 1961 it was 178 per cent more than in 1950.

Nitrate production experienced a constant decline for 1950–1961. Average production in the 1960's has scarcely reached 1.02 million tons, which is 38 per cent lower than the average for 1950–1951.[40] It must also be noted that the share of Chilean nitrate in world production has been decreasing since the end of the nineteenth century.[41] So unparalleled is this reduction that according to statistics, Chilean nitrate has dropped from 65 per cent of the world production to only 4 per cent in the last fifty years. The increase in world demand has been more than amply met by synthetic nitrate produced elsewhere at a lower cost than that of the Chilean product. A government corporation, *Corporación de Ventas del Salitre y Yodo* (COVENSA), buys and exports nitrate of all Chilean companies, distributes the profits and sees that the government receives its share. The two most important companies are the *Compañía Anglo-Lautaro,* which works the *salitreras* of María Elena and Pedro de Valdivia, and the *Compañía Salitrera de Tarapacá y Antofagasta,* which exploits extensive deposits in these two provinces.

In 1956 the Chilean Congress approved an ad-referendum agreement between nitrate producers and the government. Dictated by reasons similar to those which motivated the "New Deal" copper law — namely, to encourage investment and increase production — this legislation, commonly known as the "Nitrate Referendum," permitted producers to include items such as amortization, interest on loans, and transportation expenses in their industrial costs. It also established a fairer system of distributing profits among the nitrate companies and of determining the government's share, and made imports of these companies duty-free. In return, the nitrate companies pledged themselves to put into effect specific development plans calling for the investment of $36 million in a five-year period.

Employment furnished by the nitrate companies is the largest in the mining industry since numerous men are employed in the process-

40 Instituto de Economía, Universidad de Chile, *La economía de Chile en el período 1950–1963* (Santiago, 1963), Vol. I, pp. 103–104.

41 See "Informe de la misión Klein-Saks sobre el salitre," *Panorama económico* (June 7, 1957), pp. 265–269.

ing as well as in the extraction of the ore. During the period 1940–1956 the number of nitrate workers exceeded 20,000 except during the years 1944 and 1955.[42] Naturally, this figure fluctuates according to production levels. In some instances, unemployment has reached considerable proportions, such as in 1944 and more recently in 1957 and 1961, with the inevitable sequence of social unrest.

Iodine production has recently shown a slight tendency to decrease, and, in general, has been subject to considerable fluctuation. The coal industry, almost wholly Chilean-owned, has been producing over two million tons annually during the period 1940–1955. However, in the last decade there has been a consistent decline of coal production. In 1960 only 1.5 million tons were extracted, the lowest amount since 1933. Widespread use of electric energy is the chief cause of the decline. The coal industry has the largest proportion of employees among the "small" and "medium" mining concerns.[43] Periods of unemployment have often worsened the social problem arising from the sublevel state of labor conditions.

Gold production has also diminished in recent years as the result of increasing costs of production and a fixed international buying price. Production in 1955–1959 was 64.6 per cent below that of 1950–1959. Manganese and silver have experienced a relative boom, with the exception of the period immediately following World War II.

The importance of mining as a dynamic force in Chilean economic development has diminished rather significantly. During the period 1950–1961, mining contributed only 5.5 per cent to Chile's gross domestic product. It is true that the "large" mining industries have continued to increase their output, but the fact remains that there are numerous "small" and "medium" mining concerns which, despite a protectionist policy, have proved unable to follow course. Evidently mining will not be capable in the long run of spurring the economic progress of the country unless its productivity increases substantially. In recognition of this fact Chilean government policy towards the large foreign interests involved has changed radically.[44] In many ways, this is the Chilean manifestation of a recent trend which has been growing in Latin America, namely, a marked change in the attitude and philosophy toward foreign capital dictated by a conviction that this capital is indispensable if the process of economic development is to be carried out. Government policies in Mexico, Venezuela, and Peru are other examples of attempts to improve the climate of investment.

[42] *Ibid.*, pp. 158–159.
[43] *Ibid.*, p. 160.
[44] *Ibid.*, p. 9.

The political attitudes derived from ideological alignments resulting from this policy and its implications in general are discussed on a party basis elsewhere in this work. In social terms, the complete dependence of desert and coal-mining areas on the mineral economy, and the large number of people who are indirectly supported by it are matters that involve the stability of the whole country.

Industrialization

Chile is often cited as a successful example of Latin America's zeal for industrialization. Motivated like all underdeveloped countries by a desire to liberate itself from dependence on raw material exports and to raise its living standards, Chile has taken impressive strides on the road toward industrialization. But industrialization, as it has been said, "is never solely a technical and economic development. It is a social and cultural process as well, and in underdeveloped countries nowadays it is also likely to have profound political repercussions.[45] These repercussions have been particularly felt in Chile where new political elements have been brought into play by industrialization. The rise of labor as a force in politics and the emergence of a new industrial technician class are two symptoms suggestive of the impact experienced by Chilean society. New patterns of political behavior are emerging as a result of the economic and social metamorphoses. Elsewhere in this book an attempt is made to trace this pattern and to describe the impact of economic development upon the structure and activities of political parties. What follows is only a historical outline of Chile's progressive and almost phenomenal industrial development.

The origins of Chile's industry are much earlier than is generally believed. Its pattern appears to have been set even before 1914 with the appearance of the first sugar refineries, cotton and woolen mills, iron foundries, cement industry, and hosiery works.[46] Two world wars and the Great Depression did much to expand Chilean industrialization but its greatest acceleration occurred after the late 1930's with the end of seven years of dictatorship and anarchy (1925–1932) and the 1938 electoral victory of the coalition leftist parties, known as the Popular Front.

Two factors have been the *leitmotif* of Chilean industrialization: the necessity for raising the standard of living and improving per capita income, and the urge to attenuate the country's vulnerability to foreign market fluctuations. A precept of policy has been added which holds

[45] Sanford A. Mosk, "An Economist's Point of View," in W. W. Pierson (ed.), "Pathology of Democracy in Latin America. A Symposium," *The American Political Science Review*, XLIV, No. 1 (March, 1950), p. 142.

[46] Butland, *op. cit.*, p. 78.

that foreign exchange should be saved by producing domestically some goods that are imported. The great majority of Chilean imports being manufactured goods, the policy of saving foreign exchange became intimately connected with industrialization.

Expansion was aided by propitious postwar circumstances such as large amounts of foreign exchange accumulated during the war, and the elimination of restrictions on the export of capital in the United States. The net result of these factors combined have been remarkable. Industrial production increased 50 per cent in the period 1946–1955 and its share of the national income went up 42 per cent from 1940 to 1955.[47]

However, in the years between 1955 and 1959 progress in manufacturing was not encouraging. After becoming stagnant in 1956 and 1957, Chilean industry has shown a very low rate of growth. Factory production increased 22.1 per cent between 1953 and 1959 at an annual growth rate of 3.7 per cent. During the same period the population increased 16 per cent, resulting in an increase in industrial production per inhabitant of 5.3 per cent in six years. Obviously an increase of 0.9 per cent a year is not sufficient if Chilean industry is to play a dynamic role in the country's economic development.[48] The contrast of those six years with industrial development in the six years from 1946 to 1952 is indeed striking. The increase per capita was then 34.8 per cent and the population grew 11.6 per cent. Industrial production expanded during those years at a rate of 5.8 per cent. The process of deterioration which began in the 1950's continued in the 1960's. Significantly, exports of manufactured products declined from 11 per cent of the total exports in 1958 to only 4 per cent in 1962. The reasons for the slow tempo of industrial expansion in recent years are many and varied. Significant changes, some political, have taken place in the industrial outlook. Establishment of new factories for manufactured imports is more difficult now that those based on domestic raw materials have been created. In 1956 a basic change in government policy brought liberalization of trade and less protectionism. An important cause of industrial stagnation was the 1956 anti-inflation program of the Alessandri administration. Credit restrictions, wage controls, and limited government expenditures featured in that program contributed further to impair the growth of the national manufacturing industry.

The principal role in this expansion has been played by the Chilean Development Corporation (CORFO), a government agency set up in 1939 and endowed with wide policy- and decision-making power.

47 Instituto de Economía, *Desarrollo económico,* p. 131.
48 Instituto de Economía, *La economía de Chile,* p. 108.

CORFO's splendid record in the development of Chile's national industries is often cited as the most successful example of national economic planning in Latin America.[49] Among the Corporation's projects, the installation of Chile's basic steel industry has required the greatest capital. In this, as well as other ventures, CORFO has been aided by international cooperation. Development of this industry whose products are essential to so many other industries has given extraordinary impetus to the entire industrialization process.

Industry in Chile, as in all developing countries, is small-scale and features numerous factories. Industrial productivity has been uneven; some industries reach efficiency levels as high as their counterparts in highly industrialized nations, others remain far behind. There is a definite trend now for industry to become a larger unit structure by consolidating and closing uneconomical plants. This tendency has already resulted in production increases and simultaneously in employment decreases in some industries.[50] From another viewpoint, the inflationary process and other factors have encouraged creation and survival of numerous small inefficient factories. Tax policies, for example, have discouraged greater industrial specialization. Some industries have added new processes, sacrificing greater specialization for the sake of avoiding payment of certain taxes.[51]

As previously noted, the great bulk of Chile's manufacturing industry is located in the Santiago-Valparaíso region, with a subsidiary center in the south at Concepción. Naturally, this location is determined by the population concentration and resulting large market and availability of manpower, energy, and communications. That Chilean industry exists primarily to satisfy demands of the internal market has been largely influential in determining its location.[52] With the growth of the steel industry and its subsidiaries, the evolution of another great industrial center at Concepción should be a healthy development.

The food industry constitutes the largest group of manufacturers and is still growing. Between 1950 and 1955 food production increased 25 per cent, the greatest increases being recorded by flour and paste, edible oils, sugar, canned and dried fruits, and vegetables. Based primarily on domestic raw materials, this industry logically developed before other industries in an agricultural country. The canned food branch has shown increased growth since the Huachipato plant began furnishing the tin but it still must manufacture its own containers at a cost equivalent to half the product's price.

49 Finer, *op. cit.*, analyzes its work and organization.
50 Butland, *op. cit.*, p. 80.
51 Instituto de Economía, *Desarrollo económico,* p. 131.
52 Butland, *op. cit.*, p. 85.

Except for milk, fruits and vegetables make up 60 per cent of the canning industry; the rest is fish, shellfish, and meats. The four milk manufacturers consume as much tin as all the fruit and vegetable processing plants combined.[53] The potential availability of a great variety of products capable of being processed foretells a promising future for this industry. Until now, however, development of the food industry has been seriously affected by the stagnation of agricultural production.

The textile industry developed rapidly, showing more than a 43 per cent production increase in the period 1946–1955. Factories are still small but larger than those in the food industry and almost entirely geared for the domestic market. The most notable development has been in cotton, but woolens and silk are also manufactured. During the war years a new rayon industry was introduced which has greatly expanded since that time. A linen industry has also appeared. In general, the textile industry still depends largely on imported fibers. This has meant the occurrence of periodical crises caused by shortages of foreign exchange.

The metal and metal-product industry, including machinery, depended largely on imports before the Huachipato mill went into production in 1950. Until that time, iron production had been limited to a scrap-band industry in Santiago and a high-cost production plant at Corral. Since output was small, a large part of the iron and steel needed by Chilean industry had to be imported. Establishment of the Huachipato plant made possible the birth of many metal-working industries, which now manufacture utensils, tools, containers, etc. It also laid the foundations for heavy industry in Chile. In 1952 a plant for the manufacture of metallic structures was installed. Production of railroad cars, using 90 per cent Chilean materials, will make it possible to renovate State Railroads equipment at considerable savings in foreign exchange, since each imported passenger car costs around U.S. $40,000.[54] So great has been the domestic demand in recent years that the *Compañía de Acero del Pacífico* (CAP) has been forced to restrict its exports measurably.[55]

Along with steel, cement production is one of the cornerstones of Chilean industrial development. Stimulated by a construction boom, annual production steadily increased over a long period, reaching 650,000 tons in 1955. Production was expanded with the installation of new plants, and in 1951 Chile was able to export roughly 90,000

[53] Instituto de Economía, *Desarrollo económico,* p. 133.

[54] *Ibid.,* p. 135.

[55] For a description and appraisal of the CAP's operations, see Eduardo Figueroa Geisse, "Desarrollo de la producción de acero en Chile," *El Mercurio,* January 25, 1957.

tons to Argentina. However, almost the whole production is used for domestic consumption, only 7 per cent being left for exports and reserves. Although cement production is larger now than the country's demands, the industry has not been able to develop a stable foreign market in competition with other cement-producing nations such as Japan and Germany.[56]

The chemical industry which produces alcohol, acids, soaps, paints, and fertilizers, ranks second in growth among Chilean manufacturing enterprises. It now satisfies the domestic demand for certain acids and is even exporting small quantities, but is still handicapped by dependence on imports for machinery and some raw materials. This is one reason that Chile, with its wealth of mineral salt deposits, has been slow in developing this industry. Production of pharmaceutical supplies has made remarkable progress in the last decade. Shortages of exchange and deliberate policies by the Chilean government have induced several foreign chemical, pharmaceutical, and dye firms either to establish plants in the country or license Chilean firms to manufacture their products. Much has been done, in general, by the CORFO to integrate this industry with the basic heavy iron and steel enterprises and oil refining.

Chilean paper and cardboard production is the greatest per capita in South America. Having grown more rapidly than the country's needs, it has permitted a drastic reduction in cellulose and paper imports. Almost the entire output is produced by the *Compañía Manufacturera de Papeles y Cartones,* which, with financial assistance from the International Bank for Reconstruction and Development, installed a new sulphate-cellulose plant with 60,000 tons annual capacity. Planned by the CORFO, financed by wood and rayon interests, it was put into operation in 1958. By 1960, according to estimates, Latin America's paper and cardboard consumption was over two and a half million tons per year. Since a good part of this supply must come from the Latin American countries themselves, the cellulose industry could play an important role in Chile's foreign trade.[57]

The manufacture of rubber and leather goods, especially shoes, is a small but important industry. With a few exceptions, the shoe industry meets present internal demands. Production has fallen slightly in recent years due to high costs and prices and shortages in the supply of domestic hides and skins resulting from difficulties in the cattle industry.

Construction work, considerably greater since the end of the war, has encouraged development of the lumber industry which reached a peak production of 36 million inches in 1945. Lumber exports which

[56] Instituto de Economía, *Desarrollo económico,* p. 134.
[57] *Ibid.*, p. 137.

were relatively high in 1949 have been, however, insignificant in recent years as a result of the ever-present foreign exchange problem. It seems surprising that Chile, with enormous reserves of utilizable timber, has not developed a solid, efficient lumber industry, but the reasons are understandable. The inaccessibility of forest areas and the lack of transportation facilities have contributed to the problem, and much needs to be done to modernize the industry with the use of new processes and equipment. In order to experiment with modern methods of exploitation, the CORFO supports an experimental station at Curalelfu, which is contributing much to scientific and rational planning of forest exploitation. There can be little doubt, considering the varied industrial uses of woods and the immense natural forest resources, that this industry is significant to Chile's future economic development as an additional source of much-needed foreign exchange.

After this brief survey of Chile's manufacturing industry the following observations can be made. In the first place, the tendency towards industrial concentration, evidenced by analysis of production statistics,[58] seems to indicate that the country is gradually emerging from the early stages of industrial development, characterized by a large number of small and diversified units which are responsible for the bulk of production.[59] There are inherent dangers in this development, since greater concentration may well lead to the extension of monopolistic practices. In Chile's case, this would be further stimulated by the relatively small market and the limited availability of capital, thereby restricting the benefits of modern techniques to only a few enterprises.

Secondly, it seems that Chilean industrial development will be directed three ways, represented by the metal, chemical, and cellulose industries. The metal industry, after the initial impetus given to it by the Huachipato steel plant, continues to develop at an accelerated pace. The chemical industry has been sparked by two factors: the important by-products of the coke production at Huachipato and of the oil industry will enable it to produce tar, creosote, ammonium sulphate and fertilizers, as well as plastics, detergents, and insecticides; and the absolute decline of Chilean nitrate caused by development of the synthetic product has served to demonstrate the need for utilizing this mineral salt and its subproducts to create a heavy chemical industry. Scientific reforestation, principally of pine, carried out in recent years, should be a factor in the expected exporting ability of the cellulose

[58] *Ibid.*, pp. 131–152.

[59] "Tendencias del crecimiento económico de Chile en 1956," *Panorama económico,* X, No. 167 (May 24, 1957), pp. 252–254.

industry. By 1965 seven new factories, five to be established by the CORFO and two others by the Paper and Cardboard Manufacturing Company, will start production.

In addition to these three important branches of Chilean industry, others hold promise of future development. The sugar industry should soon be capable of supplying one fourth of the national demand for their product. A system of refrigerated transport throughout the country will mean a notable improvement in food marketing. Other plans include expansion of the production of edible oil, flour, and canned fish.

Foreign Trade Problems

In general, no fundamental change has taken place in Chile's foreign trade pattern for many years. The country is still chiefly an exporter of minerals and some agricultural products and an importer of manufactured goods and agricultural commodities which cannot be grown domestically. As we have seen, copper and nitrates remain the country's most important exports. Extractive industries make up 74–85 per cent of the annual value of exports and provide the government with about one third of its total revenues; foreign trade taxes contribute half the cost of government.[60]

This does not mean, however, that there have been no important changes, for there have been significant alterations in the structure of foreign trade. While at one time nitrate accounted for the largest percentage of exports and copper's share was relatively small, in 1960 more than 50 per cent of all exportations ad valorem was attributable to copper alone, and nitrate represented only one tenth. Also significant is the fact that while agricultural products have remained about 12 per cent of the value of exports, the expansion of Chile's industry has meant that industrial goods climbed from 3 per cent to 11 per cent of the export total in 1953 (an increase of 750 per cent in thirteen years).

Changes on the import side are evidenced by the tendency to increase pastoral, agricultural, and mineral exports, in relation to manufactured goods. In recent years there has taken place a notable decrease in the importation of consumer goods, compensated by an increase in imported capital goods. These changes are, of course, explainable by the greater demand for foreign raw materials by Chilean industry, the growing dependence on imported foodstuffs, and the increasing importance of fuels. Increases on the import side are accompanied by shifts in composition, as shown in the case of raw materials. While steel imports have dipped, and vegetable oils are practically no longer

[60] Instituto de Economia, *Desarrollo económico,* pp. 69–70.

on the list, fuels have risen spectacularly in recent years.[61] Fuels and raw materials represented 48 per cent of the value of all imports in 1954, while capital goods were 25 per cent of the total. These structural shifts are exceedingly important, for they mean that from now on a decrease in foreign exchange will not only result in the reduction of imported consumer goods, but also will become a deterrent to the importation of capital goods on which the expansion and maintenance of Chilean industry depends. The industrialization program is then intimately related to the foreign exchange and trade situations which are further complicated by credit and debt factors.

Very significant changes have also occurred in the geographic distribution of Chile's foreign trade, mainly due to world politics. Before 1914 most Chilean exports went to the United Kingdom and other European countries, but two world wars dislocated the pattern so that her foreign trade, as all Latin American foreign trade, became hemispherically oriented.[62] The United States became the most important country in Chile's foreign trade. At present, over half of its exports usually go to the United States, and over half of its imports come from there. Exports to other countries in the Western Hemisphere fluctuate between 10 and 20 per cent of the total value of all exports, while imports — mainly oil, petroleum, and tropical agricultural commodities — amount to about 20 per cent, but are tending to drop. Peru, Argentina, Brazil, and Venezuela are the chief Latin American suppliers of Chile's import needs. This shift in the direction of trade was made at the expense of Europe, once Chile's principal export market and source of imports. Now Europe accounts for about 20 per cent of Chile's imports and slightly over 30 per cent of her exports.[63]

The United States, then, as Chile's largest single customer and exporter, is basic to Chilean foreign trade. Consequently, favorable trade relations with the United States are fundamental to Chile's industrialization program. The large copper companies are United States-owned and the major market for mineral production is the United States. Perhaps even more important, the United States has become the principal source of credit for private and public investment as well as the chief supplier of modern techniques and equipment.

Although Chilean trade only rarely shows a deficit on paper, in reality sales of exports from the large foreign investments in minerals do not return in foreign exchange the total value of the selling price.

[61] For background materials see Comisión Económica para América Latina de las Naciones Unidas, *Antecedentes sobre el desarrollo de la economía chilena, 1925–1952* (Santiago: Editorial del Pacífico, S.A., 1954).

[62] Butland, *op. cit.*, p. 91.

[63] Instituto de Economía, *Desarrollo económico,* pp. 186, 195.

One quarter and one half of the export value of copper and nitrate, respectively, can safely be deducted from the apparent trade balance [64] Despite increases in the value of exports during the early postwaı period, a greater increase in the price of imports resulted in an unfavorable balance.

The process of economic development in underdeveloped nations tends to produce a chronic deficit in their balance of payments. Chile is a typical case. Its exports do not increase in proportion to the growth of income and population, and its import demands rise with changes in consumer needs. It is necessary to obtain abroad the capital goods needed for industrial development, and agricultural production remains relatively stagnant. Under these circumstances Chile has been forced to resort to credit and direct foreign investment with the logical increase of payments for amortization and service of loans. In general, the largest amounts obtained from foreign sources come from loans rather than direct investments and are applied to finance development programs undertaken by various government agencies.

Foreign trade developments in the 1960's have resulted in a growing trade imbalance. Export earnings grew over the five-year period 1957–1962 at a slightly slower rate than real national product, achieving an overall increase of only about 17 per cent. During the same five-year period, however, imports, due to the high proportion of raw materials and foreign capital goods needed for industrialization, grew much more rapidly, leading to trade deficits in 1960 and 1961. This trend, accompanied by heavy flight of capital, has brought about a critical balance of payments situation. In 1961 the Central Bank's net international monetary reserves decreased by $118 million and by a further $75 million during the first seven months of 1962. In July of that year, the gold and foreign currency reserves of the Bank totaled $51 million as against $257 million in external obligations.[65]

The United States has been the most important source of investment since 1939; this country was prompted by a desire to keep Chile away from Axis influence during World War II and later from Soviet influence, to strengthen the Chilean economy so as to prevent political instability, and to expand her own foreign markets and at the same time assure her supply of strategic materials. Additional sources of capital have been the International Bank for Reconstruction and Development, investments of foreign companies, particularly in mining, which in recent years have amounted to about 50 per cent of the total

[64] Butland, *op. cit.*, p. 93.

[65] Inter-American Development Bank, *Social Progress Trust Fund, Second Annual Report, 1962* (Washington, D.C.: Inter-American Development Bank, 1963), p. 208.

investment.[66] Foreign investments and credits, in millions of dollars, were made up as shown in Table 5.[67]

Totals by countries for the years 1948 and 1953 appear in Table 6.

The importance of foreign trade in the formation of capital in Chile is illustrated by the fact that almost 90 per cent of the total investment in machinery and equipment is imported. As is the case with all underdeveloped economies, Chile's domestic savings and ability to import have not been sufficient to finance expansion of the productive capacity which is the basis of economic development, with the result that the country continues to depend heavily, for this purpose, on foreign trade. Chilean exports, however, have not increased appre-

Table 5

	1937	*1948*	*1953*
Government bonds, securities	434.8	141.9	227.1
Agriculture	—	6.9	4.1
Mining	402.0	383.0	524.1
Industry	17.7	35.0	47.8
Trade	37.0	34.9	36.7
Electricity, railroads and other public utilities	206.7	99.7	72.9
Miscellaneous	—	85.3	100.8
Totals	1,111.12	793.3	1,020.5

Table 6

	1948	*1953*
United States	536.0	813.1
Great Britain	198.4	127.7
International Bank	8.8	22.1
Switzerland	5.0	9.8
France	4.8	9.6
Argentina	29.9	6.7
Germany	0.2	5.0
Belgium	2.2	4.8
Sweden	0.9	2.9
Uruguay	0.0	2.8
Japan	—	2.7
Other countries	7.1	13.3
Totals	793.3	1,020.5

[66] See United Nations Department of Economic and Social Affairs, *Foreign Capital in Latin America* (New York, 1955), pp. 61–67.

[67] Source: Carlos Keller R., "Inversiones extranjeras en Chile," *El Mercurio,* May 11, 1957.

ciably; to satisfy its import needs, then, the country depends almost exclusively on the foreign exchange situation and on foreign credit and investment. With the deterioration of the foreign exchange situation and the consequent difficulties in the balance of payments, there has been increasing need for foreign assistance in the form of direct investments as well as loans. Furthermore, financing the government budget also depends largely on foreign trade. It is easy to understand, then, how fluctuations in the world demand for Chilean basic products have perturbed its economy so deeply.

The Banking System

Apart from commercial banks, Chile's banking system is composed of a Central Bank and a State Bank. The former is in charge of formulating and controlling currency policy, for which it has ample powers. Although legally autonomous in policy matters, because of its board membership it has always followed the course determined by the government and Ministry of Finance. The Central Bank was set up in 1925 with control of currency issue and a currency based on gold. In the depression years, the gold standard, however, had to be abandoned, since it made currency circulation too dependent on the fluctuations of foreign trade. Beginning in 1931, when free convertibility was abandoned, a series of laws, representing a complete reversal of policy, inaugurated an expansionist policy of domestic credits and loans, which was instrumental in Chile's recovery but which also led to a serious inflationary condition. This expansion policy, with minor changes, has continued to this day.

The inflationary trend caused the Bank to assume new functions related to the management of exchange rates and administration of exchange controls. As a result, a very complex system evolved which features the centralization of practically all international transactions under the authority of a single board.[68] In 1953, the Central Bank which had continued functioning under the original act, sometimes even in violation of its statutes, was endowed by a new Organic Law, which gave legal basis for its greater authority over currency matters.

The other key institution in the banking system is the State Bank of Chile which was established in 1953 by consolidating various *cajas* or funds, among which were the National Savings Fund, the Industrial Credit Institute, and the Agrarian Credit Fund. This amalgamation meant the assumption by the new State Bank of such functions as acting as financial and banking agent of all government agencies, stimulating savings, financing, wholly or partly, plans for investment, etc.

[68] Seymour Harris, *Economic Problems of Latin America* (New York: McGraw-Hill Book Co., 1945), p. 315.

There is no question that industrialization, particularly since 1931, has been favorably affected by the protection awarded by a system of multiple exchange rates and the manipulation of exchange control and depreciation, and that, for the most part, credits have been applied to generally productive purposes.[69] At the same time, however, it is equally true that expansion of the money supply is one of the principal causes of the inexorable rise in prices suffered by Chile since that same year, and that this policy translated into unrestricted loans by the Central Bank, as well as commercial institutions, is largely responsible for the inflationary current.

Attempts to introduce changes into the system were unsuccessful in 1946 and 1950, but after 1955 a new economic policy gradually began to emerge. It attempted to control the inflationary process by restricting credit, to hold down wage and salary increases, and to economize governmental expenditures. In 1956 new credit controls were established, complemented for the first time by restrictions in the use of rediscounts, a device which was responsible for much of the inflation. At the same time, the government attempted to finance its fiscal deficit without resorting, as it is legally authorized to do, to the banking system.[70]

The Tax System

The Chilean system for the collection of revenue, in spite of the country's great efforts toward economic development, includes almost no devices to channel productive resources into certain activities, and does not establish any relation between taxes and increases in production or investments. It is basically designed to finance government expenditures, since approximately 90 per cent of public revenues are derived from taxation. It is a highly centralized system; municipal taxes constitute less than 6 per cent of government tax collections, and the provinces have no independent tax revenues at all.

In recent years, however, there has been a tendency to use the taxing system to create incentives for the expansion of agriculture, mining, and industrial activities. Rewards for expansion and investment in the form of tax reductions, are, however, dispersed among numerous laws and regulations, the most significant being the *Nuevo Trato* law for the copper industry which established the principle "Greater production of copper, fewer taxes." From a different angle, the tax system has served, on occasion, as an instrument for decentralization, as in

[69] Butland, *op. cit.*, p. 96.

[70] For a general appraisal see Felipe Herrera, "Política económica y política monetaria," *Panorama económico,* (November 2, 1957), pp. 751–758.

the case of new industries to be set up outside the Santiago area. In 1953 special tax privileges were offered to encourage the industrial development of the northern province of Tarapacá, and Chiloé, Aysén, and Magallanes in the southern tip.

Deceptively simple at first glance, the Chilean tax system until very recently was in fact very complex and lacked effective controls against evasion. The existence of numerous taxes which produce little and are difficult to administer and of many laws establishing special taxes tended to complicate the picture. Since the tendency was to spread the tax burden as much as possible, the same object might be taxed by different laws, creating further administrative problems. For instance, four distinct taxes created by different laws are levied upon a single movie ticket.[71]

Chile's gross national product per capita in 1962 was estimated at $458. In the same year the ratio of tax collections to gross national product was 14 per cent and to total government revenue 93 per cent. This ratio is among the highest in Latin America. According to a report of the Central Bank of Chile, the fiscal burden increased in real terms (on a 1958 basis) from 91.50 escudos per economically active person in 1950 to 163 escudos in 1959 and 137 escudos in 1962.[72] Between 1959 and 1962 while the gross national product increased by only 56 per cent, tax revenues were augmented about 74 per cent. The yield from income and property taxes increased from slightly over 20 per cent to nearly 24 per cent of total fiscal income, while levies on mining company profits decreased from 17 per cent to 12 per cent. Custom duties and sales taxes are the principal indirect taxes: each provides about 20 per cent of the total tax income, while taxes on production yield about 9 per cent.

Taxes in Chile, in general, continue to be mostly regressive in nature and centered upon consumption levies. In 1961, indirect taxes accounted for 53.6 per cent, and direct taxes for 34.4 per cent of all public revenues.[73] Also characteristic of the Chilean system is its heavy reliance on import and export taxes as the two principal sources of revenue. Slightly more than two thirds of tax revenues come from consumption and foreign trade levies and from taxes on profits of the mining companies. In this respect it is possible to distinguish three periods in Chile's economic history. From the beginning of the republic to the War of the Pacific the pattern of the

[71] Instituto de Economía, *Desarrollo económico,* pp. 175–177.

[72] Banco Central de Chile, *Evolución de las finanzas públicas de Chile, 1950–1960* (Santiago, 1963).

[73] Inter-American Development Bank, *Social Progress Trust Fund, Second Annual Report, 1962,* p. 208.

economy was oriented "internally" and productive activities developed evenly. The government, limited in its role, financed its modest budget with proceeds from customs duties and internal taxes. For fifty years after 1880 the economy was "externally" oriented; internal taxes lost all importance and public finance depended entirely on nitrate taxes which produced at least half the total national revenue until the appearance of synthetic nitrate in the world market. The third period, which began with the collapse of foreign trade in the depression years, is marked by a return to an "internally" oriented economic pattern: the policy of industrialization and the search for new internal sources of revenue. The importance of export and import taxes is gradually subsiding although they still are dominant factors in the fiscal picture.[74]

Indirect taxes, as mentioned, generally account for a considerable part of revenues. The variety of these taxes in Chile is remarkable, ranging from the tax on whale hunting, which yields practically nothing, to the sales tax, which alone furnished 14 per cent of the 1955 fiscal budget.[75] Prospects are that indirect taxes will continue to be preferred, because they are productive and easier to administer than other taxes.

The sales tax, formerly paid by the producer or manufacturer, has been imposed since 1954 at the retail level instead. Two principal types of import taxes are utilized, one being specifically levied by customs tariffs on a unity basis (kilo, meter, liter, etc.) and the other ad valorem which is imposed once the goods are admitted into the country. A series of other minor indirect taxes, such as the stamp tax and levies on tobacco, gasoline, alcohol and horse-race tickets, account for relatively small revenue.

Direct taxes fall into two main categories: (1) income taxes levied upon persons and corporations, and (2) property and inheritance taxes. Income taxes were adopted in 1924 and their rates vary according to the source of income. They still constitute a small fraction of the national revenue although their proceeds have increased consistently in the last twenty years as a result of the rise in the number of wage-earners concentrated in urban areas where evasion is more effectively prevented.

Property taxes, which became more significant after 1928, represented only 8.2 per cent of the tax total in 1961. Between 1929 and 1954, taxes on real estate had increased only 12 per cent. The almost insignificant yield as well as the negligible increase in a period of twenty-five years is partly attributable to the irregularity of the system

[74] Instituto de Economía, *Desarrollo económico,* p. 180.
[75] *Ibid.,* p. 181.

Direct Taxes (in millions of escudos 1950)[76]

	1940	*1950*	*1961*
On personal income	1.6	2.1	2.7
On national industry	1.0	1.6	3.7
Property taxes	1.0	1.9	2.0
On mining industry	2.6	2.2	3.3
Totals	6.2	7.8	11.7

of evaluation, appraisals being made at long intervals (from five to ten years). During these periods currency value has changed radically because of the unchecked inflation, with the result that land values have not kept pace with rising prices. The government attempted to correct this situation in 1954 by establishing an automatic reappraisal to be made each year after January 1, 1958.[77] Value readjustment, according to the law, is to be made in each commune, considering the cost of living, costs and value of urban properties, and the general net profits of agriculture for farm lands. Nevertheless, to obtain a fair share of revenue from agricultural lands will always be a difficult problem. Any attempt to increase taxes on land or its production, or to enforce collection effectively would meet with great opposition from the powerful and well-organized agricultural interests.

Taxes paid by the big mining companies should be set in a separate category since a special tax system, applicable to them, has gradually evolved as a way of securing larger revenues for the exchange budget as well as the nation's ordinary budget. In 1954, direct taxes paid by the foreign-owned mining companies, principally copper, accounted for 48 per cent of the total of these taxes. Three factors concurred to make possible this substantial contribution of the big mining companies to Chile's revenue: a law of 1942 which increased profit taxes to 50 per cent, and later to 60 per cent; the price-freezing of copper bought by the Central Bank at 24 cents a pound in 1951 so that the government received the difference between this price and the sales price; and, finally, the recovery of copper prices at the end of World War II.[78]

[76] Adapted from Instituto de Economía, *La economía de Chile,* Vol. II, p. 155.

[77] Instituto de Economía, *Desarrollo económico,* p. 188.

[78] The grave decline of the copper market in 1958, besides other serious repercussions, meant for Chile a loss of $90 million in its exchange budget that year. According to the statistics of the Budget Bureau, copper revenues that year represented only 12.3 per cent of the total revenues, while in 1956 and in 1955, the proportion was 25.2 and 28.1 per cent, respectively. *Ibid.,* p. 188.

In 1961 the Alessandri administration announced plans for sweeping tax reforms subsequently passed by the Congress.[79] At the same time, new regulations were adopted to improve control and collection procedures. A bill changing the land tax, approved in November, 1962, revised the system used to determine land values for tax purposes, modified the tax rates, and broadened the base on which gift and inheritance taxes are assessed. In December, 1962, Congress passed a law empowering the chief executive to reorganize the Internal Revenue Service, the Treasury, the Customs administration, and the Fiscal Defense Council. It is expected that such a reorganization will improve tax collection and combat evasion.[80] New regulations for the Internal Revenue Service were approved in 1963.

Two other bills which included reforms of the income tax and the gift and inheritance tax were also passed in that year. The gift and inheritance tax bill established a flexible rate scale based on the official "living wage" (*sueldo vital*),[81] so as to maintain the progressive feature of the tax against changes in the cost of living and the purchasing power of the currency. In addition to providing for taxation of property located abroad this bill embodied more realistic methods of valuation. Reforms provided by the new income tax bill are to be applied in two stages. First, the present classification by source of income is to be simplified and the Complementary Global Tax (*Impuesto Global Complementario*), a sort of "overall surtax," will be increased. Changes will also be made affecting corporate projects, capital gains, real estate income, dividends, etc.[82] At the end of 1963 the govern-

[79] Fernando Gonzalez R., *La reforma tributaria frente a la economía chilena* (Santiago: Editorial del Pacífico, 1962), contains criticisms of the tax reform bills sent to Congress in August, 1962.

[80] Some of the measures included are: criminal penalties for tax evasion, additional tax inspectors, establishment of an agency for the investigation of tax infringement, decentralization of services, installation of modern equipment, etc.

[81] This minimum "living wage" is based on the cost of living and must be paid to white collar employees of private concerns. In 1961, the *sueldo vital* in Santiago Province was the equivalent of $73 per month.

[82] Prior to the tax reform the categories and rates established under the Chilean tax system were: (1) income derived from real estate: no base tax, but for purposes of the surtax, urban property was presumed to return gross taxable income equal to 7 per cent of its assessed value; (2) income from interests, dividends and annuities, 33 per cent; (3) income received from commercial, industrial, agricultural, and brokerage activities, 25 per cent; (4) income from metallurgical activities and mining (except the large copper companies), 32 per cent; (5) income derived from wages, salaries, bonuses, 3.5 per cent; and (6) income derived from professional activities or lucrative occupations, 15 per cent. Inter-American Development Bank,

ment set new goals involving modification of tax exemptions, of some provisions of the Fiscal Code (*Código Tributario*), and various taxes such as the sales tax, stamp and sealed-paper taxes, and taxes on business transactions.[83]

The outstanding feature in public spending today is the emphasis on the promotion of economic development. While in 1940 state expenditures of this nature were less than one fourth of the total, at the mid-1950's they were one third of such expenditures and development activities had become the most important function of government. A large part of this increase is represented by large disbursements in the form of subsidies to railways and to air, maritime and urban transport. Capital outlays represented nearly one fourth of all government expenditures in 1962, as compared to 22 per cent in 1959 and 16 per cent in 1957. Overall fiscal expenditures increased by 33 per cent (in real terms at 1958 prices) between 1959 and 1962, while capital investments rose by more than 47 per cent, amortization payments decreased, and ordinary costs expanded by less than 35 per cent. During the years 1960–1962 the budgetary deficit, despite the trend of rising revenues, increased by almost 300 per cent as a result of the magnitude of public spending for development (a more than 130 per cent expansion through subsidies to state enterprises, increased investments, payrolls and transfer payments to the private sector). The net deficit (excluding amortizations) in 1962 amounted to 243 million escudos, compared to 155 million in 1961 and 143 million in 1960. These deficits were largely financed internally with loans obtained from the Central Bank and commercial banks, and also from the sale of government bonds.[84]

The table on page 178 also indicates a notable increase in the funds for education but it is necessary to add that a substantial share of the education budget is earmarked for administrative expenses and not for teaching personnel. In addition, subsidies for private educational institutions constitute an important state expenditure. In 1961, 8.4 per cent of all government expenditures was devoted to education.[85]

Social Progress Trust Fund, First Annual Report, 1961 (Washington, D.C.: Inter-American-Development Bank, 1962), p. 65.

[83] Albert Gailord Hart, "Tax Policies in Chile." A paper presented to the Tax Institute Symposium on "Tax Policy and United States Investments in Latin America," (Washington, D.C., 1962), is an incisive analysis of the present tax system and proposed reforms by an economist who was involved in the reform process itself as a United Nations adviser.

[84] Inter-American Development Bank, *Social Progress Trust Fund, Second Annual Report, 1962*, pp. 208–209.

[85] Luis Escobar Cerda, *Organización para el desarrollo económico* (Santiago: Editorial Universitaria, 1961), discusses financing problems of higher education.

Table 7 National Government Expenditures

	1940		1947		1954	
	Thousands of 1950 pesos	*Percentage of total*	*Thousands of 1950 pesos*	*Percentage of total*	*Thousands of 1950 pesos*	*Percentage of total*
I. Promotion of economic development	3,522,886	23.27	5,042,896	26.11	8,497,896	32.90
Transport and communications	1,496,802	9.88	2,076,142	10.75	4,214,993	16.32
Agriculture	273,147	1.80	548,039	2.84	638,316	2.47
Industry, commerce, mining and energy	936,858	6.20	938,800	4.86	1,649,555	6.39
Primary Education	816,079	5.39	1,479,915	7.66	1,995,032	7.72
II. Nonprimary education and sports	673,313	4.44	1,001,058	5.18	2,199,986	8.52
III. Public health and social services	2,836,594	18.73	4,464,125	23.10	5,449,082	21.10
Social prevision and welfare	2,074,112	13.70	3,536,465	18.30	5,219,069	20.21
Housing	762,482	5.03	927,660	4.80	230,013	.89
IV. Internal and external security	3,773,827	24.91	5,569,505	28.82	6,257,644	24.23
Police and courts	1,645,355	10.86	1,762,927	9.12	2,147,026	8.31
National defense	2,128,472	14.05	3,806,578	19.70	4,110,618	15.92
V. Administration, etc.	4,340,720	28.65	3,244,308	16.79	3,422,899	13.25
General administration	835,355	5.51	1,129,280	5.84	2,167,269	8.39
Financial payments	3,302,218	21.80	1,372,224	7.10	1,051,810	4.07
Devolutions	203,147	1.34	316,069	1.64	177,302	0.69
Miscellaneous	—	—	426,735	2.21	26,518	0.10
Totals	15,147,340	100.00	19,321,892	100.00	25,827,507	100.00
Remunerations	5,060,386	33.41	6,988,006	36.17	10,973,386	42.49
Goods and services	1,709,335	11.29	3,130,059	16.20	2,282,481	8.84
Transfers	5,191,162	34.27	5,372,188	27.80	7,808,340	30.23
Investment	3,186,457	21.03	3,831,639	19.83	4,763,300	18.44

From Instituto de Economía, *Desarrollo económica,* p. 192.

The Welfare State

Expenses for health and social services represent more than one fifth of the budget and have shown a considerable increase in the last decade, making it the highest percentage in Latin America. The percentage of total expenditures of the central government devoted to public health was 8.7 in 1961.[86] Expenses for social services amounted to 14.8 per cent in the period 1955–1959. During the three years of this period these expenses absorbed 17.2 of all government expenditures.

This expansion in social services can be explained in terms of the constant unstable conditions of the national economy which have caused wage-earners to press the government for some mechanism to alleviate the relentless currency depreciation. First to resort to this defense mechanism were the workers, but gradually public as well as private employees joined in. With inflation having practically eliminated all possibilities of personal savings, the pressure for an expansion of the existing social prevision system (providing health benefits, accident insurance, old age pensions, unemployment benefits, family allowances and savings funds to practically the whole Chilean population) became strong. To the need for enlarging the social services resulting from population growth and urbanization was added pressure by many groups, principally white-collar workers, interested in having the system serve not only as a defense against inflation but as a source of personal loans for making purchases, etc. Under this new impetus, the Chilean social security structure has emerged and continues to expand, not only keeping pace with the changing social structure of the country, but also as a useful mechanism in a chronically unstable environment. The problem now is that in some ways it has aggravated that very economic instability, the effects of which it sought to ameliorate.[87]

It may be opportune at this time to outline briefly the development and structure of Chile's social welfare system. The transition from a traditional policy to active state participation in social affairs dates from the first Alessandri administration (1920–1925), which laid the basic pattern of social security. Subsequent governments, especially the Popular Front administration in 1938, strengthened and extended its structure, building a system only equalled in Latin America by Uruguay and far ahead of most European countries. Practically all Chileans, as indicated above, are directly or indirectly related to the social prevision system. A compulsory *caja de previsión,* or guild

[86] Inter-American Development Bank, *Social Progress Trust Fund, Third Annual Report, 1963,* p. 176.

[87] Instituto de Economía, *Desarrollo económico,* pp. 194–196.

structure, is the basic unit. Social benefits to workers are administered through some forty-two independent *cajas,* differing substantially in kind and scope. The active population of Chile covered by the existing *cajas* totals more than 1.5 million, that is to say about 80 per cent of the labor force.

There are specific *cajas* for the large public and semiautonomous employee groups as well as for numerous categories of private employees. Fourteen *cajas* can be classed as the major social benefit organizations. The types of benefits offered members of various *cajas* generally include retirement pensions, loans for house construction, funds for debt payments and other purchases, medical and dental care (including hospital costs and paid sick leaves), bonuses for dependents, mortuary bonuses, separation payments, and miscellaneous forms of social assistance. In the public sector, the *Caja de Previsión de la Defensa Nacional* and the *Caja de Empleados Públicos* are the most important, while the *Caja de Previsión de Empleados Particulares* and the *Servicio de Seguro Social* are the most important in the private sector.

A few details of their benefits would furnish a glimpse of how the social benefit mechanism operates in Chile. In general, members of the armed forces retire after thirty years of active service, but voluntary retirement for certain causes after only ten years of service is also possible. The normal full pension is equivalent to the last salary received and is readjusted whenever active salaries are changed. In cases of premature retirement, this pension may be only 40 or 50 per cent of the last salary. A full pension, known as a *montepío,* goes to the widow, children, parents, sisters, or brothers, when an active or retired member of the armed forces dies. This pension is also subject to readjustments. These, with separation payments, dependent bonuses and other benefits, are financed by employee contributions of 8 per cent of their salaries, which, with other incidental deductions, provide 25 per cent of the needs of the *Caja.* The government provides the balance. These benefits are also extended to laborers in various industrial units belonging to the armed forces and to pilots of the Chilean National Airlines (LAN).

Public employees may retire at the age of sixty-two with full pension if they have completed a minimum of ten years of active service in the government. Retirement for certain causes will be granted with fewer years of service and amounts to 50 per cent of the average salary during the last thirty-six months of employment. Full benefits will also be paid after thirty years of contributing to the *Caja* and thirty-five years of public service. These benefits are financed by a 10 per cent deduction from salaries of public and semiautonomous institutions, supplemented by a 5.5 per cent contribution from the government.

In the field of private enterprise, the *Caja de Previsión de Empleados Particulares* is by far the largest. It has branch offices in all the larger cities of Chile and offers a full range of social benefits. Private employees may retire after thirty-five years of service or at the age of sixty-five years. In the former case, they receive a pension amounting to the average of their last sixty monthly salaries. In the latter, pensions amount to 1/35 of the average salary multiplied by the person's years of contribution to the *Caja*. Widows' pensions amount to 50 per cent of the normal retirement pension. In cases of temporary unemployment, the *Caja* pays 75 per cent of the minimum salary plus the bonus for dependents for three to six months. Loans for house construction and purchase can be obtained in accordance with priorities established by the *Caja's* regulations. Interest rates and loan periods are highly attractive in relation to normal facilities available. General loans may also be granted. The extensive benefits provided by this *Caja* are financed with funds provided by employers, approximately 35 per cent of the amount paid as salaries, plus 8 per cent deducted from employees' salaries.

Laborers are provided social benefits through the *Servicio de Seguro Social*. Workers may retire at the age of sixty-five after having completed at least 800 weeks of registered work in the case of men and 500 weeks in the case of women. They receive a minimum pension of 50 per cent of their average salary during the last sixty months of employment, adjusted annually to compensate for inflation. Disability compensations, widows' and orphans' pensions, dependent and mortuary bonuses, plus extensive medical services are also provided. The *Servicio* invests part of its funds in joint housing projects with the *Caja de la Habitación,* selling homes to workers on easy terms on a priority system. It also grants loans to laborers. All these benefits are financed by a contribution of 10 per cent of the salaries of the employers, 5 per cent contributed by the employee and a 5.5 per cent government contribution.

Persons not belonging to any of the *Cajas* enjoy no organized social benefits with the sole exception of a restricted free medical care offered through the *Servicio Nacional de Salud* (National Health Service) which also provides medical attention to the members of the *Cajas*, except those which have their own services. The National Health Service provides beds and treatment for 70 per cent of the population and gives at least part-time employment to over three quarters of Chile's 4,000 physicians.[88] Private welfare institutions provide for the indigent population not eligible for *caja* service.

[88] K. H. Silvert, "Medical Personnel and Facilities in Chile" (Santiago: American Universities Field Staff Letter, April 15, 1957), gives an interesting account of the Service and its relations with physicians.

Caja Income

(Percentages of salaries indicate the employer-employee contributions to several major *cajas.*)

1. Manual workers	37.50	5. National defense	72.43
2. Private employees	45.36	6. Railroad employees	68.49
3. Public employees	47.24	7. Commercial and state bank employees	75.53
4. Municipal employees	37.76	8. Merchant marine workers	57.66

Except for the armed forces' *caja* and that of the bank employees, all *cajas* are under the supervision of a government agency, the *Superintendencia de Seguridad Social.*

The burden to the national economy which this vast and complex system of social welfare represents is becoming more onerous every year. Receipts of the various institutions of social welfare amounted to 21,519 million pesos in 1953 compared with a national total tax collection of 33,189 million pesos that same year.[89] The extremely high number of retired persons is burdensome and represents a significant drain on the nation's manpower. The total number of retired government workers amounted to 65,000 in 1953, which means that there was one retired employee for every two active public servants. Of this number 27,000 came from the armed forces, 17,000 the police force, and 21,000 the civil service. A total of 4,242 million pesos was earmarked for this purpose.[90] Retirement plans based on lower estimates of average life expectancy than in other parts of the world make it possible for the worker to claim benefits on reaching an age lower than that required in other countries. Cases of premature retirement for causes other than age are very common, resulting in a large number of relatively young persons who are assured a life income.[91]

A sharp controversy has existed for some time between a group composed of government officials plus some political leaders who claim that social benefit payments are absorbing as much as 20 per cent of the national income, and others who maintain that the figure is more nearly 8 per cent. A large part of the discrepancy revolves upon the kind of accounting employed to calculate the national income, particularly in the treatment of the capital investments of the various *cajas*. An additional controversy has arisen concerning the lack of uniformity among the various *caja* systems and their incomplete

[89] Carl Hudiczek, *Economía chilena: Rumbos y metas* (Santiago: Editorial del Pacífico, 1956), p. 162.

[90] *Ibid.*, p. 169.

[91] For an account of the cost of social services in fiscal terms, see "Presupuesto fiscal y gastos de seguridad social," *Panorama económico,* XI, No. 183 (January, 1958), p. 6.

coverage of the population. There has been discussion of possible centralization of the whole system into possibly two large social benefit institutions with uniform coverage. Whatever the outcome of such controversies, the fact remains that the expense involved in such an extensive social security and welfare system as demanded by Chilean labor groups is having a disturbing and restrictive effect upon the expansion of capital accumulation which is necessary in order to promote a higher standard of living. Political groups may not agree about this fact, but it is doubtful that any would ever advocate drastic changes or a policy of austerity in what the mass of the Chilean people consider its greatest "social conquest."

Several ad hoc government committees at one time or another during the last decade have been charged with studying reforms in the social welfare system. The last such group, appointed by the Alessandri administration in 1959, submitted its report in 1962. This report included a proposal to simplify and streamline the system. However, nothing had been done in 1964 to introduce any bills in the Congress designed to achieve that purpose, and the social security system remained untouched.[92]

The Military Establishment and the Bureaucracy

The table on page 178 indicates that expenditures for internal and external security have experienced a slight increase since 1940. Military establishments (armed forces and police) cost Chile more than 20 per cent of its total national expenditures, a situation not uncommon to Latin America. Military and police personnel account for 30 per cent of the body of persons in public service. The high cost of such a military apparatus is a major drain on the country's foreign exchange resources, since all purchases of military equipment are made abroad. But regardless of how obvious the need for economy may be here, the possibilities of reducing these expenditures are remote, to say the least, when one considers that the Chilean military, although not an active participant, is a veto group in national politics.

As regards administrative expenditures the table reflects a notable increase in public personnel from 71,947 to 116,191 in the period 1940–1955. This increase of the bureaucracy (60 per cent) is even more disproportionate, since the country's active population expanded at a rate of 23.5 per cent during the same period. One of its chief causes is, undoubtedly, the incapacity of the private sector, resulting from the low level of capital accumulation, to absorb the enlargement of the economically active population.[93] Another is the increasing share of responsibilities by the government in the sphere of economic

[92] Instituto de Economía, *La economía de Chile,* pp. 166–167.
[93] Instituto de Economía, *Desarrollo económico,* p. 203.

activity. This disproportionate size of the bureaucracy, with its adverse effect on the national economy, and the failure to maintain high standards of selection and efficiency in the civil service are presently the objects of much criticism. However, economy as well as standard improvement appears to be insufficiently explored to date. Among political groups, the Christian Democrats, more than any other, have been concerned with this problem, insisting upon the urgent necessity of a thorough reorganization and modernization of Chile's public administration.

The Housing Problem

Housing is another socio-economic problem which besets Chile and therefore always elicits government interest. As early as 1908, a Council on Workmen's Housing was established and followed by other institutions in subsequent years. In 1943 the *Caja de la Habitación* (Housing Fund) was created as an independent agency in charge of housing. Five years later, the "Pereira Law," which is still in effect, was passed to encourage low-cost housing construction. In 1953, the Housing Fund and the Reconstruction Corporation were combined into a new Housing Corporation, *Corporación de la Vivienda* (CORVI). This corporation's chief source of funds comes from annual budgetary appropriations, 5 per cent of the net profits of industrial, mining, commercial, and agricultural enterprises, and an annual percentage of the surpluses of the Social Security Service and welfare institutions. Loans granted by CORVI are protected against inflation by provisions which permit adjustment of payments to fluctuations in the wage and salary index. Banks, insurance companies, corporations, and semi-governmental institutions must set aside for low-cost housing construction a minimum of 20 per cent of the portion of their capital reserve invested in property to be leased.[94]

In spite of the fact that the pace of low-income housing construction has accelerated notably since 1959, CORVI estimates made following the severe earthquakes of 1960 indicated that Chilean housing shortage was approximately 550,000 units. This deficit was expected to increase in the following years at the rate of 38,000 units a year, taking into consideration homes needed for new families and replacement of old units.

The Housing Corporation has greatly expanded its activities since the 1960 Act of Bogotá and the launching of the Alliance for Progress. In addition, a system of private savings and loan associations under the supervision of a Central Savings and Loan Fund (*Caja Central de Ahorros y Préstamos*) which insures their deposits and exercises redis-

[94] Inter-American Development Bank, *Social Progress Trust Fund, First Annual Report, 1961,* p. 69.

count functions was established in 1960. By the end of 1963 more than 80,000 families had savings accounts in 22 associations operating in various parts of the country.[95]

The Ten-Year Development Plan prepared in 1961 envisaged construction of 200,000 new housing units over a period of five years, the program to be carried out by CORVI and the savings and loan associations. In 1962 more than 42,000 new dwellings were completed, a rate of construction greater than the average required to meet the initial five-year goal. However, it must be noted that generally efforts have benefited the lower-middle income groups rather than the members of the lowest economic strata, who are unable to pay for homes even when assisted by loans at low interest rates.

The serious nature of Chile's housing problems and its social and political effects is underscored by the prevalence in all cities, but particularly Santiago, of *poblaciones callampas* (mushroom towns), slum areas made up of shacks which have grown almost overnight without authorization or control. Anyone who has seen these *callampas* is not likely to forget their outrageous squalor. It is easy to understand how such slum areas can be ideal breeding ground for political extremism. Also indicative of the seriousness of this problem is the fact that although housing investments are typical among slow-return investments, the Ten-Year Plan contemplates devoting to housing about 20 per cent of all public investment from 1961 through 1970. Even this intensive concentration is expected to do no more than keep the housing deficit from mounting in the face of population growth.[96]

The Inflationary Spiral

In Chile, inflation has been a fact of life for over eighty years and an acute and serious problem for the last two decades. Whereas the cost of living between 1939 and 1950 rose about six times, the increase between the latter year and 1956 was six times more, making it about 35 times higher than it was in the prewar years. Between 1950 and 1958 prices increased fifteen fold, and the money supply expanded seventeen fold.[97] While the cost of living index, based on an arbitrary 100 for 1940 had risen to over 3,000 in 1957 the real income of the Chilean wage-earner, his purchasing power, had risen only 40 per cent since 1940. The extent of Chilean inflation can be gathered from

[95] Inter-American Development Bank, *Social Progress Trust Fund, Third Annual Report, 1963,* p. 185.

[96] *Ibid.,* p. 185.

[97] On the subject of Chilean inflation there is abundant literature. A few publications are: Instituto de Economía de la Universidad de Chile, *Chile y la inflación* (Santiago, 1956); Jorge Alessandri, *La verdadera situación económica y social de Chile en la actualidad* (Santiago: Confederación de la Producción y el Comercio, 1955); United Nations Economic Com-

the fact that in the period 1952–1957 the price of rice went up from 22 to 78 pesos a kilogram, sugar from 8 to 85 pesos, meat from 50 to 500 pesos, and an ordinary man's suit from 3,000 to 21,000 pesos. These figures become more meaningful after considering salary levels: an unskilled worker in 1957 averaged 15,000 pesos monthly, which equaled about $24 at that year's rate of exchange. A white-collar employee averaged 50,000 pesos.[98]

To generalize about the basic causes of Chilean inflation is practically impossible for, as it has been said, analyzing these causes is like inquiring about the chicken and egg.[99] In general, however, explanations tend to be based on two different approaches, one emphasizing what are called "structural factors," and the other emphasizing the financial manifestations of inflation.[100] Those belonging to the so-called "structuralist" school point to the slow development of the national income and blame inflation on the struggle between groups in society to obtain a larger share of this income. According to them, the exiguous growth exhibited by the national income is due to the influence of several factors. Effects of the Great Depression years were so profound the country has not yet recovered from the damage. Foreign trade has declined in comparison with pre-depression times, originating difficulties in the supply of raw materials and capital goods. Inefficient methods of production and an anachronistic land-tenure system are responsible for the failure of agricultural production to keep up

---

mission for Latin America, "La inflación y la política anti-inflacionista," in *Estudio económico de América Latina, 1957* (Santiago: CEPAL, 1958), 216–229; David Felix, "Structural Imbalances, Social Conflict and Inflation," *Economic Development and Cultural Change,* VIII, No. 2 (January, 1960); Universidad de Chile, Instituto de Economía, *La economía de Chile en el período 1950–1963* (Santiago: Instituto de Economía, 1963), pp. 42–88; Jorge Ahumada, *En vez de la miseria* (Santiago: Editorial del Pacífico, 1958), pp. 119–158; Aníbal Pinto, *Chile: un caso de desarrollo frustrado* (Santiago: Editorial Universitaria, 1959) and *Ni estabilidad ni desarrollo* (Santiago: Editorial Universitaria, 1960); Max Nolff, Felipe Herrera, and others, *La inflación: naturaleza y problemas* (Santiago, 1954); Osvaldo Sunkel, "La inflación chilena: un enfoque heterodoxo," *El Trimestre Económico,* Mexico, No. 100 (October–December), 1958, pp. 97–130; Francis H. Schott, "Inflation and Stabilization Efforts in Chile, 1953–1958," *Inter-American Economic Affairs* (Winter 1959), pp. 7–20; *Panorama Económico,* the excellent Santiago semimonthly has published numerous articles dealing with inflation. Among recent contributions is a brilliant essay in Albert O. Hirschman, *Journey Toward Progress* (New York: The Twentieth Century Fund, 1963), pp. 161–223.

98 Tad Szulc, "Chile's Nightmare — Case Study of Inflation," *The New York Times Magazine,* October 13, 1957.

99 K. H. Silvert, "Diagnosticians and Inflation" (Santiago: American Universities Field Staff Letter, November 22, 1956), p. 1.

100 Instituto de Economía, *Desarrollo económico,* pp. 17–18.

with population growth. The rigidity of public expenditures and heavy subordination for revenues on an ever-fluctuating income from exports have also contributed, according to this analysis, in upsetting the national budget. Then, since productivity is low, pressure from employers, workers and government begins to build up, the less favored elements attempting to keep their incomes in line. Gradually each group evolves its own defensive system against the pressures of the other. For some, a credit and pricing mechanism is the weapon; for others automatic annual rises of wages and salaries serve the purpose, with the resulting wage and salary inflationary spiral of prices. This explanation, however, fails to take into account the accumulative character of inflation.[101]

The second set of explanations, ascribed to the so-called "monetarists," gives preferential attention to financial factors, stresses the maladjustment between the expansion of currency and the development of production of goods and services, establishing a cause and effect relationship between currency expansion and price increase. The former, of course, would be, in this theory, intimately related to matters such as fiscal deficits, and some institutional mechanisms.[102] Most of the prescriptions recommended to cure Chile's major illness are based chiefly on this type of thinking, and they all advise, in general, a more rational tax policy, budget cutbacks, and restrictions on prices and credit.

In further simplification it may be said that for the "structuralists" inflation is a natural accompaniment of growth and cannot be curbed through monetary or fiscal means without provoking stagnation. "Monetarists," on the other hand, hold that inflation has ceased to promote development and that it must be stopped quickly before it degenerates into explosive tensions. Both sets of explanations leave many questions unanswered; equally unsatisfactory are the common single-cause explanations, which simplify the problem by saying it is the case of a nation which has been living beyond its means, that stagnation of Chilean agriculture is the key, or that the country's burdensome program of social legislation is the culprit. Obviously, just as Chilean inflation is not unique in the world, its causes are also many and of sundry nature. As in all inflationary processes, Chile's case combines effects of "structural" factors with others of accumulative character which, once set in motion, act independently of the original factors. It even contains elements which are psychosomatic, as evidenced by the tendency since 1955 to spend according to ex-

[101] See the essays by Roberto de Oliveira Campos, Joseph Grunwald, and David Felix in Albert O. Hirschman (ed.), *Latin American Issues* (New York: The Twentieth Century Fund, 1961).

[102] Instituto de Economía, *Desarrollo económico,* p. 18.

pected rather than actual income caused by the automatic-raise system, and also by the heavy hoarding of goods in expectation of new price rises.

The strictly financial line of argument maintains that Chile was not immune to inflation before 1939 and has been experiencing it since the last century, when new elements swept into power with the Popular Front government and created demands by the lower economic groups that accelerated the inflationary spiral. The country embarked on a costly program of social legislation. In order to pay for it the government was thrown into continuous deficits and forced to print more money, thus depreciating the currency. Wages began to climb; all the complex mechanism of credit and price changes appeared; and the spiral rose. Whether all this benefited those lower economic groups is questionable, for statistics show that the share of wages in the national income fell from 27 to 21 per cent between 1940 and 1953, even though the percentage of wage-earners in the active population remained constant at 57 per cent. Significantly, total salaries at the same time increased 135 per cent, the income of the self-employed 100 per cent, and profits and dividends over 90 per cent.[103]

With the softening of the Chilean peso for immediate fiscal reasons, the postwar years brought a definite simultaneous worsening of the situation because neither agriculture nor industry was able to supply what an expanding economy and a growing population required. Agriculture failed to raise production per capita; in the five-year period 1948–1953, the population increased by 10 per cent and agricultural production by only 2 per cent.[104] Food production continued to fall off, bringing new inflationary increases. The failure to increase productivity forced Chile to depend on costly imports for many key foods.

In industry, old-fashioned techniques and lack of capitalization resulted in scarce and expensive products. The rise in prices inhibited capital investment by making potential creditors reluctant to invest quickly depreciating money in the expansion of plants when returns were greater in import transactions or in traditionally preferred real estate. As the inflationary balloon rose, the proportion of the gross national product invested in fixed capital decreased. Central Bank figures indicate that gross national capitalization is annually about 2.5 per cent of the gross national product, after deductions for replacement of machinery and equipment, and allowances for population increase are made. Nearly half of this amount is channeled through government undertakings. Construction work, exclusive of government or semigovernment projects, accounts for a large amount of the total gross investment. Insufficient capitalization is, in the opinion of

[103] Silvert, "Diagnosticians and Inflation," p. 2.
[104] *Ibid.*, p. 2.

many Chileans, the key element in a vicious circle: less is produced for lack of adequate capital investment, production decreases, and, consequently, capitalization becomes more difficult. Socially speaking, inflation has affected the pattern of saving and spending in a way that profoundly discourages capital accumulation within the country. This is illustrated by the case of bank savings which benefit those persons who secure them as bank loans, but which are returned to the owners in depreciated form. Despite the present system of bonuses and readjustments, the case of insurance policies is similar. Large sums from the compulsory savings of the *caja* system have been channeled into home-building loans, to the benefit of roughly only 10 per cent of the contributors. Those who acquire a home through the *caja* system pay for it in money whose value is constantly decreasing, while 90 per cent of retired members are receiving fixed small pensions. Even after readjustments are irregularly paid by the government, these pensions are in most cases insufficient to meet the cost of living.[105] This explains in part why the proportion of savings and gross investment to the gross national income has not changed in the last 15 years, although profits have risen 70 per cent. It also accounts for the high propensity to consume among those profit-sharing persons who have spent 90 per cent of their net income after taxes and saved only 10 per cent.[106] To be sure, historical and traditional factors affect the pattern of saving, but inflationary pressures have strengthened the tendency. Even if investment by private persons partly relieved the government from its heavy burden for direct capital expenditures, the foreign exchange deficiency would remain a critical factor. The huge sums being spent by the government on development programs in the fields of steel, petroleum, electric power, etc., have been extremely beneficial in that they have made it possible to replace imports, thereby saving foreign exchange; but the new national products are not capable of augmenting the available supplies of exchange. This is important in view of the fact that the annual exchange budget is estimated at approximately $400 million.[107]

As in most underdeveloped countries, the problem of capital accumulation in Chile is made more difficult by intense popular pressure for a higher standard of living. Workers cannot be made to produce under previous conditions or for the wages of the past; they demand additional benefits, such as dependent bonuses, public housing, and the like. A Chilean writer once gave a blunt diagnosis: "We want to consume as a civilized people while we produce as barbarians." An-

[105] José M. Navasal, "La capitalización insuficiente: raíz profunda de los problemas nacionales," *El Mercurio,* May 19, 1957.
[106] Silvert, "Diagnosticians and Inflation," p. 3.
[107] *Ibid.*, p. 3.

other Chilean, former President Dávila, claimed that the economic problems of Chile as well as those of the rest of Latin America boiled down to the sharp and sometimes disproportionate rise in living standards experienced in this century.

Remedies proposed are as numerous as diagnoses, but they contain some common ingredients: holding the line on salaries and wages, stamping out tax evasion, steady investment of domestic capital, restrictions of credit, and austerity in public expenditures — particularly for the military, which consumes nearly 30 per cent of the budget.

A United States firm of business consultants was employed by the Chilean government in 1955 to draft an anti-inflation program. The Klein-Saks Mission felt that price controls would be unenforceable and argued that the way to slow down inflation was to create a healthy economic climate. To accomplish this it proposed measures designed to make Chile live within its means, by a drastic cutback in governmental expenditures. It suggested that monopolistic practices be abandoned, and that the free play of competition be allowed to raise productivity and lower prices. Tax evasion by the well-to-do must be eradicated, thus more fairly distributing the burden of saving the country from inflation. Chilean capitalists should be persuaded of the importance of eliminating tax evasion in their own economy.[108] These measures were only partially successful.[109] Chile has been assisted in great measure by intergovernmental loans, by the International Bank for Reconstruction and Development, and by a steady flow of private United States capital. By 1957 the rate at which inflation was progressing had been arrested. The inflationary spiral was not stopped, but it was materially slowed down. Whereas the cost of living in 1955 rose 88 per cent, the increase in 1956 was only 38 per cent and in 1957 17 per cent, but the problem was far from being solved, and the government, in essence, was only buying time.

Early in 1956 two measures were adopted to combat inflation: restriction of credit and price stabilization together with a reduction of the automatic raises of salaries and wages. Of course, both were directed to arrest the inflationary spiral rather than solve the basic causes

[108] For the mission's report see: *El programa de estabilización de la economía chilena y el trabajo de la misión Klein-Saks* (Santiago: Editorial Universitaria, 1958).

[109] A good case can be made by those who claim that the technical contributions of the Klein-Saks mission were minimal and that actually its real accomplishment was a political one. Most Chilean technicians had already agreed on the technical measures needed to stem inflation and before the coming of the mission had advocated such measures. The mission suggested only a few new devices. On the other hand, the Klein-Saks group served a useful political role as a binding agent for the newly emerging and extremely loose coalition of the Ibáñez forces with the two traditional right-wing parties (Conservatives and Liberals).

of the phenomenon, and both involved certain dangers. A third measure, which freed foreign exchange from previous controls, forced importers to make substantial cash deposits prior to placing their orders.

Until January, 1956, workers were legally entitled to an automatic annual raise equivalent to 100 per cent of the increase in the cost of living during the previous year. In that year, Law 12,006 established the so-called freezing of prices, salaries and wages. This law did not create a rigid system of price control, actually freezing prices, but simply attempted to maintain the current price level, at the same time authorizing increases justifiable by higher costs, and fixing the prices of certain articles of prime necessity. The law did not freeze salaries and wages either but established raises equivalent to 50 per cent of the increase in the cost of living in 1955 and the first fortnight of 1956. While raises for government workers were limited to no more than 50 per cent and not less than 48 per cent of the cost of living increase in that period of time, the law imposed no such restrictions on the salaries of private employees.

In spite of the apparent lack of teeth in this legislation, in practice it had some effect. In 1957, the across-the-board wage increase was just over 30 per cent, while the overall rise in the cost of living in 1956 had been cut to 37 per cent from 88 per cent in the previous year.[110] Along with the wage restrictions, tighter regulations on bank credit were imposed and the foreign exchange system was revamped. These measures were supported by financial assistance ($75 million) from the International Monetary Fund and from United States agencies.

Prices rose only 17 per cent during 1957, but in 1958 the stabilization program began to falter and the rate of inflation climbed back to 33 per cent. Even worse, there occurred a drop in the rate of economic expansion and per capita income actually declined. Disappointment over the performance of the Chilean economy in 1956–1958 and hostility to the Klein-Saks mission resulted in the great majority of the country's economists joining the "structuralist" school. This group of economists was to have a significant effect on policy-making in the early 1960's when institutional innovations such as land and tax reform began to be pushed vigorously.

New attempts at stabilization were launched in 1959. President Alessandri, in tacit alliance with the Radical Party, proceeded after his 1958 electoral victory to push a new program of economic expansion and stabilization. The system of credit controls was strengthened, a new currency unit (one escudo = 1,000 old pesos) established, and the exchange system was definitely unified. The new stabilization measures were relatively successful. For the first time

[110] Szulc, *op. cit.*, p. 41.

in over twenty years prices virtually stopped rising in August, 1959. Wage and salary increases were held to between 10 and 20 per cent early in 1960, and prices continued fairly stable throughout that year despite the economic disruption resulting from severe earthquakes. On the other hand, industrial production, after making a good beginning toward recovery in 1959, sagged again in 1960. Hence, it could be claimed, as Hirschman does, "that, just as in 1956–57, stability was again being bought at the price of development.[111]

By mid-1961 inflationary pressures increased again and were further accompanied by an accentuated capital flight. The cost of living climbed by more than 27 per cent in the course of 1962. The level of consumer prices in Santiago went up 28 per cent during that year and another 45 per cent in 1963.[112] Toward the end of 1962, the government applied to the International Monetary Fund for a one-year 40-million-dollar loan, under the terms of which a new stabilization program was to be put into effect in January, 1963.

The effects of inflation upon the Chilean society and body politic are incalculable. The inflationary process is causing important alterations in the political and economic patterns. As one writer puts it: "persistent inflation will arouse or strengthen demands for basic social and economic reforms; and a society that is unable to make the relatively small intergroup adjustments required to end inflation is likely to find itself faced with strong and persuasive demands for much more fundamental social changes."[113] The Chilean laboring mass, historically better off than its counterpart in other Latin American countries, is now being forced into social and economic regression and resents it bitterly. The middle class, like the workers, is also suffering from inflation and the current anti-inflationary measures. Since as a key consumer of domestic and imported goods this social group plays the most important role in the economic life of the nation, its well-being is essential to the country's future industrial development. Inflation has seriously affected, if not arrested, the healthy evolvement of this middle class upon which Chile's political and economic stability so heavily depends. A new class of Chilean wealth has emerged, composed of importers and exporters who have profited through foreign trade transactions and speculators who have managed

[111] Hirschman, *op. cit.*, p. 219.

[112] Inter-American Development Bank, *Social Progress Trust Fund, Third Annual Report, 1963*, p. 178.

[113] Hirschman, *op. cit.*, p. 216. However, this author suggests elsewhere in this book that in the Chilean case inflation may have provided the country with additional room for social maneuvering during a critical stage of its development by permitting the maintenance of a militant stance on the part of contending groups in the society while playing a game in which everybody wins sham victories.

to build considerable fortunes in the near chaos of the situation. There are others who have been lulled into a false sense of prosperity by the constant influx of money, although their basic material position has not really been bettered.[114] A bright note in this otherwise dismal picture is the remarkable resilience and inherent dynamism of the Chilean population, particularly its middle class, which has learned to live with its problems.

The Ten-Year Development Plan

As suggested above, the high rate of inflation and the series of restrictive measures applied by the government to reduce inflation resulted in economic stalemate and stagnation. In January, 1961, in order to solve this problem as well as to establish a basis for economic and social reform, the government initiated a national development plan, the Ten Year 1961–1970 Economic Development Program, which had been prepared by CORFO. This program envisages the investment of the equivalent of $10 billion and a gradual increase in the rate of capital formation from 10 per cent by 1970. The program is aimed at achieving an annual GNP growth rate of 5.5 per cent which would mean a 3 per cent per capita increase. It contemplates a 63 per cent increase in farm production, 70 per cent in mining production, 76 per cent in industrial output, and 97 per cent in electric power. Financing for the Plan would come from increased public and private savings, complemented by some external capital. About 45 per cent of the required capital outlay is expected to come from the private sector and 55 per cent from the public sector. National savings will have to triple the present level and external funds amounting to $1.98 billion will have to be obtained if established goals are to be attained.

Subsequently approved by the Committee of Nine of the Organization of American States, in accordance with the procedures of the Punta del Este Charter and of the Alliance for Progress, the Ten-Year Plan was put into effect in 1961. A Committee for Economic Programming and Reconstruction (*Comité de Programación Económica y Reconstrucción,* COPERE) composed of cabinet members and other top economic officials is charged with advising the government on development studies and projects, and with coordinating and supervising the implementation of approved programs. Various public and private organizations are also conducting research aimed at perfecting the Ten-Year Plan. The second half of the program (1966–1970) is to be revised as results of this research become available.[115]

[114] Silvert, "Diagnosticians and Inflation," p. 4.

[115] Inter-American Development Bank, *Social Progress Trust Fund, Third Annual Report, 1963,* p. 181.

It is too early to evaluate results of the Ten-Year Plan. Institutional reforms have barely started and progress in financing the Plan has been slowed by the failure of the economy to generate the required volume of savings. The gross domestic product increased at the same general rate contemplated in the program during 1961 and 1962, but the disappointing progress in agriculture, mining, and manufacturing provides a negative aspect. The only significant expansion occurred in construction, and public services.[116]

Politics and Economic Development

It is hoped that the preceding sections have convincingly shown how difficult it would be to analyze the process of Chile's political development without some reference to the socio-economic context, for herein lie the roots of most current Chilean political problems. The prolonged economic depression, characterized by the decline of industrial output and mounting unemployment, was threatening by 1964 to break up the delicately balanced coalition of Center and Right, which until then had safeguarded the status quo. This danger was first clearly realized by the near victory of the Socialist-Communist coalition in the 1958 election and its impressive gains in subsequent congressional elections. President Alessandri's austerity program of stabilization failed to cure the general social and economic malaise. After this failure, a new balance between the two objectives of stability and growth was sought, and Alessandri's cabinet of *gerentes* (business executives) again turned to the politicians. Some revival of industrial production occurred, but the negligible increase in employment, the increased inflation, and the rapid rise of food prices once again brought the wage-salary adjustment conflict to the political stage.[117] That conflict in time would break the Rightist-Radical alliance.

The most obvious conclusion derived from the preceding sketch of Chile's contemporary economic pattern is that the country has embarked upon an economically nationalistic program of industrialization which is the result of a national consensus of the necessity for economic elaboration. But the lack of socio-economic coalescence in the structure of society, in turn reflected in a great diversity of organized political groups, is a typical feature of Chilean life. In the short run, the present administration may be able to reduce the economy's structured imbalances and ease social tension for a time, but in the long run there is little doubt that if Chile is ever going to attain a viable and dynamic economy it will depend principally on whether she can create a substantial balance between social means and

[116] *Ibid.*, p. 181.

[117] Adamantios Pepelasis, Leon Mears, and Irma Adelman, *Economic Development: Analysis and Case Studies* (New York: Harper & Brothers, 1961), p. 322.

social ends, something which has thus far been lacking. This situation has been accurately described in these words:

> Rights and duties have not been equalized nor are they equally felt along the social scale, for there are vast differences of productive capacity, political power and social acceptability among the various layers of society. The government must act in the interest of socio-economic sectors, some of which are semi-feudal, others of which may demand governmental intervention in the economic structure for a variety of reasons, and still others of which want an internal policy of *laissez-faire,* that cowers behind a high tariff wall. No organized groups of importance press for a traditional Liberal political-economic policy. While the Chilean *fundo,* or *hacienda,* still makes use of a labor force strongly tied to the soil, the Chilean coal miner is a member of a vertical union and is conversant with all standard forms of political militancy, choosing his leaders among such groups as the Christian Socialists, Communists or Anarchists.[118]

In spite of these divisions and party fragmentation, there do exist accords, the most important of which are related to economic policies. To quote from the same source, "Chilean politicians may argue as to which side of the economic street should be occupied, but not whether the route itself is the correct one."[119]

The idea of active state participation in the industrial and social welfare of the republic dates back to the first government not dominated by the Conservatives, the Alessandri government in the early 1920's, although there were evidences of interventionism even before the political retreat of the rightist forces. It was then that the first symptoms of a conflict between the institutional structure and national economic development appeared. Under the leadership of Alessandri, new juridical institutions concerning social welfare and the economic machine were forged in response to the amorphous but pressing popular desires for improvement. Had it been possible then to give strong impetus to Chile's economic development, there would have been no problem. But the national product lagged behind, and the country began to carry the burden of a program of social benefits which was disproportionate to its financial means. The rudimentary beginnings of an economic development program crumbled during the world crisis of 1930. By 1938, however, an impressive institutional structure for economic development had been built. A momentous event in this institutional development, which thereby received new impetus, was the creation in 1939 of the *Corporación de Fomento de la Producción*

118 K. H. Silvert, "A Political-Economic Sketch of Chilean History from 1879." (Santiago: American Universities Field Staff, January 27, 1957), p. 2.

119 *Ibid.*, p. 2.

(CORFO) under the Popular Front government. For the first time the state took the initiative in economic activities other than its traditional ones to channel its efforts directly toward industrial development. With acceptance of CORFO came agreement throughout all sections of the population that Chile's problems required broad government planning.

Consensus had been reached years before on the question of political democracy when the landed gentry, then no longer masters of the destiny of the nation, acquiesced in the matter because they could not prevent the rise of competing groups and because mere political participation by these groups did not essentially endanger their social and economic status. When the demand for governmental programs of social service and labor legislation became strong, consent was achieved again and the rightist forces acquiesced in these programs in return for assurances that there would be no attempts to tax the land or to destroy the *hacienda* system. Now, all parties again were agreeing on the desirability of economic nationalism and state interventionism, in some degree or another.[120]

There are many explanations to this agreement. All groups realize that given the lack of available capital, the desire for economic expansion cannot possibly be achieved without government investments. For historical and traditional reasons, there exists no particular emotional apprehension against state intervention among most Chileans. A large number of those who control the largest industrial enterprises started their careers as government officials and therefore have knowledge and appreciation of the state's role in economic development. Most groups realistically, although perhaps unwittingly in some cases, accept the need of outside assistance and with it the governmental intervention that permits the official guarantees generally required for intergovernmental or international loans. Lastly, both extremes of the political spectrum are characteristically malleable and the Right especially has a long tradition of adaptability. The Chilean political atmosphere is traditionally one of sobriety and austerity, and the country is proud of its political sophistication and tolerance. There is rarely any name-calling or mud-slinging in the political arena, and as a small country, its political leaders are often related by personal ties.[121]

The question now, however, it not the transition from a traditional policy to a new one, for the change desired has already taken place and

[120] The above does not necessarily mean that opposition is lacking. An example of adverse opinion is Luis Correa Prieto, *Aspectos negativos de la intervención económica,* (Santiago: Zig-Zag, 1955).

[121] *Ibid.,* p. 19. Professor Silvert advances most of these reasons as applicable to the specific case of the creation of the *Corporación.* There is no reason, however, why these statements could not apply to the general agreement about economic development.

state-directed industrialization has been under way for twenty years. The issues today concern the question of organization and the problem of coping with new changes brought by economic expansion. Contemporary political debate concerns real policy differences about the means of expanding what already exists and of providing solutions to the fundamental public problems — the high cost of living and inflation — which are continuously widening the distance between the segments of society. The solution may require far-reaching modifications of the institutional structure,[122] and political consent may collapse precisely on the question of economic democracy. This was the significance of the presidential elections of 1964. The roots of the national economic problem, in the opinion of many, lie in the necessity of making the sacrifice of restricting living standards without restricting political democracy.

Party competition within the frame of political democracy seems to be failing to meet the demands of politically important segments of the population, and new lines of consent, involving deep changes, will have to be found by the parties if the governmental process based on party government is to function. The inability of organized political groups to meet these demands led a frustrated and angry electorate to turn its back to the parties in 1952 and to return General Ibáñez to power in hopes that a paternalistic authoritarianism would succeed where coalition politics of the Left had failed. This popular discontent was also responsible for the senseless Santiago and Valparaíso riots of April, 1957, in which nearly thirty persons were killed and one hundred injured. In the 1960's Chile is at a crucial point in her economic and political development, and the present situation cannot long continue before producing serious social unrest. After all, it is often said with a certain justice, that the half of Chile represented by groups which are able to defend themselves against the effects of inflation has been living off the other half which has been unable to so protect itself.

The 1952 election of a *passé* charismatic leader, like Ibáñez, in a country of such temperate political moods as Chile was the counsel of desperation, and can only be explained as a manifestation of the people's desire for far-reaching and comprehensive programs to relieve inflationary pressures which had been beyond the capacity of the parties. The Ibáñez administration proved to be an even greater disappointment. Instead of austerity, probity, and firm handling which

[122] "La acción anti-inflacionista no es patrimonio de un gobierno o partido; es deber de todos los ciudadanos," *El Mercurio,* June 2, 1937. This report of a lecture given by René Silva Espejo on the subject "Inflation and Juridical Normality" expounds the need for legal reforms to combat inflation.

Chileans had sought in the former "strong man," the country found itself in the hands of a pilfering, nepotic, inefficient, weak and ineffectual government which led it to near economic chaos. The Ibáñez administration's great weakness, during the first years of its term, was the absence of support of organized political forces. Counting himself above politics, Ibáñez, accompanied by a political brigade of strange bedfellows with contradictory ideologies, sporadically applied improvised laws and methods without any preconceived or coherent plan of action. In the early years of the administration a legislative deluge, inspired by the Socialist faction which then supported the government, resulted in widespread interventionist practices in all parts of the economic machine. At the same time what could be termed the great offensive for political spoils by Ibáñez's own Agrarian Labor Party resulted in an enlargement of the bureaucratic apparatus. These two factors had damaging effects on the administration's finances and worsened inflationary pressures.

As could be expected, the hybrid political conglomeration soon broke down, and its most important components went to the opposition. For almost two years the regime floundered in a parliamentary vacuum, faced with serious resistance and conflicts. A series of local and general strikes in 1955 and 1956 gravely threatened the political stability of the country.[123] Under these conditions, the almost miraculous survival of the administration was due to two circumstances: Ibáñez' nonpartisanship which permitted ministerial changes otherwise improbable, and his military status which assured the loyalty of the armed forces. However, when confusion was reaching its peak, the regime made a desperate appeal to the rightist forces. With parliamentary assistance and counsel of the Conservative and Liberal parties, an economic policy emerged to deal with inflation by essentially attempting to remove government restrictions and allowing market adjustments to create an area of stable interplay. In a sense, the policy was late in arriving, for three years of experimentation and disconnected measures had played havoc with the economy. Some serious differences developed later between the administration and the political groups which had responded to its call. To financial deterioriation was added political isolation which further weakened the government's prestige. The Ibáñez regime survived its two remaining years (1957–1958) amidst the most dangerous instability in the history of the country.

Inflation and the administration's financial program became the only issues in the parliamentary elections of 1957. Electoral results clearly indicated that the mood of the people had swung again towards the

[123] For an account of the effects of frequent strikes in Chile's economic life, see Moisés Poblete Troncoso, "Las huelgas y el progreso económico-social," *El Mercurio,* October 15, 1956, p. 3.

major established political groups. The Radical Party, forsaken in 1952, again became a powerful force; the new and dynamic Christian Democrats made an impressive showing; the Liberals among the rightist forces scored considerable gains; and the Left, even with some losses, retained its position without substantial change. The losers were the *callampa* parties (mushroom parties) hurriedly organized to jump on the Ibáñez bandwagon in 1952, and the now almost insignificant Agrarian Labor Party. The ballot boxes definitely confirmed the administration's discredit and loss of public confidence, but more important, they demonstrated once more the traditional political sanity and good sense of Chileans who, now convinced of the impossibility of running the country within a democratic framework without restoring party government first, wisely decided to turn again to the established representative groups.

As in the 1957 congressional elections, the economic issues were crucial in the 1958 presidential campaign. All four candidates had one thing in common: a critical attitude of the Ibáñez administration's handling of inflation and other economic ills, with differences only in respect to emphasis. In general, they all maintained that the greatest fault of the policy of stabilization was lack of unity and coherence, and neglect of such essential elements as fiscal economics and encouragement of production. In other words, the economic policies of the government had been designed to remedy the financial aspects of inflation but had made only feeble efforts to attack the basic causes of Chile's economic ordeal. The Alessandri administration was not appreciably more successful than its predecessors, and in the presidential elections of 1964 once again economic development and political reforms were to be the *leitmotif* of the campaign.

Chile is sliding backward, and what is worse, the economic indexes are showing no improvement at the same time that the demands of Chileans are more pressing. In recent years per capita income has changed little, unemployment has increased, food production is not keeping pace with population growth, and so on. The same old dilemmas have been producing the same old irresolution. Chile's development policy of the last twenty years has been an application of the mixed-economy approach. The Chilean experience may suggest to economists the need to determine the conditions for the success of this mixed approach more clearly. Japan is an example of the successful application of the mixed-economy approach to a backward society because Japan has been able to do what Chile has not, namely, to accumulate capital by heavy land taxes and by depressing wages and salaries. Another type of mixed-economy approach in India emphasizes public investment financed by heavy income and consumption taxes. But as one writer has pointed out, Chile has wavered between the two approaches. It has sought to encourage private accumulation of capital by low and regressive taxation and to protect the agricultural status quo in a setting where the actual consumption of the propertied classes has resulted in a low level of new private investment. But while adhering to these inducements and the requisite tax policy, it has sought to compensate for that low level with public investment and to appease egalitarian pressures with ambitious welfare measures. "Inflation has not succeeded in reconciling the inherent conflict of ends. As long as the political rigidity responsible for these inconsistencies prevails, Chilean development will probably continue to limp along."[124] Industrialization in Chile has been hampered by inadequate governmental policies, and a further complication has been created by the constantly increasing gap between the middle and bottom layers of society. There is a greater distance today between classes in Chile than ever before in its modern history. It would seem that Chilean society is not sufficiently open to accomplish democratically the radical alterations now demanded. The question is whether this society is likely to become sufficiently pressed so as to be forced to undertake such changes along different channels.

At this point what may happen in Chile is not easy to predict. All that can be safely said is that conditions will not remain static and that an even greater readjustment among Chile's power groups will occur. If any range of possibilities is to be established by those who are fond of playing Cassandra's role, it may be useful to conclude by attempting to give an abstract of the position of each of the four major groups contending in Chilean politics today on the questions of development.

A distinction must be made between the two broad elements of the rightist forces, which during the Alessandri administration had the responsibility of governing (perhaps for the last time). The Conservative Party espouses economic doctrines of a curiously precapitalistic, paternalistic, antistatist nature. It offers not much more than the return to order and authority, to the sobriety and temperance of nostalgic years, at a time when the nation has become accustomed to adventure and danger and expects bold and imaginative thinking. The Conservative formula is now clearly rejected by the electorate, as the returns of the 1965 election demonstrated: the defeat the Conservatives suffered then can be described as nothing less than a debacle. The Conservatives would have an "orderly" country, slowly and cautiously picking its way and always in danger of serious stagnation, rather than a nation with the vigor and ambition governments with a popular

124 Adamantios Pepelasis, Leon Mears, and Irma Adelman, *Economic Development: Analysis and Case Studies* (New York: Harper & Brothers, 1961), p. 323.

impetus customarily provide. The Liberal Party, on the other hand, has shown much greater flexibility, as evidenced by its success in attracting some of the new technicians and professionals. Contrary to what might have been expected, it accepts the concept of government intervention in economic affairs, being in favor of a modified form of economic liberalism and the Chilean version of free enterprise. Philosophically the Liberal Party is the moderate wing of the Right and even shows symptoms of moving a little to the Center, as indicated by its near nomination of Eduardo Frei, the Christian Democrat leader, in 1958. Had it not been for the sudden death of the Liberal's elder statesman, Raul Marín Balmaceda, immediately following a dramatic speech opposing Frei's candidacy and defending the "sacred" Liberal-Conservative alliance, the Christian Democrat leader might have been awarded Liberal support despite the party's ideological opposition to his program. If this had happened, the Conservatives would have had to follow course, and the Right, not too happily, would have enlisted under the banner of Christian Socialism. As it turned out, a group of professionals, businessmen and technicians clustered about Alessandri, who had been elected to the Senate in 1957 as a Liberal but called himself an independent. The Conservatives, afraid of a fifth electoral defeat, threw their lot with Alessandri and the Liberal Party. Six years later Conservatives and Liberals, concerned with the clear possibility of a leftist victory, disregarded all ideological differences to throw their support behind Christian Democratic presidential candidate Frei.

The Liberal-Conservative alliance emphasized the authority and austerity personified in its leader from 1958 to 1964, President Alessandri, an aloof and successful businessman unadorned by any political attributes except a magic family name and a reputation for ability and honesty. His economic program stressed the need to set an example of sacrifice and austerity to the nation by drastically eliminating all superfluities and introducing rigorous fiscal economies. The Liberal-Conservative bloc advocates the restriction of new state economic activities, no matter how advantageous they may be for the country's progress. That is, only those state enterprises that are already extant or may be regarded as indispensable are to be continued, while all others must be postponed until the country's economy has recovered its balance. In time, the savings derived from a rational administrative reorganization, a more effective tax collection system, and the increasing scope of private economic activities could be employed first in works that are traditionally within the state's economic province and, later, in industrialization plans which cannot be undertaken by private enterprise. Alessandri maintained that the nation was deceived into believing that it had sufficient means to accelerate economic development and simultaneously to improve the standard of living of wage earners, and that it was only selfishness on the part of the wealthy class which prevented it from achieving that end. Coupled with this belief, his government claimed, came the erroneous notion that the wealthy class could assume greater responsibility in capital investments. Since that is only an illusion, it is indispensable to create a favorable investment climate in order to attract foreign capital. Convinced that Chile's present dire economic difficulties have been brought about by an unrestrained urge for development, the Liberal-Conservative alliance desired for the country, in short, a plan of development which would not endanger its stability.[125] However, toward the end of his administration the economic policy of the government underwent a change: stability remained an important concern but economic growth was given priority again.

The Radical Party, traditionally the major Center group, shared responsibility for the ultimate failure of the administrations of the period 1938–1952 to utilize to the country's advantage the new economic power that their accession had given Chile. Perhaps for this reason, the Radical plank today lacks much definition. It regained favor with the electorate in 1957 chiefly by attacking the Ibáñez policies, but it did little to expound specific solutions. During the struggle for the presidency in 1958, and again in 1964, the Radicals were only relatively more explicit. They put emphasis on the need for agrarian reform, based not on the elimination per se of the *latifundio,* but on the proper utilization of abandoned and unproductive land properties. They emphasized that an insufficient production of foodstuffs is one of the causes of the inflationary process, and found a partial solution in an adequate exploitation of the land. The party believes that capitalization can be increased by reducing superfluous consumption of the high-income groups and that moderate sacrifices by the latter would suffice to allow the economy to develop rapidly. It defends state intervention and participation in economic life as the greatest safeguard for the protection of the most vulnerable groups of society from monopolistic dangers during the present crucial stage of transition toward full industrialization. Cooperating with the Alessandri administration, until the dissolution of the "Democratic Front," a few months before the 1964 presidential elections, the Radicals held a precarious balance of power in Chilean politics but exercised only a secondary influence on economic policy.

The other great Center-Left force, the Christian Democratic party, is the most articulate group in the expression of economic thinking. For the Christian Democrats, Chile within a democratic framework

[125] For details on Alessandri's electoral program see "La acción de un mal gobierno gravita con más fuerza sobre los grupos más desamparados, dijo Jorge Alessandri," *El Mercurio,* October 27, 1957.

o solve its economic and political ills. The first ttack against inflation through monetary, credit, s. If the tolerance of the country were not ex- proach might be a feasible way to stop the in- estrict consumption, and balance the economy, , the Christian Democrats believe that when new investments would fall, poverty would be- dimensions of the economy would be reduced. n general resembles that offered by the Right, d stagnation, and would be acceptable only for ency and not as a permanent solution. The sely approximates the Radical Party position, would consist of allowing full freedom in consumption and the consequent race of profits, salaries, wages, and prices, with the hope that production some day would catch up with inflation. The country has had bitter experiences with this method, the Christian Democrats claim, and knows full well that although it may bring brief periods of deceptive prosperity, it leads eventually to moral as well as economic bankruptcy. The third solution which they discuss — and the one they have embraced — is a strict and orderly policy of restriction and economy over a long term, clearly coordinated with a vast program of economic development based on priority investments that would give preference to activities which are basic and directly productive. The Christian Democrats claim that their economic development program would increase Chile's national income 70 per cent in nineteen years, doubling the working-class standard of living and providing a 30 per cent increase in the income of the other social groups.[126] They would start with the acute question of urban housing, proceed to the reduction of public expenditures (including a thorough revision of the social security system), and then attempt to bring about monetary stability in conjunction with an increased program of industrialization. Considering that unless changes are made in the agricultural picture, programs of reforms in other areas may prove useless, this Christian Democratic approach accentuates the need for a rational agrarian reform which would contemplate long-term credits, transportation and refrigeration systems, irrigation projects, farm cooperatives, and colonization of state lands. As regards statism, the Christian Democrats maintain that it is unrealistic to create a conflict between state economic intervention and free enterprise. A governmental economic mechanism within a democratic framework and oriented toward basic activities, they claim, can (with the cooperation of private enterprise) achieve wonders in a period of ten years. With respect to social con-

[126] "Con Frei, Chile tiene la seguridad de alcanzar el gobierno que necesita," *El Mercurio,* December 20, 1957.

ditions, Christian Democrats make an appeal for "a national offensive" against poverty and the wretched living conditions of three million Chileans. The wide gulf which separates social classes must be narrowed by achieving a fairer distribution of income. Equalization cannot be accomplished by a futile redistribution of the present scarce income, but rather of an income that is constantly increased by virtue of higher productivity. The Christian Democratic principles are to be applied by Chilean professionals with Chilean-oriented techniques, for an impersonal nationalism seems to set the tone of Christian Democratic thinking. It is precisely this nationalism and the accompanying emphasis on a neutral government of technicians, together with the call for a national regeneration crusade, that have made such a strong appeal to all professionals and many other groups, as represented in the impressive gains of the party since the 1961 elections.

The diagnosis of Chile's ills given by the fourth political coalition, the FRAP (Popular Action Front), the formidable alliance of the extreme Left, does not differ basically from the analyses of its antagonists except on the question of locating the blame for the illness. For the extreme Left, the fundamental ailments derive directly from a socio-economic backwardness proceeding from the country's antiquated semifeudal and semicolonial structure. That structure is sustained by the obstinacy of a privileged minority and by the moral decadence of all social levels, but particularly the upper groups. The FRAP's economic prescription, in contrast to those which have been already examined, calls for drastic changes in the political as well as economic structure of the country. Its formula, chiefly elaborated by the key organizations in the coalition (the unified Socialist Party and the Communist Party), requires a political framework other than the existing one. Aiming towards a revolution for socialism, a step toward integral socialism rather than an immediate socialist revolution, the FRAP advocates what it calls a "workers' democratic revolution" and the creation of a "popular democracy."

The FRAP maintains that it would admit the participation of private enterprise in the economy "only in whatever measure it could contribute to the national effort in the establishment of an efficient, popular state." It also maintains that Chile should not depend, like a mendicant people, on foreign capital and ideas for its progress, and it proposes that the state establish a monopoly upon all basic production sources. Copper and nitrate must contribute larger sums to the government for industrial and agricultural development. These mining industries should be nationalized and all mineral exports should be controlled by the state. The FRAP considers urgent the expansion of Chile's commercial relations with all the Latin American countries, aiming at an eventual economic integration of the Southern Hemisphere and also at the re-establishment of trade relations with the Soviet Union and all other socialist states.

To the FRAP, the only solution to Chile's agricultural problem is a drastic agrarian reform which would put an end to the *latifundio* system, distributing land among the peasants and supplying them with modern equipment, as well as modern agricultural techniques. The FRAP would allow just compensation providing they do not oppose expropriation. Nationalization of all banks and insurance business, as well as the petroleum and sugar industries, is proposed. Both mixed and state-controlled enterprises would exist in heavy industry. Agricultural reform and industrial development are to be financed chiefly by revenues derived from the nationalized foreign companies and from foreign trade.

These postulates are part of a doctrinal platform which the FRAP parties proclaimed in 1958 in answer to those who argued that the Chilean Left had become stagnant and in a sense conservative, dependent on worn-out slogans and lacking in positive and appealing new formulas to capture the imagination of the people. This new Left, inspired mainly by the Socialist-Communist alliance, proposed in that year, and again in 1961 and 1964, a program frankly in opposition to traditional Chilean leftism, which had always been loyal to the prevailing institutional order and in these circumstances had often aligned itself with other political organizations of both the Right and the Left. For the first time, the coalition of the extreme Left agreed that a revolutionary change of the status quo is necessary which will put an end to the system it considers to be only formally or externally democratic.

The Chilean Socialist-Communist group represents what is called "the Marxist alternative," of recent appearance in Latin America. As is the case with Europe, the Latin American peoples will have to choose between creating a new socio-economic order within the principles and methods of Western democracy or achieving this end under Marxist ideas and formulas. Chile, because of its racial homogeneity, its long record of public participation in governmental affairs, the nature of its natural resources, and the irresistible internal pressures for fairer and more efficient forms of social and economic integration, will be one of the Latin American countries to which the "Marxist alternative" is sure to be vigorously offered. What Chile clearly cannot afford is to continue struggling ahead under a confused, defective, and ineffective political system which has failed to make the adjustment demanded by modern conditions.

5

Elections and Electoral Procedures

Election Laws

Elections in Chile are regulated by national laws and are under the supervision and control of national bodies. The Constitution of 1925 established a proportional representation system. In compliance with this constitutional mandate, on September 19, 1925, an "Electoral Law of the Republic" established the electoral districts for the congressional elections.[1] Since that time, electoral legislation has frequently been revised and amended. The last extensive revision was made in May, 1962,[2] and included three major innovations: (1) the proscription of electoral pacts in congressional and municipal elections; (2) the strengthening of penalties for failure to register; and (3) the establishment of permanent voter lists.

[1] Carlos Estévez Gazmuri, *Elementos de derecho constitucional* (Santiago: Editorial Jurídica de Chile, 1949), pp. 152–178.

[2] This decree, No. 542, was modified by Decree Laws 590, 592, 650, 710, 721 and 725 of October 7, 9, and 22 and November 6, 18, and 20, 1925, respectively. Later it was modified by Law 4,763 of January 6, 1930; by the Decree with Force of Law 300 of May 20, 1931; by Law 4,996 of October 1, 1931; by Decree Law 638 of September 21, 1932; and by Law 5,806 of February 5, 1936, Law 6,250 of September 3, 1938, and Law 6,825 of February 11, 1941. On February 17, 1941, a new text, Law 6,834, revised and codified all electoral legislation. New amendments were later introduced by Law 8,987 (Law for the Permanent Defense of Democracy) of September 3, 1948, which outlawed the Communist Party, and by Law 9,292 of January 8, 1949, extending suffrage to women in national elections. All electoral laws were modified again by the General Electoral Law No. 9,334, March, 1949, and Laws 12,891 and 12,918 of August, 1958. Since 1958 the electoral law has been amended five times.

Legally speaking, voting in Chile is both a right and a duty. All literate Chilean citizens over twenty-one years of age who are registered may vote.[3] Those excepted are: noncommissioned officers and enlisted men in the armed forces and in the police; those whose citizenship has been suspended because of physical or mental disability; those charged with or convicted of punishable crime (*pena aflictiva*);[4] and men under twenty-five who have not fulfilled their military obligation. Foreigners who have lived in Chile for five years are entitled to vote in municipal elections only.[5]

Registration and voting are obligatory for those who are eligible. An eligible voter who fails to register is subject to a prison term of up to sixty days or a fine of a half an escudo a day. If he fails to vote, he is subject to a similar sentence plus the loss of citizenship rights for a period ten times as long as the prison term. Registration of eligible voters is further encouraged by a requirement for proof of registration in order to transact business with banks, credit institutions, and government agencies.[6]

Prior to the 1958 and 1962 reforms, numerous obstacles to registering seriously hampered the Chilean system and resulted in a relatively small number of registered voters. Voter records were kept for ten years, and then all registrations become invalid and re-registration was necessary. Registries were open only for the first eight days of each month, except for the six months before the election and ninety days after it. In the case of closely scheduled elections, registration periods were reduced in practice to fifteen or twenty days (eight days every month). In 1962, registration lists were made permanent, and they now become invalid only if fifteen or more names have been removed because of death, change of residence, or other reasons specified in the

[3] Constitution, Art. 7.

[4] For which a sentence of not less than three years and one day in prison was imposed.

[5] Mario Bernaschina, *Cartilla electoral* (Santiago: Editorial Jurídica de Chile, 1958), pp. 26–27.

[6] *Chile: Election Factbook*, ed. Charles H. Daugherty (Washington, D.C.: Institute for the Comparative Study of Political Systems, 1963). This excellent publication includes a resumé of Chile's modern political history, a description of political parties, an analysis and results of various elections, a description of the electoral system, and biographical sketches of leading political leaders. The Institute, a division of Operations and Policy Research, Inc., has published a series of booklets containing similar information on elections in various Latin American republics. This author is much indebted to the Institute for allowing him to examine its files and to use some tables prepared by its staff.

law. Hours for registration have also been extended. There are three kinds of registration lists: male, female, and foreign. These lists contain up to 300 names. Voter registration is conducted by boards composed of officials of the national administration. As a result of easier registration procedures as well as stronger penalties for abstention from voting, the percentage of the population registering and voting has risen substantially in recent years.

The districts for the election of members of the Chamber of Deputies are drawn to coincide with the provincial boundaries in twenty-one of Chile's twenty-five provinces. Exceptions are the province of Santiago, which has four electoral districts, the province of Ñuble, which has two, and the provinces of Llanquihue and Aysén, which together form one district. From one to eighteen deputies are elected from each district in the nation. The Constitution prescribes that one deputy be elected for each 30,000 inhabitants or fraction of 15,000 or more. Strangely enough, although more recent population counts are available, the 1930 census is still being used to determine representation in the lower house. Senators are elected under a system of constituencies or groups of provinces numbered from north to south — five senators being elected for each of nine senatorial districts. (See map, and Table 8.)

Elections for both houses of Congress are held on the same day in March every four years. Deputies are elected for four years and senators for eight. The entire Chamber of Deputies — 147 members — comes up for election each time, whereas twenty-five and twenty senators are elected alternately. Municipal elections were formerly held every three years, but a constitutional amendment adopted in 1959 stipulates a four-year term of office for councilmen and specifies municipal elections be held two years after congressional elections, in April every four years. Only twice in the past have these elections coincided with congressional elections. The 1959 amendment will now prevent this from ever happening. Presidential elections, as we have seen, are held every six years. Although there is no provision preventing the holding of presidential, congressional, or municipal elections at the same time, they have very seldom coincided.[7]

Voter Participation

The size of the electorate in Chile is limited by the literacy requirement for voting and by the fact that only about half of the population is over twenty-one. Some three quarters of this half are literate. At present, of a total of a little over seven and a half million Chileans,

[7] *Ibid.*, p. 8.

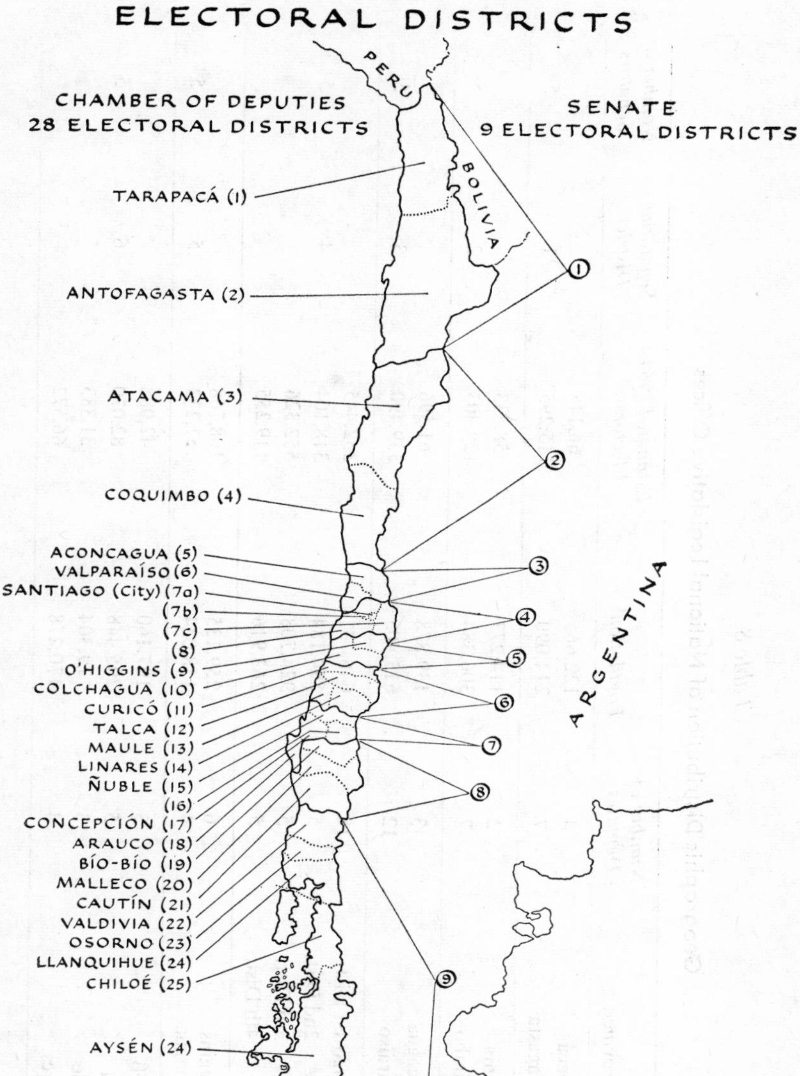

ELECTORAL DISTRICTS

CHAMBER OF DEPUTIES
28 ELECTORAL DISTRICTS

SENATE
9 ELECTORAL DISTRICTS

PERU
BOLIVIA
ARGENTINA

TARAPACÁ (1)
ANTOFAGASTA (2)
ATACAMA (3)
COQUIMBO (4)
ACONCAGUA (5)
VALPARAÍSO (6)
SANTIAGO (City) (7a)
(7b)
(7c)
(8)
O'HIGGINS (9)
COLCHAGUA (10)
CURICÓ (11)
TALCA (12)
MAULE (13)
LINARES (14)
ÑUBLE (15)
(16)
CONCEPCIÓN (17)
ARAUCO (18)
BÍO-BÍO (19)
MALLECO (20)
CAUTÍN (21)
VALDIVIA (22)
OSORNO (23)
LLANQUIHUE (24)
CHILOÉ (25)
AYSÉN (24)
MAGALLANES (26)

1
2
3
4
5
6
7
8
9

Source: *Chile: Election Factbook* (Washington, D.C., Institute for Comparative Study of Political Systems, 1963). By permission.

Table 8

Geographic Distribution of National Legislative Offices

Chamber District	Province	Number of Deputies	Population[1]	Estimated 1964 Electorate[2]	Senatorial District	Number of Senators
1	Tarapacá	4	122,665	66,145	1	5
2	Antofagasta	7	214,090	115,295		
3	Atacama	2	114,277	58,333	2	5
4	Coquimbo	7	306,384	129,403		
5	Aconcagua	3	139,878	61,596	3	5
6	Valparaíso	12	613,405	339,490		
7[a]	Santiago 1st Dist.	18	646,731	352,445	4	5
7[b]	2nd Dist.	5	594,184	318,104		
7[c]	3rd Dist.	5	924,708	552,326		
8	4th Dist.	5	263,916	119,255		
9	O'Higgins	6	259,135	108,768	5	5
10	Colchagua	4	158,024	57,233		
11	Curicó	3	107,160	42,088	6	5
12	Talca	5	205,448	82,070		
13	Maule	3	79,304	31,383		
14	Linares	4	170,278	66,572		

15	Ñuble 1st Dist.	3	93,140	31,085		
16	2nd Dist.	5	191,376	78,850	7	5
17	Concepción	9	537,711	260,587		
18	Arauco	2	89,211	33,022		
19	Bío-Bío	4	167,286	64,385		
20	Malleco	6	174,185	63,300	8	5
21	Cautín	10	393,041	155,157		
22	Valdivia	5	255,109	75,534		
23	Osorno	3	143,955	64,059		
24	Llanquihue	3	165,959	72,551		
	Aysén	3	37,085	16,971	9	5
25	Chiloé	3	98,662	41,424		
26	Magallanes	1	73,037	44,512		
	Total	147	7,339,546	3,501,943		45

[1] Based on 1960 census. Total population includes 202 persons in Chilean Antarctic.

[2] Estimates of literates 21 and over in September, 1964.

Source: *Chile: Election Factbook* (Washington, D.C.: Institute for the Comparative Study of Political Systems, 1963). By permission.

about three and a half million (44 per cent) are eligible to vote. Of this number about 33 per cent were registered in 1963, and 27 per cent actually voted in the municipal elections that year. Since 1958 the normal rate of voter absenteeism has been running between a low of 16 per cent in the presidential elections that year and a high of 30 per cent in the 1960 municipal elections. An examination of election statistics for the last two decades indicates that voter participation was fairly stable during the 1940's — between 8 and 10 per cent of the population. This percentage rose considerably in the early 1950's (16 per cent in 1952) because of two factors: the impact of the 1949 law giving women the right to vote and the strong personalist appeal of Carlos Ibáñez's campaign in 1952. Voter turnout continued to climb in the presidential elections of 1958 (18 per cent), and in the 1961 and 1963 elections (19 per cent and 27 per cent, respectively). (See Table 9.)

The rate of participation varies from region to region and is normally lower in the rural areas, but these variations are not significant. Two extremes are the provinces of Magallanes and Aysén, with voter turnout percentages of 26 and 13 respectively. However, in contrast, the absolute number of voters in the various provinces may vary considerably. The great majority of the Chilean population and electorate reside in the central region of the country. Electoral registers for 1963 indicated that over half of the total number of eligible voters lived in an area 250 miles long extending from Aconcagua Province south to Talca. A recent electoral study asserts that if this region were extended to 750 miles, all but 15 per cent of the potential voters would be included, although the section covers only one third of the national land area.[8] For instance, the geographic distribution of voters in the 1961 congressional elections resulted in more than half of the ballots being cast in this central region, which includes seven provinces. Only 8.5 per cent of the national land area is included in the central region.[9]

As might be expected, presidential elections have always attracted the largest number of eligible voters. Municipal elections, until the recent extension of suffrage to women, produced very small turnouts. Congressional elections have previously resulted in substantial turnouts, although never as large as those for presidential contests.

The Feminine Vote

Without any doubt, the most significant factor determining the substantial increase of voters in the part few years has been the feminine

[8] *Chile: Election Factbook,* p. 32.
[9] *Ibid.,* p. 14.

Table 9

Who Votes

Year	Type of Election	Population[1]	Registered Voters	% of Population Registered	Votes Cast	% of Registered Who Voted	% of Population Who Voted
1963	Municipal	7,735,990	2,570,291	33.22	2,070,188	80.54	26.76
1961	Congressional	7,394,187	1,858,980	25.14	1,385,676	74.54	18.74
1960	Municipal	7,243,971	1,769,681	24.43	1,229,503	69.48	16.97
1958	Presidential	6,984,507	1,497,902	21.45	1,250,350	83.47	17.90
1957	Congressional	6,738,699	1,284,154	19.06	878,229	68.39	13.03
1956	Municipal	6,588,483	1,184,882	17.98	731,449	61.73	11.10
1953	Municipal	6,083,211	1,106,709	18.19	759,379	68.62	12.48
	Congressional		1,100,027	18.08	786,811	71.53	12.93
1952	Presidential	6,001,275	1,105,029	18.41	957,102	86.61	15.95
1950	Municipal	5,773,859	833,460	14.44	619,724	74.36	10.73
1949	Congressional	5,687,539	591,994	10.41	470,376	79.46	8.27
1947	Municipal	5,534,819	657,485	11.88	552,034	83.96	9.97
1946	Presidential	5,488,339	631,257	11.50	479,310	75.93	8.73
1945	Congressional	5,368,819	641,495	11.95	449,930	70.14	8.38
1944	Municipal	5,295,779	765,092	14.45	498,434	65.15	9.41
1942	Presidential	5,096,579	581,343	11.41	466,507	80.25	9.15
1941	Congressional	5,050,099	575,625	11.40	450,248	78.22	8.92
	Municipal		700,143	13.86	488,904	69.83	9.68
1938	Presidential	4,844,666	503,871	10.40	443,888	88.10	9.16

[1] Based on 1940, 1952, and 1960 censuses. Each figure represents an extrapolation to the month of the election based on estimated rate of growth.

Source: *Chile: Election Factbook,* Institute for the Comparative Study of Political Systems (Washington, D.C., 1963). By permission.

vote. Until 1949 women could vote only in municipal elections. In that year, amendments to the electoral law granted women the right to vote in national elections. Exercising their newly won right for the first time in the 1952 elections, women cast 30 per cent of the valid votes for President. In the 1958 elections, women's votes accounted for 35 per cent of the total number of ballots cast. In spite of these impressive figures, registration of women voters still lags considerably behind that of male voters. In 1963, for example, the electoral registries included some 1,450,000 men but only 1,100,000 women, even though there are slightly more women than men among the Chilean population and literacy rates of the two groups are essentially the same.[10] However, all indications are that there has been a strong trend recently toward increased registration of women. It is reasonable to expect this trend to continue for a number of years. Naturally, a continued increase in women registration will be paralleled by an increase in vote percentages. A comparison of voting statistics for men and women in the 1952 and 1958 elections indicates that the participation of women had increased from one election to the other by 150,000 and that of men by a few thousand less. (See Tables 10 and 11.)

It may be concluded, then, that women have come to play an almost decisive role in Chilean elections. In 1952, Ibáñez, although supported by a slightly larger percentage of men, obtained a clear plurality among women voters. In the 1958 elections, the feminine vote was crucial to such an extent that Alessandri probably owed his election to it. Indeed, so narrow was the margin of victory that Salvador Allende, the FRAP candidate and second runner, actually led Alessandri among male voters by 17,500. While the leftist coalition of 1958 was able to draw a third of the total male vote, it failed to poll as much as a fourth of the female vote. There are many who attribute the impressive gains made by the Christian Democrats in the 1963 municipal elections to the successful appeal of their candidates for female support.[11] Being well aware of the electoral influence of women, Chilean political parties are following the example of their Latin American counterparts by assiduously courting this segment of the electorate. Convinced that the two keys to victory in the 1964 presidential contest were the votes of women and of rural workers and *inquilinos,* both major contenders concentrated their most strenuous campaign efforts on these two groups. That this strategy was wisely founded can be

[10] *Ibid.*, p. 32.

[11] "Las mujeres tejieron la victoria del PDC," *Ercilla,* April 10, 1963, pp. 14–17.

Table 10

Vote for President, September, 1952

Candidate	*Total*	*Per cent*	*Men Per cent*	*Women Per cent*
Carlos Ibáñez	446,439	46.8	48.4	43.0
Arturo Matte	265,357	27.8	26.0	32.0
Pedro Alfonso	190,360	19.9	19.8	20.2
Salvador Allende	51,975	5.5	5.8	4.6

Table 11

Vote for President, September, 1958

Candidate	*Total*	*Per cent*	*Men Per cent*	*Women Per cent*
Jorge Alessandri	389,909	31.6	30.2	34.1
Salvador Allende	356,493	28.9	32.4	22.3
Eduardo Frei	255,769	20.7	19.0	23.9
Luis Bossay	192,077	15.6	15.2	16.1
Antonio Zamorano	41,304	3.3	3.2	3.6

Source: *Chile: Election Factbook,* (Washington, D.C.: Institute for the Comparative Study of Political Systems, 1963). By permission.

amply demonstrated by the briefest examination of the final results of that election, particularly of vote distribution on the basis of sex and of geographic location of the totals polled by each candidate.

Proportional Representation

The Constitution of 1925, we have noted, provided that a system of proportional representation be employed in the election of senators, deputies, and municipal councilmen. The specific system adopted by Chile, in compliance with this constitutional principle, was developed by the Belgian Victor D'Hondt at the end of the nineteenth century. It is unquestionably one of the most complicated of all proportional representation schemes. More than any other system, it tends to encourage party proliferation as well as adventurous individual candidacies. The D'Hondt method, also known as the "dividing number" or "electoral quotient" system, has often produced odd results in Chile. In the past, for example, candidates with fewer popular votes were frequently elected to office over others with more votes, both within a given party slate and among the various party lists. The vagaries of the system, prior to the 1958 and 1962 reforms, were such as to produce an extraordinarily confusing political picture, with a consequent adverse reaction on the part of the electorate. Since the system encouraged the development of peculiar blocs designed to take advantage of the law's complexities, some candidates ran at the same time under the banner of two parties that were irreconcilably opposed, perhaps from the two ends of the national political spectrum. At times clericals, anti-clericals, rightists, and leftists all got together on the same list, especially in the provinces.

Among other defects of the system is the disproportionate number of votes required for election in the various electoral districts. For example, while in Santiago's third district this number — the electoral quotient — is usually more than 19,000 votes, there are districts in South Chile (i.e., Malleco or Chiloé) where the quotient hardly ever reaches 3,000. Consequently, a party whose strength is concentrated in districts with a high electoral quotient must often secure, in order to elect one deputy, two or three times the number of popular votes required by another party with strength concentrated in districts with a low electoral quotient. Likewise, a political party whose strength is dispersed over the entire country has greater difficulty electing deputies than another with blocs of votes strategically located in only a few areas.[12] Since the scheme produces a certain number of "left-over" or excess votes for each party, it inevitably encourages electoral combinations or pacts among parties that lead to the peculiar situations described above. Operation of the system prior to the elections of 1961 was so complex as to defy description.

Reforms introduced in 1958 eliminated electoral pacts in elections for deputies and councilmen. In 1962 the prohibition was extended to senatorial elections. The long-sought elimination of all electoral pacts is the most significant innovation introduced in the history of Chilean electoral legislation. It dealt a mortal blow to the *callampa* or fly-by-night party that flourished under the old system. With the disappearance of many minor political groups, the party system has become tighter and better defined, and political forces tend to align themselves with the six major traditional parties that truly represent social and economic interests. The trend toward development of three great blocs — the Right, the Center, and the Left — has continued steadily, since its beginnings in the twenties, given impetus by these electoral reforms. In the 1964 presidential election the support of the Center-Left, represented by Christian Socialism, by the Right caused a tem-

[12] Carlos Fortín Cabezas, *La supresión de los pactos electorales,* Colección Estudios Políticos, No. 1 (Santiago: Instituto de Ciencias Políticas y Administrativas, 1961), pp. 2–3.

porary polarization of forces and a further simplification of the party picture. It remains to be seen, however, whether that polarization will be permanent or not.

The proportional representation scheme used at present is not nearly so complex. Parties prepare slates which may include the names of as many candidates as there are seats to be filled in any particular election. In the past, the order in which the candidates' names appeared on the ballot was decided by the party, and each party printed and distributed its own ballots. This order as well as the sequence in which party slates appear on the ballot is now determined by lot after registration closes. The voter receives a single, official ballot, which contains all party slates for any single type of election in his district. In case of congressional elections he receives a separate ballot for candidates for the Senate and candidates for the Chamber of Deputies. Essentially, then, the vote is cast for an individual and not for a party. Prior to the 1962 reforms, a voter could either select a single party ballot or could vote for individuals on more than one party ballot. Something similar is indeed a common practice in other proportional representation systems.

SENADORES

B. PARTIDO DEMOCRATA CRISTIANO

— 1 IGNACIO PALMA VICUÑA

C. PARTIDO CONSERVADOR UNIDO

— 2 HECTOR CORREA LETELIER

E. PARTIDO RADICAL

— 3 EXEQUIEL GONZALEZ MADARIAGA
— 4 QUINTIN BARRIENTOS VILLALOBOS
— 5 PELEGRIN MEZA LOYOLA

G. PARTIDO COMUNISTA

— 6 CARLOS CONTRERAS LABARCA

I. PARTIDO LIBERAL

— 7 CARLOS ACHARAN ARCE
— 8 JULIO VON MUHLENBROCK LIRA
— 9 SERGIO SEPULVEDA GARCES

J. PARTIDO SOCIALISTA

— 10 ANICETO RODRIGUEZ ARENAS

K. PARTIDO DEMOCRATICO NACIONAL

— 11 JORGE LAVANDERO EYZAGUIRRE
— 12 FRANCISCO RAMIREZ SOTO

Source: *Chile: Election Factbook* (Washington, D.C., Institute for the Comparative Study of Political Systems, 1963). By permission.

As the best means of explaining the electoral quotient let us consider a hypothetical senatorial election in a particular district or group of provinces entitled to five Senate seats. There are in this electoral zone five party lists of proposed candidates for the five openings. The first step is to total votes by party. The result is what is called the "list vote." Seats will be awarded to the competing parties on the basis of these "list votes."

Party	*Candidate*	*Candidate Preference Votes*	*Party List Votes*
A	1	14,350	14,350
B	2	15,930	33,657
	3	7,965	
	4	9,762	
C	5	3,982	3,982
D	6	5,300	19,433
	7	10,600	
	8	3,533	
E	9	4,864	4,864
F	10	27,093	27,093

To find now specifically how many seats are to be awarded to each party the "dividing number" or "electoral quotient" must be determined. Each "list vote" is divided by an ascending sequence of numbers — one, two, three and so on (however many are necessary in the next step). The resulting quotients for each of our hypothetical lists (which we have divided only by 1 and 2) are:

Party A	*Party B*	*Party C*
14,350 ÷ 1 = 14,350	33,657 ÷ 1 = 33,657	3,982 ÷ 1 = 3,982
÷ 2 = 7,175	÷ 2 = 16,828	÷ 2 = 1,991
Party D	*Party E*	*Party F*
19,433 ÷ 1 = 19,433	4,864 ÷ 1 = 4,864	27,093 ÷ 1 = 27,093
÷ 2 = 9,716	÷ 2 = 2,432	÷ 2 = 13,546

A number of quotients equivalent to the number of seats to be filled is then arranged in descending order of size. (The order is noted in parentheses above.) Since there are in our example five seats to be filled,[13] our group of five quotients is:

1. 33,657
2. 27,093
3. 19,433
4. 16,828
5. 13,546

The last number in this group is the "electoral quotient," or *cifra repartidora.* To complete the process of determining how many seats fall to each party, the *cifra repartidora* is divided into the "list votes," disregarding fractions.

Party A	14,350 ÷ 13,546 = 1 seat
Party B	33,657 ÷ 13,546 = 2 seats
Party C	3,982 ÷ 13,546 = no seats
Party D	19,433 ÷ 13,546 = 1 seat
Party E	4,864 ÷ 13,546 = no seats
Party F	27,093 ÷ 13,546 = 1 seat

Party slates C and E received no seats. Party B received two seats. It ran, however, three candidates. Its candidates 2 and 4, with the highest number of votes on that party list, are therefore elected. Parties A and F each received one seat and ran one candidate; therefore candidates 1 and 10 are elected. Party D also received one seat but ran three candidates; again candidate 7, with the highest number of votes in that party list, is elected.

Registration of Candidates

Candidates are registered by party or by independent groups. Those nominated must be literate citizens and registered voters. An individual who has been convicted of a punishable crime is barred from becoming a candidate for public office. Age requirements are thirty years for the office of President, twenty-one and thirty-five for deputies and senators, respectively.

The law provides that each candidate (except presidential nominees) must declare before the Board of Electoral Registry (*Dirección del Registro Electoral*) that he has been a member of the political party sponsoring him for a minimum of 180 days, or if he is registered by an

[13] Note that, though a division by the figure one above is possible, no division by a number larger than the number of seats at stake can be necessary.

independent group, that he has not belonged to any political party for the same period. Candidates for the Chamber of Deputies and Senate must officially register 120 days before the election, but presidential candidates may register up to forty-five days prior to election day. The number of candidates presented by each party may not exceed the number of seats to be filled. Independent candidacies are in practice discouraged under the system, since the law requires that registration for the races for deputy, senator, and President must be supported by signatures of 2,000, 5,000, and 20,000 eligible voters, respectively. Furthermore, each of these signatures must be executed in person in the presence of election officials.[14] From 100 to 2,000 signatures are required to register independently as a candidate for municipal councilman, depending on the district. The percentage required is generally high.[15]

New political parties are also required to register by presenting a written application to the Board of Electoral Registry, accompanied by the party statutes, a description of its program, a list of the members of its executive committee (*mesa directiva*), and the signatures of 10,000 registered voters. No party can be denied official status if it fulfills these requirements and if it applies for registration not later than 240 days before an election. However, a party may be stricken from the books by order of the Director of the Electoral Registry if it fails to maintain representation in Congress after an election.

Voting

On election day voters from a given district appear with their identification documents at the polling place where they are registered. As previously noted, each registry contains 300 names, for which an "electoral table" (*mesa receptora*) is formed. From among the names appearing in the registry five persons (and substitutes) are elected by lot at each *mesa receptora* to supervise the voting, count the ballots, and make the appropriate report. No compensation is given for the performance of this civic duty. Men and women vote at separate polling places, and the results are tabulated independently, a method that facilitates the analysis of voting patterns by sex.

[14] It is estimated that it would take a minimum of fifteen to twenty hours to comply wth this requirement. See Mario Bernaschina, *Manual de derecho constitucional* (Santiago: Editorial Jurídica de Chile, 1958), Vol. I, p. 122.

[15] In one commune to register as an independent candidate in 1963 required the signatures of 25 per cent of the voters. *Chile: Election Factbook,* p. 42.

A single ballot, printed by the government, for each electoral contest being held is given to the voters at the polling place by the members of the *mesa.* The ballot, which self-folds into an envelope, is of a different color for each contest. On it appear the names of all candidates for one office. The single ballot was only recently introduced. In past elections, as is noted elsewhere, the ballots were prepared by the various parties or by party combinations. Voters picked them up at party booths before going to the polls or at the polling places themselves. Loyal party people preferred to get the ballots in advance, for fear that opposition partisans might have defaced ballots other than their own at the polling places.[16]

On the ballot the candidates are listed according to party and in an order determined by lot. The order of party lists is also fixed by lot. The upper-right-hand corner of the ballot is detachable, and on it a serial number is printed. Election officials record this number alongside the voter's name on the registry, before handing him the ballot. To insure secrecy the voter enters a booth, draws a curtain, and only then marks the ballot. To mark the ballot a vertical inked line is drawn through the printed horizontal line which appears alongside each candidate's name. A check or a cross drawn in ink over the printed line will invalidate the ballot (see model of ballot on page 222).

After sealing the ballot the voter delivers it to the *mesa* official, who checks the number, detaches the number corner, and returns the ballot to the voter. He, in turn, drops it into the ballot box. Any mark on the ballot other than the one prescribed or a write-in vote will be cause for automatic invalidation.

Preliminary count of the vote is taken by *mesa* officials immediately after the polls close at 4 P.M. The first step is to count the voters' signatures in the book of registry and the number of stubs corresponding to the ballots deposited in the box. Then, the ballot box is opened and votes are counted. Poll watchers designated by the parties stand by while the ballot boxes are opened and witness the vote count. In fact, a number of provisions of the Electoral Law insure the right of party watchers to observe all stages of the electoral process, from the setting up and operation of information booths before the election to the witnessing of the proceedings of the electoral qualification courts that certify the elected candidates.[17] Reports on any election irregularities or complaints are mailed together with the totals, to electoral

[16] K. H. Silvert, "Elections, Parties, and the Law" (American Universities Field Staff Letter, March 10, 1957), p. 8.

[17] *Chile: Election Factbook,* p. 44.

BALLOT MODEL (1958 Election)

gummed flap

SERIES NO. 580368

PRESIDENT OF THE REPUBLIC

1 — JORGE ALESSANDRI RODRIGUEZ

2 — LUIS BOSSAY LEIVA

3 — ANTONIO RAUL ZAMORANO HERRERA

4 — SALVADOR ALLENDE GOSSENS

5 — EDUARDO FREI MONTALVA

scrutinizing boards called Departmental Colleges (*Colegios Departamentales*).[18] Two days after the election, these boards select the Departmental Scrutinizing Colleges (*Colegios Escrutadores Departamentales*).

18 All materials pertinent to the election are transmitted by registered mail, and the Postmaster General and his subordinates are responsible for their safe-keeping. Two copies are made of every record. These are sent by different officials to different specified authorities.

Like the *mesa* officials, these bodies have no authority to settle disputes on the count. They simply check and total the results for their department and send them to specially constituted courts. In municipal elections results are sent to the appropriate Provincial Qualification Tribunal (*Tribunal Calificador Provincial*), which certifies the election of councilmen. National election results are submitted to the National Qualification Tribunal (*Tribunal Calificador de Elecciones*) for the certification of elected congressmen and to the Congress for the certification of the President. Neither the Departmental Scrutinizing Colleges nor the Qualification Tribunals re-tally the ballots unless results are being contested.

It has been the good fortune of this writer to witness a number of electoral campaigns and elections in Chile, at both the national and local levels. In every instance the mechanics of the election were exemplary. Parties were formed, candidates were nominated, campaigns were conducted, and voting took place in absolute freedom. Even at the height of hotly contested elections, when he is the target of all the modern techniques of political propaganda, the Chilean voter seems to preserve a remarkably sane and a bit skeptical attitude toward politics. That is understandable, of course, when, as in recent years, a large segment of the population has lost faith in the ability of political groups to provide the type of leadership needed for a better future. Just the same, observers cannot but be impressed with the model behavior of the Chilean electorate. Elections are honest and peaceful, votes are properly counted, and electoral controversies are settled without resorting to force. There are, to be sure, the enthusiastic mass meetings, the huge demonstrations, the posters that litter the city streets and country roads, and the volumes of incessant radio propaganda typical of electoral campaigns anywhere. Sometimes there are isolated incidents of violence: a homemade bomb is thrown at a party headquarters, or street demonstrators clash. Every now and then cases of fraud and bribery crop up, but they are neither numerous nor significant.

A very common technique, used by all the political parties to capture votes by financial inducement without violating the letter if not the spirit of the law, is known as the *voto gratificado* (rewarded vote). Its practice is made possible by the infrequent renewal of books of electoral registry and the existence of a large floating population, composed principally of migratory workers. For example, a voter may be working in Santiago at election time but may be registered in Talca, where he must vote. He may be approached by a party worker who offers to pay, in return for his vote, expenses of a trip to Talca, plus whatever wages he may lose by missing his job. The offer is generally attractive to a worker away from home and eager to visit relatives or friends. He is provided with money for food or else is given instructions about where he can be fed at no expense. On arrival, he is generally "convoyed" (in the current political jargon) by the party representatives who meet him at the station to provide him with local transportation and lodgings and generally to keep an eye on him. *Afuerinos* (migratory workers), who slowly move southward from one *fundo* to another working on the wheat and grape harvests, constitute the bulk of the *votos gratificados*. Sometimes a voter, having heard of this practice through friends or acquaintances, appears at party offices on his own initiative, requesting assistance to be able to fulfill his civic duty. He is rarely turned down if his credentials are in order and he can show his registration number. Although the Radical Party may have utilized this practice more frequently than others, all political parties make some use of it. Several ingenious devices are used to insure that the voter will fulfill his part of the bargain.

Prior to the use of a single, government-printed ballot, when ballots printed by each party were deposited in official envelopes, a clever electoral trick, known as the system of the *sobre brujo* (bewitched or magic envelope), was widely used. The first step was for one individual to sacrifice his vote by obtaining from the *mesa* officials the official envelope duly stamped, retaining it, and depositing in its stead an ordinary envelope (which, of course, invalidated his vote). Then the official envelope, now with the ballots of the party in question inside, would be given to another voter who, after voting, returned the unused envelope he in turn had received at the polling place. The operation could be repeated indefinitely, and the risks incurred were not serious, since mere possession of the envelope was considered improper but not a violation of the law.[19]

A certain national pride in political serenity and a certain political sophistication characterize Chilean elections. Many Chileans believe that even under the stress of social upheaval or of a government inspired by Marxist principles, the country would conduct a "Chilean experiment" unique in the context of Latin American politics and quite different from the one conducted in Castro's Cuba. Indeed, the freedom and peace of Chilean elections are striking symptoms of political health, though they are somewhat paradoxical in view of the country's grave social and economic evils. One is led by them to ponder the nature of the relationship between political practices and socio-economic difficulties.

[19] The system has been employed in other Latin American countries. In Cuba it was known as the *boleta viajera* (the "traveling ballot").

Electoral Administration

The organization and conduct of elections is a responsibility of the Office of Electoral Registry (*Dirección General del Registro Electoral*), headed by an official known as the Director of the Electoral Registry. He is appointed by the President with the consent of the Senate and cannot be removed without the approval of that body. Traditionally a nonpolitical appointee, the Director enjoys the same constitutional immunities as members of the Congress. He has responsibility for the general supervision of all electoral bodies and custody of the Archive of Electoral Registries; and he prepares the alphabetical roll of all eligible voters. In addition, he serves as secretary of the National Qualification Tribunal and issues regulations concerning the application and interpretation of the electoral laws.[20]

Every department into which the country is divided has an Electoral Board in charge of selecting polling officials, determining the location of polling places, and performing routine electoral functions. Registration of voters in each department is accomplished by a Registration Board (*Junta Inscriptora*). The Registration Boards draw up the official lists of voters used at the polls.

Vote counting and certification of elected candidates are functions, as we have seen, of the polling officials, the Departmental Colleges, and Departmental Scrutinizing Colleges. The Departmental College is composed of all presidents of *mesas* in a department. In turn it elects the Departmental Scrutinizing College, which totals the vote in the department. Besides certifying the results of elections (see page 223, above), the Provincial Qualification Tribunals and the National Qualification Tribunal execute justice. The National Qualification Tribunal[21] hears and decides all electoral claims at the national level and settles appeals from the decisions of the Provincial Qualification Tribunals in cases arising from municipal elections. The decisions of the National Tribunal are final; not even the Supreme Court can countermand its orders.

The National Qualification Tribunal is organized in this way: fifteen days before congressional elections are held, a commission headed by the Chief Justice of the Supreme Court and composed of the president of the Senate, the president of the Chamber of Deputies, and the president of the Court of Appeals of Santiago meets in the office of the Director of the Electoral Registry. The commission elects the five individuals who will compose the national electoral court from

[20] Mario Bernaschina, *Manual de derecho constitucional*, Vol. I, p. 112.

[21] For a history of this court see José Guillermo Guerra, *La constitución de 1925* (Santiago: Balcells & Co., 1929), pp. 417–430.

among the following: one from among former presidents and vice-presidents of the Senate; one from among former presidents and vice-presidents of the Chamber of Deputies; two from among the justices of the Supreme Court; and one from among the judges of the Court of Appeals of Santiago.[22]

Charges of election irregularities and petitions for nullification are submitted to the *juez letrado* within the particular jurisdiction. These charges must be made within ten days after the election. The *juez letrado* merely hears the case and then sends it to the National Qualification Tribunal for a decision. Any cases involving a declaration of ineligibility of a candidate are decided by the body to which he is seeking election before the first day of June (approximately three months after congressional and municipal elections).

Election of the President

Qualifications required of presidential candidates are specified by the Chilean Constitution: (1) birth in Chilean territory; (2) age of at least thirty; (3) valid registration as a voter; and (4) absence of any conviction of "punishable crimes" (*delito que merezca pena aflictiva*).[23] The President is chosen by direct vote for a six-year term and cannot succeed himself for the following term.[24] Presidential elections are held sixty days before the expiration of the term of the incumbent. Voting is by secret ballot on which the names of the candidates appear in an order determined by lot. The procedures for balloting and counting are essentially the same as those used in congressional elections. The voting results received by each candidate and totaled by the National Qualification Tribunal are submitted to a joint session of the Congress, which declares the winner — the candidate receiving a majority of the popular vote. The quorum required for this joint session is a majority of the combined total of incumbent senators and deputies (not a separate majority of each chamber). The Congress cannot engage in debate or modify in any way the results of the scrutiny performed by the Qualification Tribunal; it can only "proclaim" the President-elect. If a quorum is not available the first day, a second session is held the next day and a vote is then taken regardless of the number present. A majority of those attending the session is needed for certification of an election.

[22] *Constitution,* Art. 79.

[23] *Constitution,* Arts. 4, 7, 27, and 61. For a definition see page 107.

[24] *Constitution,* Art. 68. During the last two years of Jorge Alessandri's administration there was a great deal of political talk concerning a constitutional amendment to permit Alessandri's re-election. The President finally put an end to the rumors by disavowing any intention to run again.

In case no presidential candidate obtains a majority in the popular election, the Congress, again in joint session and by secret ballot, chooses between the two candidates who poll the highest number of votes.[25] It should be noted that, given the multiplicity of parties since adoption of the Constitution of 1925, Congress has frequently had to exercise this prerogative. Beginning with the election of 1946, four Presidents in succession were chosen by the Congress. In 1946 and 1952, the leading presidential candidates, González Videla and Ibáñez, had substantial margins over the rest of the candidates. In 1958, however, the candidate chosen by the Congress, Jorge Alessandri, had only a slim lead over the candidate in second place.[26] (See Table 12.)

Table 12

Vote for President

1946		*1952*	
Gabriel González Videla	192,207	Carlos Ibáñez	446,439
Eduardo Cruz-Coke	142,441	Arturo Matte	265,357
Fernando Alessandri	131,023	Pedro Alfonso	190,360
Bernardo Ibáñez	12,114	Salvador Allende	51,975
1958		*1964*	
Jorge Alessandri	389,909	Eduardo Frei	1,406,002
Salvador Allende	356,493	Salvador Allende	975,692
Eduardo Frei	255,769	Julio Durán	124,869
Luis Bossay	192,077		
Antonio Zamorano	41,304		

Nevertheless, in each of these cases, the Congress always overwhelmingly elected the candidate who ran first in the popular vote, although there is no doubt that legally it could have chosen the runner-up in popular vote. Also, in each case the candidate who came in second conceded the election without waiting for the decision of the Congress.[27] This tradition is so well established that when in 1964 there was some speculation that, if the Popular Action Front (FRAP) candidate led in the popular vote and the election were nevertheless

[25] Constitution, Art. 64, 2°.

[26] Complete vote.

[27] In 1958 candidates Frei, Bossay, and Zamorano promptly conceded victory to Alessandri, but Allende, claiming an inaccurate vote count, refused to capitulate at first. Of 187 congressmen participating in the election, 26 voted for Allende. FRAP leaders had previously announced that they would vote for Allende but abide by the congressional decision if Alessandri were chosen.

Party Glossary

PCU	United Conservative Party* (*Partido Conservador Unido*)
PL	Liberal Party (*Partido Liberal*)
PR	Radical Party (*Partido Radical*)
PDC	Christian Democratic Party (*Partido Demócrata Cristiano*)
PS	Socialist Party (*Partido Socialista*)
PCCh	Communist Party of Chile (*Partido Comunista de Chile*)
PADENA	National Democratic Party (*Partido Democrático Nacional*)
PD	Democratic Party (*Partido Democrático*)
VNP	National Vanguard of the People (*Vanguardia Nacional del Pueblo*)

* Often referred to simply as *Partido Conservador* (Conservative Party).

thrown into the Congress, this body might exercise its legal right and ignore Allende's lead, the other major contender, Christian Democrat Frei, hastened to say that if he were the one chosen under those circumstances he would not accept the presidency. The 1964 election could indeed have been a strong test of respect for this tradition, since 57 per cent of the members of the Congress at that time belonged to political forces of the Liberal-Conservative-Radical coalition. Although the coalition disintegrated prior to the election, Liberals and Conservatives had supported the Frei candidacy, and the Radicals had backed a candidate of their own (Julio Durán) in hopes of maintaining their influence in the making of future governments. Composition of the Congress was fairly one-sided in favor of the Center-Right, as Table 13 shows:

Table 13

	PCU	PL	PR	PDC	PADENA	PS	PCCh	VNP	Ind
Chamber	17	28	39	23	12	12	16		
Senate	4	9	13	4	0	7	4	1	3
Total	21	37	52	27	12	19	20	1	3

Conservatives and Liberals had a total in both chambers of 58 members, Radicals had 52 (the largest single congressional party representation), Christian Democrats had 27, and the leftist bloc consisted of 62 deputies and senators.

Campaigns

According to the Electoral Law, campaigning for congressional and municipal elections is limited to a two-month period and for presidential elections to a six-month period. This restriction, however, is in practice applied only to electoral propaganda in the news media and on posters, circulars, and similar vehicles, in which case it is rigidly observed; otherwise electoral campaigns in Chile are lengthy. Presidential candidates are often in the field over a year and a half before the scheduled election. In all Chilean elections, the interplay of interests and the adjustment of differences that normally mark the campaigning of candidates representing competitive political groups take place early. Posters, banners, and other similar materials fall under the jurisdiction of the municipal councils, which limit them in the manner described above.[28] Although in general few efforts have been made to regulate campaign financing, an electoral provision does limit newspaper and magazine charges for political propaganda on their pages to the normal advertising rates for the preceding six months.[29] The rule that all propaganda must cease forty-eight hours before the polls open is rigidly observed. It is a customary and legal practice for the political parties to set up information booths in the polling places during the last two days before an election.[30]

As the base of the electorate broadens, parties are utilizing every possible device to reach back-country districts heretofore the private electoral preserves of conservative landholders, who were able to control the votes of the *fundo* workers. Much of the recent success of the leftist FRAP and of the Christian Democrats is a result of some of these new campaign techniques. A good example is the zealous and astute campaign conducted by the FRAP in Curicó, a typical Conservative-dominated province, for the special by-election of May, 1964. During that campaign, which resulted in a stunning victory for the leftist candidate and the disintegration of the Radical-Conservative-Liberal alliance, FRAP's top national leaders and local workers honeycombed the entire province, pleading, cajoling, and often dispensing medicines and foodstuffs. Into the central squares of remote villages, teams of young FRAP students drove trucks loaded with portable generators to provide power for movies or public address systems. At

28 It is noteworthy that in Santiago, in contrast to other Latin American capitals which remain literally covered with banners, posters, slogans painted on walls, etc., for months after an election, municipal workers start removing all propaganda materials within hours after polling places close.

29 *Chile: Election Factbook,* p. 44. There are practically no data available on this important subject of campaign financing, with the exception of some extremely rough estimates made by political commentators from time to time. For example, in the 1957 election it was estimated that a candidate for senator in the Santiago district spent an average of 40,000,000 pesos. The same article estimated a total of 490,000,000 pesos spent in that year's campaign. See *El Debate,* January 30, 1957, p. 1.

30 *Chile: Election Factbook,* p. 44.

other times, these students set up in these trucks temporary dispensaries to provide medical services, thus gaining the sympathy of thousands of peasant laborers. In the Curicó election, both the FRAP and the Christian Democrats appealed most effectively to the voters' pocketbooks. They attacked the futile efforts of the government to stem the spiraling cost of living and criticized its delay in handling a wage-readjustment bill. While these economic issues contributed to swinging the electorate to the Left, the FRAP campaign tactics undoubtedly added to the margin of its candidate's victory. In the first place, by nominating Naranjo, son of the deceased deputy who formerly represented the district, FRAP appealed to the voters' sentimentality. The image of the popular physician Naranjo, as projected by the leftist propaganda, was of a doctor who worked with "apostolic dedication," ministering to the poor.[31] Another noteworthy aspect of the Curicó campaign was the importation by the government coalition and the landowners of several well-known former prize fighters. This move had the double objective of capitalizing on whatever popularity the fighters might have had and of intimidating the opposition. In contrast, the FRAP and the PDC imported popular figures in show business and well-known intellectuals. Furthermore, in a dramatic maneuver to minimize electoral bribery, FRAP and PDC followers laid siege to a local bank after learning that its employees had worked overtime to packet 250,000 escudos into bundles of five- and ten-escudo bills. Even though the FRAP and PDC did not prove that the money was intended to buy votes, the government forces lost face. Following the incident, while the Conservatives denounced the local military forces for not breaking up the demonstration, Allende, the FRAP presidential standard-bearer, found himself in the convenient position of being able to commend the army for its exemplary behavior.[32]

Recent Electoral Trends

An analysis of the elections held in Chile in the last twelve years indicates the presence of some political trends of major significance. First, there has been a substantial increase in the size of the electorate. Not all of the increase can be attributed to the growth of the population; a sizable portion has resulted from greater participation of groups previously excluded from the political process. The entry of women into national politics in 1952 had unquestionably a large influence.

[31] *Hispanic American Report,* XVII, No. 3 (May, 1964), pp. 255–256. Hereafter cited as *HAR*.

[32] *Ibid.,* p. 256.

Since that year the percentage of votes cast by women has been rising steadily in all elections. Indications are that the percentage will continue to climb and may eventually reach 40 to 50 per cent of the vote. Many new voters, male and female, have been added to the voting lists as a result of zealous proselytizing by dynamic political organizations such as the Christian Democratic Party and the Left coalition.

Other trends to be noted are the remarkable decrease in the number of political parties with the extinction of the "accidental" organizations and the increasing polarization in the alignment of political factions. This phenomenon became distinct in the 1964 election. Important shifts have occurred in the political party system: the Radical Party, which held the key to coalition politics for the past twenty-five years as leader or partner of Center-Left and Center-Right alliances, has surrendered the balance of power to the Christian Democrats. The latter have risen spectacularly in the past few years. Accompanying these events is evidence of a strong swing to the Left on the part of the electorate and a growing radicalism on the part of the intellectual leadership, which is searching for new solutions to Chile's old social and economic ills. This intellectual revolutionary potential and the effects it may have upon politics should not be underestimated.[33] Recent legislative reforms have brought about the elimination of many vices that marred the Chilean electoral system. Principally, they have put an end to party coalitions in congressional and municipal elections which had led to so many disreputable practices. These reforms have contributed considerably to the decrease in the number of parties.

The 1952 Presidential Election

Results of recent elections illustrate the trends suggested above. In the 1952 presidential elections, the Ibáñez victory was essentially a personal one. He was supported by a miscellany of groups from Right to Left that produced a catch-all political platform. His election marked the end of the fourteen-year period of Radical control of the presidency. The principal lesson to be derived from the Ibáñez election was that for the first time in the history of the country a majority of *fundo* workers and tenant farmers defied control of the rightist landowners in order to vote for Ibáñez. The majority of the leftist forces supported him, in spite of the Socialist candidacy of Allende. For the first time these leftist forces made inroads into the rural districts of central Chile — traditionally solid conservative territory.

[33] For comments on Latin America's intellectual rebellion, see Tad Szulc, *The Winds of Revolution* (New York: Frederick A. Praeger, Inc., 1963), pp. 293–302.

Ibáñez led in seventeen provinces, while the rightist candidate Matte led in six and the Radical Party standard-bearer Alfonso led in two. Ibáñez received a clear majority in several provinces, including Santiago and Valparaíso, and came close to obtaining a majority in other important provinces, such as Concepción and Cautín.

Municipal Elections of 1956

The results of the first elections held during the Ibáñez administration in April, 1956, were not unexpected, but they were nevertheless significant. Approximately 45 per cent of the Chilean electorate went to the polls to choose some 1,500 councilmen in 263 communities throughout the country. The newly established leftist coalition, the Popular Action Front (*Frente de Acción Popular,* FRAP) obtained some important victories, polling a total of about 26 per cent of the vote. Simultaneous elections in the provinces of Tarapacá and Valparaíso were held to fill vacancies in the Chamber of Deputies caused by death. The FRAP contributed substantially to the victory of the Radical candidate in Tarapacá and won a victory for its own candidate in Valparaíso. The Radicals polled 24 per cent of the vote. Results showed that many of the small parties, notably the Agrarian Party, that had supported Ibáñez in 1952 had all but disappeared. Moderate successes were achieved by Conservatives and Liberals, who together polled 31.4 per cent of the vote; but the greatest gains were made by the leftist wing of the Radical Party. The *Falange* (Christian Democrats), still a small party at that time, polled only 6 per cent of the vote.

Congressional Elections of 1957

In the March, 1957, congressional elections a definite swing to the Center occurred. The Radicals became the largest single bloc in the lower house, with thirty-six seats. The leftist FRAP coalition lost sixteen seats, retaining only twenty-one out of the total of thirty-seven deputies who had represented it in the Chamber prior to the election.[34] The big losers, however, were the Agrarian Laborites (supporters of Ibáñez), who secured only eleven seats, as against the twenty-three they had held in the previous Congress. The Christian Democrats (then called *Falange Nacional*) made impressive gains. The party's representation in the Chamber increased from five to sixteen, while its leader Eduardo Frei received the largest vote (60,000) of any senatorial candidate in Santiago. The Santiago senatorial race also indicated a resurgence of the Liberal Party with the impressive victory of its

[34] *HAR,* X. No. 3 (April, 1957), p. 145.

candidate Jorge Alessandri. After the election Frei and Alessandri were recognized as strong aspirants for the 1958 presidential race.

The 1958 Presidential Election

Alessandri narrowly won the plurality in 1958 — 31.6 per cent of the vote — and the presidency. Geographically, the voting pattern of the election was complex. Alessandri fared well in many provinces but failed to obtain a clear majority in any single province.[35] In the urban province of Santiago, which accounted for 29 per cent of the national vote, 35 per cent of the ballots went to Alessandri, as opposed to 28 per cent for Allende. On the other hand, in the northern mining provinces of Tarapacá, Antofagasta, Atacama, and Coquimbo and in the south-central coal mining and industrial districts of Concepción and Arauco, the FRAP candidate Bossay's votes, although small in number, were geographically dispersed.[36] Significant, however, was Bossay's failure to obtain more votes in the central region, where his percentage fell far below his national average of 15 per cent. Christian Democrat Frei received the steady support of roughly 20 per cent of the electorate throughout the country. His percentages fell below 15 in only three small districts out of 29; and they went over 25 in another three, including Valparaíso. Although (as we have seen) leftist strength was highest in the northern provinces and in Concepción, traditional strongholds of leftism, Allende also did very well in the second Santiago district and in several scattered small provinces, and his provincial percentage only twice fell below 20.[37] He led Alessandri in the southernmost provinces of Aysén and Magallanes. In fact, his lead in Magallanes was five to one.

The most significant feature of the 1958 election was its confirmation of the trend initiated in 1952, when the rural conservative-dominated districts went to Ibáñez. Observers had predicted a strong FRAP showing in the industrial and mining regions, and a FRAP victory in those areas was therefore not surprising. What was indeed a surprise, however, was the remarkable strength shown by the leftist candidate in the agricultural areas of the central Valley — traditionally oligarchical strongholds.

Municipal Elections of 1960

Two years later in municipal elections, Chilean voters indicated approval of the Alessandri administration by giving the Liberal and

[35] *Chile: Election Factbook*, p. 36.
[36] *El Mercurio*, September 8, 1958, p. 1.
[37] *Chile: Election Factbook*, p. 36.

Conservative parties that had sponsored him a strong endorsement. The Conservatives obtained 14.7 per cent of the vote and the Liberals 15.3, making the total share of votes obtained by the rightist group 29.4 per cent. But again the centrist Radical Party, which was then following a policy of independence while supporting Alessandri's program, proved to be the favorite at the polls. The FRAP coalition suffered significant losses in the 1960 election. The rightist political bloc which supported Alessandri obtained 645 seats, the Radicals 414, and the Christian Democrats 251. The FRAP was last, with 240 councilmen. Although it is true that in Chile municipal elections ordinarily attract considerably fewer voters than national contests, the FRAP losses from a 1958 total vote of 356,493 to a 1960 vote of 276,045 were substantial enough to indicate a decline in favor with the voters.[38] All symptoms pointed to the electorate's continued move toward the Center-Right, indicating approval of Alessandri's economic and social programs.

Congressional Elections of 1961

The 1961 congressional elections clearly indicated that the political pendulum was again swinging to the Left. Judging by the results of those elections, a strong anti-government sentiment had developed among the voters.[39] Disillusioned by the slowness of reforms and impatient with Alessandri's austerity program, the Chilean voter gave solid support to the leftist coalition and to the Left-Center Christian Democrats. The FRAP obtained more votes than any other party or political bloc. The Communist Party obtained five of the twenty-five senate seats being contested and secured sixteen seats in the Chamber of Deputies. The FRAP now controlled 27.5 per cent of all seats in the Chamber. The Christian Democratic Party also made dramatic advances, receiving more votes then the Conservatives and coming into control of 14.6 per cent of the Chamber's seats. The Conservative and Liberal Parties, components of the rightist bloc, both lost seats. However, the Liberal-Conservative-Radical (the Radical Party had joined the government in 1960) government coalition managed to retain its majority in both houses of the Congress, thanks to the support of the Radicals, who made no gains but at least retained their congressional strength. Once more the Radical Party had become the

[38] *HAR,* XIII, No. 4 (June, 1960), p. 268.

[39] A good comparative analysis of the 1961 election is Germán Urzúa V., "Análisis de las elecciones parlamentarias de diputados de 1957 y 1961," *Boletín chileno de ciencias políticas,* No. 11 (September-December, 1962), pp. 134–160.

key to a coalition government, this time of rightist coloration, and was to wield the actual power in the Congress, since it controlled 27.6 per cent of all seats in the lower house.[40]

After disputes over several seats were settled,[41] the new Congress which convened on May 21, 1961, was composed as follows:

Table 14

Party		Chamber of Deputies		Senate	
Right-Center Coalition	Conservatives	17	84	4	26
	Liberals	28		9	
	Radicals	39		13	
Center	Christian Democrats	23	23	4	6
	Independents	—		2	
Left (FRAP)	Socialists	12	40	7	13
	Communists	16		4	
	Partido Demócrata Nacional	12		—	
	Vanguardia Nacional del Pueblo	—		1	
	Independents	—		1	
	Totals		147		45

Table 15

Congressional Elections 1961

Party	*Total Votes*	*Percentage*
Conservative	198,260	11.4
Liberal	222,485	16.5
Radical	296,828	22.0
Christian Democratic	213,468	16.0
National Democratic	95,179	7.1
Socialist	149,122	11.2
Communist	157,572	11.3
National Union	3,394	1.0
Democratic	772	
Comandos Populares de Chile	96	
Independents	2,720	
Void and blank votes	45,780	
Total	1,385,676	

[40] *Statistical Abstract of Latin America, 1963* (Los Angeles: Center of Latin American Studies, University of California, 1963), pp. 36–37.

[41] A particularly heated dispute between the Radical and Christian Democratic parties involved a senatorial seat from the provinces of Tarapacá and Antofagasta.

Party vote percentages provided further evidence of the dramatic trend begun in the 1961 election. On the Right, Conservative strength which had grown steadily in the 1940's, reaching its peak in 1950 with 25.8 per cent (the highest percentage polled by any party that year), dropped to 11.4 per cent of the vote. The Liberal Party, on the other hand, obtained 16.5 per cent of the vote, climaxing a slow climb from a low of 10.8 per cent in 1953. On the Center, the Radical Party fully recovered from the Ibáñez landslide of 1953, when it polled only 13.3 per cent of the vote. After reaching a high of 22.5 per cent in 1956, it had maintained a percentage slightly over 20 and in 1961 received 22 per cent of the vote. On the Center-Left, the Christian Democratic Party continued the steady growth it had begun after the Ibáñez period. It had indeed a remarkable record of increasing strength from only 4.7 per cent in 1950 to the 16 per cent which the party received in 1961.[42]

Results of the 1961 election were a good omen for the parties of the Left. The parties of the FRAP coalition together polled in 1961 almost 31 per cent, about one third of the total vote. The Socialist Party polled 11.2 per cent, well within its percentage average for the last two decades.[43] The Communists saw an increase in their vote from 9 per cent in 1960 to 11.3 in 1961. Although still far from the 16.5 per cent which it polled in the 1947 election just before it was outlawed, its 1961 vote nevertheless indicated a remarkable recovery. The other two FRAP partners did not fare well this time. The National Democratic Party (*Partido Nacional Democrático,* PADENA) lost its six senators but was able to elect twelve deputies. Its percentage of the vote was 7.1.[44] The other minor FRAP party, the National Vanguard of the People (*Vanguardia Nacional del Pueblo*) received about 1 per cent of the vote.[45] In total, only seven of the thirty-two political parties which had existed in the 1953 elections remained.

After the election the Radical Party, the Liberal Party, and the Conservative Party joined forces in the election of the new presiding

[42] *Chile: Election Factbook,* p. 22.

[43] The Socialists, who once (1941) had received 18 per cent of the vote (plus an additional 5 per cent of other socialist-oriented groups) hit bottom in 1947, at the height of their internecine struggles, when the entire socialist faction polled only 8.9 per cent of the total vote. They recovered during the late 1940's and 1950's with the unification of their forces.

[44] No early percentages are given because PADENA was formed only after the 1960 municipal elections from a variety of non-Marxist groups that had been followers of Ibáñez. Its two principal nuclei were the former *Partido Demócrata* (PD) and the *Partido Nacional Popular* (PANAPO).

[45] *Chile: Election Factbook,* p. 22.

officers of the two houses of Congress and the committee chairmen and cooperated in filling othei important offices. This arrangement indicated that the Radicals, who had refused some half-hearted overtures from the Left and from their Center-Left rivals in the Center, the Christian Democrats, had decided to continue supporting the Alessandri administration. Hoping to gain popular backing to win the presidency in 1964, the Radicals were now sponsoring several reforms, including an agrarian reform bill.[46] The two rightist parties, Liberal and Conservatives, disturbed by their losses in the elections, began an examination of conscience, studied policies, and laid new plans. In the leftist camp, Communists and Socialists agreed to intensify their propaganda in the rural areas, a strategy which obviously was paying handsome dividends. The Christian Democrats, meeting in a convention to determine future policy, discussed three possible courses of action: first, to encourage friendly relations with the rightist parties, to which many young party stalwarts had belonged before the founding of the party; second, to seek a coalition of sorts with the Moderate Left; and third, to veer definitely to the Left, offering a strong reform program, and to make an attempt at gaining the presidency alone in 1964. The latter course was the one essentially approved by the party convention.[47]

Municipal Elections of 1963

As the municipal elections of 1963 approached, it was obvious that the government, if not Alessandri personally, had lost prestige. The national mood was one of discontent and impatience. A record number of voters participated in the election-abstention at the polls — only 22 per cent of the number registered. In all, 2,070,188 persons voted, and as has been true since 1949, women accounted for a substantial segment of the vote. The percentage of female voters had increased from 19 in the 1961 congressional election to 27. Although every political grouping claimed a victory of some sort,[48] if there was one winner in particular it was clear that it was the Christian Democratic Party. Unallied, this party managed to pile up 452,987 votes (22 per cent of the total), which was more than twice its vote in the 1961 election, and it elected 314 municipal councilmen. As a result of the Christian Democrats' victory, their organization became the single strongest party in Chile. Obviously their triumph had been at the expense of both the government Right-Center coalition and the FRAP.

[46] *Ercilla,* April 15, 1961, p. 17.
[47] *HAR,* XIV, No. 4 (June, 1961), 351.
[48] See for example, *Las últimas noticias,* April 8, 1963, pp. 3–4.

COMPARATIVE STRENGTH OF POLITICAL BLOCS

	NATIONAL DEMOCRATIC FRONT (Conservative, Liberal, Radical)	POPULAR ACTION FRONT (Socialist, Communist, National Democratic, National Vanguard)	CHRISTIAN DEMOCRATIC PARTY
1961	718,345 votes 49.9%	405,267 votes 30.6%	213,468 votes 16%
1963	940,729 votes 47.2%	589,315 votes 29.5%	452,987 votes 22.7%

Liberals, Conservatives, and Radicals together received an impressive total of 940,729 votes, and elected 952 municipal councilmen. From the standpoint of total votes, they too could claim victory, but based on terms of percentage, their share of the votes slipped from 53.2 in 1961 to 47.2. All three partners in the government coalition experienced losses. The Conservatives saw their percentage drop from 14.7 in 1961 to 11.4, and the Liberal vote decreased from 16.5 to 13.2 per cent. The Radicals did better, losing less than 1 per cent, from 22 in 1961 to 21.6 in 1963.

The Popular Action Front (FRAP) received 589,315 votes altogether and elected 339 municipal councilmen. In total number of votes, the performance at the polls of the two major leftist parties could instill much hope among their followers. The Communist Party, which in 1961 obtained only 157,572 votes, received 252,735 in 1963, thereby becoming the fourth largest single party in Chile. The Socialists took fifth place by getting 229,645, in contrast to the 149,122 received in 1961. In doing so, they managed to edge out the Conservatives by about 2,000 votes.[49] On a percentage basis, however, FRAP suffered

[49] *Vistazo,* April 9, 1963, p. 3.

some losses. Its parties slipped from a total of 30.6 per cent of the vote in 1961 to 29.5. Significantly, figures for the two major partners in the leftist coalition showed some slight gains. The Communists reached 12.7 per cent (11.7 in 1961) and the Socialists 11.5 per cent (11.2 in 1961). Clearly the two other minor allies accounted for the overall loss suffered by the Left. The National Democratic Party (PADENA) fell from 7.1 per cent in 1961 to 5.2, and the National Vanguard of the People Party dropped from 1 to 0.1 per cent of the total vote.

The Christian Democrats were naturally jubilant at the results of the election. The rightists acknowledged the loss of strength of the *Frente Democrático* (government coalition) but attempted to minimize it by attributing it to the "natural attrition" experienced after a period of time by any group in power. The Radicals had at least clearly shown the justice of their demand to head the *Frente Democrático* ticket in 1964 with a presidential candidate from their ranks. Leftist leaders commented that the "participation in the election of 700,000 new registered voters, without political experience and consisting mostly of female voters, who are most susceptible to propaganda of the Radicals and Christian Democratic Party, constituted a difficult test for FRAP."[50]

The rise of the Christian Democrats had indeed been dramatic. Their strength in northern and central Chile was amply demonstrated. In the northern provinces of Tarapacá, Antofagasta, Atacama, and Coquimbo, traditional areas of Communist strength, the Christian Democratic vote was surprisingly large. In central Chile it was equally impressive. In the province of Valparaíso, for example, the PDC received 53,480 votes, leading the Radicals by 16,000 votes and the Communists and Socialists together by roughly 6,000. Such a party upset had not occurred for twenty years in Valparaíso. In Aconcagua province, an area in which the party had made few inroads until this time, it received nearly a majority of the vote, trailing the Liberal Party by the incredibly slim margin of thirty-five votes. The Aconcagua returns were interpreted as good evidence of the party's success in attracting the vote of rural workers. In general, all indications were that a good portion of the new Christian Democratic votes were the result of desertions from the ranks of the rightist parties.[51] The success was of such magnitude that it caught the Christian Democratic leadership by surprise. It was a serious blow to the Radical Party, for besides removing it from the top of the political totem pole, the

[50] *El Mercurio,* April 10, 1963, p. 1.
[51] *Ercilla,* April 10, 1963, pp. 16–17.

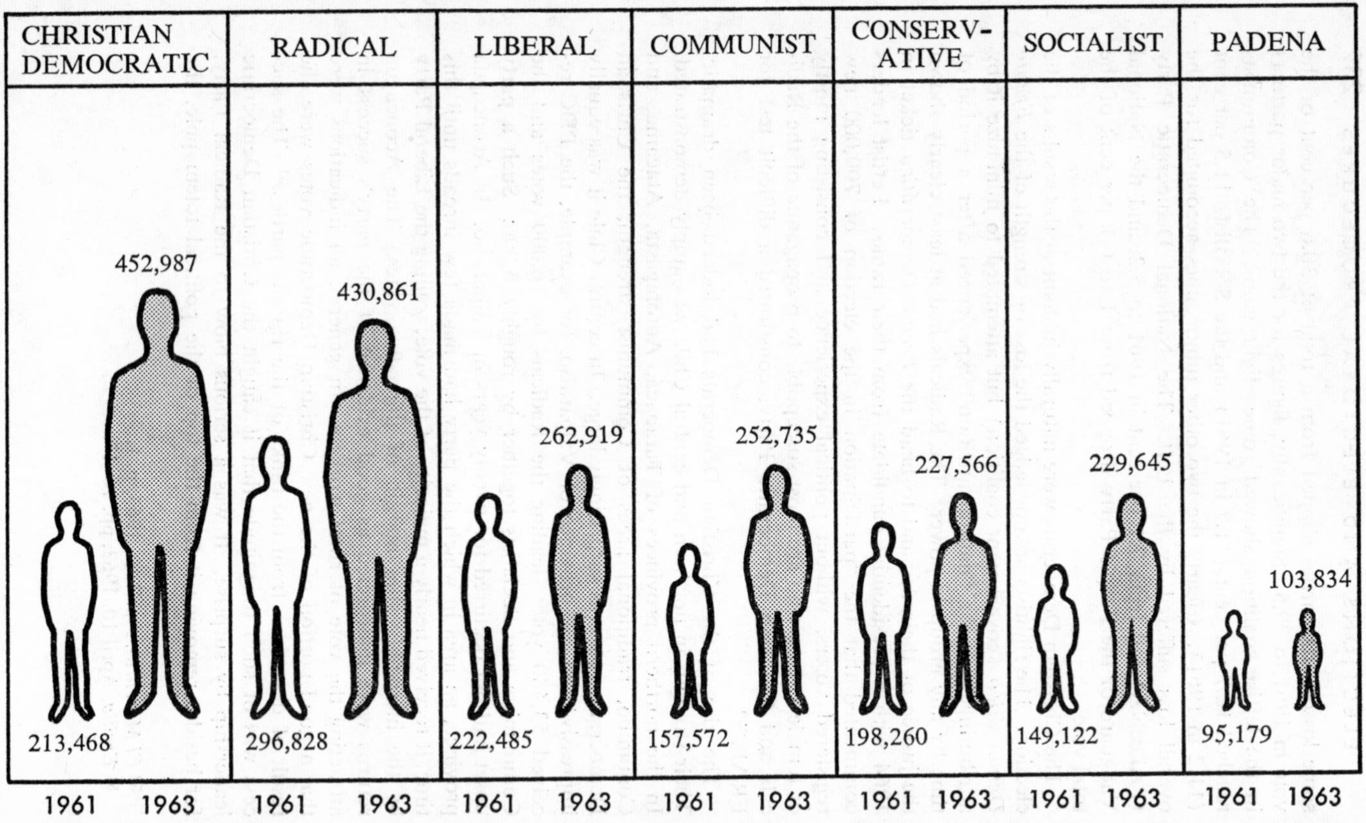

	CHRISTIAN DEMOCRATIC	RADICAL	LIBERAL	COMMUNIST	CONSERV-ATIVE	SOCIALIST	PADENA
1961	213,468	296,828	222,485	157,572	198,260	149,122	95,179
1963	452,987	430,861	262,919	252,735	227,566	229,645	103,834

PDC also threatened to dislodge it from its long-held monopoly of the Center (as representative of the professional and labor middle-class elements) in Chile's Left-Center-Right framework. (See Figure 4.)

From another angle the 1963 elections could only be interpreted as a complete repudiation of the government and a manifestation of the country's desire for change and for some basic transformation of the socio-economic status quo. The combined opposition vote was so formidable as to render only one verdict possible — the majority of Chileans wanted another policy. To many the 1963 election, more important than revealing the popularity of presidential candidates, served as an indicator of how the Chilean voter felt about the monetary devaluation, the rise in the cost of living, and many other economic and social issues.[52]

Shortly after the election, eighty top leaders of the Christian Democratic Party decided to support a PDC candidate in the 1964 presidential election and to close the door to alliances with any other party or group of parties. Senator Eduardo Frei appeared as the most likely PDC candidate. The Radicals, in turn, submitted to their partners in the *Frente Democrático* a list of six candidates headed by Senator Julio Durán, who eventually became the presidential candidate of the government coalition. The leftist bloc announced its determination to back the candidacy of the Socialist leader Salvador Allende.

The question of whether the outcome of the 1963 elections provided a sound basis for predicting the results of the presidential elections of 1964 immediately became the subject of much speculation. There were those who argued that, since the Radicals, Liberals, and Conservatives together had polled approximately 47 per cent of the vote in 1963, a candidate supported by this coalition could be expected to get approximately the same percentage of the 1964 vote. A popular opposing view, however, resorted to historical evidence to show that, although political parties had occasionally been able to maintain their voting strength from local to presidential elections, more often they had not. The case most often cited in support of this view was the 1958 presidential contest. In this election candidates Alessandri and Allende polled vote percentages which were close to the ones obtained in 1956 by the parties supporting them in 1958. Alessandri polled 31.2 per cent of the vote, compared with 31.4 per cent polled by Liberals and Conservatives together in 1956. Allende obtained 28.5 per cent, compared with the FRAP total of approximately 26 per cent in 1956. But in the same presidential election, the Radical candidate Luis

[52] *HAR*, XVI, No. 4 (June, 1963), 388.

Bossay received only 15 per cent, compared to his party's 24 per cent in 1956. Furthermore, on the same occasion, Frei, the Christian Democratic candidate, got 20 per cent of the vote while his party had received only 6 per cent in 1956. The 1958 election is not an exceptional case, and Chilean electoral records in the last quarter of a century abound in similar instances. There cannot be much validity to generalizations about the carry-over of voting strength from one election to another if it is not supported by historical fact. In as fluid a political environment as Chile's, where conditions and tensions fluctuate and new issues are constantly arising, many other factors besides the voting strength shown at the preceding election are likely to play an important and even decisive role in any presidential race.[53]

The Curicó Election of 1964

The truth of this assertion was soon to be demonstrated, at least in part, by the outcome of a special congressional election in Curicó province, about a year later. In this province, which is 90 per cent rural and had always been considered a conservative stronghold, the FRAP coalition scored a remarkable victory in March, 1964. In this election the candidate supported by the Radical-Liberal-Conservative coalition was able to poll only 32.5 per cent of the vote in the province, a 17 per cent drop. The FRAP forces augmented their 1963 showing in Curicó by 10.1 per cent, from a total of 29.1 per cent in 1963 to 39.2 in 1964. The Christian Democrats, who in 1963 had obtained 21.5 per cent, increased their Curicó polling strength by 6.2 per cent, receiving 27.7 per cent of the vote.[54] In addition to the dramatic gains made by the FRAP and the PDC, voting statistics indicated that it was the larger and more assertive male vote which had swung the Curicó electorate to the FRAP candidate. The Curicó election caused, in Allende's words, "a veritable earthquake" in Chilean politics. Immediate consequences of the rightist debacle were the disbanding of the *Frente Democrático,* the withdrawal of its candidate Durán (who later was renominated by his party as the Radical standard-bearer), and the subsequent unconditional endorsements of Christian Democrat Frei by the Liberal and Conservative parties. In less than one year since the 1963 municipal elections, the Chilean political picture had radically changed, and the fortunes of all parties had been affected. The Curicó episode, besides reflecting a growing disenchantment with the Alessandri administration, portended a shift to the extreme Left

[53] *Chile: Election Factbook,* p. 38.

[54] For details on the Curicó campaign, see pp. 229–230.

in Chilean politics. Durán's withdrawal of his Democratic Front candidacy "showed the fundamental weakness of an alliance of a middle-of-the-road Radical Party, eager to appeal to the mass of voters now swinging leftward, and the right-wing Conservative and Liberal Party identified with the business and landowning classes."[55] Old-guard Radicals hoped their party might drain enough votes from both the Christian Democrat and the FRAP candidates to improve their bargaining position in a future government. The rightist forces, in near panic at the prospect of a FRAP victory, accepted the only alternative: to make a plea for the unification of non-Marxist forces to fight the strong Left and to support the candidacy of Senator Frei. Thus, as the 1964 presidential elections approached, political forces solidified into two blocs, both leaning toward the Left of the political spectrum: on one side a non-Marxist democratic Left-Center bloc led by the Christian Democrats with the support of the rightist parties, and on the other a confident Socialist-Communist-dominated FRAP coalition. Torn between these two blocs stood the Radical Party, still the most important party in Congress, trying to hold together the heterogeneous components that its organization contains. The outcome and implications of the 1964 election, the most important in Chile since 1920, are discussed in the concluding chapter of this book.

[55] *HAR,* XVII, No. 4 (June, 1964), 353.

6

The Party System

Chile is the only Latin American country where political forces are clearly and distinctly aligned, as in many European countries, into three great blocs: the Right, the Center, and the Left. The resemblance of the Chilean party system to that of much of Europe and particularly to the system which existed in France during the Third and Fourth Republics is striking and has been noted by many observers. Students of comparative politics who are familiar with both countries are prone to compare Chile's Radical party and the French Radicals of the Third Republic, to conclude that both are similar and both have played an almost identical role in their respective systems as the middle-of-the-road, bureaucratic party, representative of middle-class interests. It is equally tempting to compare the working alliance of Communists and Socialists in Chile with the present cooperative arrangement between their counterparts in the Italian Republic or to attempt to determine to what extent the Chilean Christian Democrats have been influenced by the Christian Socialist movement of Germany and Italy. Chilean politics are undoubtedly more nearly "European" than is the case elsewhere in Latin America, but yet there are features that are uniquely and typically Chilean. Ideologically speaking, "the Chilean political scale is overbalanced to the Left: the Conservatives and the Liberals have accepted existing liberal democratic institutions and therefore cannot be called extreme rightist parties in the same sense that European monarchist or fascist parties can. The Right and the Left are almost equal in the number of votes received, with each getting a little over a quarter of the total; the Center receives almost half."[1]

Chile is also often cited as the best example of the multiparty system which is common, although in somewhat different forms, throughout Latin America. It comes close to having parties representing the entire

[1] *Chile: Election Factbook*, p. 22.

range of political tendencies. In the period of approximately one hundred years during which the multiparty system has functioned in Chile, the number of parties in existence has varied widely, reaching a maximum of thirty-six in 1953. However, for more than thirty years six major parties, which with one exception are all over half a century old, have dominated the political field. As the preceding chapters make clear, the majority of the voters have been flocking in recent years to these six traditional forces. In the present chapter, Chilean parties will be analyzed from three perspectives: (1) of the nature of their program and its doctrinal foundations or ideology; (2) of the characteristics of their rank-and-file members, and (3) of the elements of their internal structure and organization. Chilean political blocs and their component parties will be discussed from Right to Left. Ideological approaches to economic issues and problems of development have already been presented in Chapter 3.

The Right

The Right is composed of the United Conservative Party and the Liberal Party. These two parties, either officially or unofficially allied, have since 1933 established national policy or at least wielded a generally effective veto power over it. Although originally divided by religious issues, they have been in accord in their opposition of reform measures advocated by the newer political groups. The failure of middle-class leadership reinforced the power of these two traditional groups which culminated in Jorge Alessandri's election in 1958. In 1961, the Radical Party joined the administration coalition, and in October, 1962, the three parties joined forces in a Democratic Front. In 1964, the new coalition disintegrated, and Liberals and Conservatives separately endorsed the presidential candidate of the Christian Democrats.

The Conservative Party

The oldest and first ruling party in Chile, the Conservative (now officially known as the United Conservative) Party traditionally has been the party of the wealthy landed aristocracy. It emerged from the turmoil of the early 1930's in better condition than any other political organization, with its economic base intact. In their 1932 convention, the Conservatives reaffirmed a position on the extreme Right, opposed to any kind of socio-economic liberalism.[2] From that time until very recently the Conservatives' economic strength — the land system —

[2] *Programa y estatutos aprobados en la Convención General del Partido Conservador efectuada en Santiago, 24–25 de septiembre de 1932* (Santiago, 1933).

has never been in any danger from expropriation or confiscatory taxes.

Ideology. The foreword to the Conservative Party platform adopted in 1961 declared that the party's fundamental doctrine conforms to the teachings of the Church. Although it accepts the presidential regime as the most workable in the present circumstances, it advocates re-establishment of a parliamentary system whenever circumstances permit. It favors restriction of the President's veto power as well as of his authority to urge Congress to enact legislation through "special procedures" (*sistema de urgencia*);[3] it proposes that Senate approval of Vice-President designees be required; and it advocates the immediate creation of administrative tribunals. The party platform contains declarations in favor of: the delegation of certain legislative powers in some circumstances; a decentralized system of administration; electoral reforms designed to eliminate minor political parties; and "the development of a corporate spirit."[4] In the area of education the platform supports the freedom to teach but advocates the right of the Church to give religious instruction in all state and private institutions.[5]

In foreign policy, the Conservative program proposes the strengthening of the United Nations and the Organization of American States. Specifically mentioned are international recognition of the Holy See and the principle that no state has the right to intervene in the internal affairs of another. The platform urges respect for existing treaties and the peaceful solution of international controversies. It recommends Chile's participation in regional arrangements, such as common markets, free trade zones, customs unions, and other economic associations aimed at raising the standard of living of the Chilean people.[6]

In economic matters the 1961 Conservative program marked a substantial departure from past pronouncements. After declaring private property a natural and inviolable right, it recognized that property had a twofold character, individual and social, and distinguished between the right to own and the responsibility to use property. It admitted

[3] See pages 102–103.

[4] *Declaración Fundamental, Programas y Estatutos del Partido Conservador, XVII Convención General, 1961* (Santiago: Talleres Claret, 1961), pp. 1–3.

[5] Good sources on Conservative ideology are: Marcial Sanfuentes Carrión, *El Partido Conservador* (Santiago: Editorial Universitaria, 1957); *Partido Conservador: Programa y Estatutos* (Santiago: Dirección General de Prisiones, 1933); *XVI Convención Nacional: Partido Conservador Unido* (Santiago: Imprenta Chile, 1955); José María Cifuentes, *El Partido Conservador tradicionalista* (Santiago, 1953); and Jorge I. Hubner, *El comunismo y los cristianos* (Santiago: Impresos Ober, n.d.).

[6] *Declaración Fundamental: Programas y Estatutos del Partido Conservador,* pp. 4–5.

restrictions on property in the interest of social well-being. If property is expropriated, moreover, there must be just compensation. The Conservative plank gives strong endorsement to free private enterprise as a key factor in the development process. Among other measures, the Conservatives propose to control inflation, abolish exchange controls, restrict price controls, reform taxes, seek participation of foreign capital, and promote domestic savings. Other features of the Conservative philosophy of economic development have already been discussed in Chapter 3.

The main departure from previous Conservative programs is concerned, significantly, with agrarian reform. For the first time in its long history, the Conservative Party timidly espouses the division and sale of state lands to individuals in order to create what the party calls "economic unities" and to promote development of a new rural class of owners of medium-sized farms.[7]

Fundamental to an understanding of the ideological position of Chilean Conservatives is the recognition that religious issues still play a very important role in party thought. There are many party members who believe that although the historical "theological question" may have been solved, some aspects related to family, marriage, and schools, particularly, are still valid policy issues. These Conservatives have the image of their party not chiefly as the defender of vested economic interests but as the sustainer and defender of Catholic ideals in politics.

[7] *Ibid.*, pp. 8, 18 and *passim*. Other important party documents which shed light on Conservative ideology are: *La Gran Convención Conservadora de 1878* (Santiago: Imprenta Roma, 1881); *La Convención Conservadora de 1895* (Santiago: Imprenta Roma, 1895); *Convención del Partido Conservador: 29 de septiembre de 1918* (Santiago, 1918); *Programa y estatutos aprobados en la Convención General del Partido: 29 de septiembre de 1918* (Santiago, 1918); *Convención del Partido Conservador: 19–21 de noviembre de 1921* (Santiago, 1921); *Programa y estatutos aprobados en la Convención General del Partido efectuada en Valparaíso: 12–14 junio de 1925* (Santiago, 1927); *Bases y reglamentos de la Convención Conservadora de 1929* (Santiago, 1929); *Programa y estatutos aprobados en la Convención General del Partido efectuada en Santiago: 24–25 de septiembre de 1932* (Santiago, 1933); *Memoria de la Convención General del Partido Conservador de 1933* (Santiago, 1938); *Convención General del Partido Conservador: 27–29 junio de 1947* (Santiago, 1947); *Acuerdos sociales de la decimaquinta Convención del Partido Conservador: 2–4 noviembre de 1951* (Santiago, 1952); *XVI Convención General Nacional Partido Conservador Unido: 12 octubre de 1954* (Santiago, 1955); and *Partido Conservador XIV Convención Nacional 1947 — Notas Históricas 1823–1947*, compiled by Ignacio Artega Undurraga (Santiago: Imprenta Chile, 1947). Recent and also useful are: Marcial Sanfuentes Carrión, *El Partido Conservador* (Santiago, 1957); and José María Cifuentes, *Cuestiones contemporáneas* (Santiago, 1956).

Religion is to this group, then, the *raison d'être* of the Conservative Party, and the Conservative "masses" are Conservative because they are Catholic. I myself was somewhat surprised to find that this image of the party was held by a substantial number of Conservative leaders interviewed, who discarded as unimportant any regional or class basis for their organization. In examining the records of previous campaigns it is not difficult, however, to find evidence of Conservative use of religious issues, particularly in the rural areas. In areas controlled by the big *fundo* owners, the local priest in his sermons was often given to counseling the parishioners to vote for those who "offered guarantees to the Church," without necessarily mentioning candidates' names. It is the change in these conditions, caused by the new independent voting behavior of the farm worker, that has had a profoundly damaging effect on the electoral fortunes of the Conservative Party in recent years. There are still provinces, like Chiloé, where religion is a lively issue in almost all political campaigns. On the other hand, there are those Conservatives who, without disagreeing with the predominantly Catholic nature of the party, maintain that only 50 to 60 per cent of their sympathizers follow the party out of religious convictions. In addition, one also encounters those Conservatives who criticize their party for what they consider excessive emphasis on ideological content, considering that its approach is too intellectual and that it fails to appeal to emotional factors, to attract the masses. They, this writer was once told, "are not to be convinced but to be courted like a woman, by appealing to their emotions and not to their ability to reason."

The party's attitude toward foreign affairs is based on what Frederick Pike has called "anti-United Statesism." He claims, and correctly, that since the nineteenth century the Chilean right has been consistent in its dislike of United States culture and life and steadfast in its desire to maintain the traditional and allegedly superior Chilean culture and civilization. Chile's Conservative aristocracy, even if it concedes the need for social reform, is committed to the stratified, hierarchical, closed society. The political and social concepts of the Chilean Right and its anti-Americanism are closely related, then. At the same time, however, close political association with the United States is regarded as a necessary bulwark against the radicalism espoused by competing parties from the Left.[8] Often indistinguishable from anti-United Statesism is the cult of Hispanism (exalting the importance of the Spanish heritage) so often encountered among Chilean Conservatives.[9]

[8] Frederick B. Pike, *Chile and the United States 1880–1962* (Notre Dame: University of Notre Dame Press, 1963), pp. 250–256.

[9] A distinguished exponent of spiritually-culturally motivated anti-Americanism and of Hispanism is Jaime Eyzaguirre. See his book *La fisonomía histórica de Chile* (Santiago: Editorial del Pacífico, 1948).

Composition. Traditionally, the core of the Conservative Party has been the high-status groups, the socially notable, represented by the large landowners and the old aristocratic families. Today, however, many loyal Conservatives are deep in modern business activities and may no longer be dependent on income derived from land ownership. Still, the tap root of Conservative strength is chiefly rural, and the number of landowners in the party and the influence they exert in party affairs is greater than the number and influence of industrialists and businessmen. It would be a misrepresentation to say that the party has no popular base of any kind and that it consists only of the small aristocratic élite, for the fact is that among Conservative voters — if not among active party members — there are at least some representatives of the lower-middle and rural working classes. This is, in fact, a characteristic of the Chilean political party system, wherein it is not possible to find a single party to which access is denied to the lower socio-economic groups. All parties receive some degree of support from these segments of society. To be sure, this support diminishes consistently as one moves from the right to the left end of the political spectrum. Also worth mentioning is the fact that in recent years the Conservatives have been relatively successful in proselytizing among youth groups. While the powerful national organization, the Student Federation of Chile, was the exclusive preserve for many years of Radicals, Communists, Socialists, and later of Christian Democrats, today there exists within the student movement a vigorous and well-organized, if small, Conservative movement. As for the urban worker, even if he is Catholic and Conservative by family tradition, once he becomes a member of a union he almost invariably deserts the Conservative Party, since the Marxist influence is deeply felt in labor organizations.

The leadership of the Conservatives belongs primarily to the upper class. There are, however, notable exceptions; some extremely gifted men of modest antecedents have been able to rise to a high position in party councils. The national president of the party in the late 1950's was not an aristocrat but a man from lower-middle-class, almost proletarian, origins who had become wealthy. An influential young Conservative leader in Congress at that time came also from a lower-middle-class background. A member of a family of twenty-one children, he was brought up in the strongly Conservative province of Colchagua. His record first as a student in the Catholic University and later as a lawyer and professor had called him to the attention of Conservative leaders. He worked his way up in the party hierarchy, and six months after having been elected president of the Conservative Youth (a unit of the party), he was holding a Conservative seat in the Chamber of Deputies.

But these cases are rather rare. The generalization can be made that Conservative leadership at least 70 per cent of the time originates in the landed aristocracy and that party positions at the provincial level are most frequently occupied by individuals with a solid middle-class heritage. A member of the latter group can only occasionally rise to party prominence, in spite of his social origins, if he demonstrates outstanding personal qualities. Invariably such individuals have in the course of time become wealthy in their own right. They often marry into the Conservative élite, which then accepts them as its own. This is suggestive of the differences in recruitment patterns and party careers of the Conservative Party as compared to other organizations. While in some of these parties, individuals reach high circles through a fairly rigid "merit system" and by gradual promotion from the lowest party levels, in the Conservative Party leaders are usually elevated to their high rank on the basis of qualifications other than long and meritorious party service. As regards public office, however, the requirement of having served as *alcalde* (mayor) seems to be established. A party member referred to this practice as the *universidad de las alcaldías* (literally, the university of the mayoralties). Almost invariably, Conservative political figures start their public service in a local elective office, pass on to the Chamber of Deputies, and later are elected to the Senate. The case of a Conservative gaining a congressional seat without previous experience at the local level is exceptional. Homogeneity of social base and a high degree of internal discipline are the chief characteristics of the Conservative organization. It is a small party in terms of registered members — having perhaps not more than 5,000 active members — but its electoral following is, of course, greater than that figure indicates. As a party official put it, "Those who are part of the mystical body of the church are precious few but those who share its soul are legion."

Structure and Organization. Party organization is somewhat reflective of the hierarchical character of Conservative forces. The principal levels of authority in the party are, beginning with the lowest: The Communal Assembly (*Asamblea Comunal*); the Communal Committee (*Directorio Comunal*); the Departmental Committee (*Directorio Departamental*); the Provincial President (*Presidente Provincial*); the Provincial Council (*Consejo Provincial*); the President of the Party (*Presidente del Partido*); the High Commissions (*Comisiones Superiores*); the Executive Committee (*Junta Ejecutiva*); the General Directory (*Directorio General*); the Supreme Tribunal (*Tribunal Supremo*); and the National Convention (*Convención Nacional*). In addition the party has the following branch organizations: The Feminine Section, the Conservative Youth, the National Organization of

Conservative Workers, and the Department of Conservative Trade Unions.[10]

The Communal Assemblies, one for each *Comuna,* are composed of registered voters who have been party members for at least six months. They elect the members of the Communal Committees and nominate candidates for municipal councilmen and deputies. Candidates are selected from a list of names containing twice the number of nominations to be made. This list is made up by the respective Departmental Committee and by the Communal Committee. Candidates for the Chamber of Deputies are chosen from a list containing four times the number of candidates to be selected. Half of this list is submitted by the Departmental Committee and the other half by the Executive Committee.

Each Communal Committee is composed of eleven members, but this number may be altered by the Executive Committee. In each departmental seat there is a Departmental Committee composed of the president, the vice-president, and three delegates of the corresponding Communal Committee; the presidents of the rest of the Communal Committees of the department; three members elected by the Communal Presidents of the department; the Provincial Presidents of the Conservative Youth, the Feminine Section, and the National Organization of Conservative Workers; and the Provincial President of the party.

The president and vice-president for each province are elected for one year by a special provincial commission, chiefly composed of Conservative congressmen and ex-congressmen and councilmen in that province. The real locus of party authority is the Executive Committee, headed by a president. Its members are elected by the General Directory and are: the president (who is the national head of the party); two vice-presidents; nine other members of the Directory; the national president of the Conservative Youth and the president of the Feminine Section; the secretary general; the treasurer; and five members elected from the party's representatives in the Congress. The Executive Committee has always been at the summit of the party's organizational structure and serves as arbiter of intra-party problems and disputes. It has broad power over financial and personnel matters, and its power over lower party levels is all pervasive. The Executive Committee may make pacts or agreements with other parties; it authorizes party members to accept Cabinet portfolios, diplomatic posts, and other high offices; it oversees the conduct of Conservative members of the Congress; and it implements decisions of the Convention and

[10] See *Estatutos del Partido Conservador* (Santiago: Imprenta Claret, 1961), Arts., 11, 12, 28, 45, 46, 62, 66, 67, 69, and 70.

the General Directory.[11] The vast powers of this body are indicated by its authority to nominate party candidates for the Senate. The General Directory, a large (approximately 600 persons) body composed of all important party officials at the various levels and an additional 100 members elected by the Convention, chooses the members of the Executive Committee and designates the party's presidential candidate. The Supreme Tribunal is the disciplinary organ of the party.

National Conventions are held every four years, with extra sessions held on call of the Executive Committee. Usually the Convention provides the opportunity for formalizing decisions that have been made beforehand in official and unofficial group meetings of party leaders. The duties of the Convention are: review of the activities of other organs of the party, evaluation of the policies of the government in light of the party program, and formulation of the principles and program of the party. Invariably the Convention is manipulated by the party leadership, which sees to it that the desired decisions are reached.

The Conservative Party is a highly disciplined organization in which the so-called "principle of authority" is sacrosanct. Very little power is allowed the lower party echelons. All important decisions are made by the leadership, and there is remarkably little evidence of any desire on the part of the members to assert themselves. The president of the Committee is by far the most influential individual in the party. More than from any personal qualifications he may possess, his power and authority emanate from the prestige of the office itself. Conservatives are fond of speaking of "impersonal government," a concept reminiscent of the Portales era. Decisions of the Committee are always put into effect, even when the choice of candidates is imposed on the local party level from above. Often candidates without any local roots are selected by the national leadership, and always they are passively accepted by the local party units. According to a party leader, revolt is impossible because those who refuse to accept decisions "are disgraced for several generations." They are socially as well as politically isolated and are repudiated by their fellows in the aristocracy. Furthermore, communication between the national and local leadership is very limited, and there is little emotional or spiritual cohesion between leaders and the rank and file.

The Liberal Party

As we have seen, the other wing of the Chilean Right, the Liberal Party, had its origins in the 1840's in the opposition of the commer-

[11] Mario Verdugo Marinkovic, "Programas y estatutos de los partidos políticos chilenos," *Boletín chileno de ciencias políticas,* No. 12, (1963), pp. 48–49.

cially oriented segment of the upper class to the authoritarian and ecclesiastical bias of the Conservative Party. Originally inspired by the intellectual movement of 1842 and advocating separation of church and state, extension of civil liberties and suffrage, and limitation of executive authority, the Liberal forces came to power in 1861 and ruled securely until 1891 during the so-called "Liberal Republic." In this period, Liberal administrations encouraged the expansion of the country into the northern and southern territories. A dynamic economic atmosphere led the Liberals to pass a series of reforms removing control of marriages and birth and death registration from the Church and eradicating property and income qualifications for voting. With the disappearance of the religious issue after the fall of Balmaceda in 1891, no substantial difference separated the Liberals and the Conservatives. In the 1920's relations between the two parties tended to deteriorate, as Conservatives reacted unfavorably to the support that many Liberals gave to the campaign to separate church and state. However, in the 1930's the majority of the Conservatives became reconciled to the decline of the religious issue in order to cooperate with the Liberal Party in protecting the social order that both espoused. Having arrived at a consensus that both commercial and agricultural interests could be safeguarded without damage to either, today Liberals and Conservatives are solidly united in Chilean politics.

Ideology. Traditionally, the Liberal Party has been open-minded toward change, espousing individual freedom, favoring the rights of the legislative branch over executive prerogatives, and upholding local autonomy against central control. The Liberals are also, if only very mildly, anticlerical, in consonance with the history of their party. Ideologically speaking, differences between them and the Conservatives are so tenuous they can be reduced to matters of degree and sometimes almost of inflection or tone. Thus, for instance, usually Liberals, although they are nationalists, tend to be less vehement in this respect than dyed-in-the-wool Conservatives. The foreword to the Liberal Party platform declares that its fundamental doctrine is one in which "social justice, freedom, and human dignity are paramount." It further proclaims an adherence to the system of free enterprise and declares that "the State is a means and not an end, and that therefore its authority should not exceed beyond what is indispensable for the harmonious development of the individual and of society."[12]

Like the Conservatives, the Liberals advocate a parliamentary system on the basis of strong and well-organized parties, but, given the present stage of political and social development, admit the necessity of a presidential regime, with some modifications designed to

[12] *Programa y estatuto orgánico del Partido Liberal* (Santiago: n.p., 1962), pp. 1–3.

strengthen the supervisory attributes of the legislative branch. In foreign policy, the Liberal platform advocates the right of "international free determination" and champions a system of cooperation and solidarity among the nations of the American continent, based on the principle of juridical equality of all nations and freedom from external interference. Free enterprise and private initiative are held by the Liberal Party to be the basis of all human progress and social well-being. Its program specifically disavows the displacement of private enterprise by the state and, in fact, declares that it is a primary function of government to protect and promote private activities aimed at developing national production.[13] A section of the Liberal program deals particularly with social problems. Though it is worded somewhat vaguely, it seems to center around a fervent mystique of national dedication to service, and it reiterates the conception that the only role of the state is to serve as arbiter between capital and labor. To combat strikes it advocates severe measures, to be taken without any limitation by the laws.[14] In spite of this policy, it is interesting to note that the Liberals, flexible as they are in view of their own rapidly increasing economic power and the kind of political nimbleness demanded by growing industrialization, recently have been making a strong bid for the labor vote and have extended their thinking, with some success, to fit the demands of a broadly national society.[15]

Composition. The core of the membership and support of the Liberal Party comes usually from groups which, while belonging to the upper stratum of Chilean society, do not predominantly depend upon agricultural activities but are connected with industry and business and in a few cases with the professions. Almost invariably the leadership comes principally from moderately progressive and modern-minded businessmen and industrialists like President Jorge Alessandri. In recent years the political base of the Liberal Party has broadened with

[13] *Ibid.*, pp. 8–10.

[14] Some sources on the history and political philosophy of the Liberal Party are: Carlos Walker Martínez, *Balance del liberalismo chileno* (Santiago: n.p., 1888); Enrique Gallo Márquez, *El liberalismo en el poder* (Santiago: n.p., 1889); *Discursos pronunciados por los senadores Francisco Bulnes Correa y otros en el debate al proyecto sobre defensa de la democracia* (Santiago: n.p., 1948); Edgardo Garrido Merino, *Espíritu y acción del liberalismo* (Santiago: n.p., 1934); Ladislao Errazuriz Pereira, *La doctrina liberal y la cuestión social* (Santiago: n.p., 1935); José Maza Fernández, *Liberalismo constructivo* (Santiago: n.p., 1942); Marcial Martínez, *Nociones sobre teoría liberal* (Santiago: n.p., 1905). Useful works by the prominent Liberal Party leader Raúl Marín Balmaceda are *Derechas o izquierdas* (Santiago: n.p., 1948) and *No demagogia* (Santiago, 1955).

[15] K. H. Silvert, "Elections, Parties, and the Law" (Santiago: American Universities Field Staff Letter, March 10, 1957), p. 16.

the participation of some middle-class and even working-class elements, giving rise to a "Liberal revival" of sorts. This broadening of electoral support manifested itself clearly during the period between 1953 to 1961, when the party's percentage of the vote climbed slowly but steadily, as a result of disillusionment with the Ibáñez administration. The party has therefore been able to develop and maintain some popular support in rural as well as urban areas, in contrast to the Conservatives, whose strength has continued to be chiefly rural. This support, as far as the urban centers are concerned, comes primarily from the *empleado* class (white-collar employees) of large industrial and business enterprises. In the rural areas it often derives from small farmers and others like them.

Despite these phenomena, the Liberal is chiefly the party of the wealthy industrialist and financier. Representatives of the party in both houses of the Congress, but particularly in the upper chamber, are usually prominent men in industry and finance, closely connected to the great mining, coal, shipping, and banking interests. However, as is the case with the Conservative Party, there are individuals of modest social derivation who manage to reach positions of responsibility in the party hierarchy and who may also be elected to office on the Liberal ticket. Again, these individuals have for the most part gained access to the upper class through successful careers in business or industry. A successful party career is not necessarily the result of long dedication to the party, and there are cases of rapid ascent based on exceptional personal circumstances. A good illustration is the case of González von Marees, leader of Chilean fascism at one time, who shortly after the admission of the fascist movement into Liberal ranks became a member of the highest echelon of the party.

Another Liberal characteristic is the relative abundance of party cliques, with consequent intergroup struggles from time to time. Some of these groups, such as those constituted by the Alessandri, the Castro, or the Opazo families, are significant centers of influence and have strong and often decisive voices in party deliberations. This in turn results in some notable differences with the other rightist party. The importance of cliques and family groups among the Liberals results in a somewhat less homogeneous organization than that of the Conservatives. There is, consequently, a smaller degree of discipline, and the organic party structure is to some degree more fluid. If among the Conservatives authority and influence are derived mainly from party position, as we have seen, personal factors such as wealth, business connections, and financial prominence count more heavily in the ranks of the Liberal Party. However, despite their differences, one characteristic that both rightist parties have in common is the pragmatic approach exhibited by their upper-class leadership and their ability to adapt themselves to changing political circumstances.

Structure and Organization. The principal organs of the party are, beginning with the lowest: the Assemblies (*Asambleas*); the Departmental Group Councils (*Consejos Agrupacionales*); the Executive Committee (*Junta Ejecutiva*); the National Council (*Consejo Nacional*); the General Directory (*Directorio General*); the Supreme Tribunal (*Tribunal Supremo*); and the General Convention (*Convención General*). In addition there are three branch organizations: the Liberal Youth, the Feminine Section, and the Trade Union Organization.

Theoretically, the General Convention is the supreme organ of the party. It must meet at least every three years. It is for all practical purposes a rubber-stamp body. Among its duties are: to introduce changes in the party statutes, to revise the party program, to resolve controversies submitted to it, and to elect the one hundred members of the General Directory. The Supreme Tribunal is entrusted with enforcing party discipline. Similar to its counterpart in the Conservative Party, the General Directory is composed of all important officials at various levels. It ratifies pacts governing presidential nominations made with other political parties by the Executive Committee or the party's president.

The National Council may present recommendations, if approved by two thirds of the members present, to the Executive Committee, and it also ratifies all agreements with other political organizations except those related to presidential nominations. The Assemblies, at the local level, nominate candidates for municipal offices in the number fixed by the Departmental Group Council and submit a list of precandidates for deputy, whose final selection is left to the Group Councils.

As is the case with the Conservative organization, the most powerful party organ is the Executive Committee. It is composed of the president and vice-presidents of the party; four senators elected by all Liberal senators; eight deputies elected by the Liberal members of the lower house; twelve members named by the General Directory; and the national president of the Liberal Youth. It selects candidates for the Senate from lists submitted by the *Consejos Agrupacionales,* and it freely chooses all candidates for congressional by-elections. Again, communication between the leadership at various command levels and the party rank and file is poor; the party is run from the top with little participation by the mass of members. There is little of the ideological fervor and *esprit de corps* characteristic of the parties of the Center and Left.

The Center

The center in Chilean politics is presently occupied by the Radical Party on the right wing and the Christian Democratic Party in a left-of-center position. Throughout the development of the Chilean party system, the Radical Party has been the medium of political expression of the middle class. Indeed, until the 1950's the growth and political inclinations of the Chilean middle class have so closely paralleled the Radical Party's doctrinal development and political action that many authors have deemed it proper to examine them together.[16] During the last two decades, the Christian Democratic Party, by means of its Roman-Catholic-oriented reform program, has succeeded in attracting large numbers of sympathizers from among the middle-class groups that traditionally constituted the electoral of the Radicals. The Center is now composed of these two forces, one old but strong and rich in traditions of European radicalism, the other young, dynamic, and a leader among the Christian Democratic forces in Latin America.

The Radical Party

From 1932 to 1964 the Radical Party had greater voting strength and generally received more support than either party of the Chilean Right. During its early period, the Radical Party subscribed to an orthodox nineteenth-century liberal point of view, deeply influenced by the ideals of French and Italian radicalism. The basic principles of that radicalism were: universal suffrage, freedom of the press, freedom of association, equality before the law, and obligatory, free, and secular education. Chilean radicalism, like its predecessors in France and Italy, arose as a reaction against oligarchical authoritarianism and in defense of individual liberty. By the first part of the twentieth century the Radical Party had evolved a collectivist orientation to meet the demands for social justice made by segments of the Chilean population. In the 1930's it cooperated with the leftist parties in working for reform. Taking the form of a Popular Front movement, this cooperation resulted in 1938 in the capture by these allies of the presidency, which they retained for the next fourteen years. During the 1940's the party lost much of its reformist zeal and gradually moved toward a position right of center, which after 1958 permitted it to unite in the Liberal-Conservative coalition under the second Alessandri.

Ideology. Much has been written about the basic schizophrenia that has beset this great political party since its very inception and more

[16] An example is John J. Johnson, *Political Change in Latin America* (Stanford: Stanford University Press, 1958), pp. 66–93.

particularly since early in this century. Among Radicals there has always existed a leftist branch advocating sweeping social reforms, even socialism, and a rightist wing identifying its political philosophy with that of Conservatives and Liberals.[17] This split has both social and ideological origins. Sociologically speaking, Chilean radicalism was led by the middle class of Chile's provinces. The core of its leaders was formed in the state secondary schools and in the University of Chile under the guidance of the great figures of Chilean liberalism who achieved the laicization of education. Anticlericalism was the chief ideological ingredient of this movement, and its development was closely linked to the influence of the Masons and to educational reform. Another important pillar of the movement was the upper-class landowners of the south, naturally of Conservative inclination, who became Radicals mainly because of their desire for clerical reform and their distrust of the spreading centralization that was placing more and more authority in Santiago.[18]

Reflecting their ties with agriculture and commerce and industry, the Radicals' attitude toward agriculture was much the same as that of the Conservatives and Liberals; and in general they supported the cheap-money policies that prevailed after 1890. They were also caught up in the spoils scramble that was a characteristic of the "parliamentary republic." Until the end of that era, the Radicals, as spokesmen for the individualists, were "doctrinaire liberals in their politics and laissez-faire adherents in their economies."[19] After the famous convention of 1906, the Party began to reflect the growing demand for reform made by the emerging working elements and the depressed salaried groups in its ranks. In the early 1930's it reaffirmed its belief in socialism and in 1932 at the Viña del Mar convention accepted the concept of the class struggle. Despite the doctrinal shift away from the original individualism of the party toward a socially oriented position,

[17] The dual nature of the Radical Party is discussed in Chapter 2, p. 56. A prominent Radical leader told this writer that the right wing of the party, although highly influential, was relatively small. His estimate was that it constituted only 5 per cent of the party's membership.

[18] For the history of the Radical movement, see Francisco Barría Soto, *El Partido Radical: Su historia y sus obras* (Santiago: Editorial Universitaria, 1957); Florencio Durán Bernales, *El Partido Radical* (Santiago: Editorial Nascimento, 1958); Enrique Vera Riquelme, *Evolución del radicalismo chileno* (Santiago: n.p., 1943); Terko Koscina, *El radicalismo como partido político: Su génesis y su doctrina* (Santiago: Editorial Universitaria, 1956); Darío Poblete and Alfredo Bravo, *Historia del Partido Radical y del Frente Popular* (Santiago: n.p., 1936); Angel C. Espejo, *El Partido Radical: Sus obras y sus hombres* (Santiago: n.p., 1911).

[19] Johnson, *op. cit.*, p. 75.

many members still held the paternalistic view that lower classes should rely on the tutelage of the middle class and should not contend with their social superiors.[20] Nevertheless, there were similar social and economic aspirations among the Radicals and the working groups. Most members of the party favored a more equitable distribution of the national income and accepted the role of the state as the arbiter of socio-economic differences.

In spite of internal differences created by its heterogeneous composition, after "the revolt of the electorate" in the 1920's the Radical Party was chiefly responsible for orienting Chilean politics to the socio-economic issues which today are fundamental. The victory of the Popular Front in 1938 launched the period of socio-economic liberalism.[21] In the course of this period the Radical Party has suffered from continuous indecision and vacillation. Veering at times to the Right, pushed by those within its fold who respond to traditional interests and reject the influences of the parties of the extreme Left, and at other times being impelled to the Left, under pressure from its Marxist-oriented segments, it has suffered changes in leadership, policy, and even principle.

Although a useful means of avoiding extremism, Radical dependence on coalition government, with its fragmentation of purpose and method, has inevitably resulted in vague and undefined ideology and hollow and expedient programs. A consistent feature of Radical philosophy, however, has been its reliance on improving the lot of the lower classes by evolutionary methods rather than by revolutionary. It is a firm Radical philosophy that vital economic issues can be solved by peaceful means through evolutionary development.[22] Official party declarations define its ideology as based on "socialist democratic doctrine" and proclaim the party's faith in the secular state and the system of political parties, its endorsement of free obligatory education, and its opposition to all forms of dictatorship or totalitarianism.[23] More specifically, the Radical platform proposes constitutional reforms aimed at the establishment of a parliamentary system with these characteristics: (a) a unicameral organization or the restriction of the upper chamber to merely an administrative or supervisory role; (b) presidential political responsibility; (c) Cabinet responsibility to the legis-

[20] Pike, *op. cit.*, p. 262.

[21] John Reese Stevenson, *The Chilean Popular Front* (Philadelphia: University of Pennsylvania Press, 1942), pp. 144–145.

[22] Speaking of this belief in evolutionary development, Radical President González Videla allegedly said once that "the Radical Party was so evolutionary that it could some day become anarchist."

[23] Mario Verdugo Marinkovic, *op. cit.*, p. 27.

lature; (d) the vesting of ample powers in the legislature; and (e) presidential authority to dissolve Congress.[24] The Radical platform is not much more explicit on socio-economic problems; it advocates reforms in agriculture, education, taxation, social welfare, and mining and advocates institutional changes aimed at the achievement of national economic development. It favors the gradual extension of state control over the basic means of production and supports nationalization of economic enterprises, if necessary, to obtain the economic and social goals of national development.[25]

In foreign affairs, the party supports the United Nations and favors the maintenance of diplomatic relations with all nations. It also advocates strong support of the Inter-American system, Latin American disarmament, the principle of nonintervention, and Latin American political and economic integration, and it is opposed to dictatorships. One element of its original philosophy that the party still supports without compromise is the emphasis on secularism. The Chilean Radical Party, like its European counterparts, can always be found in opposition to any issue that would tend to increase the power of the Catholic Church or in any way to reduce the freedom of religious preference. Furthermore, it is apparently impervious to nationalism. As products of the nineteenth century, the Radicals do not seem to understand nationalism, essentially an ideological phenomenon of the twentieth century.

Composition. No other party in the Chilean political system has as varied a composition as the Radical Party. While each of the other parties represents a relatively narrow segment of the population, the Radical Party encompasses a wide variety of people in its membership, from landowners to workers. It includes northerners from the mining districts, southern landowners, small merchants, professionals, intellectuals, artisans, and many skilled workers. In addition, it is supported by many members of the so-called *clase acomodada* — ambitious bourgeois who are attempting to rise into the upper class. At one time, retired military officers played an important role as supporters of the party. This group for the most part became followers of Ibáñez in later years.[26] In the main, however, the characterization of the

[24] *Acuerdos aprobados en la XXI Convención del Partido Radical* (Santiago, 1963).

[25] For details on Radical ideology on socio-economic issues, see Germán Urzúa Valenzuela, *El Partido Radical: Su evolución política* (Santiago: Academia de Ciencias Políticas y Administrativas, 1961).

[26] Upon his return from exile, Arturo Alessandri drastically reduced the size of the officer corps of the Chilean army. Some time later when the Radical Party withdrew its support of Alessandri, this group of officers who had been forcibly retired joined it in order to oppose the government.

Radical Party as representative of middle-class urbanites holding white-collar jobs is accurate. Despite the presence in the party of "radical millionaires" and minority groups of non-Marxist workingmen, the backbone of the organization is the middle class. Much of Radical Strength has come from the geographical extremes of Chile, since it has in the past represented the dissatisfaction of provincial bourgeoisie with the centralization of the country's resources and administration in Santiago. Proof that it also reaches the lower socio-economic groups is the presence of leaders from such groups at all party levels.

A significant development since 1938 has been the linking of the Radicals with the business and industrial world, an alliance that came about because the party was in power when the expansion of governmental participation in the economic life of the nation began to take place. The Radical Party has won thoroughly to itself the Chilean bureaucracy, which grew by leaps and bounds after 1938 under the administration of successive Radical Presidents. When the government began to assume the key role in industrial development, Radical bureaucrats came in close contact with industrialists and businessmen, and there was a consequent influence upon party leadership. Through its leaders, the party established for the first time in its history intimate ties with large industrial and commercial enterprises. Many prominent Radical leaders became big businessmen, improving their economic and social status in the process but remaining faithful to the party.[27] Only exceptionally was there anything irregular about such improvements, and when there was what had happened was that advantage had been taken of opportunities and information provided by access to key governmental agencies engaged in the promotion of industrial development.[28] In similar fashion, a bond was established between the Radicals and the large foreign-owned mining enterprises.[29] Regardless of the history of their political affiliation, those professionals and technicians most effectively trained to assume responsibility for the many new economic activities being undertaken by the state were by reason of

[27] Examples are numerous. Senator Ulises Correa, a modest civil service official in the provinces in 1938, is today a wealthy wine merchant. Another Radical senator, of modest origins in Copiapó, is connected with four important mining enterprises and is an important olive grower.

[28] Radical administrations have not always been free of scandal. A famous one, concerning what was popularly referred to as the "hoyo radical" (Radical hole), involved the acquisition of valuable land in downtown Santiago for the construction of a large building destined to house the party's headquarters. Other cases had to do chiefly with the importation of automobiles and other foreign-made products, the purchase of which was restricted by the government.

[29] Several prominent Radicals are lawyers or hold executive positions in the Lautaro and Anaconda mining companies.

their middle-class origin, inclined toward the Radical Party. In addition, as the new industrial enterprises sought to recruit already experienced, well-trained men, by coincidence they found more of them among the Radicals than among any other political organization.[30]

Because it is the most democratic of all Chilean parties (from the organizational point of view), opportunities for ascent in Radical Party ranks are open to all members regardless of social origin.[31] A considerable number of Radical leaders are sons of school teachers, an ambiguous social category, particularly in the provinces and in the great *fundos*. Teachers are not farm workers or *inquilinos,* but neither do they sit at the *patrón*'s table. Having enough education to feel some resentment because of their social and economic inferiority, they make all the sacrifices that are necessary to give their children a higher education. The primary school teacher may elevate himself and become the head of the province's education department or director of a primary school, or he may even come to occupy a higher post in the national educational bureaucracy. Invariably, persons in this category and their families are loyal Radical followers. A typical pattern of recruitment and party career might be the one followed by an influential party leader who was once awarded the highest distinction a party can bestow: nomination to the presidency. This leader, a typical representative of the provincial intellectual bourgeoisie, began his political career at age seventeen in Concepción. Initially attracted to the party by studying its literature and listening to speeches by its members, he became a member of the Propaganda Center of the party in that city. At age twenty-one he was elected secretary of his *asamblea* (local party unit)and later moved to Santiago to continue his education and his party activities there. Six years later, after a spirited party struggle, he was nominated and elected deputy for Santiago. Prior to this election he had represented the province of Aconcagua and been selected secretary general of the party's Central Committee. In time he became a member of the party's powerful Executive Committee and its vice-president.

Although most students of Chilean politics would agree that ethnic groups do not play a significant part in electoral contests, it should be

[30] Evidence of how economic development may establish new ties between the political leadership and economic interests, with the consequent significant effects, is not difficult to find in Chile. The author, in examining the composition and political affiliation of the boards of directors of all important banks, credit institutions, and industrial corporations, was able to find a rather impressive number of members of the Radical Party.

[31] There are Radical leaders who deplore some of the consequences of the democratic nature of the organization. They maintain that it has sometimes led to lack of respect for the party intellectuals and has made possible the rise of political adventurers.

noted that Jews and Arabs are numerous in the Radical Party. One of the most distinguished senators of the party is Jewish and is strongly supported by the Jewish colony of Santiago. However, the so-called *turcos* (literally Turks, a term applied to all immigrants from the Middle East), many of whom are wealthy industrialists and merchants, tend to avoid identifying themselves with any particular party and make heavy campaign contributions to all political camps. Another important ethnic group, the Germans in southern Chile, are generally divided politically on the basis of religious affiliation: the Protestants join the Radical Party and the Catholics the Conservative. A typical case is the city of Puerto Varas, where the German colony, almost without exception, is divided along these lines. In general, however, in Chile it is not possible to speak of ethnic vote blocs in the sense in which they exist, for example, in the United States.

Structure and Organization. Much of the remarkable vitality of the Radical Party is derived from its cohesive organization. The core of this organization is the *asamblea,* the local unit. Usually there is one *asamblea* for each commune, though in some cases there may be more. In order to become a party member, an individual must apply for admission to and obtain the approval of an *asamblea,* a procedure which takes approximately thirty days. The *asambleas* meet once a week and elect officers in April of every year. In order to vote in party elections, members must have paid their dues and must have held membership for at least a year before the election. Aside from elections of their officers, the *asambleas* participate in the elections of candidates for municipal councils and the Congress, in the selection of delegates to the respective Provincial Council and to the National Convention, and finally in the nomination of presidential candidates. The site of the *asamblea* generally serves at the same time as a social club, with restaurants and other facilities always open to members. Party activities at the local level thus combine with recreation, a fact which contributes much to creating an atmosphere of conviviality and comradeship among the *asamblea* members. The attractions of social gatherings, coupled with the characteristic faithfulness of the Radical rank and file, tend to insure a high rate of attendance at party meetings. They provide a place to meet friends and acquaintances over drinks, to exchange pleasantries and political gossip, or to engage in serious intellectual discussion. Through the activities of the *asamblea* the individual becomes involved in party affairs to the extent that his political affiliation is an important part of his life — a far more important part than if he merely supported a political program or voted for nominees.

Two other party organs have their roots in the *asambleas:* the Provincial Council (*Consejo Provincial*) and the National Convention

(*Convención Nacional*). The Provincial Council, formed by one delegate from each *asamblea,* is the body entrusted with implementing at the provincial level orders emanating from the top executive organs of the party. Representatives of the Provincial Councils participate in turn in the selection of the National Council (*Consejo Nacional*), with authority over all other party bodies except the National Convention. Each *asamblea* is represented at the Convention by one delegate or more if it has more than two hundred members). Finally, there is a central executive organ, the National Executive Council (*Consejo Ejecutivo Nacional*, CEN), composed of the chieftains of the party.

The National Council is composed of: the members of the CEN; three senators and three deputies; three members of the Radical Youth; three members and all the directors of the departments of the CEN; one representative for each deputy in the province, selected by the Provincial Council every two years; and nine persons elected by the National Convention. The National Convention is composed of: the National Council; the Supreme Tribunal; all cabinet members of the party; all the party's members and former members of Congress (the latter have no vote); the presidents of the Provincial Councils; fifteen members of the Provincial Councils; fifteen members each from the Radical Youth and the labor unions; ten municipal *regidores;* the directors of the CEN departments; one delegate from each *asamblea* (more if it consists of more than two hundred persons); and all persons who have been members of the party for fifty years.

The National Executive Council, CEN, consists of nine members elected by the Convention, two senators, two deputies, one municipal councilman, the president of the youth organization, and the national secretary of the labor group. The officers of the CEN, who constitute the *Mesa Directiva,* are the president (he may be a member of CEN or may be selected from any *asamblea*); the vice-president; the secretary general; and the treasurer.[32]

In addition to the party organs described above, there are a number of technical departments which are attached to the National Executive Committee. These are the Departments of Finance, Control and Organization, Electoral Campaigns and Recruitment, Political Studies and Indoctrination, Cultural Action, Propaganda, Education, Foreign Policy, and the Professional and Technical Department. The Provincial Councils meet monthly, the National Council every three months, the CEN once a week, and the Convention every four years.

[32] For further details see *Partido Radical, Estatutos Aprobados en la XXI Convención Nacional Ordinaria* (Santiago, 1962); Germán Urzúa, *op. cit.*, pp. 7–12; and Mario Verdugo, *op. cit.*, pp. 53–54.

Among the most important functions of the CEN are: to make party policy; to implement the decisions of the Convention; and to organize or dissolve other party organs, with the exception of the National Council and the Supreme Tribunal. It also authorizes party members to accept the presidential appointments they may be offered. The party's motion of censure against a Radical member of the Cabinet must produce his resignation within twenty-four hours, or else he is automatically expelled from the party. As the supreme authority of the party, in theory at least, the National Convention must approve the party platform.

Relationships among party members are distinctive. The PR is an "individualistic" party, which does not exhibit the evidences of teamwork found in the other Chilean parties. Party struggles tend to be rough-and-tumble affairs, particularly when they center about presidential politics. This ebullience, plus the inherent lack of definition in the party's economic platform, impedes somewhat the efficacy of the technical groups which prepare reform programs. Their efforts are often frustrated by the free-for-all skirmishes within the *asambleas,* which sometimes degenerate into what is called in political jargon a *choclón,* a confused and chaotic political gathering. Relations between the national leaders and the Radical masses are twofold: there are direct contacts with the grass roots of the party and there are indirect ones through the hierarchical structure. No leader can hope to maintain his influence without immediate connection with the *asambleas,* since these bodies often enough can manage to make or unmake candidates by their stubborn resistance to submit to impositions from above. Therein lies the main difference between the PR and the rightist parties. However, it should be mentioned that it is frequently reported that some distinction exists in this regard between periods when the party is in power and those when it is not. In the first case a greater influence from the national leaders of the party is apparently discernible. It is also pointed out that when differences arise between a Radical President and party leaders the latter invariably prevail.[33]

Another characteristic of the PR is the absence of any rigid discipline. As one Radical leader puts it, the PR is "a party of short memory." Even in the most extreme cases of insubordination there is always the possibility for the prodigal son to return. The highly emotional ambiance of the *asamblea,* however, makes appealing to their sentimentalism and persuading them to readmit a repentant

33 The party decision at one time to abandon the administration of Radical President González Videla had its origin in a wave of hostility against his policies that swept the *asambleas* and forced the Executive Committee to take such action.

fellow member a difficult matter.[34] It seems indeed incredible that Juan Antonio Ríos was once expelled from the party only to become some years later President at the head of the Radical ticket.

The Christian Democratic Party

The Christian Democratic Party is the left wing of the Chilean Center. In an earlier chapter the origin of this party and its neosocialistic economic and democratic political ideology were discussed. Coming into existence in 1938 as the National Falange (*Falange Nacional*), this offshoot of the Conservative Party, led by a group of brilliant young Catholics such as Bernardo Leighton, Manuel Garretón, Radomiro Tomic, and Eduardo Frei, moved to conquer some of the most important figures in intellectual circles, in the labor movement, and in many of the new government-sponsored industries.[35] Also influential in Falange's development was Rafael L. Gumucio, a patrician figure of the Conservative Party who temporarily joined the new party and is now considered by many as the "spiritual father" of the Christian Socialist movement. Small in numbers, the party lacked a large popular base like the huge administrative system that rolls up consistent and predictable votes for the Radicals. Nevertheless, it grew in influence, even among some anticlericals, as it demonstrated its ability to satisfy the political needs of important policy groups. In the 1940's it had to compete with another Catholic reformist group led by a man of great prestige, Eduardo Cruz-Coke, who, after abandoning the ranks of the Conservatives, founded the Conservative Social Christian Party (*Partido Conservador Social Cristiano*). This party, however, was short-lived and dissolved in the late 1950's. Many of its supporters

[34] Sentimental attachment to the party is found in the PR more than in any other party. There are some wealthy landowners in the provinces who support the party not because they adhere to its principles but because of family tradition. The author had the opportunity to meet many of these "sentimental" followers of the PR. One, an eighty-year-old gentleman, a typical Manchesterian Liberal, had tears in his eyes whenever he spoke about the party.

[35] The split with the Conservatives led to violent attacks from that direction against the "heretical" inclinations of the Christian Democrats — their belief in pluralism, secularism, and the open society. For examples, see Carlos Aldunate Errázuriz, *Polémica sobre Maritain* (Santiago, 1940); Sergio Fernández Larraín, *Falange Nacional, Democracia Cristiana y Comunismo* (Santiago, 1958), and *Aspectos de la división del Partido Conservador* (Santiago, 1950); Jorge Iván Hübner, *Los católicos en la política* (Santiago, 1959); and Monsignor Luis Arturo Pérez, *Maritain* (Santiago, 1938). The opposite point of view is represented by Jaime Castillo, *En defensa de Maritain* (Santiago, 1949), and Falange Nacional, *El Partido Conservador* (Santiago, 1938), attacking the political and social backwardness of the Conservative Party.

later swelled the ranks of the Falange, which began to call itself the Christian Democratic Party (PDC) in 1957. Growing slowly but steadily, this young organization led all other parties in popular support for the first time in 1963, receiving 23 per cent of the vote. By that time, it had won the allegiance of large numbers of intellectuals and technicians and of a substantial segment of the women and had developed an effective organization with a well-organized corps of volunteer workers. "The combination of convinced women and doubting intellectuals," as Silvert puts it, "is a singularly sophisticated political brew."[36]

Ideology. The development of Christian Democratic philosophy in Chile is marked by three distinct periods or phases. For lack of better nomenclature these phases can be designated by the names of three prominent Falange figures who directed the ideological current of the party during each of those periods, namely, Manuel Garretón, Bernardo Leighton, and Radomiro Tomic. The party of the Garretón era was strongly influenced by the Belgian movement known as Rexism, which although Catholic was also somewhat tainted with Nazism.[37] Following this period, the party under Leighton's influence developed a lively religious and democratic idealism. A man of strong spiritual qualities, Leighton changed the Rexist orientation of the Falange, purifying it from its Nazi overtones and transforming it into a truly democratic movement.[38] The conversion of Garretón to the more democratic ideology added strength to the new current. The party became strongly anti-Nazi, populist in nature, and fundamentally Christian in philosophy. In the third period, with Leighton's ascendancy fading, the powerful influence of Tomic emerged. Favored with an appealing personality, unusual and versatile talents, and an outstand-

36 K. H. Silvert, "Interview with a Candidate" (Buenos Aires: American Universities Field Staff Letter, August 30, 1957), p. 1.

37 The similarity between the famous twenty-six-point program of Falange Española (the Spanish Fascist Party) and the declaration of principles of the Chilean Falange in the Garretón era was striking. This program remained almost unchanged until 1948. The following anecdote throws some light on party thinking at the time. When Arturo Alessandri offered a twenty-five-year-old Bernardo Leighton the Labor portfolio in his Cabinet and the latter accepted it as a duty to assist Alessandri's reformist administration, Garretón sent Leighton a telegram: "Impossible to accept position in the Cabinet. For a leader of the movement nothing but the leadership of the nation." (Alessandri liked Leighton's youthful enthusiasm. "He talks just like I did at his age," the old "Lion of Tarapacá" is supposed to have said.)

38 For an interesting sketch of Bernardo Leighton, see Ricardo Boizard, *Cuatro retratos en profundidad: Ibáñez, Lafertte, Leighton, Walker* (Santiago, 1950).

ing oratorical ability, he exerted an intellectual influence that soon permeated the party.[39] But more than ideological, the differences between the Leighton period and the Tomic were tactical. No doctrinal changes could be really detected, the most significant difference being one of style, perhaps of greater reliance on personalities than on ideas. External circumstances had much to do with the transition from one stage to another. The first ideological shift from Garretón to Leighton was partly a consequence of World War II. During the second period, the Falange made its first successful excursion into the trade union movement. With the end of World War II and the rise of the East-West conflict, it became more difficult to continue the left-inclined approach towards the working classes (the policy of *abrazo popular*); instead the party concentrated its efforts on attracting all Catholics to the Christian Democratic fold. Progressive-minded Conservative dissidents gradually swelled Christian Democratic ranks, and the party moved slowly to the Center in order to reduce to a minimum its differences from other political sectors and to broaden its popular base. In the 1960's this policy combined with a very active movement to proselytize the working elements was to yield handsome dividends for the party, under the leadership of Eduardo Frei.

The Chilean Christian Democratic movement from its inception has always espoused change, state interventionism, and the full range of civil liberties. In the late 1940's, a period of rising Communist power, the Christian Democrats hoped to attract the leftist protest vote. Failing to win this mass vote, it did attract, however, many formerly orthodox leftist intellectuals and then began moving to the Center and the Right for its popular base.

The essence of Chilean Christian Democratic doctrine is the belief in social pluralism and political democracy. The party's neo-socialistic economic platform, derived from the acceptance of the need for a limited class struggle as a means of achieving social justice, is discussed elsewhere in this book. Most Christian Democrats see themselves as leftists and Catholics. As Catholics they consider themselves anti-Marxists, but as leftists they cannot allow themselves to be undemocratic in their anti-Marxism. They criticize capitalism on the United States model as being opposed to Christian morality. Old-style liberalism is considered thoroughly un-Christian and pernicious by many

[39] Tomic is a controversial figure in the party. Some regard him as an extremist and a bit of a demagogue. He probably leans more to the left than any other Christian Democratic leader. Tomic is also charged by some with irresponsibility and frivolity, and he is criticized for frequently absenting himself from the high councils of the party. Many others, however, consider him a truly exceptional specimen of the modern "white caudillo."

Christian Democrats. Some important leaders of the Christian Democratic Party are in actuality not distant from Marxism in their political philosophy. In advocating what they term the "communitarian society," they agree with Marx that private capital is the root of nearly every evil and therefore they support the abolition of private ownership of all property save consumer goods.[40] In general, Christian Democrats have no particular commitment to the free enterprise system and would abandon it if they thought it wise to do so. In writings and speeches, Eduardo Frei, who stands in the philosophical center of the Party, constantly hammers away at the need for replacing the obsession for profit that inevitably vitiates capitalism with the spirit of Christian brotherhood.[41]

The active Catholicism of the movement is always a point of contention in partisan struggles. Ideologically, Christian Democrats attempt to refute the frequent charges of their political adversaries that they are a "confessional" or Church party by pointing out that they accept religious pluralism as an established fact in Chile and that in working toward a just social order they are willing to cooperate with any group, whatever its religious beliefs. They also point out that the party now includes persons of many religious faiths and that it has from time to time had serious differences with a good part of the Church hierarchy, so much so that in 1948 there was one attempt to cast the party out of Church councils altogether. It should also be noted that the Christian Democrats' appeal to a sort of impersonal nationalism within a democratic framework has also served to counteract these charges and to overshadow the clerical color inherent in the party.

Christian Democratic acceptance of the need for at least a restricted form of class struggle implies the need of encouraging the masses to acquire the means of giving their demands a political articulation. According to the party's philosophy, the masses will then be in a position to secure from the upper levels of society those fundamental changes that ordinarily the latter could never have been induced to accept. Once a new social order has been established in this way, the Christian Democrats except the class struggle to be replaced by cooperation between the different social classes.[42] Deeply influenced in their thinking

[40] Pike, *op. cit.*, p. 261. See also Jacques Chonchol and Julio Silva Solar, *Hacia un mundo comunitario: Condiciones de una política social cristiana* (Santiago, 1951).

[41] Frei is a prolific writer. Some of his most important works are: *Aún es tiempo* (Santiago, 1942); *La política y el espíritu* (Santiago, 1946); *La verdad tiene su hora* (Santiago, 1955); and *Pensamiento y acción* (Santiago, 1958).

[42] Pike, *op. cit.*, p. 260.

by the papal encyclical *Quadragesimo Anno* (1931), Christian Democrats, critical of the evils of communism as well as of capitalism, which in the party's eyes have been linked in their basic development, have evolved their own concept of a "middleway" or "third alternative." It consists of the involvement of the worker in management and ownership, the promotion of intermediate groupings between the individual and the state, and state intervention to restrict the power of large economic interests. Statism is to be controlled, however, to prevent the creation of huge bureaucratic structures which consume the resources they are administering so that the mechanism created by man destroys man rather than saves him. "The action of the state," writes Frei, "cannot be an absorbing and paralyzing intervention but must respect intermediate organisms — the family, the city, the region, the trade union, the business enterprise. It must exert an effective authority for orientation, planning, and leadership.[43]

Advocating a "revolution with freedom," the Christian Democratic plank for the 1964 presidential elections specified the means by which this new social order might be achieved. They included democratization and modernization of political structures through constitutional reforms designed to give the chief executive authority to consult the people directly concerning fundamental measures; extension of the franchise to all twenty-one-year-old Chileans; enumeration in the Constitution of labor rights, such as the right to strike, to form trade unions, to receive fair compensation, and to have social security; and the introduction of reforms to expedite the lawmaking process and the administration of justice, to improve public administration by establishing administrative decentralization, and to make municipal autonomy a reality by providing for popular election of local government officials. Other sections of the Christian Democratic electoral plank espoused sweeping alterations in the land system, in education, and in the organization of urban areas and advocated profit-sharing plans for industry, the abolition of monopolies, and the expansion of mining, agricultural, and industrial activities.[44]

In international affairs the party regards itself as anti-imperialist and opposes foreign intervention. It advocates peace, universal disarmament, proscription of nuclear weapons, the pacific solution of international controversies, and it supports the creation of political

[43] Eduardo Frei, *Pensamiento y acción* (Santiago: Editorial del Pacífico, 1958), p. 63.

[44] A summary of this program, known as the "declaration of the Third Millahue Meeting" (approved at Millahue, a mountain town in Chile, April 19, 1964), is found in *Noticias para el exterior: Partido Demócrata Cristiano de Chile,* Año I, No. 2, pp. 3–6.

institutions aimed at Latin American integration. As regards relations with the United States, it maintains that no Latin American nation can successfully follow a policy of overt anti-Americanism, whether or not such views are coupled with pro-Sovietism. This realization does not imply, however, either economic or political submission on the part of Latin America but rather the establishment of an international partnership.[45]

Composition. The hard core of the PDC consists of Catholic members of the middle class. For this group, the Party is "a kind of Radical Party which is not anticlerical."[46] As suggested above, the rise of the Christian Democrats has confronted the Radical Party for the first time in its history with a rival for the electoral support that traditionally has been the base of Chilean Radicalism. As the original group of dissident young Conservatives developed into a separate entity, at first small but finally large enough to constitute a major political force, the Party began to win adherents in intellectual circles, among many non-Marxist-romantic leftists, and finally among the women. Today, more important perhaps to the life of the party than any other group are the professionals and technicians, for they have given it the organizational talent necessary not only to win electoral battles but also to formulate specific plans of government. According to a PDC leader, over 90 per cent of the professionals are members or followers of the party. The attraction these individuals have to the Christian Democratic Party is understandable.

[45] There are many useful works dealing with Chile's Christian Democratic movement. Pike, *op. cit.*, Chap. 9, n. 23, provides an excellent list. In English, Paul E. Sigmund, Jr., ed., *The Ideologies of the Developing Nations* (New York: Frederick A. Praeger, 1963), pp. 309–320, contains excerpts in translation from Frei's *Pensamiento y acción.* Other important books and pamphlets are: Manuel Garretón and Radomiro Tomic, *Definición de una actitud: Tres discursos* (Santiago, 1942); Manuel A. Garretón, *Hacia un ideal político* (Santiago: Ediciones Lircay, 1934); Radomiro Tomic, *Fundamentos cristianos para una nueva política en Chile* (Santiago, 1945), and *Comunismo, capitalismo y democracia cristiana* (Santiago, 1948); and Bernardo Leighton, *Partido Demócrata Cristiano* (Santiago: Academia de Ciencias Políticas, 1957), and *Los conflictos del trabajo y su significado social* (Santiago, 1945). Julio Silva and B. Parra, *Nociones para una política demócrata cristiana* (Santiago, 1957), throws much light upon Christian Democratic thinking. A useful party pamphlet is *El abc de la democracia cristiana* (Concepción: Instituto de Estudios Políticos, 1962). Particularly useful are the Christian Democratic periodicals *Nuestro Tiempo, La Libertad, La Voz,* and *Política y Espíritu,* a biweekly which was first published in 1945. This last journal is indispensable for the student of the movement in Chile.

[46] K. H. Silvert, "Election, Parties, and the Law" (Santiago: American Universities Field Staff Letter, March 10, 1957), p. 15.

In terms of the division of generations, the Chilean political and social renewal in the 1920's produced a group of distinguished University of Chile graduates, intellectuals and professionals, who shared a desire for social change and political progress. After the emergence of Alessandri as the champion of the masses and with the rise of the middle classes, this "generation of 1920" was able to play a significant role in laying the foundations of social welfare and labor legislation. It also established a series of administrative agencies in imitation of similar institutions in Europe and the United States. The "generation of 1920" lacked any scientific background in economics; its knowledge of economic problems was not acquired through systematic training but came second-hand and informally. Neither the new social legislation nor the administrative services created for the purpose of modernizing the country were therefore, with few exceptions, the result of technical studies and a thoroughly prepared national plan. Both were the products of improvisation, of projects haphazardly and unsystematically put together, with little attention to methods of financing. Functions and responsibilities of the newly created agencies grew at a rapid pace as the country moved toward industrialization, but their organization remained in its original precarious state. As this situation became more critical, yet a newer generation, many of its members well-trained professionals — engineers, architects, economists, and the like — educated abroad and all much better prepared than their counterparts in the Alessandri era, grew disillusioned with that lack of organization and the progressive bureaucratization that accompanied it. They began agitating for a "technification" of the public services. In search of a political party responsive to their demands, they felt strongly the appeal of the Christian Democrats' technically oriented, interventionist program to remedy the economic defects and establish honest and efficient government and began to enlarge its ranks. These technically oriented groups had sometimes supported the rightist parties merely out of a desire for efficiency. Despite the ordinarily leftist inclinations of many of these groups, the characteristically disorganized and fragmented Left could not satisfy their desire for orderly government. They turned then to the PDC, where, with the exception of the area of religious philosophy, they could feel ideologically comfortable. In the 1958 elections some of them tended to cluster about Jorge Alessandri, who despite his official Liberal-Conservative candidacy has always called himself an independent. That such a technically and professionally oriented segment of the population did not turn to the Radical Party and to the FRAP is an interesting and well-noted phenomenon, which is most often explained in the terms I have employed above. Another explanation sometimes encountered is that the "conservatism" of the Chilean Left — which did not move much until recently to adjust itself to new demands and possibilities — had something to do with the alienation of the technical class. Whatever the reasons, this group has made notable contributions to the Christian Democratic movement. Economists have been working for years preparing reports and studies for the party to be put into effect as soon as it took control of the government. Many other professionals concerned with the public services and though not party members sympathizers with it have been engaged in economic planning, housing research, and other projects they hoped the PDC will carry out. All of these individuals cherished the thought of a sort of political truce under the PDC that would endure for a period during which a "government of technicians" directed by a neutral governmental mechanism and operating within a democratic framework could achieve needed aims.[47]

Essential to Christian Democratic success has been the young professional educated in the Catholic institutions. This recognizable type among party members, well-educated and articulate, is in general intellectually superior to his counterpart in the Radical Party. After completing their training, these young professionals frequently establish themselves outside Santiago in the provinces. This diffusion proves advantageous to the party, for there is a notable missionary zeal among Christian Democratic youth, and the result is that soon after arriving in the provinces these professionals found new PDC groups and engage in an active political program. Most provincial communities now have a small but enthusiastic group of Christian Democrats. It is this element which provides the party with its small (probably around 300) able group of leaders, men almost without exception of high intellectual and personal qualities.

The pattern of the party career among Christian Democrats, because of the relatively small size of the party, differs fundamentally from the pattern among Radicals. The homogeneous nature of the membership makes the PDC a party in which personal relations and the bonds of friendship are extremely strong. Parliamentary and other government positions are assigned principally with the interests of the party in mind and not much in accordance to seniority or party rank. A remarkable community of interest and purpose has existed in the party leadership, coupled with an unusual ability in accommodating differences. This oneness of understanding is probably due in some measure to the intimate friendships in the small group of national leaders, and it contributes to the immense prestige that these leaders enjoy among the party's rank and file.

[47] Silvert, "Interview with a Candidate," p. 8.

While, as we have observed, membership has been drawn extensively from the Catholic middle-class elements of the electorate, efforts have also been made to attract Protestants, agnostics, atheists, and Jews, in order to transmute the party into a genuine non-confessional movement. As a political "union" aspiring to represent the Center and the mass of independents, the Chilean Christian Democrats, like their German counterparts, are seeking something broader than a party in the customary sense. The objective is to develop and represent a cross section of various groups and to concentrate on those problems and interests that are common to the political community as a whole, thereby serving a "national cause." In the long run, however, this strategy may affect the internal cohesion and discipline which have characterized the party since its inception. Occasionally, fissures appear within the party between the stronger leftist and centrist elements, particularly on problems related to the "social question," but thus far it has been able to withstand the strain of internal differences. Acceptance of the support of the rightist forces in 1964 has contributed in some degree to intensifying some of those tensions.

Structure and Organization. The structure of the Christian Democratic Party consists of two types of organs: political and special or technical. Every political organ of the party has an executive group of elected officers known as a council (*consejo*), which functions at the three levels, communal, provincial, and national. The special or technical party units are known as departments (*departamentos*) and are charged by the various political units with the preparation of party programs. Among the latter the principal ones are: the Communal Assembly (*Junta Comunal*); the Provincial Assembly (*Junta Provincial*); the National Council (*Consejo Nacional*); the Plenary National Council (*Consejo Nacional Plenario*); the National Assembly (*Junta Nacional*); and the Party National Congress (*Congreso Nacional del Partido*).

The two most important party agencies are the *Junta Nacional* and the *Consejo Nacional*. The first body, according to the party statutes, is the supreme organ of the party. Its duties include reviewing activities of the other party organs and establishing the principles, program, and statutes of the party. Though the party statutes attribute both to it and to the National Congress supreme powers, the *Consejo Nacional* is the source of real political power in party affairs. The National Council directs all national functions of the party, as well as controlling most of its provincial and local activities. It exacts observance of the party program and implements decisions of the other national agencies. The National Council authorizes party members to accept cabinet posts, diplomatic positions, and all other presidential appointments. It directs party policy in Congress through instructions to the party's senators and deputies and exercises control over any parliamentary pacts for legislative action. Party statutes establish sanctions against party members in Congress who may fail to follow directions emanating from the National Council. In addition, any kind of political agreement or pact of a national nature, as well as agreements subscribed to by party leaders at international meetings of the Christian Democratic movement, must be ratified by the Council. The *Consejo Nacional,* because of both its position in the formal structure of the party and the prestige of its members, is in short the key to the entire party.

Christian Democratic candidates for public office are selected by a number of methods. Candidates for municipal councilmen are nominated by the local unit of the party, the *Junta Comunal,* and elected by the *Junta Provincial.* In the case of deputies and senators, the *Juntas Comunales* submit lists of nominees, and the National Council makes the final selection. The designation of the candidate for the presidency or any decision related to the party position in a presidential election is the responsibility of a specially convoked meeting of the *Junta Nacional.*[48]

As the organizational structure described above suggests, the Christian Democratic Party, like most Chilean parties, is a highly centralized national political organization in which the influence of the top leaders is paramount. Although there may be internal struggles, in every case the will of the national leaders has ultimately prevailed. Since the Christian Democrats are a relatively small party, discipline is further assured by the personal ties which have been mentioned.[49]

The work carried out by the party's technical departments is of the utmost importance. This sector of the party has great responsibility in solving problems inherent in the rapid growth in the size of the party and the complexity of the interests represented in it. As a result of the addition of individuals and groups formerly outside the party and particularly of the influx of newly enfranchised women, functional speciali-

[48] Unlike the method employed by major parties in the United States, the conduct of party business is not combined with presidential nomination in a single national convention by Chilean parties; a separate nominating convention is held.

[49] There have been cases, however, when the national leadership nearly failed to impose its will upon the rank and file. A good example is the decision to support the candidacy of Radical Pedro Enrique Alfonso in 1946. This decision was adopted by a close vote in the high councils of the party, against what appeared to be the desires of the majority of the lower echelons of the party, who favored Mewes, a prospective independent nominee.

zation has developed accordingly, and the types of party concern and party activity have multiplied.[50] Aside from the purely technical units devoted to formulating plans for the solution of national problems, the labor and feminine sections of the party, as well as volunteer organizations, have become especially significant in recent years.

The Left

The Chilean Left consists of a formidable coalition of four parties — Communist, Socialist, National Democratic, and National Vanguard of the People. The two major forces in this amalgamation are the Communist and the Socialist parties. The alliance, established in May, 1956, first united the Socialist Party of Chile and the Popular Socialist Party (the two factions into which Chilean socialism was then divided); the Democratic Party of the People; the Democratic Party of Chile; the Labor Party, and the Communist Party (outlawed at the time). Shortly after the establishment of this alliance, the so-called *Frente de Acción Popular* (FRAP), the Socialists were able to combine their forces in a single organization, and in 1958 the Communist Party regained its legal status. Shifts in the other minor parties of the coalition resulted in the present make-up of the leftist coalition.

Traditionally the political parties of the Left have been plagued by internal strife and dissension; the whole picture of leftism has been one of disarray and bitter rivalries. A principal feature in the historical development of Chile's extreme Left has been the old and deeply rooted animosity between Communists and Socialists. For the first time in Chilean history, under the present FRAP coalition these two major forces have adjusted their differences and combined their efforts.[51] Unity has paid off handsomely for both parties, for their electoral strength and political influence have risen to new heights during the present decade. FRAP's future depends entirely upon whether or not the present harmony between these two major partners of the Left can be preserved. Mutual distrust of long standing is a

[50] The activities of some of these technical groups represent some significant innovations in the Chilean political scene. On election day in 1957, the author observed the work of those in charge of computing election returns at PDC headquarters. More than 150 persons collaborated in making the most systematic and exact computation of election returns that had ever been made in Chile. By seven o'clock that evening (only three hours after polls closed) it was known that the PDC candidate for the Senate, Eduardo Frei, would obtain more than 60,000 votes. In contrast, all that was available at the Radical Party headquarters was scattered reports from the interior and news bulletins from commercial broadcasting stations.

[51] See Chapter 2, p. 80.

serious obstacle, but the prospects of electoral victory and alterations in the international situation have been strong inducements toward unified leftist action. In addition, as suggested above, the Chilean Left has now overcome the stagnation of the 1940's and 1950's, and in place of worn-out slogans and hazy programs the Left is now offering vigorous new formulas, calling for a drastic change in the status quo that strongly appeals to a considerable mass of the electorate.

The Communist Party

The Communist Party has been represented in Chile's politics longer and more consistently than have its counterparts in the affairs of any other Latin American country. It occupied a key position in the labor movement for almost forty years and during much of this period was the principal political force among Chilean workers. As a relatively small party with a limited popular following, the Communist Party has nevertheless been able to wield a disproportionately large influence because of its discipline and its faculty of exploiting popular issues. Founded in 1912 by Luis Emilio Recabarren as the Workers' Socialist Party, it had risen to a dominant place in the trade union movement when in 1921 it joined the Third International and changed its name to the Communist Party (*Partido Comunista de Chile,* PCCh). As a result of a domestic extension of the Stalinist-Trotskyite feud in the Comintern, two distinct parties developed out of the Chilean Communist Party at that time. Some years later the Trotskyite group merged with the Socialists. In 1937, as supporters of the Popular Front, the Communists won one Senate seat and sent seven members to the Chamber of Deputies. The acrid controversy between the Communists and Socialists was a principal factor leading to the Socialist withdrawal from the formal organization of the Popular Front. Taking advantage of the weakening of their chief rival, the Socialists, the party made considerable inroads among the workers during the 1940's and continued to gain ground throughout World War II. With the election of Gabriel González Videla in 1946, members of the Communist Party entered the Chilean government for the first time and served almost five months. Outlawed by González Videla on September 3, 1948, the party saw all its registered voters removed from the electoral lists and many of its leaders deported. Meanwhile Communist support in the labor movement diminished sharply; but in spite of suppression the Communist organization remained strong.

Supporting Ibáñez in the 1952 election, the Communist Party began to recover its losses in the trade unions after persuading the Socialist leaders to include the PCCh in a new unification of the labor movement. During this period the party began to extend its influence to agricultural regions that had traditionally been rightist strongholds. Re-legalized in 1958, the party continued to advocate leftist unity. As its electoral strength developed, its representation in Congress became correspondingly sizeable. In recent years the party has been able to consolidate its position, as a growing number of voters have accepted Communist claims that only the PCCh is capable of bringing about true social reform. By emphasizing the policy of collaboration with Socialists and even bourgeois groups and by professing a policy of legitimacy and relying on elections as the means of gaining political power, the Communist Party has established impressive electoral records. The PCCh is probably the most politically effective communist party in Latin America. It has produced a group of able political leaders, men such as Elías Lafferte, Carlos Contreras Labarca, Luis Corvalán, and others. Its tactic of pursuing a gradualist, "peaceful" road to power, its strong appeal in labor and intellectual circles, and its representation of itself as just another political party have helped to maintain the party's national influence. Its membership in 1964 was estimated at 25,000 to 30,000.[52]

Ideology. Like that of most other communist parties, the ideology of the PCCh is rooted in Marxist-Leninist philosophy, as interpreted by the Communist Party of the Soviet Union, with which the Chilean Communist Party has maintained a close relationship since its affiliation with the Third International. Consequently, Chilean communism considers its struggle for power as a part of the world revolution of the proletariat to be carried out in the mold of the October Revolution in Russia.

The communist political program advocated by the Chilean party may be synthesized as follows: (a) anticapitalism and anti-imperialism; (b) broad reforms toward democratization of the educational system; (c) full state participation in all economic activities (and the concomitant principles of agrarian reform, nationalization of banks and insurance companies, strict control of foreign trade, etc.); (d) electoral reforms to extend suffrage to illiterates, all eighteen-year-old citizens, and members of the armed forces and the police; and (e) reforms of the political system to achieve "a true democratic order of national liberation, under which all power resides in the hands of the people."[53]

The constitutional measures proposed by the PCCh would include the creation of a unicameral legislature with the power to elect the

[52] Bureau of Intelligence and Research, Department of State, *World Strength of the Communist Party, 16th Annual Report,* (Washington, D.C.: January, 1964).

[53] Jorge Jiles Pizarro, *Partido Comunista de Chile,* (Santiago: Academia de Ciencias Políticas, 1957), p. 21.

President of the republic, Cabinet ministers, and members of the courts; the establishment of provincial assemblies (provided for in the Constitution of 1925 but never implemented); the democratization of the armed forces, largely through a promotion system that would permit the advancement of the lower ranks and through scholarships for workers to all military schools; the strengthening of individual rights and formal constitutional protection of the right to work, the right to strike, the right to education, and other related rights.

In international affairs, the Chilean Communist Party has denounced the Charter of the Organization of American States, the Pact of Bogotá, the Rio de Janeiro Treaty of Reciprocal Assistance, and the Chile-United States Military Assistance Pact. The party considers these international agreements instruments of submission to the United States and advocates an independent foreign policy based on the maintenance of diplomatic and commercial relations with all members of the community of nations without discrimination of any sort.[54] The PCCh has generally conformed to the international party program in foreign affairs, although sometimes only after argument and delay.

The specific Chilean Communist position is that at present Chile is ruled by a native oligarchy allied to United States imperialism but that the country is now approaching a people's democratic revolution against these two enemies. The central task of the party is stated in consequence to be formation of a united front of all popular forces. This united front, often called the National Liberation Front (*Frente de*

[54] There is a vast amount of literature on communism in Chile. In English a good account of the historical development of the party in relation to the labor movement is found in Robert J. Alexander, *Communism in Latin America* (New Brunswick: Rutgers University Press, 1957), pp. 177–210. Other important works are: Juan Casillo, *Lo que ha hecho el comunismo* (Santiago, 1942); Fernando Alegría, *Recabarren* (Santiago, 1938); Ricardo Fonseca, *Chile es capaz de resolver sus problemas* (Santiago, 1947); César Godoy Urrutia, *Adonde va el socialismo* (Santiago, 1940). Elías Lafferte, the late, great leader of Chilean Communism, wrote among other books and pamphlets *Hacia la transformación económica y política de Chile por la vía de la unión nacional* (Santiago, 1945) and *Vida de un comunista: páginas autobiográficas* (Santiago, 1957). Another leading Communist, Carlos Contreras Labarca, wrote a large number of pamphlets including: *La lucha del pueblo por la reorganización de Chile* (Santiago, 1946). Strongly anti-Communist is Sergio Fernández Larraín, *Informe sobre el comunismo rendido a la Convención General del Partido Conservador Unido el 12 de octubre, 1954* (Santiago, 1954). Julio César Jobet, *Socialismo y Comunismo* (Santiago: Espartaco, 1952) is a good analysis of differences between socialism and communism. Useful party publications are *¿Qué es el P.C.* (*Partido Comunista de Chile*)*?* (Santiago: Imprenta Horizonte, 1962) and *Programa del Partido Comunista de Chile* (Santiago: Imprenta Horizonte, 1962).

Liberación Nacional) is intended to include not only the proletariat but also the urban middle class which "is interested in the progress of the country."[55] The PCCh seeks understandings with other political parties with similar objectives as a means of gaining national power. The National Liberation Front is regarded as the tool with which a people's democracy and people's government may be constructed and an independent, democratic, peaceful, and neutral Chile created. The democratic coalition of popular forces, led by the workers and the farmers, would remove the oligarchic minority from economic and political power, reforming the now reactionary social and political structures. This "people's democratic revolution" would clear the way for a full socialist revolution and the complete abolition of capitalism. That revolution, however, is anticipated as a peaceful one; the party professes to reject violence as a method of victory.

The emphasis is, then, on peaceful development that would ultimately bring about fundamental domestic changes. Total nationalization is not proclaimed as a goal for the first stage of the revolution, although the party does call for expropriation of all foreign-owned industries, banks, and insurance companies, and of most of the *latifundios*. As in all Latin American communist parties, the principal theme of the PCCh program is anti-imperialism, which in practice is anti-Americanism. The strong anti-Yankee feeling, always present in some form in Latin America, whether strong and active or faint and dormant, has served the Communists well in their efforts to direct the formidable currents of nationalism to their advantage and to conceal the inherent antagonisms between theoretical communism and nationalism. The PCCh is no exception in this respect, although in general its attacks on the United States are somewhat less virulent than those of other Latin American communist parties.

Composition. The PCCh is essentially a workers' party. Its electoral support does not come from nonunion workers but generally from trade unions that are controlled by the party. Its membership is composed for the most part of trade union workers, although there are also a segment of the *petite bourgeoisie* and a numerically small but significant group of intellectuals, writers, artists, and university professors among its followers. Until the late 1950's the working-class nucleus of the party included only the urban proletariat, but since then the party has been able to attract more and more followers from the peasant class. The popularity and appeal of the Cuban Revolution was a factor in Communist growth in the rural sectors. Communist efforts

[55] Luis Corvalán, *Hacia la conquista de un gobierno popular: Informe del Comité Central del PC rendido por el Secretario General del Partido* (Santiago, 1962), p. 39.

to woo the peasants culminated in the so-called First Congress of Peasants (*Primer Congreso de Campesinos*) staged in 1961; the Congress in turn led to the formation of the National Federation of Peasants (*Federación Nacional de Campesinos*).[56]

That the PCCh controls a substantial number of Chilean trade unions is evidenced by the fact that in 1962 there were eleven PCCh members in the National Council of the Chilean Labor Confederation. It is not possible to determine accurately the precise number of unions that are controlled by the party, but all observers agree that it is very considerable. Among the rank and file are some of the most distinguished Chilean intellectuals — the famous poet Pablo Neruda and the writer L. E. Delano, for instance. These intellectuals lend prestige and respectability to the party, but their influence within the ranks is considerably less than that of the labor leadership. In the Central Executive Committee, for instance, workers and intellectuals are represented usually in a five-to-two ratio. At the meetings of the high councils of the FRAP coalition, the Communist representatives are generally the only working-class delegates present. Also characteristic of the Communist Party are efforts to encourage and promote the organization of artistic activities, such as theater, choral, and dance groups. Programs of the kind are always stressed by the party. On the other hand, members from the professional and technical fields are not numerous, in contrast to comparable numbers in the Socialist or Christian Democratic parties. Communist groups are, however, active in the student movement and constitute the majority of the leftist elements of that sector.

The PCCh offers its members opportunities to rise to positions of increasing responsibility and to embark on professional party careers, but these advances can only be made by long and arduous work and by the unequivocal demonstration of loyal dedication to the party. Those who aspire to higher party positions are tested over and over. A minimum of ten years of service to the party is required before an individual is considered for a position of prominence and responsibility. In this particular respect, the PCCh is unique in Chilean politics, since even in the Socialist Party there are frequent examples of leaders who have had a meteoric career. It is the only party in Chile in which full-time party officers receive their full financial support from the organization.

The process of recruitment is a deliberate one and receives special attention from top party leadership. It frequently begins in the front organizations (*organizaciones de frente*), which may be variously eco-

[56] Corvalán, *op. cit.*, p. 36.

nomic, political, or cultural in nature but are supported with uniform vigor by the party. It is at this level that promising prospects are identified who may later be eventually brought into the party. Also characteristic of the PCCh is a highly organized program of political indoctrination and civic education. Political instruction is thorough and highly specialized. Seminars, political training programs, and the like are daily activities for the membership. Opportunities to travel abroad and visits to Soviet-bloc countries are available to members, as well as to distinguished nonpartisan figures in intellectual circles.

It should also be noted that of the parties associated with the FRAP, the PCCh is the most highly endowed. The party taps a variety of sources: contributions from labor organizations, obligatory monthly fees paid by all members, sale of publications, contributions from wealthy sympathizers, collections at party functions, the organization of dances, theatrical performances and similar affairs. There is, for all practical purposes, a kind of ministry of finance within the party mechanism, and it works very effectively. Commercial enterprises involving substantial investments have even been established for the party's profit. One of these, an import business, has been prospering for years.[57] Whether all these ample party funds come from such sources or a part originate outside the country, it is a fact that the PCCh has always had ample financial resources. Naturally they have proved an advantage to the party, particularly since the Chilean Left in general has been traditionally poor. Besides permitting it to have a large corps of full-time officials, a luxury no other party can afford, these resources have given the Communists an important weapon in the trade union field and are one of the principal explanations for their prominent position among labor organizations.[58] In addition, Chilean Communists as a group are hard-working, resourceful, and efficient. When their alliance with other political parties permits close comparison, Communist functionaries are noted for their readiness to volunteer for the most difficult and unrewarding tasks and their ability to perform them competently.

Structure and Organization. In the 1962 revised party organization, the main organs of the PCCh at the national level were the National Congress (*Congreso Nacional*) — the supreme organ of the party for the whole country — the National Conference (*Conferencia Nacional*), and the Central Executive Committee (*Comité Ejecutivo Central.*)[59]

[57] Among the others are said to be bus lines, real estate projects, and printing establishments.

[58] Alexander, *op. cit.,* p. 210.

[59] *Estatutos del Partido Comunista aprobados en el XII Congreso Nacional* (Santiago: Editorial Horizonte, 1962).

The by-laws emphasize that party organization is based upon the "principle of democratic centralism" and define this principle as embodying the election of all party officers, the application of strict discipline, and the obligation of the leaders to account periodically to the relevant party organs.

Chilean Communist organization at the local level corresponds to the national scheme. There are the Regional Committee (*Comité Regional*), with a corresponding Regional Conference (*Conferencia Regional*) and Regional Congress (*Congreso Regional*). The primary party unit, the Party Committee (*Comité del Partido*), is divided into cells (*células*). Each cell has an executive body and an assembly (*Dirección* and *Asamblea*). If the cells that compose the Party Committee include workers in the same type of production or service, the Committee is then called *Comité de Empresa;* in all other cases it is referred to as the *Comité Local.*

The Central Executive is, of course, the ultimate source of power. It represents the party, executes the decisions of other organs, and supervises the general activities of the party. Specifically, it convokes extraordinary meetings of the National Congress and of the National and Regional Conferences. Finally, as the top executive organ, it has the responsibility for selecting all candidates for public office. The key post in the Central Executive Committee is that of General Secretary. A series of special units — among them youth and female — and a number of front organizations complete the organizational structure of the party.

The Socialist Party

The roots of Chilean socialism are said to be the *Sociedad de la Igualdad,* founded in 1850, and the works of Francisco Bilbao and of the disciple of French utopian socialism, Santiago Arcos.[60] However, it was not until the turn of this century, at a time coinciding with the birth of the labor movement, that genuine socialistic ideas began to take hold.[61] In the early 1930's they began to spread among the salaried and intellectual classes. Not long after the demise of the so-called "socialist republic" in April, 1933, the Socialist Party of Chile was formally established as a merger of the following groups: New Public Action (*Nueva Acción Pública* — NAP), Socialist Revolutionary Action (*Acción Revolucionaria Socialista*), Socialist Order (*Orden Socialista*), Marxist Socialist Party (*Partido Socialista Marx-*

[60] See Chapter 2, p. 60.

[61] Socialist organizations that were basically nonpolitical in nature, such as the *Centro Social Obrero* (1898), the *Partido Obrero Francisco Bilbao* (1898), and the *Partido Socialista* (1901), were short-lived.

ista), and Unified Socialist Party (*Partido Socialista Unificado*).[62] Shortly after the First Party Congress was held, Eugenio Matte, regarded as the founding father of the Socialist Party, died, but the party itself continued to grow rapidly, becoming a vigorous mass organization. In 1933 it ran as its presidential candidate Marmaduke Grove, who later withdrew to throw Socialist support in 1938 in favor of Radical candidate Pedro Aguirre Cerda, the Popular Front standard-bearer.[63]

After the Popular Front victory the Socialists were given three posts in Aguirre's cabinet. It was not long before the Party suffered its first split, as a group opposed to the government formed the Workers' Socialist Party (*Partido Socialista de Trabajadores*), the members of which for the most part joined the Communist Party two years later. When the Socialist Party in 1940 withdrew from the Popular Front and thus brought about its eventual dissolution, a period of serious Socialist disintegration began. In 1942 the Eighth Party Congress decided to support the administration of Radical President Juan Antonio Ríos. As a result a new party struggle occurred and a new fraction was founded, the Authentic Socialist Party (*Partido Socialista Auténtico*) led by Marmaduke Grove. A new split in 1948 contributed to a further Socialist decline, a phenomenon already in evidence in the 1946 election, when the party received only 12,000 votes. The party was now divided into two major factions, the Socialist Party of Chile (*Partido Socialista de Chile*) and the Popular Socialist Party (*Partido Socialista Popular*). The chief cause of the new division was the enactment of President González Videla's anticommunist law. Traditionally the Socialist position was strongly anticommunist, but the new law led to a difference between those who favored suppression and those who did not. The former created the Socialist Party of Chile, which later participated in the González Videla administration. In the 1952 presidential election the other faction, the Popular Socialists, supported the candidacy of Ibáñez, while the Socialist Party of Chile nominated a candidate from among its own ranks, Salvador Allende.

But even as these events were taking place, in the late 1940's a new, young, dynamic group — typified by Raúl Ampuero, leader of the Popular Socialists — was coming into power in Chilean socialism. This group eventually played an important part in the recovery of the

[62] The principal leaders of NAP were Eugenio Matte Hurtado, Carlos A. Martínez, and Marmaduke Grove; of *Acción Revolucionaria,* Eugenio González Rojas and Oscar Schnake; and of *Orden Socialista,* Arturo Bianchi. Oscar Schnake became the first Secretary General of the new party.

[63] See Chapter 2, p. 67.

Socialist movement. After a brief period of collaboration with Ibáñez, the Popular Socialists in 1956 joined the ranks of the opposition, and the way to party unity was opened.

In May, 1956, the parties of the Left allied in the Popular Action Front (*Frente de Acción Popular* — FRAP). Included were the two Socialist parties, the People's Democratic Party (*Partido Democrático del Pueblo*), the Democratic Party of Chile (*Partido Democrático de Chile*), the Labor Party (*Partido del Trabajo*), and the now-outlawed Communists. United now in opposition to Ibáñez and with the long-standing Socialist-Communist controversy mitigated by postwar international events, the Socialists were at last ready to forget their differences. A "Congress of Unity" held in July, 1957, formalized the merger of the two factions under the simple designation, Socialist Party. The new party confirmed its adherence to the Popular Action Front. In February, 1964, the Twentieth Party Congress, held in Concepción, re-elected Raúl Ampuero as the party's Secretary General. The Left, fortified by the unification of the Socialists and the new harmony with the Communists, gave remarkably solid support to Socialist leader Salvador Allende in the 1964 presidential contest.

Ideology. At its birth, Chilean socialism was a Marxist movement taking an extremist position. Although the movement was composed of heterogeneous groups — pure Marxists, anti-Marxists, anarcho-syndicalists, "humanistic socialists," and many others — the ideological influence of the Trotskyites was probably the predominant one. This radical-Left ideological position did not correspond to the intellectual and social background of party members. Party dogma left little room for individual political difference and was definitely much more extreme than representative opinion among the Socialist rank and file. It was not until 1946 that efforts were made to clarify party ideology by developing some kind of consensus and that a program was drafted that adapted Chilean socialism to the political reality of mid-century Chile. This task was accomplished principally by the younger element in the party that, under the leadership of Raúl Ampuero, brought to an end the dominance of the elders. The party, naturally, continued to be Marxist and Socialist, but it abandoned worn-out doctrine, and its program acquired distinctly new overtones.

In the first place, the party became aware of and eventually accepted the new wave of nationalism sweeping Latin America. That reconciliation to nationalism in general serves to explain the Socialist Party's support of Ibáñez in his rise to power as well as its indifference to and even acquiescence in some particularly virulent types of nationalism, such as that characteristic of the Peronista movement in Argentina. Socialist support of Ibáñez' nationalism and the temporary

Socialist alliance with the *ibáñista Partido Agrario Laborista* is evidence also of a certain process of Chileanization that has recently been occurring in the Socialist Party. A by-product of this process has been the narrowing of programmatic differences with the Communists, who, in Chile as in most other Latin American countries, had been quick to embrace the continent's new nationalism. A third important ideological development within the Socialist movement was the adoption of a clearly antiliberal democratic position that, in turn, has tended to widen the differences with the Center forces, most particularly with the Radical Party. As a result of these modifications, Chilean socialism is now frankly in opposition to the established institutional order and maintains the necessity of eliminating the liberal-democratic system that is considered to be in actuality only externally and formally democratic. In its stead the party advocates the establishment of a new order, authoritarian in nature but based on wide popular support.

In general terms the Socialist Party labels itself as Marxist, revolutionary, anticapitalist, anti-imperialist, classist, and "Americanist" (meaning advocating the unity of all the Latin American peoples). Its philosophical base is provided by Marxist dialectics and historical materialism. But the philosophy is not applied rigidly to the interpretation of Chilean phenomena. The possibility is fully admitted that formulas applied to different situations in other countries may be inadequate when they are applied to Chilean problems. Imitation, then, is rejected, and Chile is regarded as developing best under a "Chilean socialism" which allows for indigenous circumstances.[64] "Revolu-

[64] An interesting discussion on Socialist ideology by Salvador Allende is found in Sergio Guilisati Tagle, *Partidos políticos chilenos* (Santiago: Editorial Nascimento, 1964), pp. 267–293. This work deals with the historical development, ideology, and organization of major parties in Chile. It is a revised edition of the book by the same author entitled *Caminos de la política* (Santiago: Editorial Nascimento, 1960). Other useful sources are: Salomón Corbalán, *El Partido Socialista* (Santiago: Imprenta Atenea, 1957); Partido Socialista de Chile, *Esquema económico de Chile* (Santiago: Prensa Latinoamericana, 1962); Alejandro Cheléu Rojas, *Flujo y reflujo del socialismo chileno* (Santiago, n.d.); Julio César Jobet, *Significado del Partido Socialista en la realidad nacional* (Santiago, 1940); *Socialismo y comunismo* (Santiago: Ediciones Espartaco, 1952); and, *El socialismo en Chile* (Santiago: Publicaciones del Congreso por la Libertad de la Cultura, 1956); Manuel Espinoza, *Humanismo socialista* (Santiago: Prensa Latinoamericana, n.d.); Agustín Alvarez Villablanca, *Objetivos del socialismo en Chile* (Santiago: Partido Socialista, 1946); Salvador Allende, *La contradicción de Chile* (Santiago, 1943); Oscar Waiss, *Presencia del socialismo en Chile* (Santiago: Ediciones Espartaco, 1952); Aniceto Rodríguez and Raúl Ampuero, *Democracia y revolución: Dos discursos sobre nuestra realidad política* (Santiago: Prensa Latinoamericana, 1955); Ani-

tionary" is taken to mean that the party intends to make drastic changes in the present Chilean socio-economic structure, through a "workers democratic revolution" aimed at the creation of a "popular democracy." The party is revolutionary regardless of the nature of means it may employ to attain this objective, because its goal is to change radically the existing social order.[65] The party program puts special emphasis on "integral" agrarian reform, improvement of the educational system, tax reform, and the alteration of electoral procedures. As steps towards a socialist revolution, the party advocates the progressive nationalization of the foreign-owned copper, nitrate, and iron companies and the strengthening of the native petroleum industry (*Empresa Nacional de Petróleo*). It has also proposed government control of credit institutions, foreign trade, insurance companies, and public utilities and the elimination of monopolies. Industrial enterprises, created initially by the government but now controlled by private enterprise — such as the *Compañía de Acero del Pacífico*, CAP — would be returned to state control. The Socialist program also favors economic development through the acceleration of industrialization. For this purpose it advocates centralized planning through the establishment of national economic institutions in the affairs of which the workers would participate. A Central Planning Office attached to the presidency would direct this national economic mechanism to adapt development plans to the needs of the socialist state. The agrarian reform as the Socialists envision it includes the compensated expropriation of large estates, the distribution of land obtained in this way among the peasants, and the establishment of cooperatives and state farms. Plans for educational reform include measures to eliminate illiteracy, to reorganize and centralize the school system at all levels in order to make education available to all citizens, and to promote national culture. The party plank on tax reform contemplates measures toward a fairer distribution of the tax burden.[66]

Advocating a true "democratization" of the Chilean political system, the Socialists propose constitutional reforms that include the

---

ceto Rodríguez, *Forjando la unidad popular: Cuenta política del camarada Aniceto Rodríguez al XVI Congreso General del PSP.* (Santiago: PSP, 1956); Bernardo Ibáñez, *El socialismo y el porvenir de los pueblos* (Santiago, 1946); Raúl Ampuero, *En defensa del partido y del socialismo* (Santiago, n.d.), and *El socialismo ante el mundo de hoy* (Santiago: Prensa Latinoamericana, 1964). A very important source is the Socialist monthly *Arauco,* founded in 1959 and published in Santiago.

[65] *Estatuto del Partido Socialista* (Santiago: Imprenta Plá, 1962), p. 3.

[66] See "Imagen de un líder," *Arauco* (August, 1964), pp. 3–109, which includes transcripts of a series of television interviews with Socialist leader Salvador Allende.

extension of suffrage to all eighteen-year-old Chileans, the establishment of an automatic system of electoral registration, and the protection of social rights like the right to work and to strike, to family bonuses, and to the homestead. They advocate measures to "democratize" the legislative branch of the government in order to improve its efficiency, and they favor administrative decentralization, municipal home rule, and the creation of Provincial Assemblies.

In foreign affairs the party supports disarmament, prohibition of nuclear weapons, dissolution of military alliances, and peaceful settlement of all international controversies. It condemns foreign intervention, colonialism, and racial discrimination and advocates the maintenance of relations with all nations. Finally, it declares its support for the unity and solidarity of all the Latin American states.[67]

In general, then, when the Socialists refer to themselves as a class party they mean that they rely only on certain socio-economic groups to achieve the Socialist revolution. Chilean Socialists consider that only the working class (workers and peasants) and the lower middle class are capable of leading such a revolution since, in their opinion, the middle classes proper have lost all creative capacity and have tended to preserve the value system of the upper class. According to Socialist thinking, these middle sectors "live from whatever they were able to accumulate in the past" while consuming the small additional capitalization made by the country in recent decades.[68]

Social Composition. Workers and intellectuals form the core of the Socialist Party. The latter are more influential, and they generally come from the provincial middle class. Leaders at the intermediate party level are often white-collar workers or members of the artisan class. The party's electoral appeal is principally directed to the workers and to the lower middle class, but it also attracts many professionals, students, and white-collar employees. Although its total membership is unknown, it is estimated at approximately 35,000. Among the masses, the Socialist Party has had always to engage in a hard struggle with the Communists for the worker vote. A parallel struggle for domination of the labor unions has generally been lost by a divided Socialist Party, and a consequent reduction in political strength has occurred. At present, although no specific data are available on the number of unions that are Socialist-controlled, the fact that there are ten Socialist members out of a membership of twenty-five in the National Council of the Labor Confederation (*Central Unica de*

67 *Programa del Partido Socialista: XX Congreso General Ordinario celebrado en Concepción, febrero, 1964* (Santiago, 1964). See also Mario Verdugo, *op. cit.*, pp. 27–28, 31, 33–34, 36–37, 42–43, 47–48.

68 Salomón Corbalán, *op. cit.*, p. 15.

Trabajadores, CUT) indicates a certain party recovery in the trade union field. Socialist influence among the copper miners has been traditionally strong, probably owing to the relatively higher standards of living of these workers in comparison with those of the rest of the labor force. In recent years the party, on the other hand, has consistently lost ground among the industrial proletariat of Santiago. Its influence upon the capital's working groups is almost reduced now to control over the oldest and most traditional trade unions, such as the railroad workers, printers, and similar groups, while workers in the new industries (textile and construction, among them) located in the large urban complex of Santiago have shown a definite attraction toward the Communist Party.

The weakening of Socialist strength in the capital city has been at least partially compensated by a growing strength in the provinces, where the party has successfully attracted an increasing number of the *petite bourgeoisie* and more importantly has continued to exert a strong influence among the peasantry. The more efficient organization that resulted from the unification of Socialist groups into a single party is responsible for this development. Today, Socialist strength is fairly evenly divided geographically throughout the country, although in a few scattered provinces the party receives no votes. This generally growing influence in the provinces, based on the support of provincial middle-class groups, has given the party a bourgeois coloration it lacked in the past. In Magallanes province, the Socialists enjoy what is practically an electoral monopoly as a consequence of support of the semi-industrial workers of the cattle, wool, and meat industries.

Professionals and intellectuals constitute a group of special importance in party affairs. They give the party prestige and respectability, and their work in the various technical commissions of the party is significant. They also perform the important functions of serving as liaison between the party and public and private institutions — like CORFO, ECLA, the University of Chile — and pressure groups — like the National Association of Agriculture.

The patterns of recruitment and party career show the influence of the group of Socialist professionals and intellectuals. Within Socialist ranks there are two ways in which an individual may rise to high party levels: by gradual promotion beginning at the base of the pyramid through a fairly rigid merit system — and this method is like that prevailing in the Radical Party — and by immediate elevation to high rank because of special intellectual and personal qualifications. Instances of the last method are numerous, since Socialist ideology has always held a special attraction for Chilean intellectuals, and opportunities for a distinguished career and rapid advancement in a party based principally on the proletariat are naturally greater than in other organizations not so based. Chileans of special intellectual gifts have frequently occupied positions of responsibility in the party.

Relations between national leaders and the provincial and village leaders are characteristically close in the Socialist Party. The role of the local organization is active and dynamic, as is true also of the Radical Party. National leaders travel constantly in order to maintain intimate contact with the party's substructure, while local leaders are in frequent contact with the national headquarters in Santiago. Internal coordination and command seems effective, and there appear to be no problems of communication. The national leadership is aware at all times of local issues and problems.

Three distinct types of leadership seem to recur in the history of the Socialist Party. At present these are exemplified by three notable political figures: Eugenio González Rojas, Raúl Ampuero, and Salvador Allende. González, presently Rector of the University of Chile, is a prestigious figure, greatly admired, seldom involved in internal politics, but carrying great weight in party deliberations when he does speak out. Ampuero is the tough, resilient type of leader, dynamic and knowledgeable, capable of inspiring strong personal loyalty. His personality has something of the charismatic about it (Chileans might call him a "white caudillo") and has attracted the solid following of those who are sometimes known as *ampueristas.* His relationship with the rank and file of the party is closer and much more personal than that of González. Allende is representative of a third type of leadership, nearly as charismatic as Ampuero's but calmer, characterized chiefly by tact, extraordinary political intuition, ability, and knowledge, and a remarkable capacity for diplomacy and compromise.

Structure and Organization. The organization of the party according to its statutes, is based on the principle of "democratic centralism."[69] Its main organs are the Nucleus (*Núcleo*) or cell, the Sectional Committee (*Comité Seccional*), the Sectional Conference (*Conferencia Seccional*), the Regional Committee (*Comité Regional*), the Regional Congress (*Congreso Regional*), the National Plenum (*Pleno Nacional*), the Central Committee (*Comité Central*), and the General Congress (*Congreso General*). A *Núcleo* is formed by not more than nine and not less than five members. Three or more *Núcleos* in each commune or subdelegation join to form a Sectional Committee. Every party member is required to join a *Seccional.* A Sectional Conference must be held once every year. In each province there is a Regional Com-

[69] *Estatuto del Partido Socialista* (Santiago: Imprenta Plá, 1962), Art. 13.

mittee, composed of representatives of a minimum of three Sectional Committees. A Regional Congress is organized every two years.

The *Pleno Nacional,* a group composed of Central Committee members plus all regional secretaries, ordinarily meets every six months to discuss political matters and to resolve organizational, electoral, or trade union problems that have arisen in putting into effect decisions of the party's General Congress.

The Central Committee is the supreme executive body during the period between meetings of the General Congress. It is composed of the Secretary General, seventeen members elected by the party's Congress, the head of the Socialist Parliamentary Brigade (*Brigada Parlamentaria Socialista*) — which is composed of all Socialist deputies and senators — the Secretary General of the Socialist Youth, and the national director of the Federation of Socialist Women (*Federación de Mujeres Socialistas*). The Central Committee has ultimate authority in all party matters. It is entrusted with the direction of party affairs, and it selects all candidates for elective office as well as party functionaries. In addition, it is authorized to negotiate all kinds of pacts and agreements with other political parties. Candidates for the municipal councils, however, are the exception. They are selected through party elections held at the local level and convoked by the respective Regional Committees.[70]

The General Congress, ordinarily held every two years, consists of delegates elected by the Regional Congresses. It determines general party policy, and it must approve the report (*cuenta política*) of the Central Committee. It can also issue calls for national conferences of a consultative nature.

There are a number of auxiliary party organs, among which the following are the most important: the Office of International Affairs; the Office of Technical Studies; the Recruitment Commission; the Agrarian Reform Commission; and the Departments of Organization and Control, Trade Unions, Propaganda, Political Education, Elections, Finances, Municipal Administration, Solidarity, and Action and Defense. Special organs, as we have observed, are the Socialist Parliamentary Brigade, the Federation of Socialist Women, and the Socialist Youth (party members between fifteen and twenty-six years of age). Special party tribunals (*Tribunales de Disciplina*) are charged with disciplinary functions and propose sanctions to the Central Committee, which actually imposes them.

Given the highly centralized structure described, party decisions generally are made by the leadership with little or no participation by the

[70] Guilisati, *op. cit.*, p. 264.

rank and file. However, there are certain types of issues that, because they are of particular and personal interest to party members or because they are strictly regional and local in nature are exceptions to this general rule; in the resolution of these the party mass may participate actively. In matters of general policy, nevertheless, subordination of the rank and file to the party hierarchy is characteristic of the Socialist organization. In all decisions of an economic nature, the reports of the respective technical departments carry great weight, and they are almost invariably accepted by the national leaders with no alteration.

The process of decision-making can be at times long and laborious. An example is the question of whether or not to support the Ibáñez candidacy in 1952. Originally, there existed an inarticulate but favorable disposition among the Socialist rank and file that eventually reached the higher echelons of the party. The matter was debated at great length in a *Pleno Nacional,* which finally recommended to the Central Committee that the party support Ibáñez. Discussion in this body lasted five months, and it was only as a result of considerable pressure from the party grass-roots that final action was taken. Altogether, more than six months were required for the party machinery to produce this decision.

The Socialist Party, it is interesting to note, preserves much of the clandestine character that it had at its inception. Records of party deliberations, the registry of members, and all other important documents are kept secret and are unavailable to outside investigators. Its cellular, semisecret structural pattern is also reminiscent of the early revolutionary period of the proletarian rise to political participation.

Minor Parties

It has been mentioned that the increasing polarization of the Chilean electorate, combined with recent reforms in electoral procedures, has brought about the disappearance of practically all the small parties. Those which remain in existence are not influential and receive an insignificant percentage of the national vote. The principal minor parties are the Democratic Party (*Partido Democrático*), the National Democratic Party (*Partido Democrático Nacional*), and the National Vanguard of the People (*Vanguardia Nacional del Pueblo*).

Only a small fragment remains of the once powerful Democratic Party. After setting a remarkable record of survival during the many political storms after the 1920's, this party disintegrated rapidly following the *ibáñista* period. Its traditional weakness was the lack of ideological substance and the absence of intellectual leadership. Characterized by political opportunism, the Democratic Party became a bureaucratic machine run by local political bosses. Its main support was centered in Santiago, Valparaíso, Concepción, and Cautín. It maintained ties with both the Left and the Right, and it managed for many years to obtain at least one Cabinet portfolio in every administration. In 1958 it became so splintered that there existed Democratic groups supporting each one of the presidential candidates. Its small remnants were allied in 1964 with the Right-Center parties.

The National Democratic Party (PADENA) came into existence after the 1960 municipal elections as an alliance of scattered leftist groups which had supported the Ibáñez administration. When the Agrarian Labor Party (*Partido Agrario Laborista*), the mainstay of the Ibáñez government, began to disintegrate in 1958, some of its members joined an offshoot of the Democratic Party and founded a new organization, the National Popular Party (*Partido Nacional Popular,* PANAPO). This group some time later gave its support to the Christian Democrats, and eventually some of its members officially joined the ranks of the Christian Democratic Party. PANAPO had a short life, and in time many of the non-Marxist groups that formed it—especially those with nationalistic inclinations—joined ranks with various splinters of the Democrats and founded PADENA. This party lost all of its six senators in the 1961 congressional elections but, against all expectations, was able to elect twelve deputies. Its strength resided in some rural sections of the central and frontier regions. The PADENA percentage of the vote fell from 6.9 in 1961 to 5.2 in the 1963 municipal elections.

As the 1964 presidential elections approached, the PADENA underwent a series of internal crises. One group maintained the necessity of an alliance between Christian Democrats and the FRAP in support of a leftist candidate other than Frei or Allende. Another group as strongly advocated support of the Christian Democrats. Consequently the PADENA split, with some of its members joining the Christian Democrats and others establishing a new organization, Agrarian Labor Democracy (*Democracia Agraria Laborista*), which also supported Frei's candidacy. The rest of the *padenistas* remained within the FRAP coalition and supported Allende.

The National Vanguard of the People Party was formed by the fusion of the Labor Party (*Partido del Trabajo*), a small personalist faction of the leftist leader Baltazar Castro, with various Marxist and Trotskyite groups. In 1964, the VNP, although remaining in the FRAP coalition, suffered several divisions as a result of personal rivalries, and two other small personalist groups emerged, the Marxist Popular Vanguard (*Vanguardia Popular Marxista*) and the Worker's National Alliance (*Alianza Nacional de Trabajadores*). None of these parties is more than an insignificant faction formed around some political personality, and they are destined to be short-lived.

Also within the FRAP coalition there are a number of organizations that are not truly parties but played an important part in the 1964 campaign. Among them are the Radical Doctrinary Party (*Partido Radical Doctrinario*), a group of dissident Radicals, and a number of "movements" created by individuals who sympathized with Allende's candidacy but were, for one reason or another, reluctant to join formally any of the FRAP coalition parties. One of them, the Leftist Independent Movement (*Movimiento Independiente de Izquierda,* MIDI), besides being larger than any of the minor parties, has among its ranks some distinguished professionals and technicians. Two other organizations formed by retired military officers are also important among the independent leftist forces: the Military Civic Front (*Frente Cívico Militar*) and Stronghold of the People (*Baluarte del Pueblo*). An organization of independent middle-class women (mostly wives of FRAP leaders) known as the *Comando Independentista de Mujeres Allendistas* (CIMA) played a role of some importance in the 1964 campaign by competing with the Christian Democrats in social work activities. This women's organization and the MIDI combined their activities under a national federation, the *Federación Nacional Allendista.*

Pressure Groups

Very little is known about this subject in Chile. As in most Latin American countries, the concept of interest groups in the sense that it has been applied in research in political behavior in the United States has scarcely been considered. What follows, therefore, is only a brief sketch generally describing some of the structures of power of economic and social importance. I should note that a full survey of interest groups, both of associational and informal-grouping types, of their history, organization, aims, and methods, ought to be made available to students of Chile.

Among the associational types, the National Agricultural Society (*Sociedad Nacional de Agricultura,* SNA) is one of the most influential. It is always well represented in the Congress, and it traditionally has had easy access to the rightist parties. Formed by all the large landowners, the SNA exercises indirect influence not only because of the economic power it represents but also because of the social prominence of its members. The great majority of the members of its governing board are prominent Conservatives and Liberals. Only a few Radicals are among them, though in recent years, because of the Radical affiliation of some new large landowners, relations between that party and the SNA have become much closer than they were in the past.

A counterpart of the SNA in the mining industry is the National Mining Association (*Sociedad Nacional de Minería,* SNM). Mining concerns, both foreign and domestic, are frequently allied with the Right and the Center parties, and many of their lawyers and other official representatives are men of some political distinction. Foreign-owned companies in general it should be said, employ persons of all political affiliations as lawyers, public relations executives, and the like.

Among the banking groups distinctions can be made between the large institutions and the small concerns belonging to wealthy families. The great banks, such as the Bank of Chile, have very close associations with the agricultural and mining interests, as well as with the big insurance companies. Although maintaining ties with significant figures in every political area, this group of great banks tends to identify itself with the Liberal Party. The small banks, some owned by wealthy families of Middle-Eastern origin, operate of course at a different level. In politics, these institutions make contributions to all parties. A third group of banking institutions is formed by a number of small concerns owned and operated by foreign nationals, such as the Spanish Bank and the Israelite Bank.

The merchants' association (*Sociedad General de Comercio*) is an influential group. Founded at the initiative of the CORFO (Chilean Development Corporation), it is composed chiefly of young progressive entrepreneurs. It is now completely independent from the government. Politically, it is strongly linked with the Liberal Party. The manufacturers' association (*Sociedad de Fomento Fabril*) is another important group. It has opposed, frequently with success, stabilization policies which it has considered adverse to its interests. The relatively small group of major exporters is closely connected with the rightist parties.

Sometimes the interests of these powerful economic groups coincide with those of the working class. Thus, for example, representatives of the "small" mining industry (*pequeña minería*) and nitrate trade union leaders frequently combine their political influence in order to put pressure on the government in favor of certain economic measures, such as currency devaluation.

The importance of the Catholic Church as a pressure group is only secondary. With the exception of Chiloé province, where members of the clergy are militants in local politics, the ecclesiastical establishment is not politically active. Only occasionally does the Church intervene in political matters, and in such cases it exercises only indirect influence through Catholic lay groups. Naturally, the Church's strongest ties are with the Catholic-oriented parties, the Conservative and the Christian Democrat. Young, reform-minded clerics always prefer the latter.

The influence of Masonry in politics has been declining for some time. The period in which it was a significant factor extended from 1915 to 1940. During that period its influence grew mainly as a consequence of the rise of the Radical and the Democratic parties. Masons were a significant factor in the Radical struggle for power, but once the Radicals gained access to the government the Masons were apparently relegated to a secondary role. As their influence declined, Catholic lay groups began to win important victories in the field of education. State subsidies to private educational institutions are not infrequent now, and Catholic institutions are authorized to grant university degrees as valuable as those given by the national university. The practical monopoly of the Radical Party over the educational system was broken largely by the ability and dynamism of Catholic teacher and student groups.

The armed forces can be considered as a veto group, but they have no relationships with political parties as such. In national politics they simply exercise by consensus a right to veto those policies which may affect their institutional interests, and they rarely become involved in other governmental affairs.[71] The army officer corps is for the most part composed of persons of middle-class origins, with only a few officers possessing an upper-class background. Although some may be described as "progressive" and interested in social and political reforms, the sense of discipline among Chilean officers is stronger than political sympathies. They are repelled by radicalism and by the expressions of it in strikes, riots, and other destructive disorders. These officers do not appear to be as strongly nationalistic as their counterparts in other Latin American countries, and there are no vestiges among them of uncritical anti-imperialist sentiments. The navy, as also is often the case in Latin America, is politically "liberal" in the best English tradition.

With regard to organized labor, it must be recalled first of all that it is political in the highest degree in Chile. The role of the trade unions as pressure groups, therefore, is always a reflection of the political orientation of their members. All political parties have a "labor department" (*departamentos sindicales*) designed to direct the activities of their members in the labor field and also to influence decisions in workers' organizations. The first party which undertook such activities in a systematic way was the Communist, when in 1931 it

[71] See Chapter 3.

began to organize cells and "fractions" in factories, workshops, and national labor federations. The Socialist Party soon followed the example by organizing "labor brigades" at local and national levels. In 1938 the Radical Party started to take an active interest in the labor movement, and it has been followed more recently by the Christian Democratic Party. Even the Conservative and the Liberal parties have now put emphasis on proselytism among trade union members.

In the present national labor confederation (*Central Unica de Trabajadores,* CUT) there are Communist, Socialist, Christian Democratic, Radical, Anarchist, and Trotskyite ideological currents. The group of independents is very small. In the Third Congress of the CUT, which took place in August, 1962, elections were held for the national executive secretariat, a body that, together with the delegates selected by the national federations, constitutes the National Executive Council of CUT. Out of a total of fifteen members elected on that occasion, six were Communists, five Socialists, three Christian Democrats, and one a Radical.[72] It must be noted, however, that the CUT does not include all of Chile's labor force and that there are a considerable number of small, nonaffiliated unions. It is to these that a majority of workers belong.

Most recent trends in the organized labor movement are the decrease in Communist influence, the strengthening of Socialist factions, the stagnation of the Radical Party, the consistent advance of the Christian Democratic forces, and the elimination of anarchism as a significant political element.

[72] A recent and useful study of the Chilean labor movement is Jorge Barría Serón, *Trayectoria y estructura del movimiento sindical chileno, 1946–1962* (Santiago: Instituto de Organización y Administración, 1963).

7

The Peaceful Road to Revolution

In the last half a century Chile has experienced three presidential elections which can be considered as turning points in the country's political history. The first was the 1920 election of Arturo Alessandri, the "Lion of Tarapacá," as a result of what has been called "the revolt of the electorate." The second was the 1938 contest which brought about the "Popular Front" and the election of Pedro Aguirre Cerda. The third was the election of September 4, 1964. This election was, essentially, a contest between two reformers and champions of the common man: Eduardo Frei, the Christian Democratic leader, who wanted a "Revolution in Liberty"; and Salvador Allende, the leader of the FRAP, the Socialist-Communist coalition, who called for thoroughgoing changes in the economic and social structures of Chile.[1]

As we have already noted,[2] the 1964 presidential campaign began early. The FRAP's showing in the 1963 municipal elections had not been overly encouraging. This had the effect of galvanizing the leftist coalition into an early mobilization of forces, for they knew that the road to the presidency was to be a hard one. The Christian Democrats, their star in the ascent, were nevertheless not overconfident and also worked strenuously and effectively among the voters. The last six months of 1963 were filled with hard campaigning and the candidates

[1] The following discussion of the 1964 presidential elections includes portions of a monograph by this author and Charles J. Parrish entitled *The Chilean Presidential Election of September 4, 1964* (Washington, D.C.: Institute for the Comparative Study of Political Systems, 1965). Used by permission.

[2] See Chapter 6, pp. 242–243.

were constantly touring the country from north to south drumming up support.

The outcome of the Curicó election in March, 1964, and the rightist debacle which caused the disbanding of the *Frente Democrático* delighted the Christian Democrats. They could not have been happier over the results had they won themselves, rather than the FRAP. They had joined the battle reluctantly, fearing that the expected victory of the *Frente* would help the Radical candidate Durán and hurt Frei's chances in September. The effect of the election was precisely the opposite: it eliminated Durán as a serious candidate, and, as we shall see, assured Frei's victory in the subsequent presidential election. After their stunning defeat, the rightist parties had only one choice left: to throw their support to the Christian Democratic candidate.

Few important changes took place in the campaign after May, and the propaganda on both sides increased in intensity and in its vitriolic aspects. By then, when the Christian Democrats were faced with Allende as a serious candidate, they began to find a strong emphasis on anti-communism very appealing. The effectiveness of the attempt to identify Allende with communism was reflected in his public statements, for he defended himself against the charge frequently throughout the campaign, stoutly maintaining his independence from communism.

The principal lines of argument were constant throughout the campaign. Indeed, these points of emphasis, as far as the FRAP was concerned, had been developed in the 1958 campaign. The leftist fundamental appeal was for a basic change in the economic, social, and political structure of the country. The large industrialists, the great *fundo* owners, the foreign investors, and the major financiers all came under fire from the FRAP.[3]

Dr. Allende and the FRAP promised that if elected they would seek to implement the following specific proposals: (1) a reduction of the voting age to eighteen, (2) abolition of the literacy test for suffrage qualifications, (3) establishment of an automatic system of voting registration, (4) a series of fundamental social welfare rights would be guaranteed all Chileans, (5) all workers would be given

[3] The following summation of the programs of Salvador Allende and Eduardo Frei is based primarily on newspaper reports, articles in periodicals, and campaign literature. Two articles by Rubén Corvalán, "Dos hombres, dos programas," Part I, *Ercilla,* May 20, 1964, pp. 14–15, and Part II, *Ercilla,* May 27, 1964, were particularly useful. For the FRAP, the document *Las bases técnicas del plan de acción del gobierno popular* (Santiago: Editorial Universitaria, 1964) was also useful.

the right to strike and to unionize, (6) higher social welfare payments to workers' families (rural and urban) would be guaranteed to those now being paid them and they would be extended to new groups, (7) unions would be guaranteed the right to belong to both national and international federations, (8) old age and children's benefits would be extended, (9) a free education would be guaranteed, (10) the independence of the judicial power would be assured, and (11) the army democratized. To be certain that the measures would be eventually passed, the FRAP called for a parliamentary reform to make Congress more democratic and to assure a majority representation to the Chilean working class. The implementation of these and the other reforms summarized below would, in the long run, need the promulgation of a new Constitution, but at the present time, Allende maintained, many changes could be made within the present framework.[4]

Senator Allende proposed a building up of the power of the provinces and an eventual decline in the power of the office of the chief executive. Also promised was the implementation of the provision of the 1925 Constitution providing for the creation of provincial assemblies which had hitherto been ignored.

In the economic field, very detailed proposals were put forward by the FRAP, which created the *Oficina Central de Planificación* (OCEPLAN) to coordinate economic and social plans for both propaganda purposes and for the forthcoming administration, should Allende win. OCEPLAN was headed by the economist Max Nolff, and many leftist Chilean social scientists and planners contributed their services to it. Under Nolff's direction, OCEPLAN produced an analysis of the present economic situation of Chile and detailed action plans.[5] The FRAP plans called for drastic changes in the Chilean economy: (1) the minerals of Chile would become the property of the state; the copper, the nitrate, and the iron mining would be nationalized, and eventually the petroleum distributing companies would be nationalized also; (2) the national banking system would be reorganized and private banks nationalized; (3) the government would also nationalize public utilities and insurance companies and would exert strong control over foreign trade; (4) the state would take the lead in promoting the development of heavy industry; (5) income would be redistributed through such measures as a tax reform that would put the inactive resources of the well-to-do to work through state investment; (6) to protect the purchasing power of the mass of people, controls would be placed upon the distribution of consumer goods; and (7) the rights of small businessmen would also be protected by the state.

[4] Corvalán, "Dos hombres, dos programas," Part II, *op. cit.*

[5] *Las bases, loc. cit.*

One of the most persistent themes of the FRAP candidate was the necessity for a solution to the problem of agriculture's low productivity. Under the program proposed by Allende, the *latifundios* would be expropriated and the *fundo* system would give way to a new system based upon mixed state, collective, and private farms. The *minifundia* that abound in Chile would be abolished and the land now divided into very small holdings would be consolidated into larger, more economically viable plots. Allende indicated that no more than 35 per cent of the arable land would be taken over by the state or collectivized. The remaining amount would remain in private hands. The FRAP proposed that the government pay for the expropriated properties by thirty-year bonds with an annual interest of 4 per cent and with provisions to compensate for inflation. It was also pointed out that there would be some readjustment for the collection of back taxes owed by many of these landowners.[6] The government would also expand the irrigation facilities, provide for the unionization of the peasants, and prohibit the resale of the land to avoid the development of a new concentration of land-holding.

In the international field, the FRAP position was clear. If Dr. Allende became the Chilean President, immediate steps would be taken to disentangle Chile from certain of its ties with the United States. The military pacts with the United States would be abrogated and "a policy of dignity" would be followed in dealings with the Colossus to the North. The FRAP program declared itself to be against racism, colonialism, and the armament race. It was for the defense of human rights in the world scene, national self-determination and, in the Western Hemisphere, very strongly on Cuba's side in her disputes with the United States. Senator Allende had made visits to China, the Soviet Union, and Cuba, and he maintained that his administration would establish good relations with all three of these countries and with other nations of the Socialist bloc.[7]

Senator Eduardo Frei also took a strong reformist line in his campaign. It differed from that of the FRAP more in tone and emphasis than in substance. The Christian Democrats promised that they too would implement electoral reforms, give the right to vote to the illiterates, and possibly lower the voting age. They also advocated legislation to limit campaign expenditures so that the large economic interests would not have such a strong voice in the campaign. Further, Frei would push for a reform of the public administration; there would be provision for the separation of private economic interests from the public administration to limit "conflict of interest" situations; and the

[6] *Ibid.*, Chap. II, p. 1213.
[7] Corvalán, Part I, *op. cit.*

administrative tribunals provided for by the constitution, but never set up by law, would be established. There would be a measure providing for the simplification of the legislative procedure and giving more power to the executive, and the executive would also obtain the power to submit projects of law to a national referendum in the event that Congress refused to pass measures requested by the President. There would be a new statute to deal with political parties, which would restrict the power of their bureaucratic structure. The judicial power would be made into a more active and independent branch of the government, and a system of popularly elected judges would be established to democratize the lower court system.[8]

In the economic field the Christian Democrats also advocated an extension of state control over the economy, although not to the degree advocated by the FRAP. Tax reforms to facilitate a more equitable income distribution would be undertaken as well as a simplification of the administrative procedure of levying taxes.

In banking, the public function of the Central Bank would be transferred to the State Bank and private banks so that the Central Bank could concentrate its activities on its role of formulator of monetary policy. Savings would be encouraged, especially among the middle and upper class, through the issuance of Social and Economic Development Bonds; provisions would also be made to prevent inflation from devaluating any money put into savings accounts. The policy of fostering economic development through the extension of state credit to private businessmen would be continued and enlarged, but provisions for insuring that the money borrowed was used for the intended purposes would also be provided.

Frei's program proposed to deal with the problem of copper by enlarging state control over the industry. He hoped that copper production could be raised in order to augment the amount of foreign exchange earned and to help secure revenue for the implementation of the government's development plans. The objective of this program would be to raise copper exports to $200 million annually, with a production increase of 600,000 tons between 1964 and 1970. Other goals listed were the refining of all Chilean copper within the country, the creation of a state monopoly to handle sales of copper in the world market, and the sale of Chilean copper to all nations, regardless of ideological considerations. If the North American copper companies refused to go along with this program, they would be nationalized. In other mining activities, iron and nitrate, the state would exercise strong controls, but their development would be encouraged by special state financing and other measures.[9]

[8] Corvalán, Part II, *op. cit.*

[9] *Ibid.*

In foreign trade, a Christian Democratic government would develop trade relations with all countries, including those of the Socialist bloc. It would exercise extensive controls on imports and exports with an eye toward building up domestic industry and the creation of foreign markets for Chilean goods. A strong endorsement of the Latin American Free-Trade area concept was also a part of the CD program.[10]

To solve the housing problem the Christian Democratic candidate proposed construction of 60,000 houses annually for six years to meet population increases. He further proposed that the national budget provide resources for massive construction, to continue the system of savings and loans but to use regulations to control the construction of luxury buildings, to create a special system of bank credit for industries and construction of cooperatives, and to establish a Housing Ministry to coordinate services, urban renewal plans, and new residential areas.

The agrarian reform proposed by Senator Frei had the same goals as those advocated by Allende's forces: a higher productivity and an increase in social justice for the *inquilino*. Large inefficient holdings would be expropriated and paid for in twenty-five-year bonds at 5 per cent interest after a 10 per cent down payment. Further, increases in agricultural productivity would be encouraged through a series of complex policies ranging from the taxation of the potential productivity of land rather than its actual output, in order to discourage leaving land fallow, to stimulating the creation of agricultural cooperatives, granting a favored status to importers of agricultural machinery, and encouraging the development of industries that are dependent upon agricultural products. The peasant would be unionized, guaranteed a minimum wage, and in many cases given his own land. There would also be an intensification of soil conservation projects both to save the land for a productive agriculture and to stimulate the growth of lumber.

In broad terms the Frei campaign was to emphasize the theme of revolution, but it was to be a "Revolution in Liberty." He promised a transformation of Chile hardly less dramatic and far-reaching than the one promised by his Socialist opponent, but he constantly stated that his would be one that would employ democratic rather than totalitarian means.[11]

It is difficult to assess the Radical candidate Julio Durán's campaign line in these same details. Since Durán represented the forces of status quo, there was no complex series of proposals to present to the public. The Radicals had taken the lead in pushing through the Agrarian Reform Law of 1962, but one could hardly term their program as any-

[10] *Ibid.*

[11] See: "Third Declaration of Millahue," *El Mercurio*, April 21, 1964, p. 27.

thing more than a promise for the continuation of the policy lines followed by the Alessandri government.

The 1964 Presidential Election

The election was held without incident and was in almost every manner exemplary of the very best Chilean democratic traditions. Soon after the polls closed, it became apparent that the Frei victory was overwhelming. Eduardo Frei achieved what no other Chilean President in this century had done — he won an absolute majority of the vote. His victory was national, for he led the balloting in nineteen of Chile's twenty-five provinces, and only 12.65 per cent of those registered failed to vote. Frei received 56.1 per cent of the vote (1,406,002 votes), Allende trailed him with 38.9 per cent (975,692 votes), and Durán placed a poor third with 5 per cent (124,869 votes).

Frei cut heavily into Allende's usual strongholds for his great victory, and Allende barely managed to carry the northern mining provinces of Tarapacá, Antofogasta, and Atacama. He held a narrow margin of slightly over 7,000 votes (out of over 165,000 votes) over Frei in Concepción, where he was expected to run far ahead, and with Arauco, adjacent to Concepción, and Magallanes he completed his total of six provinces. Frei ran far ahead in Santiago where almost one fifth of the votes in the country were cast. The Santiago totals were: 60.9 per cent (621,476) for Frei, 35.7 per cent (363,502) for Allende, and only 3.4 per cent (24,725) for Durán. In Valparaíso, Allende's home district where he was expected to do well, he ran some 65,000 behind out of slightly over 250,000 votes.

To sum up, Frei won the election everywhere and Allende lost it everywhere. That is to say, to win, Allende needed to close substantially the gap between candidates in Santiago and Valparaíso, win heavily in Concepción, do well in the rural areas, and hold the Left's traditional edge in the mining provinces of the north. He was unable to accomplish any of this. He lost heavily to Frei in Santiago and Valparaíso, won narrowly in Concepción and the northern provinces, and lost the rural areas, albeit by a narrow margin in some cases.

However, in spite of the spectacular Christian Democratic victory the FRAP generally managed to hold its own (in terms of relative strength in comparison to 1958) with the growth of the Chilean electorate, but its pattern of growth was uneven. Allende's support increased most in those areas in which he made a poor showing in 1958 and increased least in the areas where he was strongest. The crux of the problem was that, despite the generally improved showing of the FRAP in the rural areas, the increase of support was not nearly enough to overcome the combination of traditional pressure from the Conserva-

Table 16

1964 Presidential Vote

	Candidates and Supporting Parties		
	Allende	*Frei*	*Durán*
Electoral District	FRAP (PS PCCh, PADENA, VNP)	PDC, PCU, PL	PR
Tarapacá	47.1%	46.2%	6.6%
Antofagasta	48.3	45.6	6.1
Atacama	44.6	43.3	12.1
Coquimbo	45.1	45.9	9.0
Aconcagua	40.4	55.0	4.6
Valparaíso	36.1	60.3	3.6
Santiago	35.7	60.9	3.4
O'Higgins	45.6	51.3	3.1
Colchagua	36.5	58.8	4.7
Curicó	41.4	52.1	6.6
Talca	45.3	50.7	4.0
Maule	38.5	54.4	7.1
Linares	41.7	53.5	4.7
Ñuble	34.6	58.4	7.4
Concepción	49.3	45.2	5.5
Arauco	60.3	28.4	11.2
Bío-Bío	38.4	52.9	8.7
Malleco	36.5	56.2	7.3
Cautín	31.2	63.0	5.9
Valdivia	43.3	51.6	5.1
Osorno	38.2	51.4	10.4
Llanquihue and Aysén	30.7	62.1	7.2
Chiloé	32.7	53.9	13.5
Magallanes	49.9	41.9	8.2

tive *fundo* owners and Frei's promise of agrarian reform. Thus, Allende was unable to win (much less win heavily, as was necessary for him to carry the election) even in the rural areas where he attracted the greatest percentage of the new voters registered. In the urban centers, the outcome was equally disheartening for the FRAP forces. For example, in the important lower- and working-class district of San Miguel in Santiago, an area won by Allende in 1958 (55 per cent) and conceded to him by most observers in 1964, Frei received an absolute majority of the vote. The importance of the female vote in the Christian Democratic victory was also evident. While Frei obtained a majority of the vote among men, he was also overwhelmingly supported by Chilean women. There is no doubt that the female voters were strongly influenced by both Frei's strong Catholicism and Allende's

Marxist arguments. The fear of the latter probably strengthened the appeal of the former, and Frei obtained 63 per cent of the women's votes.

To conclude, the pattern of Frei's great victory was that of a national triumph. He was strongly supported in all areas of the country. In those sections in which he trailed Allende he was not far behind, and in a number of communes he was the overwhelming choice of the voters.

Durán, with nearly 125,000 votes (5 per cent) trailed both candidates in all sections of the country. As has been observed earlier, he was left with a humiliating defeat and, because of Frei's absolute majority, could not even bargain with the Radical congressional votes as he might have had Frei obtained only a relative majority.

What were the most important factors contributing to the great and unprecedented victory for Eduardo Frei in 1964? First and foremost was certainly the issue of communism, and this contention is amply supported from two directions. First, there was its role in the Chilean Right's throwing its support to Frei after the Curicó disaster. Later, the position on communism was also important in Durán's and the Radicals' decision to stay in the race instead of going over to Allende. The second aspect of the Communist controversy was its effectiveness as a campaign weapon against Allende. This matter was drummed persistently into the consciousness of the Chilean electorate, and there is no doubt of its great effect.

The second most important electoral factor was the extraordinary appeal and attractiveness of Frei and his program. Although it was difficult to predict the outcome of the election beforehand, it is difficult to see, from this vantage point of hindsight, how he could have been defeated. He was a reformer in a time when Chileans were in a strongly reformist mood; he had at his disposal a most effective political organization to run his campaign; and he had the strong political and financial support of the Chilean Right, which was willing to spearhead the major issue of the campaign, anti-communism. Thus, the theme "Revolution in Liberty" could deftly include leftists, anti-communist reformers, middle-of-the-road go-slow democrats, and status quo conservatives who hoped that the aspects of liberty in the slogan would receive stronger emphasis than the revolutionary ones. Frei became the overwhelming choice of the reformist-oriented middle class. Despite the strong tradition of anti-Church feeling among members of this group, Frei summed up their aspirations. These people are democrats, liberals, and economic nationalists, and they generally accept a strong measure of state control of the economy. The pattern of election returns from middle-class urban districts confirms their support of Frei.

These two factors, the communist issue and the personality and program of Frei, go a long way toward explaining the results of the 1964 Chilean presidential elections.

In broader terms, what was the significance of the election for the Chilean political system? First of all, the long and heated campaign had a strengthening effect on national political integration. Over one half of those voting in the 1964 election had never voted before for a Chilean President. There is no doubt that this election, then, was a powerful catalyst in the process of altering the pattern of political socialization and recruitment in Chile. Further, the fact that nearly one and one-half million voters (both old and new) supported Frei certainly portended well for the future of the Christian Democrats.

The Congressional Elections of 1965

The question of whether Frei owed his victory to rightist and centrist votes cast not for him but against communism, or whether the Christian Democrats commanded sufficient popular support in their own right to put through their reform program was answered March 7, 1965, when Chilean voters returned to the polls to elect the 147-seat Chamber of Deputies and 21 of the Senate's 45 seats. This time the centrist and rightist parties, alienated by the reform proposals of the new President and bidding for a comeback, opposed the Christian Democrats bitterly, after reconstructing the *Frente Democrático*. The FRAP coalition also put on a vigorous campaign in hopes of recovering from September's reverse. In the first few months of his administration virtually all of Frei's reform measures proposed to the Congress were stymied by congressional intransigence from both the far Left and the far Right. This strong opposition forced him to withdraw his economic and political reform measures, and to stake his political future on the March elections.

Among the measures proposed by Frei and blocked by the Congress was the Christian Democratic plan to share ownership of the giant United States copper holdings, which would lead to a doubling of Chile's copper production. In December, 1964, Frei announced to the nation that an agreement had been reached with the copper companies. In pursuance of the "Chileanization" program, production would double by 1970, while copper refining in Chile would triple by that time. The agreement included partnership of the Chilean government in several companies and in all the new exploitations; acquisition of 51 per cent of the shares of the Braden Copper Company for 80 million dollars to be paid in twenty years and to be completely reinvested in Chile; and 25 per cent of the shares of the new mines of the Cerro Corporation (Río Blanco) and Anaconda Copper Company

(Exotica). In addition, 49 per cent of the unexploited Anaconda mines would pass to the Chilean government. In turn, by the terms of the agreement the copper companies were to obtain concessions on taxes and import duties and a promise of stable rates in the future. In essence these features would mean to Chile a new investment of $416 million, an annual increase of $47 million in fiscal revenues, and an increase of $115 million in its foreign currency income. The country would increase its participation in the world copper market as well as increase its foreign currency income based on copper by 62 per cent.

Other measures Frei had introduced called for a private capital tax aimed at the rich, a nearly 40 per cent cost-of-living pay boost for Chilean workers, a slum clearance project, agrarian reform, and establishment of a state bank to provide lower interest rates. The Frei government also proposed nationalization of the United States-owned Chilean Telephone Company, which provides 95 per cent of all telephone service in Chile, and of the company that provides 20 per cent of the nation's electric power, also American-owned.

There had been considerable doubt after Frei's election as to whether he had broad support in the country. The forces that supported Frei in 1964 had done so for a number of reasons, and many of these reasons had little to do with the program he was espousing. Thus, the power available to Frei during the presidential campaign that came from these sectors was not readily transferable to a long-range support for the Christian Democratic Party. The March elections answered the question above with a strong affirmative. Running on their own, the Christian Democrats scored a smashing victory, even more spectacular than the 1964 triumph of Frei. Surpassing the most optimistic forecasts of their electoral experts, they increased their seats in the Chamber of Deputies from 27 to 82. In the Senate they won 12 of the 21 seats at stake — a gain of 11. The Christian Democratic vote represented 41.06 per cent of the total ballots cast.

The Christian Democratic victory was achieved chiefly at the expense of the rightist and the Radical forces. Conservatives obtained 5.36 per cent of the vote and the Liberals 10.05, while the Radicals secured only 12.80 per cent, and Socialists and Communists together received 21.71 per cent. In the new Chamber of Deputies, on the Right and Center, the Liberals lost 22 seats, the Conservatives 14, and the Radicals 19. On the leftist side the Communists gained 2 seats, the Socialists gained 3, and PADENA lost 9. All of the minor parties failed to elect representatives. Of the 21 seats contested in the Senate, aside from the 12 won by the Christian Democrats, 3 went to the Radicals, 3 to the Socialists, 2 to the Communists, and one to PADENA (a loss of 3 for the Radicals, no loss for the Socialists, and a gain of 2 for the Communists). Conservatives and Liberals failed to win a single senatorial seat.

Table 17

Composition and Percentage of Strength of Both Houses of the Chilean Congress by Parties
1965 Congressional Election

		Chamber			Senate			
		Number		Per cent	Number			Per cent
Frente Democrático (FD)		29		20.60		17		37.77
Conservatives	3		2.04		2		4.44	
Liberals	6		4.08		5		11.11	
Radicals	20		13.60		10		22.22	
Christian Democrats		82		55.78		13		28.88
Frente de Acción Popular (FRAP)		36		24.48		15		33.33
Others*	3		2.04		2		4.44	
Socialists	15		10.20		7		15.55	
Communists	18		12.24		6		13.33	
Totals		147		100.00		45		100.00

* Include for the Chamber of Deputies the *PADENA* and for the Senate the *PADENA* (one senator) and the *Vanguardia Nacional del Pueblo* (one senator).

Source: *El Mercurio,* Santiago, March 9, 1965. In this figure Senators Exequiel González and Jaime Barros have been included as members of the Radical and Communist parties respectively, despite the fact of their resignation. These Senate seats were not at stake in the 1965 Congressional election.

The landslide gave President Frei an effective governing majority for the next four years, saving him from an agonizingly frustrating five-and-one-half more years of office with an obstructionist Congress. His victory could now be viewed as a resounding mandate for his program of "Revolution in Liberty" and a strong rejection of both the rightist and the Marxist solution.

Despite the role played by the 1964 and 1965 elections in the national political integration of Chile there are large gaps that have yet to be filled effectively. It is true that almost every voter in Chile had at least one opportunity to see one or both of the major presidential candidates during the long presidential campaign, and for many of these people, particularly those in rural areas, it was the first time that a politician had come before them to discuss seriously national political

PERCENTAGE OF TOTAL VOTE RECEIVED BY THE SIX MAJOR PARTIES SINCE 1941 CONGRESSIONAL AND MUNICIPAL ELECTIONS*

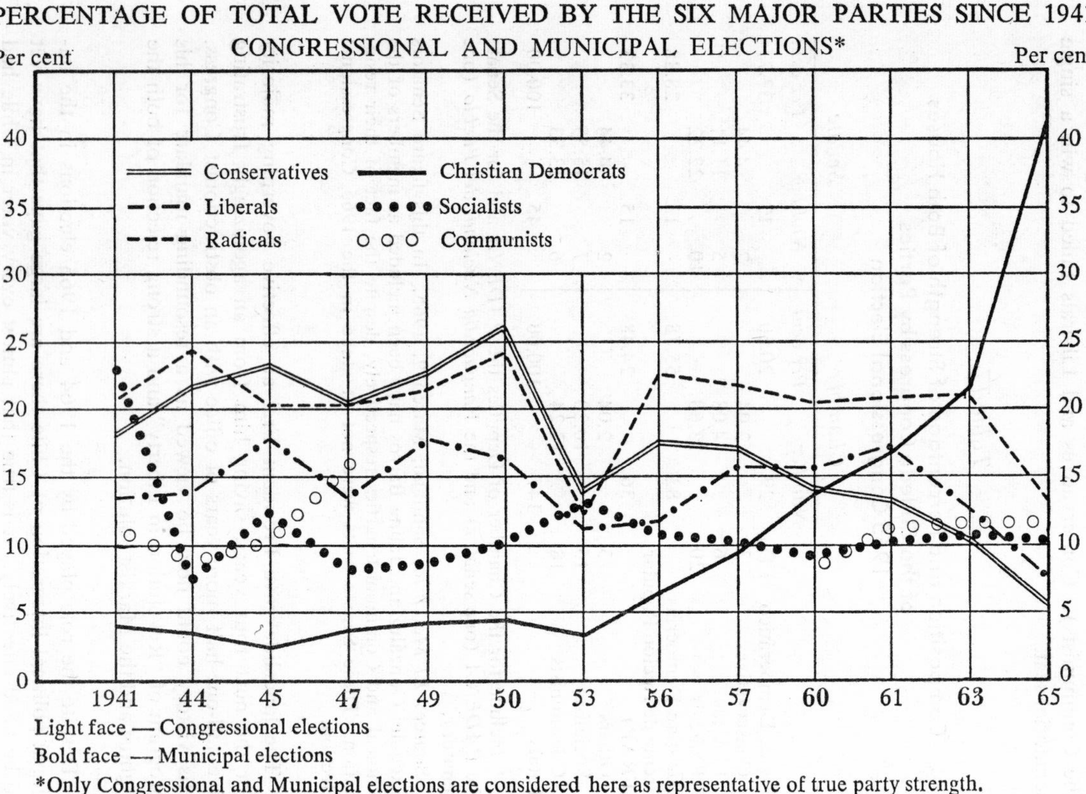

Light face — Congressional elections
Bold face — Municipal elections
*Only Congressional and Municipal elections are considered here as representative of true party strength.

issues. It is equally true that the Christian Democrats succeeded in reaching during the congressional campaign segments of the population which until recently had remained as a nation apart. These facts alone signify an important alteration in the political behavior of Chileans. However, the mere act of voting, while it is a first step, does not necessarily indicate that intermediary structures are being created that will be capable of bringing effective pressure on the political decision-makers during the long years between elections. At present, for example, there is not one organization that can be accurately described as an interest group capable of representing the demands of the Chilean peasant, even on a regional basis. Further, there is still considerable resistance to the formation of such groups by the economically powerful groups in Chile. The emphasis of Frei's program on the *Promoción Popular,* designed to integrate the urban and rural poor into effective political roles giving them a decisive voice in development plans and in solving problems with which they are directly concerned, indicates that the Christian Democrats are aware that such intermediary structures can be an important source of strength for the party in the future.

Conclusion

At the time of this writing, President Frei was preparing to use his new political power to enact without delay the reform program that, Christian Democrats are confident, will turn their administration — the first on the continent — into an example for Latin America. This program, they believe, will show how to defeat poverty and underdevelopment without curtailing freedom or upsetting constitutional government while carrying out radical transformation in Chile's social and economic structures. The political future of Chile will also depend partly on the amount of external support given the Frei government. Naturally, most of this aid must come from the United States, but the international character of the Christian Democratic movement has struck a responsive chord in Europe as well, and there are particularly close ties between the German Christian Democrats and Frei's followers. With sufficient aid forthcoming from foreign sources and with ample support in Congress for its program of reform, the Chilean Christian Democrats may well be able to make good their promise to turn their country into an example for the rest of Latin America.

There is, however, an awareness among the new Chilean reformers of the difficulties as well as the advantages in having started a new wave of hope and expectation in a country where nearly a third of the citizenry is deprived of education. There is little doubt that powerful economic interests will continue their hostility to reforms, even though the rightist parties that represented them have suffered severe and possibly fatal political setbacks. Their task, whatever measurements are applied, is a gigantic one. Summarizing what has been described in the preceding chapters, one may say that Chile is today a stagnant country. It would require sixty years to double its per capita income, as compared to the more prosperous nations which double their income in twenty years, or less. The population of the country is increasing, but the building of homes and schools is not keeping pace. There are two million inhabitants without housing and 500,000 children between seven and fourteen years of age who do not study or work. Unemployment and unproductive employment have grown. About 150,000 Chileans reach the age of fifteen annually, and most of them have little hope of higher education or employment. Agriculture has not expanded as rapidly as the population; as a result, not enough food is produced. The country supports a social security system that is burdensome, inefficient, and bureaucratized. The foreign debt has grown more rapidly than the country's economy, increasing Chile's dependence on foreign nations. The new government faces a serious budget deficit, an enormous foreign debt, a failing currency, and a chronically accelerating inflation. With regard to political development there are serious maladjustments. The split of Chilean society into two segments — the "two Chiles" observers often refer to — is a reality. Only about one fifth or perhaps even less of all Chileans live under modern conditions. This group is the effective nation. The rest consists of the underprivileged and uneducated, who have little access to and seldom participate in the political process, and who are now pressing demands for a better future. Further economic growth necessarily must involve the incorporation of these social segments into the national community.

Counterbalancing these unfavorable conditions, however, Chile has also a number of assets. First of all, the decline in public morale of the past years, caused by the loss of faith in the ability of the political machines to cope with the nation's problems, seems now to have given way to a new consciousness of national integration and unity, as demonstrated in the 1964 and 1965 elections. Secondly, the political system, as we have seen, possesses a series of characteristics normally ascribed to highly developed nations. There is respect for legality and little electoral fraud; a military establishment strongly attached to legal and civilian traditions of change; genuine democratic representation in a Congress that functions without restraints; a judiciary not subject to undue pressure; a strong political party system; an administrative system that is overdeveloped but at least is highly professional and reasonably efficient; a prevalence of honesty and morality among political leaders; a low degree of personalism in politics; and, lastly, availability of political information of all kinds and persuasions.[12] In addition, there is the high order of receptivity of the educated class to external stimuli; the vast reserves of vital human resources, represented by the underprivileged, for a determined drive for national growth; and a new consensus that comprehensive planning of all national activities and the mobilization of all disposable resources is essential.

Chile, like all of the other Latin American countries, has been shackled in its development by imponderable institutional and organizational handicaps. Its relative industrial progress furnishes an excellent example of the problems of modernization in a country hampered by institutions and behavioral patterns of a semifeudal tradition. The task undertaken by Chile's new reformers, the Christian Democrats, is that of leading the country along the road of modernity through a peaceful revolution. They have aroused much hope and dedication in the Chilean people, and if they succeed, theirs would be an unprecedented achievement in the history of developing nations.

[12] K. H. Silvert, *Chile: Yesterday and Today* (New York: Holt, Rinehart and Winston, Inc., 1965), pp. 191–193.

SELECTED BIBLIOGRAPHY

Ahumada, J. *En vez de la miseria.* Santiago: Editorial del Pacífico, 1958.

Alexander, Robert J. *Communism in Latin America.* New Brunswick: Rutgers University Press, 1957.

Almeyda Arroyo, Elías. *Geografía de Chile.* Santiago, 1955.

Alvarez Villablanca, Agustín. *Objetivos del socialismo en Chile.* Santiago, 1946.

Amunátegui, Domingo. *El progreso intelectual y político de Chile.* Santiago: Editorial Nascimento, 1936.

Arteaga Undurraga, Ignacio. *Reseña histórica de las XVI convenciones del Partido Conservador.* Santiago: Imprenta Chile, 1947.

Baltra Cortés, Alberto, Felipe Herrera, and René Silva. *El futuro económico de Chile y de América Latina.* Santiago: Editorial Universitaria, 1957.

Barría Serón, Jorge. *Trayectoria y estructura del movimiento sindical chileno, 1946–1962.* Santiago: Instituto de Organización y Administración, 1963.

Barría Soto, Francisco. *El Partido Radical, su historia y sus obras.* Santiago: Editorial Universitaria, 1957.

Bernaschina, Mario. *Los constituyentes de 1925.* Santiago: Editorial Universitaria, 1945.

————. *Derecho municipal chileno.* 3 vols. Santiago: Editorial Jurídica de Chile, 1952.

————. *Manual de derecho constitucional.* Santiago: Editorial Jurídica de Chile, 1955.

Bonilla, Frank. "The Student Federation of Chile: Fifty Years of Political Action," *Journal of Inter-American Studies,* II, No. 3, July 1960.

Butland, Gilbert J. *Chile: An Outline of Its Geography, Economics, and Politics.* 3rd edition. London: Oxford University Press, 1956.

Cabero, Alberto. *Chile y los chilenos.* Santiago: Editorial Lyceum, 1948.

Campos Harriet, Fernando. *Historia constitucional de Chile.* Santiago: Editorial Jurídica de Chile, 1956.

Chonchol, Jacques, and Julio Silva Solar. *Hacia un mundo comunitario: condiciones de una política social cristiana.* Santiago, 1951.

Cohen, Alvin. "Economic Change in Chile." (Latin American Monograph No. 11.) Gainesville: University of Florida Press, 1960.

Comisión Económica para América Latina de las Naciones Unidas. *Antecedentes sobre el desarrollo de la economía chilena, 1925–1952.* Santiago: Editorial del Pacífico, 1954.

Corbalán, Salomón. *El Partido Socialista.* Santiago: Imprenta Atenea, 1957.

Corporación de Fomento de la Producción. *Geografía Económica de Chile.* Santiago: Imprenta Universitaria, 1950.

Crocco Ferrari, Juan. *La población chilena.* Santiago, 1947.

Cruz-Coke, Ricardo. *Geografía Electoral de Chile.* Santiago, 1952.

Daugherty, Charles H. (ed.). *Chile: Election Factbook.* Washington, D.C.: Institute for the Comparative Study of Political Systems, 1963.

Declaración fundamental, programas y estatutos del Partido Conservador, XVII Convención General, 1961. Santiago: Talleres Claret, 1961.

Dirección de Estadística y Censos. *Algunos resultados del XIII Censo de Población y II de Vivienda.* Santiago, April 1962.

Donoso, Ricardo. *Desarrollo político y social de Chile.* Santiago: Imprenta Universitaria, 1943.

Donoso, Ricardo. *Las ideas políticas en Chile.* Mexico: Fondo de Cultura Económica, 1946.

Edwards Alberto. *La fronda aristocrática.* Santiago: Editorial del Pacífico, 1952.

Edwards, Alberto, and Eduardo Frei. *Historia de los partidos políticos chilenos.* Santiago: Editorial del Pacífico, 1949.

Encina, Francisco. *Historia de Chile.* Santiago: Editorial Nascimento, 1949.

———. *Nuestra inferioridad económica, sus causas, sus consecuencias.* Santiago: Imprenta Universitaria, 1912.

Escobar Cerda, Luis. *Organización para el desarrollo económico.* Santiago: Editorial Universitaria, 1961.

Estatuto del Partido Socialista. Santiago: Imprenta Plá, 1962.

Estatutos del Partido Comunista aprobados en el XII Congreso Nacional. Santiago: Editorial Horizonte, 1962.

Estatutos del Partido Conservador. Santiago: Imprenta Claret, 1961.

Estévez Gazmuri, Carlos. *Elementos de derecho constitucional.* Santiago: Editorial Jurídica de Chile, 1949.

Eyzaguirre, Jaime. *La fisonomía histórica de Chile.* Santiago: Editorial del Pacífico, 1948.

Fetter, Frank W. *Monetary Inflation in Chile.* Princeton: Princeton University Press, 1931.

Fichter, Joseph H. *Cambio social en Chile. Un estudio de actitudes.* Santiago: Editorial Universitaria Católica, 1962.

Finer, Herman. *The Chilean Development Corporation.* Montreal: International Labor Office, 1947.

Fortín Cabezas, Carlos. *La supresión de los pactos electorales,* Colección Estudios Políticos, No. 1. Santiago: Instituto de Ciencias Políticas y Administrativas, 1961.

Frei, Eduardo. *Pensamiento y acción.* Santiago, 1958.

Frías Valenzuela, Francisco. *Manual de historia de Chile.* Santiago: Editorial Nascimento, 1950.

Galdames, Luis. *A History of Chile.* Chapel Hill: University of North Carolina Press, 1941.

Gil, Federico G. "Chile, Society in Transition," *Political Systems of Latin America,* Martin C. Needler (ed.). New York: D. Van Nostrand, 1964.

———. "Genesis and Modernization of Political Parties in Chile." (Monograph Series of Latin America No. 18.) Gainesville: University of Florida Press, 1962.

Guerra, José Guillermo. *La constitución de 1925.* Santiago, 1929.

Guilisati Tagle, Sergio. *Partidos políticos chilenos.* Santiago: Editorial Nascimento, 1964.

Hanson, Earl Parker. *Chile, Land of Progress.* New York: Reynal and Hitchcock, 1941.

Heise González, Julio. *Historia constitucional de Chile.* Santiago: Editorial Jurídica de Chile, 1954.

Hirschman, A. O. *Journeys Toward Progress.* New York: Twentieth Century Fund, 1963.

———. *Latin American Issues, Essays and Comments.* New York: Twentieth Century Fund, 1961.

Hudeczek, Carl. *Economía de Chile, rumbos y metas.* Santiago: Editorial del Pacífico, 1956.

Instituto de Economía de la Universidad de Chile. *Desarrollo económico de Chile 1940–1956*. Santiago, 1956.

Jiles Pizarro, Jorge. *Partido Comunista de Chile*. Santiago: Academia de Ciencias Políticas, 1957.

Jobet, Julio César. *Ensayo crítico del desarrollo económico-social de Chile*. Santiago: Editorial Universitaria, 1955.

————. *Socialismo y Comunismo*. Santiago: Espartaco, 1952.

Johnson, John J. *Political Change in Latin America*. Stanford: Stanford University Press, 1958.

Lagos, Ricardo. *La concentración del poder económico, su teoría, realidad chilena*. Santiago: Editorial del Pacífico, 1961.

León Echaíz, René. *Evolución histórica de los partidos políticos chilenos*. Santiago: Editorial Ercilla, 1939.

Linares, Francisco Walker. "Evolución Social," in *Desarrollo de Chile en la primera mitad del siglo XX*. Santiago: Editorial Universitaria, n.d.

McBride, G. M. *Chile: Land and Society*. New York: American Geographical Society, 1936.

Maitland, Francis. *Chile: Its Land and People*. London, 1941.

Marín Balmaceda, Raúl. *No demagogia*. Santiago, 1955.

Ministerio de Hacienda. *Organización institucional de Chile*. Santiago, 1955.

Montecinos Rozas, Edmundo. *Apuntaciones para el estudio de la evolución de los partidos políticos chilenos y de su proyección jurídica*. Santiago: Imprenta Dirección General de Prisiones, 1942.

Nolff, Max, Felipe Herrera, *et al. La inflación; naturaleza y problemas*. Santiago, 1954.

Partido Radical. *Estatutos aprobados en la XXI Convención Nacional Ordinaria*. Santiago, 1962.

Pepelasis, Adamantios, Leon Mears, and Irma Adelman. *Economic Development: Analysis and Case Studies*. New York: Harper and Brothers, 1961.

Pike, Fredrick B. *Chile and the United States, 1880–1962*. Notre Dame: University of Notre Dame Press, 1963.

Pinto Santa Cruz, Aníbal. *Chile. Un caso de desarrollo frustrado*. Santiago: Editorial Universitaria, 1959.

————. *Hacia nuestra independencia económica*. Santiago: Editorial del Pacífico, 1953.

Poblete, Darío, and Alfredo Bravo. *Historia del Partido Radical y del Frente Popular*. Santiago, 1936.

Problete Troncoso, Moisés, and Ben G. Burnett. *The Rise of the Latin American Labor Movement*. New York: Bookman Associates, 1960.

Programa del Partido Comunista de Chile. Santiago: Imprenta Horizonte, 1962.

Programa del Partido Socialista, XX Congreso General Ordinario celebrado en Concepción, Febrero, 1964. Santiago, 1964.

Programa y Estatuto Orgánico del Partido Liberal. Santiago, 1962.

Ramírez Necochea, Hernán. *Historia del movimiento obrero en Chile — Antecedentes — Siglo XIX*. Santiago: Talleres Gráficos Lautaro, 1956.

República de Chile, Servicio Nacional de Estadísticas y Censos, *XII Censo General de Población y I de Vivienda*. Santiago: Guttemberg Press, 1956, Vol. I, "Resumen nacional."

Sanfuentes Carrión, Marcial. *El Partido Conservador*. Santiago: Editorial Universitaria, 1957.

Scott Elliot, G. F. *Chile*. London: T. Fisher Unwin, 1911.

Silva, Julio, and Bosco Parra. *Nociones para una política demócrata cristiana.* Santiago, 1957.

Silva Cimma, Enrique. *Derecho administrativo chileno y comparado.* Santiago: Editorial Jurídica de Chile, 1954.

Silvert, Kalman H. *Chile: Yesterday and Today.* New York: Holt, Rinehart and Winston, Inc., 1965.

————. *The Conflict Society: Reaction and Revolution in Latin America.* New Orleans: The Hauser Press, 1961.

————. "Elections, Parties, and the Law," American Universities Field Staff Letter, March 10, 1957.

————. "Interview with a Candidate," American Universities Field Staff Letter, August 30, 1957.

El socialismo en Chile. Santiago: Publicaciones del Congreso por la Libertad de la Cultura, 1956.

Stevenson, John Reese. *The Chilean Popular Front.* Philadelphia: University of Pennsylvania Press, 1942.

Subercaseaux, Benjamín. *Chile: A Geographic Extravaganza.* New York: Macmillan, 1943.

Urzúa Valenzuela, Germán. *El Partido Radical, su evolución política.* Santiago: Academia de Ciencias Políticas y Administrativas, 1961.

Vega, Julio. "La clase media en Chile," in *Materiales para el estudio de la clase media,* Vol. 113. Washington, D.C.: Unión Panamericana, 1950.

Vera Riquelme, Enrique. *Evolución del radicalismo chileno.* Santiago, 1943.

Verdugo Marinkovic, Mario. "Programas y estatutos de los partidos políticos chilenos," *Boletín chileno de Ciencias Políticas,* XII, 1963.

Waiss, Oscar. *Presencia del socialismo en Chile.* Santiago: Ediciones Espartaco, 1952.

INDEX